Combining meticulous archival research an
insights of cultural historians and missiologists,
Methodism in postcolonial Ghana. While ackn
in Wesleyan theology and holistic mission, Essa
but rather on contextualization, indigenization, ... Ghanaian Methodism he brings to life, therefore, is one that emphasizes Fante agency, Akan cultural traditions, and ethnic identity. Essamuah is not blind to the tensions and controversies involved in the evolution of Ghanaian Methodism from its nineteenth-century roots to its postcolonial identity, but his study amply demonstrates that African Christianity in general and Ghanaian Methodism in particular are no mere relics of colonialism. With a scholar's instinct and a practitioner's passion Essamuah both openly acknowledges the limitations of his study and earnestly pleads for further research on Christian churches in postcolonial Africa. His pioneering study is a testimony to the enduring missionary spirit of the Methodist tradition and to its capacity to shape and be shaped by the dynamic local cultures in which it takes root. It deserves a wide readership among those interested in African Christianity, the Methodist tradition, and religion, colonialism, and postcolonialism. *David Hempton, Alonzo L. McDonald Professor, Harvard Divinity School*

This is a scholarly study by an African of an African subject, an African Church and from the perspective of an African. It is warmly recommended for all to read especially because it reinforces the ecumenicity of Church. *Rev. Prof. Emeritus John S. Pobee, University of Ghana and Vicar General of Anglican Diocese of Accra*

It's the privilege of Bay Area Community Church to daily experience the missionary heart and life of one who is "genuinely Ghanaian," Dr. Casely Essamuah, our endeared global mission pastor. This work represents his passion for spreading the story of God's kingdom as revealed in history, ministry and missions of the Methodist Church Ghana as church with endearing ties and distinguished heritage. May the next generation of Christ followers--Ghanaians and global--learn from these insights and be better equipped to serve our Lord and Savior. *Greg St. Cyr, Senior Pastor, Bay Area Community Church*

It is impossible to come to a full understanding of Christian mission anywhere in Africa without some knowledge of the contributions of indigenous agents. Casely B. Essamuah, himself with a rich heritage in Ghana Methodism has, in this impressive volume, given concrete examples of these developments. *J. Kwabena Asamoah-Gyadu PhD, Professor of African Christianity & Pentecostal Theology, Dean of Graduate Studies, Trinity Theological Seminary Accra, Ghana*

Genuinely Ghanaian makes an important contribution to the historiography of Christianity in Africa. Essamuah convincingly argues that Ghanaians took colonial British Methodism and contextualized it appropriately, holding in tension Akan cultural identity and postcolonial Ghanaian nationality, while remaining true to a Wesleyan theology of mission. Highlighting significant achievements without glossing over internal struggles within the Methodist Church Ghana, Essamuah demonstrates in this multi-disciplinary study how Ghanaians accepted Methodism on their own terms and reworked it to fit their needs. This is a welcome book that demonstrates how Christianity introduced by foreign missionaries has become a truly African religion. *Darrell Whiteman, Vice President, Mission Personnel and Preparation & Resident Missiologist, The Mission Society*

The synod of the Methodist Church Ghana, overseen from Britain no longer, met in 1961. Francis Bartels' classic *The Roots of Ghana Methodism* traced its history from the beginnings of the Cape Coast Bible Band up to that pivotal moment. Another half-century on, it is time not only to update the record but to review the entire period from a perspective which, acknowledging its debt to both African and missionary pioneers, is authentically Ghanaian. Casely Essamuah has addressed this task with verve and passion as well as scholarship.

Genuinely Ghanaian, published in the year of Bartels' death at the age of 100, is a welcome addition to the literature of African Church History. *The Rev. John R Pritchard, formerly Africa and then General Secretary of the Methodist Church Overseas Division, British Conference*

I welcome the way Dr. Casely Essamuah's history of the Methodist Church, Ghana shows how genuinely Ghanaian that church has become between 1961 and 2000, and how more recently branches of the church have become established in other parts of the world. He shows how, in spite of problems in the church's life, members of the church have engaged in mission in their own country, have also brought new life into local churches in the United States, Britain and Holland and are sharing fully in the life of the world church. *Rev. Dr. Albert Mosley, former General Secretary, Methodist Church Overseas Division, British Conference*

Genuinely Ghanaian is an insightful historical piece that gives full attention to the phenomenal contributions of Ghanaians in the birth, nurturing and the missiological growth of the Methodist Church Ghana more especially after autonomy. *The Rev. Dr. Paul Kwabena Boafo, Protestant Chaplain, Kwame Nkrumah University of Science and Technology, Kumasi*

Genuinely Ghanaian brings a much-needed balance to the presentation of the history of the African church, and in particular, the role of Ghanaians in the establishment and development of Christianity in Ghana from the nineteenth century! Dr. Essamuah does this in a style that is both intellectually engaging and literarily captivating. *Genuinely Ghanaian* is a must-read for all those who want a balanced view of the history of the African Church! *Rev. Dr. Francis Kofi Adams, Assistant Professor, Drexel University, Pennsylvania, USA. Pastor of Spiritual Formation and Leadership Development, Victory Christian Fellowship, Pennsylvania*

Dr. Casely Essamuah has rescued the history of Methodism in Ghana from its often perverse narrative as another monument of Europe's civilizing mission in Africa. In this superbly written, bold, yet sobering book, Essamuah sees the Fante people of Ghana as the main agents in the transformation of John Wesley's theology into a "genuinely Ghanaian" socio-cultural message and institution on African soil from 1835 to 1961 and beyond. One of the many redemptive qualities of this remarkable book is its correction of fashionable fantasies about early Christianity in Ghana, and restoration of the contributions of Africans to Methodist theology to the historiography of Christianity in colonial and post-colonial Africa. *Edward Kissi, Ph.D., Associate Professor of African History, University of South Florida, Tampa*

Any student of African Christianity must study Ghana, the "Black Star of Africa." And any student of Ghana must understand the impact of the Methodist movement on Ghanaian Christianity. With close attention to detail, reflective practitioner missiologist Dr. Casely Essamuah guides us in this significant work to understand the Methodist foundation on which much of Ghanaian Christianity is founded. I highly recommend this resource to you. *Paul Borthwick, Senior Consultant, Development Associates International*

Currently, the representative Christian person on the globe is located in the Non-Western World; Africa is a heartland of contemporary world Christianity. The quality and vitality of contemporary African Christianity is extremely significant as it impacts world Christianity today. We owe current freshness and growth of the church in Africa among other factors to several responsible contextualization efforts in parts of the African Church. For the "African Church is best Christian when it is best African." Dr. Casely Essamuah's study of MCG is an important contribution to missiological works on authentic expression of biblical Christianity in the African context. The total Church, clergy and lay are involved in functional contextualization and uplift the role of women in church life. This monumental work brings out extremely important and significant missiological research findings and remarks on this segment of the African Church—the MCG. *Jude Hama, General Director and CEO Scripture Union, Ghana*

GENUINELY GHANAIAN

. . . .

A HISTORY OF THE METHODIST CHURCH GHANA, 1961 - 2000

by

CASELY B. ESSAMUAH

With a Foreword by the

MOST REVEREND DR. ROBERT K. ABOAGYE-MENSAH,

PRESIDING BISHOP, THE METHODIST CHURCH,

GHANA, *2003-2009*

Africa World Press, Inc.

P.O. Box 1892
Trenton, NJ 08607

P.O. Box 48
Asmara, ERITREA

Africa World Press, Inc.

P.O. Box 1892
Trenton, NJ 08607

AWP

P.O. Box 48
Asmara, ERITREA

FIRST PRINTING 2010

Book and cover design: *Guenet Abraham*

Library of Congress Cataloging-in-Publication Data

Essamuah, Casely B.
Genuinely Ghanaian: a history of the Methodist Church, Ghana, 1961-2000 / by Casely B. Essamuah; with a foreword by the Robert K. Aboagye-Mensah.
p. cm.
ISBN 1-59221-747-8 (cloth) -- ISBN 1-59221-748-6 (pbk.)
1. Methodist Church--Ghana--History--20th century. I. Title.
BX8322.G5E87 2010
287'.166709045--dc22

2010010619

DEDICATED WITH PROFOUND GRATITUDE

To my parents
Samuel Benyarku Essamuah
and Ernestina Oduguamba Essamuah
Your children rise up to call you blessed.
(Prov. 31:28)

To my dear wife
Angela Maria Wakhweya-Essamuah
Your people will be my people
and your God will be my God. (Ruth 1:16)

To our children
Zinhle Kristyn, Zikomo Samuel, and Zachary Noel
I have no greater joy than to hear that my children are walking in the truth.
(1 John 4)

Theological consciousness presupposes religious tradition, and tradition requires memory and memory is integral to identity: without memory, we have no past, and if we have no past, then we lose our identity.

Kwame Bediako
1945-2008

Where common memory is lacking, where men and women do not share in the same past, there can be no real community, and where community is to be formed common memory must be created.

H. Richard Niebuhr
1894-1962

What you have received as heritage, take now as task and thus you will make it your own.

Johann Wolfgang von Goethe
1749-1832

CONTENTS

ABBREVIATIONS

AACC All Africa Conference of Churches
AFRC Armed Forces Revolutionary Council
AIC African Initiated Church
CBC: Catholic Bishops Conference
CCG: Christian Council of Ghana
CPP: Convention Peoples' Party
CVC: Citizens' Vetting Committee
EMR: Evangelism, Mission and Renewal (Department of MCG)
FCB: Foundation Conference Bulletin (1961)
GCUC: Ghana Church Union Committee (1961)
GPC: General Purposes Council (formerly Committee)
MCG: Methodist Church, Ghana
MCOD: Methodist Church Overseas Division (UK)
MDCC: Musama Disco Christo Church
MMA: Methodist Medical Association
MMS: Methodist Missionary Society
MPRP: Methodist Prayer and Renewal Movement
MSUM: Mission Society for United Methodists
MUCG: Methodist University College, Ghana
NCS: National Catholic Secretariat
NDC: National Democratic Congress
NGM: Northern Ghana Mission (program of the MCG)
NIC: National Investigations Committee
NLC: National Liberation Council
NLFA: New Life for All
NPP: New Patriotic Party
NRC: National Redemption Council

OMSC: Overseas Ministries Study Center
PDC: Peoples Defense Committee
PFP: Popular Front Party
PNDC: Provisional National Defense Council
PNP: People's National Party
SMC: Supreme Military Council
SO: Standing Orders of MCG constitution
TEF: Theological Education Fund
UGCC: United Gold Coast Convention
UMC: United Methodist Church
UNC: United National Convention
WARC: World Alliance of Reformed Churches
WCC: World Council of Churches
WDC: Workers' Defense Committee
WGHS: Wesley Girls' High School
WMMS: Wesleyan Methodist Missionary Society

"Minutes" refers to Minutes of the MCG Annual Conference. The specific year and page number usually follow. Minutes were produced up to 1970. Thereafter, the denominational head office issued "Conference Tidbits."

Agenda refers to the printed reports from various dioceses and organizations distributed and used during conference.

GLOSSARY

Assessment: The amount set by the district and connexional offices for local churches (societies and circuits) to pay. This amount is calculated based on the number of members in the church.

Candidate: Someone who has applied to go to the seminary. Until recently, the national church paid for all the expenses, including tuition and room and board. Before one is accepted into the seminary in the Methodist Church Ghana one has to appear before the Leaders and Quarterly Meetings, and Synod to answer questions on one's Christian pilgrimage, call to ministry, marital status, and so forth.

Catechumen: A church attendee who is not a full member, a "seeker" in modern American terms.

Church: The denomination, Methodist Church Ghana. The context will indicate if a particular congregation is the subject.

Circuit: The group/area of the church that is supervised by a superintendent-minister. In earlier times, circuits were graded A, B, and C, depending on their ability to pay their ministers. In the poorer circuits, the district and connexional offices made up the difference in the salaries/stipends of ministers so that there was an equitable system.

Collection: The colloquial term for offering, it is used at all levels, including conference documents. On any given Sunday, a Methodist church in Ghana could collect two or three offerings. The first one is for the regular Sunday collection; another one might be for any of the various church organizations especially on founding anniversaries; and a third may be for a church project. Some churches have boxes at the exits to be used to collect moneys to be given to poor and needy people in the church and in the community. This collection is usually called the Poor Fund (benevolence or deacons' fund). It is from this fund that ministers and leaders visiting shut-ins and invalids donate to those to whom they give Communion.

Conference: The highest decision-making body of the Methodist Church. From 1961 to 1999 it met annually, but starting in 2000 it meets every other year.

Connexion: The national Conference which is referred to as a Connexion. National offices and officers are called connexional office/officers.

District/Diocese: The boundaries which are usually close to that of a political/administrative region, though heavily populated areas have more than one Methodist district. After the adoption of episcopacy, the term Diocese was substituted for district.

Fellowship of the Kingdom: The ministers association, intended to foster fellowship and spiritual renewal. It is active on both district and connexional levels.

General Purposes Committee/Council: The national representative body that meets between conferences. All bishops and heads of departments are members. Most of the time its decisions are confirmed automatically by the Conference because it is expected to have paid more attention to the details than can be done in the larger setting. Like the conference and synods on which it is modeled, it has both and equal ministerial and lay representations and sessions.

Leaders Meeting: The local leadership team of any society/elder board in a local church. Comprised of the elders recommended by other leaders and appointed by the resident ministers, they constitute the highest decision-making body of the society. They usually meet on Thursday nights. The members are normally also leaders of Bible classes. Some ministers use the leaders meeting to educate the lay leadership not only in biblical studies but also in pastoral counseling and general ministry. In some societies the leadership of various organizations are invited to sit in on the Leaders meetings.

Local Preachers: Lay men and laywomen who have passed oral and written examinations and are thus licensed to preach in Methodist churches. There are always ongoing schools for training and examining local preachers. This is also the first step for anyone who intends to become a minister. One needs to be a local preacher for at least a year and be evaluated before one is formally allowed to proceed with the process.

Minor Synod: A church court. Before a minister is called before a minor synod, they are normally suspended from the ministry.

Outstation: A town without a resident Methodist minister; a minister leaves his/her own station and goes on visitation to the outstation.

Probationer: Ministers who are commissioned as probationers. They are sent to serve under a seasoned superintendent minister. They are expected to serve a minimum of two years, complete a Long Essay on a subject to be determined by the probationer and the supervisor, and go through oral examination by synod and conference committees as well as by the entire synod and conference before they are ordained at the conference.

Society: A local church. The Methodist congregation in a locality which is called a society from the days of Methodism's founder, John Wesley.

Station: A town where a Methodist minister resides.

Standing Committee: The district/diocese version of the General Purposes Council.

Synod: The regional decision-making body, supervised by a Chairman and General Superintendent under the old system, but now is supervised by a diocesan bishop.

Transfer: The process whereby Ghanaian Methodist ministers stay at a station for a year. This is renewable up to seven years, at which time they are due for transfer to another church in another locality.

ACKNOWLEDGMENTS

THIS BOOK ON THE POSTCOLONIAL HISTORY OF GHANAIAN METHODISM is, in part, my story as well. It was during my college years at the University of Ghana, Legon that I began to appreciate the importance of the story of the Methodist Church-Ghana (MCG).

I came to understand the place of Methodism in Ghanaian society in a new and refreshing way by studying with the Very Reverend Professor Joshua Kudadjie and Professor Elizabeth Amoah (and later at seminary with Drs. Robert K. Aboagye-Mensah and Emmanuel Y. Lartey). Perhaps the single most significant contributor to my education was the course I took with the veteran Old Testament scholar Professor Kwesi A. Dickson. The course, The Old Testament and African Life and Thought, opened my mind to many of the currents and trends in African Christianity today. I took up further studies at Harvard Divinity School, with Professor Harvey Cox supervising my master's thesis on the interface of Christianity and culture among the Akan of Ghana.

In 1997, Dr. Ogbu U. Kalu challenged me to write the history of the church in the postcolonial and post-missionary eras. Over the years I have enjoyed the friendship of Dr. Tite Tienou, former principal of Alliance Seminary, Abidjan, Côte D'Ivoire, and now dean of Trinity Evangelical Seminary, Deerfield, Illinois. He opened my mind to the francophone literature on African Christianity. In September of 1997 I was privileged to be a part of an "oral history" seminar at the Overseas Ministries Study Center (OMSC) in New Haven, Connecticut. Under the guidance of Dr. Jean-Paul Wiest and Cathy MacDonald, I entered the world of oral history collection and analysis. To all these people I owe a debt of gratitude.

I am indebted to many others as well: to the leadership and members of Park Street Church, Boston, where, from Easter 1993 up till June 2005, I had found a spiritual home during my years of study in the United States, and where I had served as minister of missions; to the Board of Elders, Missions, Finance and Administration Committees of the Church for allowing me to take time off from work to write the dissertation that was revised into this book; Dr. Gordon P. Hugenberger, senior minister of the Church; David W. Rix, chair of the Missions Committee; and to Dr. Ron Barndt, the moderator of the church.

I am currently blessed to serve as compassionate outreach pastor at Bay Area Community Church, Annapolis, Maryland and have enjoyed the pastoral oversight and brotherly love of my senior pastor Greg St. Cyr and his leadership team. To them I am also very much indebted.

I also extend my profound gratitude to the Methodist Church Ghana and to the conference of 1992 for permission to do further studies at Harvard Divinity School. The 1995 conference also granted me permission to extend my time in the United States so that I could undertake doctoral studies at Boston University School of Theology. I am also grateful to the current and past MCG leadership teams for giving me unrestricted access to documentation and records of the church, especially to those in office during the research period; to the Most Reverend Dr. Samuel Asante-Antwi, presiding bishop; the Right Rev. Albert Ofoe-Wright, administrative bishop; the Very Reverend Comfort R. Quartey-Papafio, assistant to the administrative bishop; the Very Reverend Dr. Emmanuel Asante, general director of the Board of Ministries; and the Very Reverend Professor Joshua Kudadjie, coordinator of the ministers' retreat, for allowing me to conduct a survey of four hundred MCG ministers, the results of which have served as a primary source for confirming the historical content and sequence in this book.

I thank my first and second readers, Professors Dana L. Robert and M. L. (Inus) Daneel, for their meticulous supervision, insuring that the dissertation on which this book is based conforms to professional academic standards. Over the course of my studies at Boston University, Professor Robert's classes have been intellectually stimulating and spiritually uplifting. She was also very supportive in seeking financial assistance for this project in its research stage. But perhaps her most abiding influence and contribution stems from the fact that she introduced me to significant networks of missiologists around the globe. The directors of the Boston University African Studies Center deserve thanks for their generous sponsorship when I was a student as well as for underwriting the cost of one of the research trips to Ghana.

My gratitude extends to my late mother, Ernestina Essamuah, for giving me access to her personal collection of church records accumulated over the years. My mother, at the age of thirty-three, was the national president of the Women's Fellowship. During the tenure of my late father, the Reverend Samuel B. Essamuah, as president of the conference, she was the President of the Ministers Wives Association. A history buff, she had a collection of funeral programs that have served as an invaluable source of information, offering biographical data and corroborating church events. Her indispensable role in my research became more and more evident as I sought understanding of the issues behind some of the policy changes during the period under review. It was a joy to read from the Minutes and check back with her for confirmation and additional "insider" interpretation. *Maa, me da w'ase pii.*

Most importantly, I could not have completed either the dissertation or this book without the support I have received from my wife, Dr. Angela M. Wakhweya-Essamuah, and our children, Zinhle Kristyn, Zikomo Samuel, and Zachary Noel. Angela has had to take on extra duties at home to make up for my long absences. Her prayers and personal encouragement when it was tough was the single most significant contributor to the completion of this book. *Namukobe, wanyala nabi!*

In the final phase of editing, the following rendered invaluable assistance: Anne O'Donnell, who formatted, proofed and edited; the Rev. Dr. Kofi Asimpi who read the manuscript and offered substantial recommendations; and Robert T. Coote, senior contributing editor of *International Bulletin of Missionary Research*, who brought a detective's eye, a missionary's heart, and a copy-editor's expansive knowledge to the entire work. I also express my appreciation to

Dr. Jonathan Bonk, executive director of the OMSC, for allowing me the use of a room and the facilities of OMSC from time to time. The serenity of the OMSC atmosphere greatly aided the writing process. My brothers Colin and Ernest proofread earlier drafts and offered critical comments. My nephews and niece Justin, Agatha, and Bernard Williams also made New Haven a home away from home.

The following also assisted me in locating materials or provided me with copies of documents: Emmanuel Abbey (librarian at the Department of Religious Studies, University of Ghana); library staff at the Akrofi-Christaller Memorial Centre for Mission Research and Applied Theology; the staff of the Methodist Church, Ghana, Archives and Documentation Centre; Oliver Chapman of the *Methodist Times* who gave me access to all the past editions of the church newspaper; Richard Foli who supplied me copies of the video interviews with past presidents; Dr. Robert K. Aboagye-Mensah, then general secretary of the Christian Council of Ghana (CCG) who gave me videos of their celebrations; and Boston Public library that afforded me access to the Wesleyan Methodist Missionary Society (WMMS) and Methodist Missionary Society (MMS) documentation. The staff at Boston University's Mugar Library, and in particular Gretchen Walsh and her staff in the African Studies Section, were extremely helpful in locating materials for me and for speeding up the processing procedure. Likewise the staff at the Boston University School of Theology Library was very helpful. My thanks to you all.

I am thankful to the following for the use of their New England homes while writing: Edward and Lois Dowey (Charlemont), Joe and Ginny Viola (Newton Highlands), and Peter and Diana Bennett (Hingham). My brother Albert and his wife Margaret and their family hosted me on all my visits to Ghana in connection with my research. In the living room of his home my brother has a wonderful collection of photo portraits of all the leaders of early Gold Coast Methodism, which served as a source of inspiration.

In preparing this material for publication, I have benefitted greatly from the friendship of Dr. J Kwabena Asamoah-Gyadu and Jude Kwame Hama of Trinity Theological Seminary and Scripture

Union of Ghana respectively. I am thankful to Rev. Samuel Atteh Odjelua also for his ecumenical fraternity. I have also received very valuable and constructive feedback from Dr. Darrell Whiteman, vice president, Mission Education and resident missiologist at the Mission Society; the Reverend John Pritchard, formerly Africa then General Secretary of the Methodist Church Overseas Division, (MCOD-UK); Professors John S. Pobee and Joshua N. Kudadjie of the Legon Theological Studies Series, Ghana; Dr. John A.K. Bonful of the Calvary Redeeming Methodist Church, Maryland and finally Francis L. Bartels, doyen of Ghana Methodist history and author of *The Roots of Ghana Methodism*.

I do not pretend that this is the last word on this subject. I have built on the work of others and so I hope that this contribution on the history of MCG will provoke other scholars, whether by its analysis or by its omissions, to delve further into the rich and unfolding history of MCG. All my friends and family members are hereby absolved from any error in fact or interpretation. That responsibility is mine and mine alone.

The grace to undertake this assignment was given by God and so to him all glory is due.

FOREWORD

SINCE THE PUBLICATION OF FRANCIS L. BARTELS' BOOK, *The Roots of Ghana Methodism*, in 1965, some of us have been expecting another book from a Ghanaian Methodist that takes off from where he ended or a book that offers us further insight into the period that Bartels covered so brilliantly and insightfully. This is what in my view Dr. Casely B. Essamuah's book seeks to achieve. His book provides us with fresh insight into the contributions that Ghanaians particularly the Akan group of people called Fantes made in the early establishment of the Methodist Church Ghana. Whereas most books on the history of early Methodism in Ghana focus on the role played by British missionaries who gave their lives to the work of the Lord, there are very few, if any that concentrate, on and acknowledge the contributions made by, the indigenous Ghanaian Christians. This is one of the strengths of this publication.

This book is also significant in the sense that it is not like most publications today that focus on the ministries of the newer African Initiated Churches at the neglect of the mainline orthodox churches, such as the Methodist and Presbyterian churches. Dr. Essamuah has demonstrated that the orthodox churches, like the MCG have made and continue to make invaluable contributions to the life and work of Africans and other peoples. Indeed his book clearly establishes that for anyone who desires a more in-depth appreciation of the currents of Christianity in Africa, a close examination of mainline churches will bear much rewarding fruit. For in terms of national outreach, socio economic ministries, and public witness, the mainline churches in most cases far outpace these newer churches and para-church organizations.

In Ghana, the Methodist Church has been in the forefront of the Christian movement and Essamuah has provided an analytic reading of our history highlighting the singular role of early Fante Methodists and their unfailing zeal in bringing the message of the gospel to the other ethnic groups in Ghana, and even in West Africa. With such a fascinating historical background, the author has organized his book around the issues of identity, Akan culture, and Methodist missionary theology.

The enduring validity of the Ghanaian Methodist musical heritage, the *ebibindwom* is discussed, and so is the evolving missionary work among the Ghanaian Diaspora in the United States and Canada.

Another important aspect of this book is that it gives a broader portrait of the church's mission history, including issues of division undergirded by church politics, and ethnocentrism. It also examines the Methodist church's witness during the political upheaval in Ghana, as an upholder of democracy and human rights, as well as innovative ventures such as the establishment of the Methodist University College, Ghana (MUCG) to supplement government efforts to offer tertiary education to young people in Ghana. The book ends in the year 2000 with the MCG's adoption of what it terms as the Biblical Pattern of Episcopacy and the controversies surrounding it.

Essamuah challenges other scholars to participate in writing the history of the mainline churches as well as that of the newer churches, and thereby advancing scholarship and truth seeking. African Christian scholars must commit themselves to a well-sustained intellectual engagement with matters of their history, faith, and practice; for it is intelligent believers, inspired by the Holy Spirit, who offer hope for a sustained future growth and relevance of the church in Africa.

For tracing an arc of the missionary history of the Methodist Church Ghana, Essamuah's work has given us a rich missiological understanding of the role of the church in the state, and that cannot be ignored by anyone who wants to write a serious post colonial history of mainline churches.

Coming from a distinguished Methodist family, and with a deep-seated affection for his roots, Dr. Essamuah has crafted a book that would satisfy a historian's quest for objectivity and a pastor's penchant for sensitivity. He is to be commended for his courage not only in wading through a sea of archival materials, but also for combining it with written analysis and with a participant-observer's stance. I heartily commend it to the people called Methodist in Ghana especially in this year of our 170th anniversary celebration when we acknowledge the enormous and significant sacrifices that both British and African missionaries made in the early establishment of the Methodist Church Ghana.

May the Triune God, Father, Son, and Holy Spirit be praised and honored.

The Most Reverend Dr. Robert K. Aboagye-Mensah
Presiding Bishop, The Methodist Church Ghana, 2003-2009
January 2005

INTRODUCTION

Statement of the Problem

GHANAIAN METHODISM IS THE PRODUCT OF INDIGENOUS EFFORTS from 1835 through 1961, at which point Ghana achieved autonomy from the Methodists of Great Britain. The primary focus of this work is the contextualization of the church, from 1961 to 2000. The result of this process is a mainline church that is "genuinely Ghanaian." Indeed, the freedom to choose and transform elements of Methodism gives this church its unique character.

The history of this church over the last century has coincided with a period of extraordinary expansion of the Christian population in Africa. This growth is especially significant viewed against the backdrop of the political and economic fortunes of the continent. Africa began the twentieth century as partitioned colonies of European countries and ended as a continent of independent political entities. Economically, the continent continues to lag behind in the provision of social amenities to her citizens. But yet the religious landscape could not be richer. The ubiquity of Christianity in sub Saharan Africa prompted the late Africanist Adrian Hastings to remark, "Black Africa today is inconceivable apart from the presence of Christianity, a presence which a couple of generations ago could still be not unreasonably dismissed as fundamentally marginal and a mere subsidiary aspect of colonialism" (Hastings 1990, 208).

Many nationalists anticipated that political independence in sub-Saharan Africa would diminish if not altogether eliminate mission-established Christianity. Theologians devoted much attention to the "foreignness" of the Christianity imparted by Westerners.[1] Furthermore, it was alleged, "Missionary exploits prove that the Christian claim to have a monopoly on the truth inevitably leads to the oppression of other people and their culture" (Sampson 2001, 92). Because missionaries were perceived as benefiting from the political and economic presence of European powers, they were inevitably linked with the colonialists and thus were considered guilty by association. Too often it appeared that to become a Christian meant taking on Western cultural ways. Local cultures were denigrated, and it was presumed that they had to be transformed, if not destroyed, before a foundation for the acceptance of Christianity could be built.

What was often missed in such assessments was that, in spite of the failures in the transmission of the gospel in Africa, the message was transmitted and received and appropriated by Africans.[2] Kwame Bediako cites the Nigerian church historian E. A. Ayandele, who remarked at the end of a missionary-bashing conference, "Even if you came to us within the framework of colonialism, and did not preach the Gospel in all its purity, that has not prevented us from receiving the Gospel and genuinely living it" (Bediako 1995a, 123).

One could hardly find a more apt exemplar of the contextualization of the Christian faith by Africans than the subject of this study, the Methodist Church Ghana.[3] John Baur, in *Two Thousand Years of Christianity in Africa: An African History, 62-1992,* asserts, "In modern Christian Africa the place of honour among the first local churches undoubtedly belongs to Ghana, more precisely to the Methodist Church among the Fante" (Baur 1994, 117). Baur's statement reflects the perspective that I am positing, namely, that the MCG has been a remarkable African institution since its initiation. Bengt G.M. Sundkler likewise credits the Wesleyan Fante on the Gold Coast[4] for establishing a people's movement and a pace setting church (Sundkler and Steed 2000, 85).

After gaining autonomy from the British Methodist Conference in 1961, intensified efforts were expended in contextualizing Ghanaian Methodism. This work focuses on two broad areas: (1) how the post independence Ghanaian cultural and social milieu has shaped the self-understanding of the MCG, and (2) what the church has retained of its Wesleyan Methodist heritage. The analysis involves chronicling historical developments and highlighting elements of contextualization. Relevant information is derived from conference agendas, minutes, and special reports, as well as from interviews with informants who corroborated historical events. Profiles of leaders have been culled from special events programs such as induction and memorial services.

Cardinal elements in this analysis of MCG identity include Africanness, Akan tradition and identity, and Methodist missionary theology. The thrust of this book is to show that Ghanaians accepted Methodism on their own terms and reworked it to fit their needs.

Significance of the Study

THIS WORK HAS SEVERAL SIGNIFICANT FEATURES. IT IS A historical study of MCG in the last third of the twentieth century. With contextualization as the interpretive perspective, the study integrates historical, ethnological, missiological, and theological analysis, making this a multi disciplinary work. This project preserves for posterity eyewitness accounts from some of the actors in this still unfolding drama. This book incorporates oral history gathered from interviews of more than forty people with first hand knowledge of these events. This is a missiological reflection that uses history as the medium. And so the selection of material had to cover areas of both history and missiology.

Unlike much recent research on African Christian history, this study focuses on mainline Christianity and thereby helps to fill a void created by the fact that so many contemporary Ghanaian scholars have concentrated their research on African Initiated Churches.[5] As a result, some people today conceive of African Christianity solely in terms of the indigenous churches, founded independently from Western influence, usually in the twentieth century. What is needed to balance the picture is an in-depth study of older mission-founded churches. Dana L. Robert writes, "African mission initiatives in mainline-initiated churches can provide a framework within which issues of popular spirituality, theology and culture, women's role, the role of mission education in building African societies, and power struggles in the churches can be raised" (Robert 2003, 11).[6]

The present account of MCG contributes to the righting of the balance. This church was initiated by Ghanaians, developed by Ghanaians, and led by Ghanaians for one hundred and thirty years prior to its gaining autonomy in 1961. Although the story of MCG foundations has been told before, it has failed to highlight the role of the Ghanaian Fante Christians as the prime movers. This work, demonstrating that MCG is a truly indigenous African institution, is offered as a response to Hastings's statement, "What is most required at present seems to be a [series] of new publications based on archival research, personal experience and field work and focusing, regionally or locally, on mission founded Christian churches in the periods 1920–1950 and 1970–1990" (Hastings 1990, 209). This work adds to the literature on African agency in initiating and collaborating on Christian missions.

I was born in Ghana and was ordained by the 1990 Annual Conference of MCG. I served for four years as the chaplain at Ghana National College, Cape Coast, and concurrently for eight months as the minister in charge of the Abura Calvary Society of the Cape Coast Circuit. Earlier on, my circuit work had been in Ekon and in New Ebu, both stations of the Moree Circuit. In my last year of service in Ghana prior to coming to the United States to study, I served as assistant synod secretary of the premier Cape Coast District and consequently was a member of the 1992 Annual Conference.

My experience of church life dates from my infancy, for I grew up in the manse or, as Ghanaians prefer to call it, "the mission house." My father, Samuel B. Essamuah (1916–87), was the fifth president of the conference of the MCG or in current terms, the presiding bishop (1979–84). His term as president culminated more than forty years of service throughout Ghana, mainly in areas where his pioneering evangelistic and musical abilities were put to great use. My paternal grandfather was a renowned catechist of MCG. My maternal grandfather, Jacob Eduam-Baiden, and my great-grandmother, Lucy Crentsil, were lay representatives who sat in the synod of the Ghanaian Methodist Church before the attainment of autonomy. My great-grandmother was also an accomplished sacred lyric singer. In this connection I recall the words of Bediako: "Theological consciousness presupposes religious tradition, and tradition requires memory and memory is integral to identity: without memory, we have no past, and if we have no past, then we lose our identity" (Bediako 1996, 428). Hence this study attempts to highlight and sharpen the identity of MCG.

Definitions

FOUR PRINCIPAL CONCEPTS MERIT DEFINITION: CONTEXTUALIZAtion, Wesleyan theology and holistic mission theory, Africanness, and Akan.

Contextualization

THE CONCEPT OF CONTEXTUALIZATION IS A RELATIVELY CONtemporary addition to the discussion of the interaction of gospel and culture. Shoki Coe and Aharon Sapsezian, directors of the Theological Education Fund (TEF), coined the term in early 1972. According to Bruce J. Nicholls, "The TEF report for that year, 'Ministry and Context,' suggested that contextualization implies all that is involved in the familiar term indigenization, but seeks to press beyond it to take into account the process of secularity, technology and the struggle for human justice which characterized the historical movement of nations in the Third World" (Nicholls 1979, 21). More recently contextualization has been described as "the interpenetration of faith and culture" (Bowie 1999, 69). Dean Gilliland states, "Contextualization means that the Word must dwell among all families of humankind today as truly as Jesus lived among his own kin. The gospel is Good News when it provides answers for *a particular people living in a particular place at a particular time*. This means the worldview of that people provides a framework for communication, the questions and needs of that people are a guide to the emphasis of the message, and the cultural gifts of that people become the medium of expression" (Gilliland 2000, 226, emphasis mine).

Contextualization of the gospel within culture echoes the incarnational nature of the Word of God. Since God came to earth enfleshed in Jesus Christ, and Jesus took the form of a Jewish man, it is imperative that the Christian message be enfleshed in each and every culture in order to assert its authenticity. Anything short of that results in a mismatch (Shorter 1988).

The only way to maintain indigenization while minimizing the possibility of syncretism is to take two principles, the indigenizing and the pilgrim, operating simultaneously. Contextualization takes the indigenizing principle, which states that "the gospel is at home in every culture and every culture is at home with the gospel," and adds the pilgrim principle, which warns that the gospel "will put us out of step with society—for that society never existed, in East or West, ancient time or modern, which could absorb the word of Christ painlessly into its system." Thus, as Andrew F. Walls notes, the gospel is both the prisoner and liberator of cultures simultaneously (Walls 1996, 3, &15).

The theme of contextualization runs through this study of MCG; it offers a comprehensive framework for understanding the mission history of Methodism in Ghana, and for assessing past traditions as well as current realities.

Wesleyan Theology and Holistic Mission Theory

MCG EFFORTS TO CONTEXTUALIZE THE GOSPEL HAVE BEEN APPLIED within the boundaries of Methodist theology and mission theory. Methodist mission theology is grounded both in the personal authority of the Risen Christ and in the world's need of salvation (Wainwright 1995, 252). Unlike other significant leaders of Christian revival movements—such as Thomas Aquinas or John Calvin—the founder of Methodism, John Wesley, did not set about to compose a summa theologica. Instead his theology was set within the context of his life and ministry. "The vehicles for Wesley's theologizing were not scholastic but practical in nature" (Coppedge 1991, 268). Wesley never saw himself as propagating a new truth but rather "the full, primitive, scriptural, Christian faith, once delivered to the saints" (Strawson 1983, 183). The Catholic spirit of the nineteenth-century followers of Wesley is captured in these words: "Our religion is Christianity or it is nothing; but we do not call ourselves the 'Church' or 'Christians,' lest we should exclude, even by implication, those who 'are not of this fold' from the 'flock.' We are 'Catholics,' for we pray that grace may be on all them that love our Lord Jesus Christ in sincerity. We are 'Protestants,' for we deny that there is any authority in Christ's Church higher than His word. We are 'Methodists,' for we desire to be 'The friends of all, the enemies of none' (197).

Wesley, the man who ministered outside the Anglican church with great reluctance, was unwilling to define himself theologically in exclusivistic terms. His approach to theology was more eclectic, placing different and renewed emphases on various themes instead of proposing new ones. Christian perfection or scriptural holiness was regarded by Wesley as "the grand depositum which God has lodged with the people called Methodist; and for the sake of propagating this chiefly He appeared to have raised us up" (225).

> Wesley's sole theological guide was the scriptures; it was his "norming norm." The other elements of the so-called Wesleyan quadrilateral, in addition to scripture,—reason, tradition, and experience—served as secondary sources aiding the interpretation of the scriptures but never superseding the Scriptures.
>
> The Reformers leaned heavily on the language categories that describe creation, sovereign majesty, the legal world of the law court, and to some degree the language of redemption from slavery. This meant that in their understanding of God they tended to focus on his roles as creator, king, judge, and redeemer. Wesley uses all these but also adds to them categories of person-to-person relationships, the sanctuary, the pastoral scene, and most often the home. This meant that Wesley understood more clearly the roles of God as teacher/friend, priest, shepherd and father. The effect of Wesley's adding these biblical analogies to those emphasized by the Reformers was a modifying of the severity of the earlier categories. (Coppedge 1991, 281)

Wesley's holistic perspective bridged God's transcendence and immanence. His theological worldview was composed of such themes as God as Father, whose way of relating to humanity was love; hence Wesley's strong focus on the concept of assurance.

Wesley also emphasized holiness. For Wesley, "Salvation had to include an element of imparted holiness as well as imputed holiness" (284). Concern for the *practice* of the Christian faith drove his preaching and practical ministry. Finally, Wesley emphasized the concept of grace: "Grace that comes before salvation (prevenient grace), grace that leads to repentance, grace that is the basis of justification by faith, grace that is behind assurance of salvation, grace that makes possible growth in Christian experience, grace that works entire sanctification as well as its assurance, and grace that leads to further growth after sanctification until God graciously glorifies the saint" (285). Wesleyan theology can therefore be summarized as a holy Father working by grace to produce a holy people.

If Wesley's theology is difficult to categorize, his mission theology is even more difficult to unpack. Both Cyril Davey's *March of Methodism: The Story of Methodist Missionary Work Overseas* (1951) and N. Allen Birthwhistle's "Methodist Missions" in *A History of the Methodist Church in Great Britain* (1993) record the missionary activity of the Wesleyan movement but devote no attention at all to Methodist missiological theology. Several reasons account for this omission. For one, Wesley never applied the term missionary to himself or to his movement. Wesley saw as primary concern to be the immediate needs of his day, hence his oft-cited aphorism, "I look upon all the world as my parish." He referred to the world outside the ecclesiastical control of the established church and not to the world in the geographic sense. This is not to say that Wesley had no missionary sensitivities. His background and experience—the missionary influence of his mother and his term of pastoral work in Georgia—grounded him for his future ministry. The missionary endeavors of early Methodist preachers, and especially of the church as a collective institution, owed more to Wesley's young Welsh assistant, Thomas Coke—that "fireball of dedicated energy"—than to John Wesley (Vickers 1996, 135). But again this does not mean that one cannot glean the distinctives of Wesleyan mission theology from Wesley's life and ministry.

There is a natural linkage of holy living and social reform. Methodist missions have had a holistic outlook of incorporating proclamation, presence, social improvement, justice, and human development. Methodism has offered a biblically based, theologically comprehensive, and compassionate approach to ministry focused on the whole person.

The most frequently used term to describe the Methodist mission impulse is holiness theology (Robert 2000a; Lang' at 2002). Wesley understood Christian religion as being distinguishable by its social outcome: "The gospel of Christ knows of no religion, but social; no holiness but social holiness. Faith working by love is the length and breadth and depth and height of Christian perfection. This commandment have we from Christ that he who loves God loves his brother also; and that we manifest our love by doing good unto all men, especially to them that are of the household of faith," (Wright 1984, 9).

Africanness

THE NEED FOR "AFRICANNESS" BECAME A CLARION CALL IN AFRICA at the time of political independence, influencing many of the policies of governments and state institutions. This movement took many forms including the appointment of Africans to replace all the positions held by Europeans at the time of decolonization. There is a plethora of literature on the subject of Africanness especially in its political and philosophical aspects (Baur 1994, 447ff.).[7] For this study, John S. Pobee's enumeration of the six elements of *Africanness* will provide the background in determining what is distinctively African.

First, according to Pobee, Africans are human beings still seeking to attain the full potential of their humanness. Second, Africans are unable to explain life without reference to what is religious and spiritual, and therefore they cannot be satisfied with a purely materialistic and secular worldview. Third, African identity is rooted in a sense of belonging to a community that embraces the living, the dead, and the as yet unborn. Fourth, Africans perceive reality in holistic terms, shunning any dualism between material/spiritual, individual/community, religious/social, and intellectual/emotional. Fifth, the institution of chieftaincy in Western Africa is the focal point for culture and a model for leadership patterns. Therefore, any attempt at denigrating culture and converting Africans away from their communities and from their chiefs into Christian enclaves is seen as an assault on Africans and Africanness. Sixth, African culture is expressed through several media, including arts, crafts, and liturgical rites, and not only in concepts and ideas (Pobee 1996, 22–27). These six elements serve as a guideline as this work explores the question of Africanness in the history and development of the MCG from 1961 to 2000.

This study argues in concert with Lamin Sanneh (1989) that translation empowers vernacularization, and with Andrew Walls (1996) that conversion need not be culturally discontinuous, and lastly with Robert Schreiter (1985) that in constructing their own local theology, Ghanaian Methodist Christians have demonstrated a lively and concrete response to the gospel.

My research has highlighted the faithfulness of the MCG community to the ideal of Africanness. I contend that, far from being an irrelevant foreign religious institution, the MCG is an authentic African church.

Akan

THE LAST TERM NEEDING CLARIFICATION IS *Akan*.[8] THE AKAN PEOPLE form 44% of the population of Ghana and therefore constitute the majority of MCG membership. The Akan occupy the greater part of southern Ghana in the semi-deciduous forest areas. Some Akan are also to be found in the Ivory Coast. The Ghana-based Akan may be divided into their major cultural and geographic divisions, each typified by the best- known sub-group: the coastal Akan (Mfantsefo or Fante), the eastern Akan (Akuapem), and the inland Akan (Asuantsefo-Ashanti or Asante) (Oppong 1993, 23). Naturally, they share linguistic and cultural similarities. The languages are a sub-group of the Kwa language, which is found in other parts of West Africa.

A significant aspect of Akan cultural life is its matrilineal line of succession; brothers and nephews on the mother's side, and not sons, traditionally inherit property. Political succession is also matrilineal. However, the matrilineal inheritance system is no longer uniformly practiced. Christianity, Westernization, and modernity have all affected the Akan way of life, and most people in urban areas follow the dictates of a last will and testament in property distribution rather than the traditional cultural dictates. Laws have been enacted that operate should one die intestate; property is now divided equally among wife, children, and the extended family.

The Fante people form the primary subject of this study for two reasons: it is the group among whom European missionary activities began and, because I am Fante myself and a pastor of MCG, it is the group with which I am most familiar.

Initially Methodism came to the Fante on the coast of Ghana, and then, in collaboration with the European missionaries, Fante believers transmitted Ghanaian Methodism to the other ethnic groups. Ghanaian Methodism therefore bears an undeniable Fante flavor.

Research Methodology and Sources of Study

I STARTED BY CONDUCTING HISTORICAL RESEARCH IN SEVERAL archives and libraries on both sides of the Atlantic. My initial research began in the School of Theology Library, Boston University, and in the Boston Public Library. The MCG Documentation and Archival Department was used as a source of primary information. Relevant portions of the agenda and minutes of the Annual conferences of MCG from 1961 to 2000 were collected. In addition, I also referred to copies of other documents such as special service bulletins, committee reports, and newspaper articles. The offices of the publishers of the *Methodist Times* and *Christian Sentinel*, both publications of MCG, gave me copies of their magazines.

Copies of conference agendas, minutes, and special reports as well as programs/bulletins for church events such as induction services and funerals of the period under review were collected from the North Kaneshie Essamuah Family Library in Accra and elsewhere. Reports of relevant committees of MCG were also examined.

The libraries and resource centers of the Akrofi-Christaller Centre for Mission Research and Applied Theology (Akropong-Akwapim), and the Department for the Study of Religion and the Institute of African Studies—both at the University of Ghana, Legon—also served as sources of information. Dissertations by Ghanaians having a bearing on this subject were studied at these centers. Each of these institutions offered an environment for the cross-fertilization of ideas and thus sharpened the theoretical boundaries and scope of this project.

During my fieldwork, I relied on my network of friends and colleagues in MCG to help me fill the gaps in my archival search. To supplement my already acquired experience, I attended a great number of special church services and funerals under the auspices of MCG. I also gathered a significant amount of source material from the living witnesses of the unfolding history of Ghanaian Methodism. Forty interviews were tape-recorded and transcribed, with the resulting texts corroborating the historic veracity of some of the chapters of this book. In 1999 a pre-dissertation research trip to Ghana was undertaken in order to gather preliminary information and to initiate some contacts. This was followed by weeks of travel in Ghana to interview a random selection of church leaders, both lay and ministerial, who in private discussions revealed significant moments in the church's history that helped to determine the ways in which MCG has matured as an African Christian institution. In 2001 I pursued further research in Ghana and conducted additional interviews. These interviews served as sources of historical record corroborating the written documents.

This research was conducted using historical analysis of various events in the period under review. Both a chronological and topical approach were used in analyzing the data, and a measure of critical discernment was achieved by providing "profiles and minutiae that enrich and authenticate historical accounts" (Addo-Fening 2000,

38). In addition, the research gives voice to the many who have contributed to the subject matter through their writings as well as those who have lived as devoted Ghanaian Methodist Christians. Since a particular theological lens, namely, missiology, is applied in this approach, the result is a multidisciplinary investigation, combining both history and theology.

Limitations

THERE ARE BUILT IN ADVANTAGES AND DISADVANTAGES TO THE USE of a thematic treatment of MCG's autonomy history. For example, subjects are raised and treated in topical, not necessarily chronological, fashion. At times this may obscure the chronological progression of the study.

The thematic approach has also revealed that there is a veritable trove of subjects demanding a much more sustained and in-depth analysis, for instance, the role of women within MCG and society in general; the religious and liturgical traffic between MCG and AICs; unique features of MCG sermons; biographies of leading women and men in MCG; histories of church organizations and schools, and military and police chaplaincies; and a comparison of *ebibindwom* and American gospel music.

There are other self-imposed limitations in this thesis. First, the use of the missiological framework means that this investigation is not a comprehensive church history project. Only those facts that contribute to the understanding of the church's missiological stance as a contextualized African Christian institution are examined. Second, although some of its conclusions may be applicable to other denominations in Ghana and possibly outside Ghana, this study does not claim to have identified a general pattern of response of African Christian leadership to issues of theological and missiological self-understanding. It is intentionally focused on MCG and is therefore self limiting in its approach and conclusions.

Third, only the first thirty-nine years of national leadership are considered. These years, however, constitute the formative years of MCG as an autonomous institution. The adoption of episcopacy and other American Methodist church structures in 2000 was a threshold event symbolizing the informal severance of a critical link with the British Methodist Conference and the formal commencement of a significant link with American Methodism. The years under consideration represent a significant period in the life and history of MCG that allows an assessment as to whether and to what degree the church and its national leadership have faithfully served Ghanaian society.

Literature Review

CHRISTIANITY IN GHANA HAS BEEN THE SUBJECT OF WORKS BY Robert K Aboagye-Mensah, John K. Agbeti, Elizabeth C. Amoah, Emmanuel K. Asante, C.G. Baeta, Kwame Bediako, Hans W. Debrunner, Kwesi A. Dickson, and Rosalind Hackett. Others who have written on Christianity in Ghana are Paul Gifford, Joshua N. Kudadjie, Birgit Meyer, H.W. Mobley, Pashington Obeng, Mercy Amba Oduyoye, Kofi Asare Opoku, Robert T. Parsons, John S. Pobee, Peter Akwasi Sarpong, Gerrie ter Haar, and Sidney G. Williamson. Samuel Adubofuor, J. Kwabena Asamoah-Gyadu, Paul Kwabena Boafo, and E. Kingsley Larbi have also examined the contemporary scene in Ghanaian Christianity. However, no one has written exclusively and exhaustively on MCG in contemporary times. And although there have been studies conducted on Ghanaian Methodism, none of them has examined the factors reviewed in this book.

The first written work that specifically focused on Methodism in Ghana was Arthur E. Southon's *Gold Coast Methodism: The First Hundred Years 1835-1935,* which gave ample credit to the Ghanaian (Fante) initiation of Methodism, as well as to their consequent close collaboration with British missionaries in establishing what Southon called "an indigenous church" (Southon 1935, 28). Southon's work is very helpful in tracing the early days of Ghanaian Methodism, and especially in revealing its indigeneity.

Francis L. Bartels's *Roots of Ghana Methodism* (1965) built on the work of Southon, bringing the history up to the time of autonomy.

Bartels's work is probably the first full scale account of a mainline church by an indigenous Ghanaian. It highlights the Ghanaian partnership with European (mainly English and Irish Methodist) missionaries in the work of Methodism in Ghana. Bartels's approach is helpful, particularly with regard to reports in the late 1950s and early 1960s surrounding the negotiations for granting autonomy to Methodism in Ghana. Bartels concluded his investigation at the time of autonomy and so enables us to see some of the immediate social and political challenges that the new autonomous church faced.

While Bartels employed a chronological approach in examining the roots of Ghanaian Methodism, Sidney G. Williamson, a British Methodist missionary who served in Ghana, approached the same subject through a slightly larger lens and in thematic fashion. In *Akan Religion and the Christian Faith* (1944) Williamson analyzes the interface of Christianity and the traditional, pre-Christian Akan culture and religion. However, Williamson's work relied heavily on works of European anthropologists and is somewhat dated. His major Ghanaian source, J. B. Danquah's *The Akan Doctrine of God: Fragments of Gold Coast Ethics and Religion* (1968), has been criticized for adopting "disreputable and unsupported theories about the origins of some Akan words . . . and reprodu[cing] Akan thought in the dress of English philosophy of the 1920s and 1930s which he learnt as a student from Professor G. Dawes Hicks" (Ackah 1988, 3). The present book uses literature that is more current to augment Williamson's account.

Matthias K. Forson's 1993 thesis, "Split-Level Christianity in Africa: A Study of the Persistence of Traditional Religious Beliefs and Practices among the Akan Methodists of Ghana," contends that Christianity has failed to be fully integrated into the daily lives of the Ghanaian Methodist people, as evidenced in the lively persistence of the old religious traditional beliefs and practices from which the people are supposed to have been converted. I assert that the converse is true: Ghanaian Methodism is as vibrant as it is today precisely because it has not sought to eliminate completely the old traditional religious worldview and practices, but rather has adapted aspects of their form of worship while maintaining Christian integrity.

One of the more helpful guides in this investigation is Birgit Meyer.[9] Meyer notes that anthropologists do not consider the study of mission churches as exciting as that of AICs. Operating on the assumption that the doctrinal emphases of the members of mission churches are no different from that of Western missionaries, anthropologists have tended to study religious movements that they find to be more exotic and in their opinion, therefore, more "African." Meyer, however, uses ethnographic materials to demonstrate that mainline church members hold ideas that are not as Westernized as has been assumed. Rather, the beliefs of many members of mission-founded churches in Africa represent a synthesis of biblical Christianity and African culture at a very deep level. She shows that the source of the Christian doctrine and practices of regular church members is typically different from that proposed by their Western-educated theologians. Furthermore, "[The] assumption of the necessity of indigenization is founded on a fundamental misunderstanding . . . that the ideas of church members are not understood as an 'African' product of the contact between the missionaries' Christianity and the pre-Christian , traditional Ewe religion, but as a result of Western domination. However, Africanization has in fact been there since the beginning: conversion certainly did not mean the mechanical take-over of the missionary teachings, but their appropriation based on existing ideas and concepts" (Meyer 1992, 100).

The scholarly discussion of the issue of African Christian identity, and especially of the self-definition of members of the mainline churches is still in its infancy. Scholars tend to group together all mainline churches as not being adequately representative of African religious and cultural particularities. This thesis offers a much-needed corrective. Fabian was correct when he asserted thirty eight years ago, "The most serious gap . . . is that we know almost nothing about the faith of orthodox mission Christians, and I strongly suspect that improved information on that point would make any statements about the 'deviance' of 'sects' and 'separatist movements' look rather simplistic" (Fabian 1971, 165).

Chapter Outlines

CHAPTER 1 SURVEYS THE HISTORY OF MCG FROM THE FORMATION of the Fante Bible Band in 1831 to MCG autonomy in 1961. This chapter focuses on the role of Ghanaians, particularly the Fante, in establishing an indigenous church. The special contribution of the biracial missionary, Thomas Birch Freeman, is also examined. Within that context, the chapter selectively treats three aspects of the early history of MCG, all incidents of mass conversion, with a view to underscoring the role of indigenous agency. The first is the Nananom Mpow (Sacred Grove) incident; second, the life and ministry of William Wadé Harris; and lastly, the prophetic ministry of Samson Oppong. Each of the three historical aspects is examined as to its impact on the dynamic growth and theology of MCG.

Chapter 2, on mission as church planting, begins by assessing the Ghanaian Methodist leadership's self-understanding and expectations of autonomy. A few cases studies are examined to reveal MCG witness to the Ghanaian society: its encounter with Islam in northern Ghana, its witness in urban Ghana, and its witness to the Ghanaian Diaspora.

Chapter 3 considers mission as a social uplift through the provision of educational institutions and health-care delivery systems. In this chapter, four case studies are considered: Tema St. Paul's Secondary School, as an example of a local circuit initiative; the Kumasi educational initiatives, as an example of a diocesan initiative; the Methodist University College, Ghana, as an example of a connexional initiative; and finally, MCG's attempt at using health-care delivery as a means of evangelization is discussed, based on the Ankaase Faith Healing Hospital.

Chapter 4, on the subject of mission in public witness, catalogs MCG's attempts at upholding democracy and serving as an internal opposition and a human rights watchdog in the very unstable political times of Ghanaian history.

Chapter 5 examines internal conflicts within MCG as challenges to its mission. Particular attention is given to the evolution of the Fante Society into Calvary Society-North Accra Circuit; the events surrounding the designation of Stephens as the first non Fante president of MCG; and a series of issues involving the Winneba district. Two episodes involving the Reverends Micah Edu-Buandoh and Maclean Kumi are also evaluated. These crises are studied in light of the alleged effect of ethnicity and ethnocentrism in MCG.

Chapter 6 is on the subject of missiological theologizing as an expression of self identity, and is divided into four parts. The first part examines the liturgical innovations that have been emphasized within MCG during 1961–2000, and in particular the unique musical heritage of Ghanaian Methodism exhibited in its sacred lyrics (*ebibindwom*). The second part examines how MCG has redefined membership in relation to the practice of polygamy. The third and fourth parts look at these other features of ecclesiology: (1) the history and demise of attempts at church union, and (2) the debate and adoption of episcopacy as the system of church governance for MCG in 2000.

Chapter 7 concludes the study with an analysis of the factors that demonstrate the indigenous character of MCG. What is today known as the Methodist Church, Ghana began not as a Western missionary institution but simply as a group of Fante laypersons who wanted to study the Christian Scriptures. It was, in fact, African (Fante) initiated. In the course of a dynamic history that blended Wesleyan theology, Ghanaian identity, and Akan cultural traditions, Ghanaian Methodists propagated and contextualized their faith in ways that authenticated MCG's Africanness. By focusing on a mainline church, this study helps to fill a void in current scholarship and thereby presents a more in-depth picture of African Christianity.

A brief epilogue reflects on the major issues that continue to engage the attention of MCG almost a decade after the beginning of the original research of this book.

CHAPTER ONE

Foundations of Ghana Methodism

MCG, UNLIKE MANY CHURCHES IN AFRICA THAT WERE INITIATED by Western missionary societies, was indigenous from its infancy. Several foundational elements that shaped its indigenous character and ethos will be explored: (1) The formation and role of the Fante Bible band, (2) the ministry of Thomas Freeman, (3) the Nananom Mpow[10] episode, 4) the ministry of the prophet William Wadé Harris, and 5) the contribution of evangelist Samson Oppong. It was the initiative of the Fante Bible study group that led to the involvement of English Wesleyan missionaries. Freeman, a young minister of mixed race from England, who labored in Ghana and neighboring states for half a century, excelled at empowering indigenous leadership. The Nananom Mpow incident spotlighted the role of courageous laypeople in breaking the hold of a traditional cult, and the ministries of Harris and Oppong.[11] Both spirit-filled, though semiliterate, West African prophets, succeeded in areas where Western missionaries had found it impossible to make progress. To understand the dynamics of these events is to appreciate the fact that Ghanaian Methodism has had an all-embracing indigenous character right from its beginning.

Ghanaian Christianity:
EARLY FOUNDATIONS, 1471–1835

METHODISM CAME RELATIVELY LATE TO GHANA, IN THE EARLY 1830s. Portuguese explorers and Catholic missionary orders preceded Protestant missionaries by at least two centuries, and Moravian and Anglican missionaries arrived in the eighteenth century, a hundred years before the arrival of the first Methodist missionary. A review of the record of earlier European and Christian influences in Ghana will be helpful before examining the roots and development of Methodism in Ghana.

Portuguese explorers first brought Christianity to Ghana[12] in the latter part of the fifteenth century, thereby establishing outposts in Shama in 1471 and in Elmina in 1482. On January 19, 1482, Diego D'Azambuja, a Portuguese Catholic sailor, met with the Fante king, Kwamina Ansa (Caramansa), in Elmina and received permission to build a castle. D'Azambuja built a chapel inside the castle, naming it Sao Jorge (St. George), after the patron saint of Portugal. Because the Portuguese restricted themselves to their own folk inside their enclaves, they had little missionary impact on the local populace (Sanneh 1983, 20).

But a century later, in 1572, as a result of the work of Portuguese Augustinian missionaries, the Fante kings of Efutu, Komenda, and Abura, all in modern-day southern Ghana, were converted to the Christian faith. In the eighteenth century Moravian missionaries from Brandenburg, Germany, and Anglican missionaries from England sponsored by the Society for the Propagation of the Gospel in Foreign Parts, initiated pioneer missionary work in Ghana. Some of their leading Fante converts were trained and ordained in Europe as ministers: Jacobus Capitein and Philip Quaque are two of the better-known figures. Quaque was an Anglican chaplain of the colonial forts for fifty years, and Capitein, also an Anglican, was part of the first Fante Bible translation project. However, as Adrian

Hastings notes, "In missionary terms they were all failures . . . gifted individuals, blossoming in Europe but tied in Africa to a tiny white slaving community and only serving beyond it a rather nominally Christian fringe of mulattos living in the shadow of a fort"[13] (Hastings 1994, 178).

By the early decades of the nineteenth century the work of the Protestant and Catholic missions had begun to take hold. Consequently, when the seeds of Methodism were sowed in 1835, they did not fall on virgin soil. Methodism came to Ghana and to Cape Coast[14] where there were already professing Ghanaian Christians. In fact, it was Ghanaian Christians who, in effect, invited Methodism to Ghana.

The first full-scale historical treatment of MCG is Arthur E. Southon's *Gold Coast Methodism* (1934). Southon emphasizes the role played by Ghanaians, especially coastal Fante people, in establishing Methodism in Ghana. At the time of the publication of his book, the centenary year of MCG, 1935, it was unusual for histories of mission churches to give a prominent place to the initiative and collaboration of native Christians. So, the fact that Southon repeats on almost every page the fact that this particular church was an indigenous institution initiated and nurtured by indigenous leadership, is a testimony to the labor of the early founders of Ghanaian Methodism. Current scholarship on the genesis of MCG points out the significant role the Fante leaders played. John Baur argues that the story of the original Fante Methodists "is a source of inspiration for Christian evangelism" (Baur 1994, 117). "The Fante Wesleyans had created a people's movement," asserts Bengt G.M. Sundkler (Sundkler 2000, 207).

Southon's record begins with "the most inhuman traffic in the world," the slave trade (1935, 14). Dotted along the coast of Ghana are castles and forts originally used as trade posts and ultimately as holding houses for captured men and women who were placed on slave ships for passage to Europe and to the Americas. The history of Ghana cannot be told without reference to the slave trade.[15] Elizabeth Isichei rightly states, "The great weakness of the Christian enterprise in black Africa in the Middle Ages was its close association with the slave trade" (Isichei 1995, 71).[16]

The original motivation for the secular European presence in

Africa was the trade in slaves, gold, and other raw materials. The presence of the European merchants and their trade interests provided in effect the balance of power. The historian David Kimble argues,

> Economic development was the main mediating force whereby the individualist, competitive, acquisitive attitudes and values of the West were introduced into African society. The impact was least, however, during the centuries of pre colonial coastal trade, greatest during the comparatively short colonial era. The early European traders brought new means to wealth and power: their guns and gunpowder profoundly altered the balance of power among the coastal States with which they came into contact, and contributed significantly to the rise of the interior kingdoms, notably Akwamu and Ashanti. (Kimble 1963, 128)

The social changes that the presence of European traders on the coast generated affected every stratum of society. The local political structure was altered and the cohesiveness of the extended family and clan was subverted as new associations and influences were introduced.

Methodism, therefore, arrived in Ghana during conditions created by the slave trade. Its goal was to aid in creating a counter cultural establishment in this period. In a significant work, Lamin Sanneh develops the concept of "antistructure" to argue that "West African Christianity espoused the culture of radical criticism of all power structures, a demystification of ideologies of absolute authority, and a dissemination of what are often regarded as 'democratic' and 'liberal' values" (Sanneh 2000, 173; see also 1999, 3–11). Christianity, as seen by Sanneh, then became "more than a nemesis of slavery; it is the nemesis, on the right of hereditary privilege and natural entitlement, and on the left, of ideologies of power and state absolutization" (Sanneh, in Miller 2002, 26). Hastings adds that in the Ghanaian experience, "the roots of nineteenth century Christianity . . . are to be found less in the return of recaptives [recaptured, liberated slaves] than among pupils of Philip Quaque and the Cape Coast Castle school" (Hastings 1995, 340). Thus, the peculiar situation of slavery abetted by both imperial trading concerns on one hand, and native traditional authorities on the other hand, stimulated a reaction that served to produce the uniquely "democratic" Christianity in which MCG played a significant part.

Ghanaian Methodism began in the days when European powers, principally Britain, had determined to end the trade in human slaves. Britain declared the slave trade illegal in its empire as of 1807, and from 1824 slave trading was considered piracy and punishable by death; but it took quite a while to stamp it out. Christian stalwarts like John Wesley, William Wilberforce,[17] and Thomas Buxton, through their public advocacy, aroused the collective conscience of England to the evils of slavery. Many missionaries in that era went to Africa with their conscience thoroughly awakened (Walls, in Anderson 1994, 11–17).[18]

Two questions dominated the political life of Ghana in the early decades of the nineteenth century: who would control the inland country where the gold mining had shifted from the coast, and who would control the routes where commerce with the various European merchants took place? (Davidson 1976, 126). As a result, the coastal plains provided a very unstable environment. The Ghanaian coastal Fante people lived in dread of the military might of their northern neighbors, the Asante, and of becoming victims of the slave traders. The Asante kingdom made ample use of its might to capture and trade slaves from far and near. Fantes determined to settle closer to the coasts—and therefore nearer the forts—to enjoy the protection of the Europeans. The MCG was thus born at a time when the danger of war and slave raids was a constant threat on the coastal plains of Ghana.

The Fante Bible Band:
THE ROOTS OF GHANAIAN METHODISM

PERHAPS ONE OF THE MOST FAR-REACHING EFFECTS OF THE EUROpean presence was the appearance of a new elite characterized and defined more by secular achievement than by heredity. In other parts of West Africa, particularly in Sierra Leone and Yoruba land in Nigeria, Creoles, a composite of African and imported blood and culture, some of whom were from recaptives or returned slaves, were among the leading classes (Isichei 1995, 162). But in Ghana, the new elite consisted mainly of business-people and traders, many of whom received their education in schools established by Methodist missions (Kimble 1963, 131–41). It is among these people that Ghanaian Methodism originally took root and found leadership.

In a particularly enlightening study, David N. Hempton (1996; 1999), surveys the historiography of Methodist growth in Europe and North America. He finds that the predominant themes have to do with Methodist structures, organization, and theology, while little discussion is given to why people converted to Methodism. Hempton states that Methodism's attractiveness lay in its "anti-clericalism, anti-Calvinism, anti-formalism, anti-confessionalism, and anti-elitism. Empowerment was from God, knowledge was from the scriptures, salvation was available to all and the Spirit was manifested, not in structures and ecclesiastical order, but in freedom and heart religion" (1996, 10). Methodism, therefore, thrived in the "expanding crevices and margins of societies undergoing profound changes of one sort or another. . . . For a religion which itself chipped away at conventional boundary lines of clericalism, gender, age, and education, the most conducive environments were those interstitial and marginal areas where traditional hierarchical structures were either absent or perceived to be antithetical to new interests" (21, 27). Because it was "an infinitely flexible and adaptable religious species," Methodism attracted the middle class rebels and the activists of society. With equal ease, Methodism functioned within a vernacular religiosity, with all its unpredictable peculiarities, and a centralized bureaucracy (16–17). As a result, in the social and political dislocation of the first half of the nineteenth century in coastal Ghana, Methodism became the religious component of the new definition of power, influence and identity.[19]

As a result of the Anglican ministry at the Cape Coast Castle, several Fantes became Christians (Hastings 1994, 179). They formed themselves into an informal Bible band and met regularly to read, study the Bible, and pray. In his foreword to Francis L. Bartels's *Roots of Ghana Methodism*, Francis Chapman Ferguson Grant, the first Ghanaian president of the MCG Conference, highlights the devotion and activism of the early Fante pioneers of the Methodist Church: "We see them resolved to study the Word of God as the best rule for Christian living—they were Methodists before they were received into the Methodist Church—and watch them become involved in the lives of their country" (Bartels 1965, v). In this statement Grant encapsulates what most Methodists would agree is the two fold essence of Methodism—a devotion to the study of the Word of God and a corresponding involvement in the society at large. Bible study and communal involvement were the hallmarks of this group.

It is regrettable that Joseph Smith and William de Graft,[20] the Fante leaders of the group, are not given places of honor in the history of MCG. As recently as January 1, 2000, when MCG observed its 165th anniversary, the emphasis in all its literature and fanfare was on the first British Methodist missionary, Joseph Dunwell. Although Smith and de Graft and others really constituted the genesis of MCG,[21] very little attention was given in the 165th anniversary material to the members of the Fante Bible band, who were the ones who extended the invitation to the missionary.

The Fante Bible band had a practice of recording minutes of its meetings; the minutes from the original meeting, October 1, 1831, read as follows: "That, as the Word of God is the best rule a Christian ought to observe, it is herein avoided framing other rules to enforce good conduct; but that the Holy Scriptures must be carefully studied, through which, by the help of the Holy Spirit and faith in Jesus Christ, our minds will be enlightened, and find the way to eternal life"[22] (Southon 1934, 27; Bartels 1965, 8).

As in many places when people study the Bible, there soon arose differences in interpretation. DeGraft and some of the other members of the group disassociated themselves from the band because they perceived that Smith, the group's other leader, was too literalistic in his interpretation of the Bible. According to Arthur Southon, Smith:

> Read the Bible privately, and aloud to his students and what he did not understand, he passed over. Not so in the case of

> DeGraft and his companions. They were younger and more alert of mind. As has always been the case with intelligent youth in every country, they wanted to know the meaning of what they read. Bible reading in their case provoked thought and discussion. The Book contained its own authority. And in their eyes, they knew it was the Word of God, and that they must live according to its teaching. They perceived that this was not just one more God whose worship could be added to the gods of their fathers. It was a new faith, something wholly different from Africa's religions, and that in accepting it; they were compelled to break with all their inherited beliefs and customs. (Southon 1934, 25–26)

This quotation identifies the difference between Smith's simplistic and literalistic interpretation and de Graft's more sophisticated interpretation.[23]

The names of the other members of the Bible band were George Blankson (later a member of the Cape Coast legislative council), John Sam, Henry Brew, John Smith, William Brown, John Niezer, John Aggrey, Kobina Mensah Sackey, and Kwabena Mensah. One could conclude from a cursory look at the Anglicized names that these people adopted English culture, but that would be a mistaken judgment. In Ghana, now as well as then, most people have multiple names. These are used in different contexts.[24] The history surrounding this practice is explained by Alex Quaison-Sackey, the first African president of the United Nations General Assembly and later vice-president of MCG. In his book *Africa Unbound* he indicates the pervasive influence of Christian missionaries:

> Even our names were purposely anglicized in nineteenth century Ghana, in order to indicate that the "bearers" had become Christians and therefore civilized as well. My own name, for example, is Sekyi (pronounced Sechi), but it became Sackey simply because my great uncle who had become a Methodist minister before the turn of the last century, wanted it that way. Quaison, meaning the son of Kwei, was adopted by my maternal grandfather in 1896 at school to show his scholar-

> ship. Thus, Obu, meaning rock, became Rockson; Kuntu, meaning blanket, became Blankson; and Dadzie, meaning steel, became Steele-Dadzie.[25] (Quaison-Sackey 1963, 52)

In nineteenth-century Ghana, the Anglicized names signaled not only spiritual conversion but also a far-reaching cultural interaction.

By the beginning of the nineteenth century, the coastal communities of Ghana had had a lengthy association with European powers, an association that gradually changed the power and social dynamics of the country. The British, representing the most powerful European nation in Ghana, preferred the coast as a counterbalance to the Asante, while the Dutch encouraged the domination by the Asante of the coastal regions, especially Fanteland.

The Ghanaian coastal states, small but culturally heterogeneous, gained importance far out of proportion to their size. The colonial order emerged around them and enabled these coastal states to rival in importance the relatively larger centralized states of Ghana's interior. Starting at first as the centers of trade and later also as administrative, missionary, and educational loci, these West African coastal settlements served as both the frontier and the dispersion point for new ideas and beliefs, while in turn they borrowed customs and institutions from the interior, which they incorporated into the colonial situation. The coastal people's capacity for absorption as well as adaptation is well documented by Roger S. Gocking in his groundbreaking book *Facing Two Ways: Ghana Coastal Communities under Colonial Rule*. Gocking describes the interaction of the coastal states with European powers:

> Janus-like, they faced two ways and symbolized the beginning of a new order that represented a fusion of both African and European influences. . . . This process of incorporation paralleled the phases through which colonial rule in general passed. It touched the arrival of missionaries and their contributions to the spread of Western education, the development of articulate, Western-educated African elite, a flourishing newspaper and literary tradition, and an early fusion of English common law with African customary law. . . . The long history

> of European and African cultural interaction has contributed to making this area one of the best examples of how much absorption and adaptation there was in this transformative process. (Gocking 1999, 2–3)

Thus, the Anglicization of Ghanaian names reveals more than a one-way absorption of European influence. It also explains the social meanings and differences in approach that Joseph Smith's band contributed, and its later impact on the indigenization of the Methodist Church. The differences in biblical hermeneutics between the two factions within the Fante Bible band mirrored in the larger society between the chiefly class and the new educated elite, were to lead to the persecution of de Graft who fell into disfavor with the current governor who was friendlier with Smith, probably because the latter was more compliant. De Graft was briefly imprisoned and deported from Cape Coast, then resettled at Dixcove. There he came into contact with Captain Potter, whose ship made regular voyages between Bristol and the Gold Coast. When Potter learned that these Bible-believing Christians wanted Bibles, he promised to convey their request to the appropriate authorities in London.[26]

In response to Potter's intervention, the Wesleyan Methodist Missionary Society dispatched Joseph Rhodes Dunwell, a twenty-seven-year-old local preacher as a "foreign" missionary.[27] After an eleven-week sea voyage, Dunwell arrived at Cape Coast on New Year's Day, 1835. George MacLean, the president of the Council of European Merchants in Cape Coast, led his fellow merchants in offering a warm welcome to this young man. The members of the Bible band were ecstatic because for the first time they had someone who had come not as a chaplain to the Europeans at the forts and castles, but primarily as the minister to the Fante Bible band.

In his brief period of ministry, Dunwell strengthened the group by using the indigenous leadership as much as he could. On June 24, 1835, Dunwell died, entrusting the church to those Fante men and women who had preceded him in leadership, namely, Joseph Smith, John Hagan, Thomas Hughes, John Mills, Elizabeth Smith, John Martin, William Brown, John Aggrey, and Hannah Smith (Bartels

1965, 19). The most important contribution of Dunwell's ministry was the reconciliation of the two Bible bands and their leaders and also in bringing to Christian faith two Asante princes who were on their way to England (Agbeti 1986, 55).

Fifteen months later, on September 15, 1836, Dunwell's replacement arrived in the persons of the Reverend George Wrigley and his wife Harriet. In his first report to the mission society in England, Wrigley expressed his admiration for the local indigenous Christian leadership that had carried on the work in the absence of expatriate personnel.[28] The Wrigleys rejoiced when the Reverend Peter Harrop and his wife arrived in Cape Coast on a voyage from London on January 15, 1837.[29] Unfortunately, Mrs. Harrop died three weeks after landing, and her husband died three days later, on February 8, 1837. That very day Harriet Wrigley also passed away, and nine months later, her husband Wrigley died. Ghana Methodism honored these five early pioneers by burying them underneath the pulpit in the maiden chapel at Cape Coast[30] (Williamson 1965, 14).

Once again, the leadership and day-to-day administration of this isolated fellowship of Ghanaian Methodist believers rested on the shoulders of the local indigenous Ghanaians. The West African coast was proving to be the "white man's grave," and so the leaders had to consider alternative measures if they were to continue their direct connection with the London-based WMMS.[31]

With Ghana being so lethal to European missionaries, it became increasingly clear that the Fante leaders were undoubtedly the ones best placed to oversee the nascent Methodist movement. Ultimately, the Methodists were to concentrate their hopes and aspirations in one man—Thomas Birch Freeman.

Thomas Birch Freeman:
PATRIARCH OF GHANAIAN METHODISM

THE ACCOLADE, "FOUNDER OF GHANA METHODISM" BELONGS TO an Englishman, son of an African father and an English mother who worked in Ghana from 1838 to 1890. Freeman is honored not only for the length of his service in Ghana but also for the breadth and reach of his missionary zeal. He helped expand the work of Methodism to the dreaded Asante and Dahomey kingdoms. He was also the first to introduce Methodism to Nigeria. As a person of mixed race, and therefore with some sympathies for Africa and for Africans, he used his racial background to the church's best advantage, and was a bridge builder in all aspects of his work.[32] His missionary service was not confined to evangelism, but included development projects in the fields of education, agriculture, and industry. Even in later years, when he was no longer in the employ of MCG, Freeman put the interests of the local people above that of his European countrymen and countrywomen thereby invoking the ire of his English compatriots.

Information on Freeman's background in England is rather scanty, but some highlights are worth mentioning. A botanist who was forced to choose between his gardening profession and being a local preacher, Freeman chose the latter at just the time when the WMMS needed a volunteer for the West African coast (Birtwhistle 1983, 56). Isichei's evaluation of the educational and professional backgrounds of many of the early pioneer missionaries is that "the mission field gave them careers that England would have denied them . . . a social emancipation of the underprivileged classes. The facile identification of Christianity with material progress, which they so often saw as a panacea for Africans, was an extrapolation from the realities of their own lives" (Isichei 1995, 77).

Thomas Birch and Elizabeth (nee Booth) Freeman arrived at Cape Coast on January 3, 1838. The Ghanaian Methodist leader Joseph Smith accompanied them all the way from England.[33] They were warmly received by the Cape Coast Methodists who offered "a poor present of 37 fowls, 43 yams, and a few bunches of shallots" and also thoughtfully added, "a basket of corn for feeding the fowls" (Bartels 1965, 31). On their arrival, they were saddened to hear that Wrigley had died two months earlier. Within six weeks, Elizabeth Freeman, while nursing her husband who had contracted fever, fell victim to it herself and died on February 20. This was a sad fulfillment of Freeman's gloomy forecast in response to the call to Ghana: "It is necessary for me to go; but it may not be necessary for me to live" (28).

In this setting where death was a recurring disruption, and where most of the early missionaries gained little appreciation for the local culture, Freeman won the admiration of many Ghanaians by his "infinite patience with the endless ceremonies, salutations and palavers," so that he was counted as an African, and was referred to as "the great white prophet" (Birtwhistle 1983, 57; 1950, 97).

Freeman and his leadership team focused on setting up and equipping an indigenous force to perform the work. On June 10, 1838, the congregation dedicated the first chapel, the Cape Coast Wesley "cathedral." The dedication program reflected Freeman's missionary agenda. The morning featured a lay preacher's meeting and training session, followed by the church administrative Quarterly Meeting.[34] One of the first actions of the administrative board was to accept de Graft as a candidate for the ministry.[35] The day of dedication ended with a Watchnight Service with four preachers each addressing the congregation.[36] Freeman demonstrated by this celebratory program that he was interested in promoting an indigenous ministry, a shared ministry of equal participation by clergy and laity, with the worshiping community sustained by the preaching of the Word. He completed the building and dedicated the very first chapel ever to be constructed in Ghana independent of the forts. Here is further evidence that MCG had non establishment and non missionary roots and thrust, even though Freeman provided a key role.

Three months later, on September 3, 1838, Freeman organized the first missionary meeting presided over by Governor MacLean. It was a memorable day starting with a Prayer Meeting at 6:00 a.m., a marriage ceremony for six couples at 7:30 a.m.,[37] a quarterly meeting at 11 a.m., and the afternoon given to the construction of a platform for the evening ceremony to begin at 7:15 p.m. The chairing of the meeting by MacLean pioneered a practice in Ghanaian Methodism in which secular and political leaders have chaired the church's missionary meetings. At these meetings, missionaries give their reports and launch appeals for funds for the extension and expansion of their work.[38]

As a result of this meeting, Freeman and the Cape Coast Methodists received and accepted a call from a group of Fante Methodists that gathered in Accra to extend the Methodist ministry. At Winneba, where a pupil of de Graft was now serving, some twenty people regularly assembled for worship. This was to be the pattern in the expansion of the church; traders or workers would relocate and take with them their Christian faith, and in time, they would request assistance from the central office. It was in this manner that the Accra group, in the suburb of Jamestown, the hub of British commercial activity, had come into existence.

By the end of 1838 Freeman's attention turned to the greatest challenge facing the land: the menace of the political and military might of the Asante kingdom. Bartels recalls, "Members at Cape Coast had grown up in . . . undetached houses with specially designed exits to facilitate escape from one through the other in time of attack by their northern enemy. Their information about Ashanti consisted of 'tales of horror, wretchedness and cruelty,' which expanded with telling and retelling and terrified them as much as they made Freeman restless 'to commence Missionary operations'" (Bartels 1965, 37). The Fante Christians were concerned that Freeman might never return alive from such a journey or might not even be allowed to see the king of Asante, the Asantehene. Nevertheless, in an exercise of Christian hope and charity, they collected sixty English pounds toward the cost of the first missionary journey of Freeman to Kumasi, the capital of the Asante kingdom.

John Mills and James Hayford, two Fante Christians and traders in Kumasi, had been conducting Christian worship services under the supervision of the king at his palace, and so Freeman was not the first to introduce Christianity to Kumasi.[39] What Freeman brought along with his presentation of the gospel was the power of a colonial force, which, when accepted, offered the modern benefits of education and English culture. The Asantehene had placed limits on those who could worship with the Fante traders. Even though services were held with his courtiers at the palace and in his presence, outsiders were not allowed to participate in Christian worship. Ultimately, though, Freeman's visits would lead to ordinary Asante people being allowed to join in Christian services.

Freeman's record of his dramatic first visit with the Asantehene has become part of missionary lore and need not be repeated here in full. When Freeman's requests to start a church or build a school were both rejected by the king, he returned to the coast to concentrate on his circuit work, stretching from Dixcove, Komenda, Elmina, Cape Coast, Anomabu, Egyaa, Saltpond, and Winneba in the west, to Accra in the east with the help of a team of indigenous Fante Methodists. The group was comprised de Graft, then a probationer; five local preachers, Joseph Smith, John Hagan, John Mills, John Martin, and George Blankson; and fifteen exhorters. Successive chapels were opened and dedicated at Anomabu and Winneba, and others at Saltpond, Abaasa, and Komenda.

After completing the journal of his visit to Kumasi, Freeman sent it to the mission committee in London, with a recommendation by MacLean, who in the absence of a governor oversaw the interests of the British government. Upon receipt of the report in England, Freeman was invited, along with de Graft, to visit London. Accepting the invitation was easier to contemplate because just about that time Brooking Mycock and his brother Josiah Mycock had arrived from England to complement the leadership of the indigenous Christians in Freeman's absence.

Freeman and de Graft visited London at a time of financial crisis in the affairs of the missionary society. The WMMS had just closed a year with a deficit of over twenty thousand pounds (Bartels 1965, 45). And yet, they enthusiastically endorsed Freeman's proposal to extend the work to Ashanti. The two were sent to churches to preach and raise awareness and funds for the project, and none was as memorable as when de Graft preached at the Langton Street Chapel where Captain Potter had his membership and first told the story of the Cape Coast Bible band. De Graft's account bears retelling:

> I was introduced into the pulpit in fear and trembling. I preached on the text, "Behold how he loved him." After the service, the kind people pressed to shake my hands and to welcome me to their country and to strengthen me in the work of the Lord. Mrs. Potter, the widow of Captain Potter, the good man who promised to do all for us to get us a Missionary and

> Bibles, when he saw me in Africa, was present in the Chapel and was exceedingly affected and wept much for joy, that she had been spared to see the fruits of the love of God. [Said she], "Once we sent missionaries to Africa, but now here is an African also who, through our instrumentality by the grace of God, is preaching Christ Jesus unto us." (48)

This visit was significant for Ghanaian Methodism in three ways. First, because of the enormous amount of money pledged; second, due to the help that de Graft provided to an ongoing translation work, and third and most importantly, because "This leading African worker in Ghana Methodism gained considerably in stature and came back with increased self-confidence; for while Freeman talked in England about what was, and what must be, de Graft was a living example of what could be" (48).[40] In addition, this mission trip was an example of reverse mission, affirming the earliest partnership model of mission as well as the international network of Methodists. Freeman returned to Ghana with Lucinda Cowan as his second wife. Back in Ghana, after less than seven months, Lucinda succumbed to fever and died on August 25, 1841. Later on Freeman married Rebecca Morgan, an early Fante convert (Birtwhistle 1983, 61).

Back in Ghana in November–December 1841, Freeman visited Kumasi again and also ventured to Nigeria, being the very first minister to conduct a Christian worship in the palace at Abeokuta. Isichei records, "The modern missionary enterprise in Nigeria began in 1842, when Thomas Birch Freeman and a Fante Christian, William de Graft, founded a Methodist mission in Badagry" (Isichei 1995, 171).

Not having any personal assistants to keep track of expenses nor having any formal checks on his expansion projects, Freeman was found by WMMS to be inept in financial accountability, and in 1857 he was relieved of his role as head of the WMMS ministry in Ghanaian Methodism.[41] Sixteen years later Freeman returned to the fold of MCG, at the age of sixty-four, and began a second phase of ministry alongside his son of the same name. Even though he had long been out of church office, he was able to initiate several innovations, such as the popular camp meetings (Birtwhistle 1983, 69). He also preached the Jubilee sermon during the celebrations of the mission in 1885. He died in Accra on August 12, 1890.

Being a mulatto[42] was for Freeman both a bane and a blessing. With Africans, he was known as a friend who understood their culture and respected their customs. With the English and other Europeans, he was despised as being too close in sympathy to the Africans (Ellingworth 1997, 50–57). During the period after Freeman was forced to resign from WMMS, he was employed by the colonial administration and given charge of a financial division. For someone who had just been set aside from leadership in the Methodist Church for financial maladministration, it is incredible that he immediately got employment in the civil service as a financial administrator. It is especially surprising when one realizes that even if he had been adept at keeping financial records, he would have been challenged by a system which had sterling, dollars, cowries, cotton, and gold dust in use as currencies (53). It is obvious then that the pool of financial talent among the expatriate community was thin at that phase.

Freeman's popularity among the coastal people was put to the test when the colonial administration put him in charge of the unpopular poll tax. Freeman, earnest as ever, persuaded the coastal Africans to pay the tax, believing that a substantial portion of the collected income would be spent on road building and other public services. However, he was disappointed when almost the entire amount collected was spent on salaries of officials, many of whom he considered to be undeserving (53). In addition, Freeman felt that the British military officers, who often lacked tact in relating to the local population, exercised undue influence on the activities of the colonial administration.

The cumulative effect of all these issues was that Freeman ended up being dismissed from the colonial administration as well. His lack of financial management, his sympathetic predisposition toward the Africans, his disappointment with the colonial administration on the use of the poll tax, and his low regard for military officers—did not endear him to the Europeans who had employed him. But as Paul Ellingworth concludes, "He shows truly missionary zeal for the development of the country and the well being of its people; matters in which . . . his adversaries show no interest at all" (Ellingworth 1997, 56). Freeman's fate was similar to that of most persons of mixed race who were employed in the early days of the colonial administration: they experienced persecution as a result of the racial climate surrounding colonial administration (Kimble 1963, 65–67). In the larger world, racial attitudes began hardening in the 1840s with the beginnings of "scientific" racism.

Nananom Mpow:
FANTE CHRISTIANS CHALLENGE THE TRADITIONAL POWERS

AFRICAN CHRISTIANITY IS CELEBRATED AS OFFERING MANY GIFTS to the world church. One of its most enduring features is the idea of a direct, divine intervention in everyday life and the healing that the church brings to the body, soul, and mind. This characteristic is a fusion of both biblical and traditional African worldviews. Where the church has acknowledged this integration as a necessary step in inculturation, the effect has been magnetic. A significant episode in the history of MCG brings these issues to the fore.

On the way to Cape Coast from Accra, one passes through the Mankessim rotary (roundabout) that is about two-thirds of the way from Accra. Many who go that route do not see the thriving commercial activity that takes place in Mankessim, the ancient Fante city just about a quarter of a mile to the right of the rotary. The role of Mankessim in the political and religious history of the Fante people is arguably one of the least chronicled aspects of Fante society. Mankessim served as the center for the consolidation and subsequent dispersal of important Fante groups in the early days of the emigration southward from Takyiman to the Gold Coast littoral. In subsequent years, as the Fante paid their visits to Mankessim, they "acknowledged as their chief idol one . . . known as *Nanaam*" (Kemp, in McCaskie 1990, 133).[43] In addition to the written sources that attest to the central significance of the traditional primal religion of Nananom at Mankessim, oral traditions also confirm that between the seventeenth and nineteenth centuries, Nananom Mpow had a pervasive influence on the political and religious history of the Fante people. Thomas C. McCaskie, a social anthropologist and historian, chronicles the religious significance of this grove. He argues that because historians have "tended overwhelmingly to see *Nananom Mpow* in instrumental terms, as an actor in the shifting kaleidoscope of political history," they have not "accorded [Nananom Mpow] a depth of analytic discussion consonant with its looming presence in Fante oral traditions" (McCaskie 1990, 134).

According to McCaskie, the Borbor Mfantse (ancient Fante) who migrated into southern Ghana were organized into five distinct *mboron* (sing; boron, mboron are groups, quarters, or wards.). The *kurentsi amanfu boron* was the northwest; the *nkusukum boron* was the southwest, present-day Mankessim; and the *edumadzi boron* was the southeast, present-day Ekumfi. The others were *bentsir boron* (the north), present-day Enyan, and the *anaafu boron* (the east), present-day Abura (134). The Fante groups around Anomabu, Abandze, and Akatakyi are thought to have come into being through a process of fission from these groups. These were all under the leadership of three legendary leaders: Oburumankoma (whale), Odapagyan (eagle), and Oson (elephant)—patriarchs and priests who, in addition to their magical regalia, also possessed *mfoa* (short swords) signifying their judicial authority. They also represented the three-tiered system of the natural order and mastery that each animal is said to have had over its sphere (Bartels 1965, 55). The place of interment of these three leaders, in the thicket of trees some ten miles from the city of Mankessim, became in time the "habitat of ghosts [*asamanpow*] or of spiritual powers inhering in nature [*abosompow*]" (McCaskie 1990, 135). In addition to serving as the spiritual watchdog over the interests of the Fante community, the Nananom Mpow became the mnemonic of the ancient Fante's historical identity. It was here in the grove that histories of the people and especially of royal families were recounted.

In time the people of the *nkusukum boron* (the southwest ward), custodians of the Nananom Mpow, became the first among equals among the Fante groups. This development was partly because of deference to age, experience, and leadership qualities, but principally, according to McCaskie, because of the "nimbus of magical power" associated with their oversight of the ancestral grove. Even after years of decline in its real power, Mankessim continued to be recognized as having a unique mythico-historical status among the Fante as a result of the fact that it was the source and final arbiter in matters of Fante custom and law. McCaskie argues that to locate the significance of Mankessim solely in the political history of the Fante people would be a defective analysis (McCaskie 1990, 138). John K. Fynn, the leading Fante historian, agrees that even though "*Nananom Mpow* as the shrine of the Borbor Fante undoubtedly became a most sacred spot in Fanteland and its priests wielded great influence in Fante society . . . *Nananom Mpow* was certainly not a foundation upon which the Fante sought to erect a national political system"[44] (Fynn 1987, 117).

Each of the *mboron* had its own communal *abosom* (gods) from which they could seek the necessary coverage through ritual practices for communal protection, good harvests, and the resolution of individual problems. With intractable difficulties and issues of war and peace affecting all of Mfantseman (Fante nation), Nananom Mpow was the final arbiter and enjoyed the highest place in a hierarchy of efficacy. All in Mfantseman agreed that the most serious judicial and religious matters were the ultimate preservation of Nananom Mpow. In 1806, the Nananom Mpow oracle had indicated that the Fante states were in grave mortal danger and advised against military confrontation with Asante. When the war ended disastrously for the Fante states, it was further proof of the efficacy of the ancestral grove—not only in predicting defeat but also in exhibiting fairness in interethnic affairs (Christensen 1954, 16).

Describing the pre-colonial period when European accounts of traditional primal religious orders were all too derogatory, Brodie Cruickshank, the colonial judicial assessor, offered a rather salutary appraisal of the beneficial role of the *abosom* (gods) and the *akomfoo* (ritual attendants) as an "engine of civil government." It was the *abosom* and Nananom Mpow, he wrote, that were to be credited with the atmosphere of public safety and trust that prevailed in Mfantseman at that time. The British were indebted "to fetish, as a police agent," contended Cruickshank.

> Without this powerful ally, it would have been found impossible to maintain order, which has characterized the country during the last twenty years, with the physical force of the government. The extraordinary security afforded to property in the most remote districts, the great safety with which packages of gold of great value are transmitted by single messengers for hundreds of miles, and the facility with which lost or stolen property is generally recovered, have excited the astonishment of Europeans newly arrived in the country. (Cruickshank in McCaskie 1990, 136)

Thus, the belief system of the Fante people before the arrival of Europeans enabled both the Fante people and the European traders to work in a context of a harmonious and law-abiding social order. By the eighteenth century Nananom Mpow's role in Fante politics had become so significant that Fante states deferred to it not only in the areas of beliefs and social ideology but also as the representation of order in its command of communal and individual allegiances and in its symbolizing of the collective identity of the Fante people.

De Graft, the Fante pioneer of Gold Coast Methodism, recalled (albeit in an account heavily filtered by his Christian conversion), that he had been informed that the Nananom Mpow manifested itself by a whirlwind thrice a year. On these occasions, which took place at night, the earth shook and the sacred trees of the grove were seen to bow down. When an offering was made by the fifty male and female ritual attendants, its reception by the gods was signaled as it spun howling and screaming and then disappeared. De Graft argued that since one could not make an objective analysis of all the mysterious circumstances surrounding the rituals, he was inclined to accept the claim of informants that the attendants had accomplices up in the tree who hauled up the offerings. In his Christian understanding of this traditional primal religion, the entire procedure was sheer trumpery, purporting to meet a deeply felt but misguided spiritual need (McCaskie 1990, 142).

In 1831 the king of Asante agreed to peace terms with the English and their allies on the coast. The changes in Fante society in the early nineteenth century occurred on economic, political, and social fronts. First, the abolition of the slave trade by Britain and other European powers removed the role of the Fante slave merchants as intermediaries between Asante and the British and other European powers on the coast. Second, there arose a new mercantile exchange that was based on "legitimate trade" and bypassed the traditional rulers (a factor that spawned a noveau riche group and undermined the traditional concepts of hierarchy and order). Third, the Bond of 1844, which imposed English common law and the English judicial system on Mfantseman, ultimately displaced the judicial authority of such institutions as Nananom Mpow.[45]

The fourth factor, as noted by McCaskie, was the beginning of the work of the Wesleyan Methodist mission among the Fante people (144). Although the attendants of Nananom Mpow, in 1836, categorically condemned any connection with Christianity, the gospel and European cultural forces continued to advance. The advent of Wesleyan Christianity in coastal Gold Coast introduced formal schooling outside of the European preserve of the castle where it had been restricted to European and mulatto children. The introduction of Wesleyan Christianity was in the eyes of many people synonymous with the advent of the English school system on the coast. Given this background, one can sympathize with Nana Eduma Kuma, the chief of Mankessim who in 1834, is reported by Chapman to have expressed his misgivings about a fiat from the ancestral grove forbidding all contacts with Christianity. Chapman states,

> [The chief] has often been told by his fetish priests, that should he permit Christianity to be introduced into his town, consequences the most serious will be the result and the most evil effects would follow; to these assertions his reply is—I do not see how this should be the case. I look upon Cape Coast, and upon Anomaboe and various other towns where they have teachers and no evil consequences ensue, on the contrary, those places are better and more prosperous than formerly. Why then should this not be the case with my town. If I can procure a teacher, I will do it. (Chapman, in McCaskie 1990, 145)

It was in this context that the confrontation between Gold Coast Methodism and the Nananom Mpow religious institution took place. With the tacit approval of the Mankessim chief, Nana Kuma, and under the influence of the Wesleyan Methodist mission, a local Christian took up residence with a community of Christian converts at Asaafa, close to Mankessim. The Methodist Christians there engaged the attendants of Nananom Mpow in petty harassment until one of the senior leaders at the grove, Akweesi, was converted to Christianity. He then cut down one of the trees of the sacred grove and thereby incurred the displeasure of the other Nananom Mpow leaders. Up until that time the Christians had enjoyed the tacit patronage of Nana Kuma, but he was so enraged by this act that he sided with other chiefs in Mfantseman who burned down the Christian settlements and drove out the converts. The Christian refugees moved from village to village where they were refused refuge and shelter until their plight came to the attention of the British officials in Cape Coast (Sundkler 2000, 204–05).

Cruickshank, found both parties at fault. He required each side to pay compensatory damage to the other, and the Christians were barred from returning to Asaafa.[46]

The significance of the intervention of the British judicial assessor goes beyond the mere settlement of peace in an environment of fractured relationships. It marked the beginning of the imposition of British law on intertribal affairs in the Gold Coast. In one singular act it showed the chiefs of Mfantseman, themselves displaced by the new merchant class, that the British would not tolerate any challenge to their authority. But most fundamentally, this case challenged the collective Fante identity that had revolved around the Nananom Mpow. After this incident, it became obvious that multiple centers of identity could be established for Mfantseman. In this case, an alternative had been established in Fante Methodism, whereby people who were expected to pay allegiance to Nananom Mpow could flout its sacred honor and any negative consequence would be confined to being censured by British law as disturbers of the social peace, but not as religious rebels.

Fante Christians celebrated this victory in pageants as a triumph of the Christian faith over a pagan establishment that used deceit and treachery to hold captive the people of Mfantseman. The Christian religion was seen as liberation from the fear that is induced in abosomsorfo: "idol worship." (Ultimately, Freeman baptized several converts from the sacred grove.) The Christian significance of this victory over Nananom Mpow went far beyond the Fante collective cultural identity and religious coherence; it was the very usurping of the role played by traditional authorities in Mfantseman. Wesleyan Christianity was seen to have displaced the religious authority of the Nananom Mpow much as the new merchant class had displaced the financial and social authority of the chiefs (Sanneh 1999, 2000).[47]

One of the recurring criticisms leveled against missionaries was that they were the willing handmaidens of colonialism, and that expatriate missions enabled European powers to take over the lives and governance of the people. But in the Nananom Mpow episode there was a confluence of the role and interests of the colonial authorities, the missionaries, and the local Christian groups. They were all aligned on one side against an enduring traditional institution. By sheer combination of their forces, they managed to displace Nananom Mpow's importance in the Fante cultural and religious landscape.

The final word here belongs to the Ghanaian Methodist minister, Timothy Laing, who as the one in charge of the Anomabu circuit, was the direct overseer of these events:

> Great is the bloodless triumph, which Christianity has achieved over idolatry in this country. In consequence of the recent exposure of the tricks connected with the worship of fetish, the confidence of the generality of people here, and in the neighbourhood, in fetish, is very much shaken. The whole Fantes, now forsake the national gods of the Fantes, and no one goes to their grove to consult them now. The present state of the people is that they now stand halting between two opinions. Our energies are therefore required to win them for Christ.[48] (Bartels 1965, 60)

William Wadé Harris:
SUCCEEDING WHERE MISSIONARIES FAILED

ALTHOUGH THE ARGUMENT THAT THE EMERGENCE OF AICS WAS A response to the "failure in love" of Western missionaries has some validity, it can also be argued that AICs utilized and transformed mission Christianity into an African phenomenon (Barrett, 1968, 97, 154; Anderson 2001b).[49] From this perspective, AICs were primarily establishing a reformed and contextualized form of Christianity. The examples of William Wadé Harris and Samson Oppong amply demonstrate this fact.

Of Harris, a contemporary French missionary recalled, "His faith is nourished by verses borrowed from the Scriptures. He lives in a supernatural world in which the people, ideas, the affirmations, cosmology and the eschatology of the Bible are more real than the things he sees and hears materially" (Gollock 1928, 199–200). Harris had already lived a somewhat dramatic life before he experienced what he called his "second conversion." This second conversion propelled him to become the catalyst for what Hastings has called "the most extraordinarily successful one-man evangelical crusade that Africa has ever known" (Hastings, 1976, 10).

From the Glebo ethnic group, and born in Cape Palmas in Liberia, Harris was initially attracted to the (African-American) Zion Episcopal American Methodists who taught him how to read and write the English language as well as his own mother tongue. Harris also served under the ministry of the Episcopalians as teacher, warden, and principal of a small boarding school. Later on, he became an advocate for British control of the area in a period of intense conflict between the indigenous population and expatriate blacks from the United States—a political activism that landed him behind bars. In 1910 while in prison, Harris experienced three trance-visitations from the Angel Gabriel. He was told to abandon "civilized" clothing, including his leather shoes, don a white robe, and preach Christian baptism.

Joseph E. Casely-Hayford, a leading Methodist Gold Coast barrister at the time, records the following:

> Of his call, he speaks with awe. It seems as if God made the soul of Harris a soul of fire. . . . He has learned the lesson of those whose lips have been touched by live coal from the altar to sink himself in God. . . . When we are crossed in ordinary life, we never forgive. When God crosses our path and twists our purpose unto his own, he can make a mere bamboo cross a power unto the reclaiming of souls. God has crossed the path of this humble Glebo man and he has had the sense to yield. He has suffered his will to be twisted out of shape and so he carries about the symbol of the cross. (Casely-Hayford 1915, 16–17)

Harris's missionary strategy was to call on people to abandon and destroy their fetishes, turn to the one true and living God, be baptized and forgiven by the Savior, follow the commandments of God, and live in peace. He organized people for prayer and worship in their own language, using African dance rhythms and musical instruments. Wadé Harris asked his followers to "wait for the white man with the Book." His preaching and ministry was usually accompanied by exorcisms and spiritual power confrontations. As converts knelt before him, he baptized them from his baptismal bowl, placing his Bible on the heads of the people as a symbolic protection against the powers of evil, especially that which came from the possession of fetishes. While many in the mainline churches would have preferred that he offer religious instruction prior to the baptism of the initiates, Harris counter argued that a public profession of faith and commitment in an African culture was a powerful inducement to total conversion.

Within a period of eighteen months, he baptized more than a hundred thousand people. Geographically, he covered Liberia (heavily influenced by the African-American expatriate and politically independent population), the French colony of the Ivory Coast (Cote D'Ivoire), and the British area of the western Gold Coast (Ghana). He encouraged his followers to join any local church of their choosing, and as a result the number of members in Catholic, Methodist, and Baptist churches swelled as they received the fruits of his labor. The churches initially welcomed these members despite their continuing practice of polygamy, which Harris had tolerated. However, the expatriate missionaries in charge of the mainline denominations insisted on monogamy, thus causing some of the new converts to leave the churches. Where there were no local churches, Harris established Christian communities under the leadership of twelve people he appointed as apostles—hence the name of one of his successor movements in Ghana and elsewhere, the Twelve Apostles Church.

In 1914, Harris, who had come under the influence of Charles Russell, the founder of the Jehovah's Witnesses movement, predicted that the war then brewing in Europe would be a judgment on the civilized world. Even though Harris led a peaceful Christian movement, the authorities in the Ivory Coast feared a mass movement of Africans, who would not be under the control of either the mission establishment or French administration. Subsequently, Harris was barred from entering the Ivory Coast, even though he had preached submission to the authorities, denounced alcohol abuse and adultery, and generally brought about a moral as well as hygienic transformation in the Ivory Coast.

Harris's legacy was an interethnic, intercolonial, interdenominational mass movement that transformed traditional religious practices by purging its worst elements and by investing other aspects with Christian meaning. This lay-led religious movement caused a proliferation of African Initiated Churches either directly as a result of Harris's work or indirectly as a result of his example. Unlike other prophets, Harris advised his followers to send their children to the English schools, thereby breaking the initial resistance of African prophetism to education and modernity (Shank 1994, 162). Most analysts credit Harris with sowing the seeds of African Christian independency in the first quarter of the last century and with popularizing some of the earliest attempts at contextualizing Christianity (Shank 1994; Hastings 1994; Sundkler 2000). Harris's work is in continuity with the mission enterprise.

As far as MCG was concerned, Harris's influence was phenomenal.[50] David A. Shank notes that there was a general breakthrough for Protestant missions in West Africa as a result of the Harris ministry. "[I]n Ghana, the Methodist Church, was confronted with more than 8,000 people in the Axim area requesting church membership, with village after village requesting catechists and schools" (Shank 1994, 161).

The Methodists in the Ivory Coast seem to have had an upper hand when their expatriate leader, the Reverend William J. Platt, sent an emissary to Harris in 1926. The envoy returned with this testament from Harris: "All the men, women, and children who were called and baptized by me must enter the Wesleyan Methodist Church. . . . No one must enter [join] the Roman Catholic Church if he wishes to be faithful to me. Mr. Platt, the Director of our Methodist Church, is appointed by me as my successor to the Head of the churches which I founded" (Sundkler 2000, 201).

Although the impact of this testament extended to the neighboring countries of Ivory Coast and Ghana, it would have had an even greater influence on MCG except for the fact that the Methodists started to enforce monogamy and the Methodist principle of self-support and tithing. John Ahui, a chief's son in the Ivory Coast and a church choir leader, revolted against the missionary authorities. He took it upon himself to visit Harris in Liberia and returned with a message to the effect that church membership should not be based on the payment of money, and, though polygamy was not an ideal form of marriage, converts did not need to divorce their wives to be fully engaged in the life of the churches.

On one hand, Harris's ministry exposed the limitations that expatriate, non-African missionaries experienced in their efforts to evangelize Africans. As Sanneh has argued,

> Historians struck by the survival in Christian Africa of vestiges of European influence will do well to remember that it was a scholasticised faith that came to Africa, and that in its European form the church demanded little engagement with local priorities and attitudes. Jesus of Nazareth was swallowed up in abstract dogma, his early life refined as fuel for enlightened minds. Encountering such a religion, Africans soon discovered its inadequacies for the flesh-and-blood issues of their very different societies. The bracing religious commitment needed

> for innovative cultural innovation and for a radical understanding of local social systems was at odds with Christianity as a system of human cognition, and the churches as transplants in Africa were too out of step with the African experience to enable people to decide what religious foundations to put in place for constructing a new society in new times. (Sanneh 1996, 134)

Kwame Bediako further elaborates on this point when he states that "'Accepting Jesus as our savior' always involves making him at home in our spiritual universe and in terms of our religious needs and longings" (Bediako 1990, 9). For Christian preaching to connect with people, it needs to address their deepest quests and longings. For Christ to make sense to, and be a transformative influence in, African culture, there needs to be a serious engagement with that culture. And this is what many expatriate missionaries in West Africa had failed to achieve.

On the other hand, one could argue that the reason why Harris pointed his converts to the Wesleyan Church was that he was not rejecting the mission structures wholesale but rather was using and transforming the mission structures. Perhaps Harris saw in the Wesleyan Church a source of literacy, or of "English" power, or of macro systems of explanation, or a source of gospel truth. Harris was using Wesleyanism to construct a new society. Wesleyanism represented a way to transcend ethnic differences by embracing a universal vision.

Harris burned fetishes, which had a hold on the people's religious consciousness. He baptized in a symbolically appropriate way, which connected them with a new identity. He did not wait for people to be fully aware of all the demands of the gospel before accepting them within his ranks. In present-day parlance, Harris involved "seekers" in his movement, with the view that as they saw the love of the members and experienced the grace of God in the community, they themselves would become fully committed to Christ.

The synod of MCG responded to the Harrist movement by sending B. A. Markin and A. B. Dickson, both Akan-Fantes, for pastoral ministry in the Ivory Coast. They were more than a little limited by the fact that they spoke neither the local languages nor French, the colonial language of the country. Bartels reports that the local people actually began to learn Fante so that they could read the Bible in that language as well as make use of the pastoral services offered by those sent by MCG (Bartels 1965, 176). In 1923, William Platt, appointed to the Lagos District served in the Porto Novo circuit. After he had made contact with the Harris converts he was stationed in the Ivory Coast and the French West Africa District (Dahomey, Togo, and Ivory Coast). One can only conjecture what would have happened if MCG had trained its personnel to meet the demands of the Harris harvest and if the First World War had not diverted the attention and resources of people elsewhere. At the very least the Harris movement made it obvious that the standard missionary approach to evangelism was inadequate. The ministry of a second African prophet and evangelist, Samson Oppong, drove this home even more graphically.

Samson Oppong:
FROM SEBEWIE TO SEBETUTU[51]

MOST PROPHETS ENGENDER CONTROVERSY, AND SAMSON OPPONG was no exception. Analysts still debate his role in the Christianization of Asante, and question whether his activities contributed significantly to the establishment of Methodism in Asante, or whether he was a fraud. None would disagree that his ministry was unconventional. His speech was crude, his knowledge of Christian thought was limited, and he often used threats to convert people to Christianity.

His typical message as reported by Hans W. Debrunner, a leading historian of Christianity in Ghana was: "Don't believe in fetishes. Burn all your magic things. If you do not change your ways God will let fire rain down upon your village" (Debrunner 1965, 6). There is no gainsaying the fact that at least sixty thousand people were added to the Methodist rolls as a result of Oppong's ministry.[52] Oppong's success can be better appreciated when measured against the background of the relatively fruitless toil and labor of expatriate missionaries.

Debrunner visited Oppong in 1957. At that time, when he was probably more than seventy years of age, Oppong recalled that he had been born into a slave family, which was attached to the household of a rich Ghanaian named Kofi Dom. Although his family traced its origin from the western part of Upper Volta, modern day Burkina Faso, Oppong identified himself as hailing from the Brong people-group in modern Ghana, the northern neighbors of the Asante. In the course of time, Oppong came under the influence of his uncle, a practitioner and priest of the traditional Akan religion and an accomplished diviner in his own right. Oppong recalled,

> When I grew older, I became a healer (*oduruyefo*) and a magician (*osumanni*). In the course of time I gained the following medicines or amulets (*aduru, suman*): 1) *Amanfo*. An amulet that protects whoever wears it from bullets and knives. Anyone wanting to fire at the wearer of such an amulet would find the gun exploding in his hand. The knife of an attacker would break in his hand. 2) *Nsuapem*. When the enemy sees anyone wearing such an amulet he would stand as though rooted to the ground by the magical power. 3) *Wuramumu*. This amulet is shaped like a little pair of bellows. If one uses them and calls the name of one's enemy, his stomach will distend and he will suffer terrible pain. 4) *Penyan*. This amulet will help one find buyers for one's goods. 5) *Basaa*. If one throws this amulet into the air it will stay there and everyone will see that one is powerful and not to be trifled with. 6) *Ohye*. If one puts this medicine into the soup of a woman who scorns one's love, she must die. 7) *Afuto-sapu-gyina-makpe*. A powerful magic [that] will kill twelve enemies at one blow. (11–13)

This list of amulets gives a panoramic view of the fears and hopes of the Akan speaking people, including both the Fante and the Asante. Protection from enemies, the acquisition and maintenance of wealth, and the ability to overcome unrequited love, and to exhibit power and also to inflict harm on opponents—these are all modern fears and hopes as well. As someone who was not only a believer in this worldview but a practitioner and promoter, Oppong's conversion experience became very critical in success of the MCG in Asante.

Between 1896 and 1901, the British abolished domestic slavery in Ashanti, thereby freeing Oppong to travel to the Ivory Coast to work in a group that supplied wood to locomotives. He was eventually made the leader of the group, but then he ran away with their group's salaries. He was later imprisoned for the theft and for flirting with a police officer's wife. While in prison he encountered a Fante Christian called Moses who prayerfully commended him to God's keeping, much against Oppong's desires. On the night that the Fante Christian was released, Oppong dreamed of his own release, and heard a voice saying, "I am the God of Moses. Burn your magic things and beat the gong for me [i.e., proclaim my Word]" (15). The following morning the prison authorities informed him that he was to be released. As a condition for his release, he was to stay for a week at the home of the French district commissioner. Instead, he left after three days and returned to his practice of traditional medicine and magic. His story followed this pattern for some time—periods of imprisonment, dreams of release, eventual release, brief association with Christians, relapse into magical practices, and imprisonment again.

In 1910 the Methodist missionary W. G. Waterworth arrived in Asante to continue what had been a very slow growth of Methodist work. His communicants numbered just over a thousand in all of Asante consisting of mostly Fante settlers, traders, and government officials. He admittedly made no inroads into the Asante religious psyche. The reasons are many. For one, the Asante people regarded Christianity as the foreign religion of the victor. (They had been vanquished in wars with the British in 1874, 1896, and 1901.) But as Southon recalls:

> One day [in 1920], a tall strongly built Ashanti walked into the mission house. He wore a long, black robe with a red cross on either shoulder and a larger red cross in the centre. In one hand, he carried a bamboo cross and in the other a flat oval stone. There was no need for an introduction. Waterworth

> knew him immediately from the description given by scores of people. He was Sampson Opong, the Ashanti prophet, who had for several months been preaching a fiery call to repentance in many towns in the heart of the Ashanti forest. (Southon, in Debrunner 1965, 28)

Southon, according to Debrunner, describes the result when Oppong and Waterworth set out on an evangelistic campaign together:

> A dozen times a day Sampson Opong gave his message, and the missionary who had become almost heartbroken over the apathy of former audiences, saw the people break down before the Cross in hundreds. . . . Chiefs and people alike turned from idols to serve the living God. Numbers of priests joined the seekers after truth, burning their fetishes and the secret symbols of their trade. Other priests who would not yield to the compelling power of that strange movement had to flee from their towns and hide in secret. In less than two years, more than ten thousand Ashanti had been baptized and hundreds more were on the point of deciding for Christ. (Debrunner 1965, 28–29)

Oppong's ministry had a multi dimensional impact on Christianity in Asante, in particular in the Methodist community. A large church was built at Adum, Kumasi, to accommodate the thousands who had come into the church. In 1929, the Methodist synod decided to locate there its first teachers' training college, Wesley College, the first post-secondary institution of higher learning in the country. Lastly, Debrunner asserts that the effort opened the doors for Asante men to enter the Methodist ministry (35). Of course, other socio political factors also played a role: the opening up of Asante by roads and railways, the hunger for and the opening up of schools, the government's belated understanding policy toward the Asante chiefs and people, and also the realization by the Asante people that the gospel was not the singular preserve of the Fante and other coastal people. While all these factors certainly contributed, it was the ministry of Oppong that made the Asante kingdom part of

Christianized Ghana. Thus, Freeman's dream was fulfilled in ways different than he had expected and by means more marvelous than he could have imagined.[53]

Conclusion

THESE FOUNDATIONAL EXPERIENCES WERE TO MARK GHANAIAN Methodism in more ways than can be acknowledged. The locational advantages of Cape Coast as a nexus of coastal people and European cultural influences and the residence of an emerging class of African middlemen greatly enhanced the propagation of Wesleyan Christianity. As the focal point of administrative and political power, Cape Coast was a prime distribution center of imported goods and offered a distribution mechanism in the export economies of the western coast of Africa (Henderink and Sterkenburg 1975, 15). MCG was built on the foundation of indigenous initiative and mass conversions. The instances highlighted here, the Fante Bible band, the missionary career of Thomas Birch Freeman and the Nananom Mpow episode, and the conversions and ministries of William Wadé Harris and Samson Oppong, all point to the indigenous factors responsible for the dynamic beginnings and growth of MCG. MCG took root in circumstances where the Christian gospel was mediated with an understanding of the spiritual quests and needs of the Akan people. MCG grew rapidly in areas where the worldview undergirding the fears and hopes of the Akan people had been fundamentally confronted and realigned according to gospel priorities.

The church that had been initiated by Fante Christians could only see success when the Western missionaries cooperated with them and saw them as the owners and the primary implementers of the vision. As Dana L. Robert recalls in another African context, "The church becomes an inclusive body when people are considered partners rather than objects: being a mission of the people is significantly different from being a mission to the people. True inclusivity is not a program, but a result of welcoming people into the family" (Robert 1998b, 12).[54]

CHAPTER TWO

Mission Through Church Planting

"THE CHURCH LIVES BY MISSION AS FIRE LIVES BY BURNING." WITH these words, the Swiss theologian Emil Brunner summarized the raison d'être of the church (Sanneh 1996b, 555–74). John Wesley, reflecting on Matthew 28:18–20, insisted that the church's all-consuming focus must be to save souls. Missions and evangelism have been the heartbeat of MCG right from its inception. When the Reverend Francis Ferguson Chapman Grant gave the President's Address at the Inaugural Conference of 1961, he pointed out that MCG had gained autonomy so that it could more effectively do its own evangelizing (MCG Annual Report 1961, 4). Two years after autonomy, MCG invested the Quarterly Meeting (the highest decision-making body at the circuit level), the Chairmen of the districts, and General Purposes Committee, now Council, and executive committee which meets in between conferences with responsibility for missionary outreach (MCG Annual Report 1963, 9). This action was to decentralize missionary planning and implementation. MCG considered mission as key to the life of the church.

Reflecting the mood that swept over Africa in the 1950s, both the leaders of the churches as well as those in the political arena were clamoring for autonomy.[55] Ghana gained its political independence in 1957, with Kwame Nkrumah as prime minister. The story of MCG was somewhat different than that of many of the churches because Ghanaians already led the church, in actual practice if not in theory. Grant,[56] the first Ghanaian president of the autonomous MCG, in his 1960 conference address, reminisced how, in his youth, he was at the 1915 MCG synod that asked the British Conference to let MCG "undertake the support of native workers so that that support might be given to others weaker than ourselves.[57] In my lifetime, we have undertaken to bear our own burden and also support a mission in Northern Ghana. At this Synod we are asking for full autonomy" (MCG Synod Annual Report 1960, 4). He reiterated that the synod was to consider

> [a] resolution for the establishing of autonomy among us, in order that, as we believe, God may fashion us more effectively for this task in this country in our day and generation. Autonomy is not an end in itself, but a means to an end, that we may become a more fit instrument in the hands of God. The Church that our Lord brought into being by His death on the Cross was God's means of turning sinners into saints and transforming a sinful world into the Kingdom of God. Our autonomy is of no account, therefore, unless, it produce[s] saints and [seeks] to make our people a holy nation. A Church is not great because it is autonomous, or wealthy, or large. It is great when it produces saints, when it produces men and women who live in the power of God by the grace of our Lord Jesus Christ, when it is able to turn the world the right side up, or as the world will say, "These men are turning the world upside down." (4)

Toward MCG Autonomy[58]

IT WAS AN UNNAMED SECRETARY AT THE METHODIST MISSIONARY Society[59] who first mooted the idea of autonomy for MCG during the latter's Golden Jubilee celebrations in 1935. In the years that followed, MCG grew increasingly self-sufficient, reaching a stage of self-support before any other overseas Methodist district in the world under the direction of MMS (Foundation Conference Bulletin [FCB] 1961, 36). At the request of the Ghana Methodist Synod, the 1960 British Conference meeting in Liverpool unanimously consented to the setting up of a new autonomous Methodist Conference in Ghana in July 1961. Under the new dispensation, the Annual Conference became the governing body of the church, meeting in representative and ministerial sessions, composed of seventy-six ministers and seventy-six laypeople. Five districts were created, each under the auspices of a Chairman and managing its own affairs through its synod and reporting to the Annual Conference. Each district synod also was composed of representative and ministerial sessions.[60]

In the mid-1950s, the Reverend Thomas A. Beetham, a British missionary who had worked in Ghana and was at that time the Africa secretary of the British Methodist Missionary Society, mooted the idea of a West Africa Inter-District Conference. After his secretarial visit in 1953, he envisioned that if the Methodist churches in the various West African countries were to combine their resources they could "bear witness to [their] faith among Muslims" (Bartels 1965, 293). According to Francis L. Bartels, Beetham regarded West Africa more as a spiritual territory than a geographic area.

But the rank and file of West African Methodists did not share this outward looking focus. What they saw when they looked at the West African Christian community was an array of different ethnic groups under different national constitutions, at different stages of maturation, and with uneven resources at their disposal. Travel within West Africa was difficult, more so then than now. The Muslim presence and influence were underestimated. With all these factors, it did not make sense to bring together people who hardly knew each other and to charge them with the task of evangelizing their Muslim neighbors. As the synods and provincial council debated the proposal for an interdistrict conference, it became obvious that the local people did not support it. Rather it was felt that autonomy for each of the synods was the first course of action to take.

The British missionaries, on the other hand, focusing on the prospect of a church union, were not sure that moving toward denominational autonomy was the right course. In retrospect, it would appear that the underlying issue was that the missionaries found it difficult to hand over control. Ogbu U. Kalu argues, "Decolonization took the missionaries unprepared, unwilling to give up power, unable to halt the trend and anxious to create a condition which [would] enable them still call the shots from behind the curtains of the vestry or boardrooms of their metropoles. . . . Though missionaries anticipated the end of colonial rule, they did little to prepare for it, perhaps in the belief that they could survive better than the [political] colonial rulers" (Kalu 2000, 1, 7).

In the case of MCG, things were rather more complex. "The ultimate authority for the affairs of the Methodist Church in Ghana, as in the other districts rested . . . with the British Conference," argued Bartels, "yet in actual practice the Synod had complete freedom of action over a wide range of the life of the church" (Bartels 1965, 294). Therefore in requesting autonomy MCG was attempting to legalize what was already the case in practice.[61]

The Reverend G. Thackray Eddy, a veteran missionary and Chairman of the district who presided at the 1959 synod, summarized the debate: MCG, at the next annual conference, would vote on a proposal to call, select, train, and discipline its own ministry, without any reference to any other authority. Assuming an affirmative vote, the status of the Methodist ministers would rest solely on their membership in the Ghana Conference. Likewise, the Annual Conference would become the final authority on Methodist doctrine, so far as the church in Ghana was concerned (MCG Minutes 1959, 18).

In his remarks Eddy reminded the synod of the many bonds between British and Ghanaian Methodism and warned of the dangers of isolationism. If the international links are not maintained, he said, the church might be swept into a "too uncritical acceptance of a purely national outlook. . . . or subscribe to a nationalistically conceived expression of the Christian faith." He continued:

> Ghana District is a very small unit, according to the traditional Methodist conception, to be a Conference; and in some

> respects, a very unbalanced one. . . . You may be convinced that God is now leading you to be given full and final authority in your own affairs; and you may be right. But it will be a long time yet before we can produce out of the resources of the Church in Ghana alone all the wisdom and theological and spiritual insight we need: indeed, no Church can, but some are large enough to have more varied resources than others. (18)

Underlying Eddy's concerns were the relatively small size of the country (notwithstanding the fact that Ghana is about the size of Britain) and the fact that there were good prospects of uniting with other West African Methodists, in particular the relatively larger Nigerian Methodist conference.[62]

Following Eddy's remarks, Dr. Kofi Abrefa Busia[63] stated that while there seemed to be general agreement that the seat of authority should move to Africa to enable the church to play her full part, two different responses had been offered. There was the possibility of a united church of West Africa incorporating Nigeria, Ghana, Sierra Leone, and Gambia (the Anglophone former British colonies in West Africa); or the possibility of maintaining ecclesiastical identities within the various countries with the option of entering into a union with sister denominations in other countries if so desired.

The final vote, taken at the 1960 Annual Synod, was for autonomy. Each country would retain its denominational identity until the possibility of church union was realized as they wished, and then they could join hands with other churches to become a united church in West Africa. And so, MCG became autonomous on July 28, 1961, marking the end of British control of Methodist affairs on the coast of Ghana.[64]

A Witnessing Church

AUTONOMY WAS "A MOMENTOUS STEP IN THE HISTORY OF METHodism in Ghana" (President William V. S. Tubman of Liberia, in FCB 1961, 46). Ghana's president Nkrumah wrote, "The contribution which the Methodist Church, in concert with other religious denominations, has made to the progress of Ghana is invaluable. It is a record of which you can be justly proud. It is my hope that now that the Methodist Church has gained its freedom, it will, as never before, co-operate with the government in the social and educational reconstruction of the country on which we have embarked" (FCB 1961, 39).

The importance of cooperation with the government was reiterated at the Inaugural Conference of the All Africa Conference of Churches, (AACC) which met in Kampala, Uganda, in 1963. At this time, most African countries had attained political independence. Not only were the presidents Africans but also most heads of civil and military institutions were Africans as well. Some countries implemented their Africanization programs successfully while others did not fare so well. Countries that were successful were mainly those in which the colonial administration had anticipated the inevitable finiteness of its oversight and so had trained local people to work alongside colonial officials or placed them in key positions. The countries that were unsuccessful suffered for obvious reasons. In Zaire (now the Democratic Republic of Congo), there were not enough trained Africans to administer all the government departments. Ghana was in a comparatively better state, with one of the best-trained Africanized civil services on the continent already in place.

It is remarkable to note that MCG, once it had become autonomous, did not stop requesting the assistance of Western expatriate missionaries. In 1965 there were seven missionaries from the British conference working in Ghana under national leadership. In 1970 the church established a committee under the Reverend J. W. de Graft Johnson to review the whole system of vernacular studies to ensure that expatriate missionaries could function effectively. Missionaries generally served in institutions as teachers, agriculturalists, and medical personnel or in mission areas like the Northern Ghana Mission (NGM), which was a program of MCG, or in the Western Frontier Mission, rather than solely serving Ghanaian congregations.

By stationing expatriate missionaries in mission areas, MCG ensured that the resources that came from the British and American Methodist churches would be utilized in places where they were most needed. Unfortunately, this created a dependency syndrome as MCG continued to expect the overseas churches to fund its outreach programs even after autonomy. This is partly because mission areas tend to lack basic socio economic development amenities such as access to drinking water, paved roads, electricity, schools, and hospitals. Those who serve in these areas expend more energy and resources providing for such necessities than their colleagues in urban and other areas.

Mission to Muslims in Northern Ghana

THE BRITISH COLONIAL GOVERNMENT HAD BARRED CHRISTIAN missionaries from operating in northern Ghana. This policy was based on the assumption held both by the people of southern Ghana and by the colonial authorities that the north was predominantly Muslim and that any evangelization effort would result in religious conflict. What it did was delay the introduction of Christianity and Western-style education.

The first attempt to establish a Methodist community in northern Ghana was authorized by the Reverend W. R. Griffin, a British missionary in 1911. He was then the general superintendent of the Wesleyan mission, based in Cape Coast. Even though the acting British commissioner at Cape Coast overseeing northern Ghana accepted the Protestant outreach program, the local commissioner in the north opposed this program and clashed with the Reverend H. G. Martin, the Methodist minister in charge of the northern mission. The Methodists tried again in 1913 when the governor of the Gold Coast, Hugh Clifford, gave them permission to reopen the mission station in Tamale, the capital of the northern region. Again they came into conflict with the chief commissioner who, while being hospitable to the Catholics, argued that since the government had had such difficulties working with Protestant missionaries from the south, he did not want that repeated in an area where he was in control. And so right from the beginning, MCG faced formidable obstacles in its efforts to establish a witness in northern Ghana (Aboagye-Mensah 1998, 42–50; Der 1974). Not until 1953 was MCG able to post the Reverend Paul Adu as its first missionary in the North, working alongside several British missionaries.[65]

In 1962 MCG sought a partnership with the Presbyterian Church of Ghana for the evangelization of northern Ghana. It was felt that whatever the differences in theological, liturgical, and missionary history between MCG and the Presbyterians, they faded in significance when compared to the urgency of proclaiming Christ's salvation to the Muslim strongholds in the North. Unfortunately, the proposed joint ministry did not materialize, and MCG had to continue in its work alone.[66] In 1963 the Methodist Conference stationed more catechists in the northern region and authorized the employment of catechists who had not completed their middle school education but who had been vetted and approved by the local church. This resulted in a new set of local workers assigned the tasks of teaching and preaching (MCG Conference Minutes 1963, 70). Additionally, southern Methodist church organizations, which were well organized and financially able, were encouraged to help with the work of the new churches in the north by entering into a sister-church relationship with them. This action was intended to help reduce the financial burden that the new churches faced (MCG Minutes 1962, 9).[67]

Regrettably, unlike the Presbyterian Church of Ghana (Dovlo 1999), MCG has not had much success in its attempts to evangelize the North. This was such a matter of concern to the church that the 1980 conference appointed a special commission headed by J. S. Annan, a leading layperson and later MCG vice president, to look into the ways and means by which the MCG could make headway in the evangelization of northern Ghana. One of the most significant outcomes of the Annan Commission was the recommendation that the administration of the Northern Ghana Mission should be entrusted to staff indigenous to the north, headed by the Very Reverend Edison K. Tinsari. (Tinsari, who had trained at Trinity Theological College as well as in the United Kingdom, was the second person from the area to be ordained a minister of MCG.) But in spite of this, and in spite of the linking of southern churches with northern churches, the work continued to face difficulties.

Unlike workers from the Presbyterian Church of Ghana who typically volunteered for pioneer work in the north, MCG ministers who served in the north—most of whom were from the south—were there by assignment, not as volunteers (Asante 1997). The policy of stationing MCG ministers as opposed to seeking volunteers affected the quality of their work as they yearned to be stationed elsewhere.

Not the least of the difficulties since 1980 is that after local Christians were put in charge, less financial support for the work in the North than in previous years was forthcoming from churches in the South and from overseas mission partners. Even though the North is the largest geographic area of Ghana, it has only as many ministers (nine at the time of research) as the single circuit of Bantama in the Kumasi diocese in the south. By comparison, the Roman Catholic Church in the northern part of Ghana has an archbishop in Tamale, bishops in Navrongo-Bolgatanga, Wa, and Damongo, and several hundred priests and others in their religious orders.

It may be that the secret to reaching northerners is to work with the numerous workers who come to the south for employment. Many Christians in Ghanaian mainline churches are indifferent to evangelistic outreach to Muslims. Some assume that Muslims believe in God as Christians do and therefore do not need to be evangelized. Christian workers stationed in the north almost invariably find themselves in congregations of transplanted southerners working as teachers, civil servants, and so forth. In many respects, the church's role in northern Ghana mirrors the situation of the political authority in that it is the lack of trained local personnel that requires the recruitment of southern workers. The situation recalls the early attempts at bringing Christianity to Ghana, when ministers were limited to serving as chaplains to the expatriate community in the castles and forts along Ghana's coastline. In addition to the language barrier between north and south, southerners bring with them feelings of ethnic, social, and economic superiority, which feeds the attitude that northerners are unreachable.

It is not surprising then, that northerners who move to the south do not feel welcome in southern churches. John Azumah asserts that most northerners are traditionalists,[68] yet the northern communities in southern Ghana are so close-knit that they offer a social network in which most northern transplants become Muslims. Thus northerners are more likely to become Muslims when they move to southern Ghana than while staying in the north (Anquandah 1979, 81–83). "The notion of a Muslim among the majority of Ghanaian Christians is that of a dirty illiterate watchman from the north or an uncouth bunch of strangers living in the dirtiest and filthiest part of the city" (Azumah 2000, 25). With such an outlook, it is to be expected that there are not many opportunities for pre evangelistic encounters between southern Christians and northern Muslims. The Christian Council of Ghana has initiated a dialogue with Muslims, but even that faces numerous challenges, including the fact that the Muslim institutions are as fissiparous as Protestant institutions.

Islam in southern Ghana, according to J. G. Platvoet, is of two mutually exclusive kinds. The Sudanic type originated in Mali as early as the 1480s and was popular in the courts of the kings of Asante during the late eighteenth and early nineteenth centuries. Sudanic Islam stood aloof from colonial society and discouraged Western education. The other type is found in the Ahmadiyya Movement. In Ghana, the Ahmadis date from 1921 when a Methodist catechist, Ben Sam, and his congregation, after being excommunicated for failing to pay their class dues (assessed tithes), embraced the Ahmadiyya sect of Islam (Platvoet 1979, 587–89). This is the genesis of "Fante Kramo" (Fante Muslims) in southern Ghana.

On an individual and personal level, there has been considerable harmony between Christians and Muslims in Ghana:

> At the grassroots level, Christians and Muslims have on the whole lived in peace. It is very common to find members of the same family adhering to different religious traditions. Muslim relatives and friends visit Christians at Christmas to wish them well and Christians visit their Muslim friends and relatives during the festivals of Idd-ul-Fitr and Idd-ul-Adha. On these occasions, gifts and meals are shared. On occasions

> such as weddings and child naming ceremonies, and even the ordination of priests, Muslims are known to come to church and vice versa because the ceremony involves a friend or relative.[69] (Azumah 2000, 24)

But that is not to say that all has been harmonious between Christians and Muslims. Several factors, as enumerated by Azumah, account for recurring tension. The Provisional National Defense Council (PNDC) government (1979–93) in its early pro-Communist, anti-Western days gave preference to the Muslim faith as an antithesis of Western Christian faith. This government attempted to ban Christian music on national radio and television (but this caused such a rumpus the ban was lifted).[70] The government also replaced religious instruction with cultural studies in the curriculum at Christian mission schools and thus deprived Ghanaian children of some of the significant elements of education that meant so much to their parents. Eventually, the religious curriculum was restored and expanded to include non-Christian religions as well as Christianity. The infamous Religious Registration Law required all religious groups in the country to register with the Ministry of Culture and Tourism. Mainline churches viewed with great suspicion the conditions under which this registration was to be carried out and ultimately did not comply with it. Finally, the government provided financial, material, and personnel support to Muslim missionary schools, known as "English/Arabic schools." The government declared as national holidays Muslim festivals such as Ramadan and Idd-ul-Fitr. Admittedly, some of these measures were long overdue, for in a pluralistic state Muslims need to be given recognition on par with Christians. But due to the way in which the new measures were politicized it became obvious that they were meant to signal to the Christian community that the government was seeking other poles of support in the religious community, since the Christian leaders were known to be less favorably inclined toward the PNDC government.[71]

Unfortunately, unlike the Presbyterians, the Methodists do not have a coordinated outreach program focused on transplanted northerners.[72] The final evaluation of MCG's mission to the North is yet to be made, but we can say that the centrally driven mission outreach has not been particularly successful.

The story of MCG's mission to the North is not complete without returning to the work of Paul Adu. Born in 1916 at Kintampo, Adu became a Christian in his youth through the work of missionaries from Wenchi. After schooling, he started church planting in the Yeji area and then applied to the seminary for pastoral studies. His first posting after the seminary was to Agona Swedru. In 1953 he volunteered to work in the North as the first Ghanaian missionary and he spent almost all the rest of his professional life in the North. Starting from Tamale, he moved to Yendi, then Bolgatanga and Bawku, in the process gaining fluency in the Dagari, Walla, Dagbani, and Hausa languages. Unfortunately, according to Joseph M.Y. Edusa-Eyison, "Rather than the Methodist Church picking up and continuing the good work [Adu] had started, these were left unattended, and the Presbyterian Church spared no efforts at taking over. Therefore the initial contacts at Yendi, Bolgatanga and Bawku were all lost to others" (Edusa-Eyison 1999, 47).

Adu is remembered not only for his preaching of the gospel but also for the great interest he showed in the secular life of the people he served, including how he provided educational opportunities as well as teaching the people about improvements in agriculture. It is regrettable that such labors were not fully utilized by the church.

Urban Mission—Dansoman Estate

IN THE LATE 1960S AND EARLY 1970S THE GOVERNMENT OF GHANA started a new residential settlement known as Dansoman Estate. It was designed to accommodate the several thousands of families that were relocating to Accra for jobs. The majority came from the central and western regions of Ghana, strongholds of MCG in the early part of the twentieth century. To attend worship services, residents of Dansoman with Methodist connections had to commute to the Calvary Methodist Church in North Accra, about five miles away. On Christmas Eve, December 24, 1972, instead of going to Calvary, Dansoman resident G. E. Dennis led an interdenominational evening service at the home of Sister Beatrice Eshun, and a number of Dansoman residents attended, among them, MCG members Alice Lovelace-Johnson, Charles and Mavis Amonoo-Acquah, and E. A. Tieku. In August 1973 R. J. Sam, D. D. Nunoo, and J. K. J. Quansah joined the group. Along with other interested residents of Dansoman Estates, they considered establishing a united church for the Dansoman community, but ultimately the Presbyterians and Anglicans decided to organize their own churches.

The early days of the Mount Olivet Dansoman Methodist Church were inauspicious, to say the least. Eshun's residence, where the services were held, was on the premises of a tavern, and it "attracted some persons [who wanted] to taste alcohol before the worship." This led to an atmosphere that "lacked decorum" and the "singing thereafter was poor" (Mount Olivet Society Inauguration of Circuit Souvenir Program 1990). These factors necessitated a change in venue, and Florence Laast, proprietress of the St. Martin-de-Poress Preparatory School, offered the church the use of her school building. Nunoo conducted the first morning service at the school on October 6, 1974, with forty-five adults in attendance. The offering that day amounted to a grand total of 6 cedis and 8 pesewas! On September 14, 1976, the group was recognized as a preaching post of the Calvary Society, and on October 1, 1978, it became a full Methodist society. By the following year all the leaders had attended the New Life for All (NLFA) evangelistic training program and had intensified their house-to-house visitation efforts. In addition to Sunday services, the group held Wednesday congregational teaching sessions, and several prayer cells were formed. These activities were in place before the arrival of the first residential minister in the person of the Reverend J. S. Hutchful, in October 1981. The spiritual leadership of the women who formed Wednesday night prayer groups—Gladys Morrison, Comfort Sarpong-Dam, Rose Quansah, and Ruth Amoah—is credited with the attendance and involvement of several women in the early days of the church.

The first building project was a church hall, which opened for worship on July 29, 1984. In October 1989 the church became a circuit of its own, with the Reverend Isaac Bonful appointed as the first superintendent minister. The increase in the number of people attending the service necessitated a revised building plan, and so a three-story edifice was constructed. It provided an airy quadrangle of twenty classrooms and four offices.

Over a period of more than a quarter of a century, the Mount Olivet church has produced six ministers: D. D. Donkor, K. K. Asher, Susan Donkor, Dr. Maxwell Aryee, J. K. K. des-Bordes, and Ampofo Twumasi. The following organizations have enhanced its ministry in the community: The Sowers, The Evangelism Fellowship, Every Member on Evangelism Fellowship, the Methodist Prayer Mission and Renewal Program, and a counseling team. Mount Olivet operates a Christian bookshop and a bus service for its evangelistic programs. It also sponsors a funeral aid program that helps members give their departed loved ones a dignified funeral. By 1999 the church had a total membership of 2,184, excluding those who worshiped in its three daughter churches, Dansoman Last Stop, Sakaman, and Tweneboah. At the time of the silver anniversary in 1999, there were 67 Bible class leaders and 37 assistant class leaders.[73]

These remarkable developments at the Mount Olivet church were largely due to the initiatives of its lay members. Meanwhile at the 1994 conference, MCG took the step of appointing the Reverend Matthias Forson to be the first full-time Ghanaian director of Evangelism, Missions and Renewal (EMR). Under Forson's direction, MCG devised and implemented a new outreach program (Forson 1995).[74] Dubbed "5 in 95," it featured three goals which were designed to achieve a modest growth of 5 percent by the end of 1995:

1. Every church member will pray for and witness to five people.
2. Each congregation will aim at increasing its membership by at least 5 percent.
3. Each circuit will attempt to start five new preaching posts.

As an incentive for involvement by all MCG congregations, a President's Evangelism Award, to be given during the Annual Conference, was instituted. In 1998 the Reverend Michael P. Sackey

(Forson's successor as director of EMR) reported that the following districts had planted a number of new churches: Akim Oda 19, Cape Coast 15, Accra 8, Kumasi 6, Sekondi 2, Tarkwa 9, and Tema 1. The other districts reported growth in areas other than in church planting (MCG Minutes 1998). At the 1998 Annual Conference, these Awards were given to no less than eight districts, each award specifying a particular achievement. For example, the Koforidua District was honored in the category of "Restoration," that is for restoring to fellowship the greatest number of backsliders and restarting defunct preaching posts. In the category of "Church Planting" the Akim Oda District was honored for having planted the most churches during the year. Under "Church Growth" the Accra District was honored for recording the greatest increase in membership. Five other districts were similarly honored for "Budget for Evangelism and Mission Work," "Compliance" (for complying with the denominational directives on Evangelism), "Training Retreat and Fellowship" (for emphasizing follow-up work), "Soul-winning," and "Special Effort" (for their progress in spite of serious constraints).[75]

The following year the *Methodist Times* gave an upbeat report. "Over 50 Methodists of God in the army of Christ, drawn from the districts of the Connexion, descended upon the Volta region in a deliberately planned four-day evangelism mission. . . . It was spearheaded by the Methodist Prayer and Renewal Programme (MPRP)."[76] The results of the outreach included the planting of four churches in Kpedze, Sogakope, Akatsi, and Denu; four lapsed churches were restarted in Kpetoe, Adidome, Agotime Beh, and Avenue Camp; and revival was reported in four others—Tsito, Sokode, Avenui, and Anyinarawase, (MCG Conference Digest 1999,9). The report states that 684 souls were won for the Lord, and that 29 evangelists were commissioned at the Koforidua Wesley Methodist Chapel on March 28, 1999, to aid in the ministry of EMR. This MPRP initiative is in contrast to other less effective efforts stemming from the centralized coordination of evangelism and church planting in MCG.

It is the case that MCG's encounter with urban Ghana follows a pattern in which laypeople initiate and develop a new local church, and then the national office responds by sending a minister to offer pastoral care. In the example of Dansoman, an initially small and inauspicious beginning has been transformed, basically by laity, into a very active institution, one of the most significant in the entire MCG.[77]

Mission in the Ghanaian Diaspora

LONG BEFORE THE GLOBAL INTERNET, GHANAIANS WERE GLOBAL citizens. Vehicles in Ghana have "travel and see" emblazoned on them, reflecting the urge within Ghanaian society to experience something different in other lands. Factors such as the economic and political instability in Ghana's recent history have contributed to the dispersal of 5 to 10 percent of the total population of Ghana to foreign countries. "By the mid-1990s, there were 20,000 Ghanaians in Toronto alone, 14,000 in Italy, 15,000 in the Netherlands, and 30,000 in Chicago" (E. Akyeampong 2000, 208). These estimates do not take account of the countless others who live and work in these communities illegally. In 1995 Gerrie ter Haar counted seventeen Ghanaian churches in the Bijlmer District of southeast Amsterdam alone (Ter Haar 1995, 6). After more than forty years of political independence from Britain, the destination of choice remains London, and here "it is possible for a Ghanaian to rent a room in the home of a Ghanaian landlord, work for a Ghanaian cleaning company or small business, maintain a Ghanaian diet by shopping in Ghanaian grocery shops, and socialize in exclusively Ghanaian circles" (E. Akyeampong 2000, 210). Ghanaians in the Diaspora also play a significant role in the economy of Ghana. It is estimated that in the 1990s the remittances from Ghanaians abroad to their families in Ghana amounted to between $250 million and $350 million annually; statistically this far-outstripped direct foreign investment for every year between 1983 and 1990 (211).

The fact that Ghana has a growing population with relatively few employment opportunities at home makes the prospect of foreign travel attractive particularly during hardships experienced in Ghana in the 1980s and 1990s. The fact that a modest salary in a

Western country can feed, clothe, and educate families back home has encouraged many professional and non professional people to emigrate. Ghana's free and compulsory primary school education for all children, coupled with the educational opportunities established by expatriate missions, furnished Ghana with a greater number of educated people than most African countries. With the fluctuations in the political as well as economic fortunes of Ghana, the country produced several thousand professionals without outlets for employment, thus fueling the emigration of Ghanaians. Emigration in Ghana's case has been compared to that of Scotland and Ireland in the first half of the twentieth century and in the Philippines in the latter part of the twentieth century (Peil 1995, 365; E. Akyeampong 2000, 206).

Ghanaians living abroad have tended to bond with other Ghanaians for several reasons. Survival and nurture in a strange environment is enhanced when newcomers seek guidance and direction from those who preceded them. Ethnic associations are often the first place where newcomers are introduced. Increasingly, Diaspora churches have become the source of the social networks and spiritual encouragement needed for survival. This phenomenon has not escaped the attention of the churches in Ghana.[78]

Ter Haar's account of the roots of the Resurrection Power and Living Bread Ministries Church in Amsterdam is typical of many:

> A small group of believers comes together in a private apartment, praying and reading the Bible. As the group grows and the place becomes too small, they may contact a mother church in Ghana, which then sends one of its pastors to help organize them. A nuclear group will be formed from which a leader and helpers will be appointed. Once there is some form of organizational structure, the group will seek formal registration, after which the headquarters in Ghana would send a pastor to lead the church. In effect, a missionary branch has then been established, putting the church under the control of the mother church in Ghana, which will assess its leaders on a regular basis. (Ter Haar 1995,10)

Ter Haar comments that European Christians have been slow to appreciate the special gifts and traditions that these Diaspora Christians bring. "Eurocentrism so far has prevented many from seeing that a reverse missionary trend has begun" (1995, 30).[79] These Diaspora churches have on the whole attracted people of the ethnic, national, or racial background of the leader. One rarely finds congregations that are truly international in composition.

The Ghana United Methodist Church in Brooklyn provides a good case study of a Ghanaian church in the Diaspora. According to the Reverend Samuel Acquaah-Arhin, the Ghana United Methodist Church (formerly the Wesley United Church of Ghana) started as an offshoot of the Ghana Methodist Church, New York (now the Ghana United Methodist Church in the Bronx).[80] Ghanaian Methodists in Brooklyn who worshiped in the Bronx often encountered considerable travel difficulties getting to the Bronx. At the same time, there were Ghanaian Methodists living in the Brooklyn area who wished to start a local church. In April 1988 the following members formed a prayer group: The Reverend Acquaah-Arhin and his wife, Adjoa; Charles and Rebecca Kumah; Nana Kwame and Ernestina Boateng; Lydia Akesson, Kwame and Adwoa Nyanin, and Maame Efua Nyanin. Initially, the group met at the home of the Boatengs in Brooklyn. Acquaah-Arhin was appointed the pastor-in-charge. These members met during the week as well as on Sundays but joined the main group in the Bronx on the first Sunday of each month. In August 1989 the group registered as the Ghana United Methodist Church.[81] Soon the church outgrew the living quarters of the Boatengs, so contact was made with the Reverend David Henry, the minister of the Union United Methodist Church in Brooklyn, and then with the Reverend Dr. Charles Straut, the United Methodist Church (UMC) district superintendent of the UMC Long Island West District. At Straut's recommendation, the Reverend Patrick Perrin of St. Mark United Methodist Church, Brooklyn, graciously offered to host the church in St. Mark's facilities.

On May 17, 1992, the Right Reverend Professor Kwesi A. Dickson, president of the MCG Conference, came to the United States and officially inaugurated the church as an affiliate member of the conference. On April 11, 1993, through the efforts of the Reverend Pedro Perrin, who had become the district superintendent of the UMC Long Island West District, the Ghana United Methodist Church, Brooklyn was admitted into the New York Annual Conference of UMC as a congregation under the Long Island West District (now the Metropolitan South District).[82]

The story of this particular church follows a pattern observed in the missionary outreach program of MCG before and after autonomy. MCG's outreach has rarely followed centrally organized programs; rather, new churches have originated at the initiative of individual Methodists who have relocated and taken their faith with them. After they have organized themselves into a prayer group, a church follows, and then they request assistance from the mother church.

Another aspect of this history is that churches serving the Ghanaian Diaspora have dual loyalties. As Methodist churches in the United States, they typically seek some form of affiliation with the local UMC. This is for pragmatic reasons in addition to the doctrinal commonalities that Ghanaians and Americans share in the Wesleyan tradition. But being Ghanaians, expatriate Methodist congregations seek formal recognition with MCG. Unfortunately, the policy of MCG toward the Diaspora has varied from one national administration to the other.[83] There has been inconsistency in the patterns of engagement. Some Ghanaian administrations affirmed pastors and churches serving Ghanaians in the Diaspora and have gladly welcomed them into the MCG fold. Others have viewed these congregations as problematic offshoots of MCG, hijacked by expatriate Ghanaians. Since the hierarchy of MCG usually has not placed these ministers, their status in the church has been a matter of ongoing controversy. The fact that they have often played pivotal roles in the establishment and ongoing ministry of these Diaspora churches, sometimes against very formidable odds, is not appreciated. Sometimes it appears that MCG leadership is only interested in the potential financial remittances to the mother church in Ghana.

Attempts have been made to provide ministerial oversight of expatriate churches from both the Ghana offices of MCG and from the UMC in the United States as called for in the Act of Covenant.[84] However, the Concordat has yet to be given serious implementation by both organizations.

The Wesleyan mission emphasis on "saving souls" has been carried out by MCG in its years of autonomy. However, there have been weaknesses in the centralized approach to carrying out this mandate. By comparison, the individual member approach has done exceptionally well, enabling MCG to be planted in urban Ghana as well as in the Ghanaian Diaspora.

CHAPTER THREE

MCG and Social Uplift

EDUCATION HAS BEEN SEEN AS PART OF THE CHRISTIAN MISSION TO feed the hungry mind and to excite the imagination of the young. This is, as it were, part of the promised abundant life that Jesus, the Lord of the church, has assured his followers. At the very least, Ghanaian Christians have presumed that literate Christians make effective Bible teachers and evangelists. As Dana L. Robert explains in another context, "A connection between evangelism and education is precisely what fuelled Methodist expansion in the late nineteenth and early twentieth centuries. . . . The acceptance of divine love and mercy by Methodist converts was often accompanied by the urge toward sanctification, which included both moral striving and self-improvement through education" (Robert 1996, 173–74).

In the Ghanaian context MCG has been known for its achievements in the establishment of schools for its people. It must be admitted, however, that not all appreciated the value of Christian education. In the late nineteenth century, the grandnephew of the Asante king made clear his resistance to the education offered by the missionaries. "You must understand," he explained to the Reverend Mr. Picot, "that we will not select children for education, for the Ashanti children have better work to do than to sit down all day idly to learn Hoy! Hoy! Hoy! They have to fan their parents and do other work. . . . [Furthermore] we would never embrace your religion, for it would make our people proud. It is your religion which has ruined the Fanti country, weakened their power and brought down the high man on a level with the low man" (Pobee 1979, 63–64).

MCG, Pioneer in Education

DESPITE EARLY OPPOSITION FROM THE ASANTE COURT, ALMOST from the beginning of Ghanaian Methodism, Ghanaians elsewhere were very receptive to the provision of educational institutions. The record shows that MCG has been a leader—some would say the leader—in the provision of educational opportunities at all levels in Ghana.[85]

But there was another reason underlying this educational emphasis: the conversion of souls. Even though it was understood that Ghanaians would not necessarily become Christians just because they had been to school, it also seemed clear that schooling in a Christian environment provided some of the best opportunities for people to encounter Christ, gain a relevant education, and make a transformative impact on society as a result. Education sponsored by MCG was therefore designed to extend the benefits of Western civilization as well as to enable as many Ghanaians as possible to choose to be Christians.[86]

Mfantsipim, Wellspring of National Leadership

AT THE TIME OF AUTONOMY IN 1961, MCG EDUCATIONAL INSTITUTIONS had already made their mark on the political history of Ghana. Take the case of its flagship educational institution, the secondary school in Cape Coast, Mfantsipim.[87] Mfantsipim had produced Ghanaian leaders such as John Mensah Sarbah, the head of the Aborigines Rights Protection Society (heir to the Fante Confederation); Joseph Ephraim Casely Hayford, who was instrumental in the founding of the West African Congress in 1917; George Ekem Ferguson, the noted surveyor who played a significant role in negotiating and signing treaties with peoples of the northern region of Ghana (increasing the area of British control); Kobina Sekyi, the legal luminary who, in addition to serving as the last president of the Aborigines Rights Protection Society, made invaluable contributions in the fight for Ghana's political independence; and finally, the Reverend Gaddiel R. Acquaah, the first African Chairman and General Superintendent of the Ghana District of the Methodist Church from 1950 to 1954.

In a book entitled *Mfantsipim and the Making of Ghana*, Albert Adu-Boahen argues that there could not have been Ghana without the input of the Mfantsipim old boys[88] (Adu Boahen 1996, 488–511). With a very lengthy list indicating areas of service, Adu Boahen credits Mfantsipim old boys with the intellectual renaissance that fostered the newspaper culture of the late nineteenth and early twentieth centuries and that provided the push for national independence. He continues, "However, it was during the civilian regime of the second Republic that followed the short military interlude in September 1969 that the School made its greatest contribution to the political life of this country. At that time, not only the Prime Minister, K. A. Busia, and his two deputies, J. Kwesi Lamptey and William Ofori-Atta, but also the Leader of the Opposition, E. R. T. Madjitey, and his deputy, G. K. Agama, were all Old Boys of Kwabotwe [Mfantsipim]." Furthermore, he states, "It would not be an exaggeration therefore to conclude that Ghana could not be what it is today but for Mfantsipim and its products. Surely, to repeat, there are few secondary or high schools not only in Africa but indeed in any part of the world which has produced the Prime Minister, about half the members of the cabinet as well as the Leader of the Opposition and his deputy all at the same time. Mfantsipim did just that during the Second Republic of Ghana from 1969 to 1972!" (Boahen 1996, 492, 508).

The enduring significance of Mfantsipim's contribution to Ghana can be captured in the career history of one of its old boys, of whom it is most proud, Kofi Atta Annan, secretary-general of the UN (1997-2006) When the World Methodist Council gave him its 1998 Peace Award, he spoke of his Methodist roots:

> I received my schooling at a Methodist institution, the Mfantsipim School in Ghana. There, I was privileged to have teachers who understood the value of knowledge infused with a moral purpose. They knew that learning and education are the strongest bulwarks against evil and ignorance. And they taught me, in the spirit of faith, that suffering anywhere concerns people everywhere, and that the light of one candle can truly illuminate the world. . . . Looking back today—from the United Nations—I value especially the lessons my teachers taught me about how we view the world around us, and how it views us. Once, I remember, Francis Bartels [Mfantsipim headmaster], took out a large white sheet with a black dot in the middle, draped it over the blackboard and asked us, "What do you see?" We all answered, "The black dot." "Why only the black dot?" he responded. "Why only the negative? What about the vast white space around the black dot?" He was reminding us to always look beyond the obvious and beneath the surface, to bear in mind the larger picture, not to just focus on the blemishes. He was teaching us also to remember that there is more than one side to a story, and more than one answer to a question.[89] (Annan 1998)

The following case studies reveal how MCG has advanced its mission through excellence in all levels of education.

St. Paul's Secondary School, Tema

TEMA, THE HOME OF GHANA'S SECOND MODERN HARBOR, IS ALSO Ghana's foremost industrial city. (It is also the closest human settlement to the intersection of the two most significant imaginary lines dividing the world in half: the Greenwich Meridian and the equator.) Originally a cluster of fishing villages founded by a group of immigrant Ga fishermen and farmers, after the construction of the nearby Akosombo Dam, Tema became the nerve center of Ghana's industrial development.

St. Paul's Methodist Church in Tema started from the meetings of a group of Methodists who had relocated there because of the work opportunities.[90] In 1959 they met in the kitchen of Mr. Koomson for fellowship, and later on in the living room of Mr. and Mrs. Lartey. But it was the Reverend J. Yedu Bannerman, recently returned from missionary service in Gambia, who nurtured the young fellowship into a church. One of Bannerman's first acts, as their minister, was to solemnize the marriages of the earliest members: M. Anti and Comfort Afua Appiah, J. K. Bassaw and Martha Awotwi, J. M. K. Acquah and Florence Mensah, E. M. Adjei and Mary Tagoe, J. A. Bentil and Grace Mensah, and S. K. Aidoo[91] (Bannerman 1999). These men and women formed the nucleus of the first Leaders Meeting (i.e. the board of elders). They selected the name St. Paul to indicate their willingness to be missionaries for their own people, the new settlers in Tema Township. They held open-air services on Sunday afternoons using a portable pulpit and a harmonium, the latter being a donation from the Reverend and Mrs. Cook of the Barnsley Methodist Church, Yorkshire, England. On April 8, 1965, eight months after breaking ground, they completed the building of a sanctuary. In 1987, due to overcrowding, the minister, William Blankson, initiated an expansion program that made the sanctuary more spacious. Over the years, eleven stations have been established as a result of the ministry of St. Paul's.[92]

With such a vibrant community, it is not surprising that the church established an elementary school, the St. Paul's Methodist Preparatory School. Over the years, the preparatory school produced a large number of qualified candidates; there were more graduates than could be admitted into the existing secondary school stream. In response, Tema St. Paul's Methodist Society, led by the Reverend Joseph Ebe-Arthur, a career educationist opened Tema St. Paul's Secondary School in October 1983. The school was operated as a circuit project, because the intake widened to include students from throughout the area. (Apart from Ebe-Arthur, the principal actors who established the new school included Mr. Dodoo, the church steward, Mr. Lartey, Christine Kwei, and the Reverend Opoku-Nkum, the school's first headmaster.) The building of the school's physical plant, the provision of books and equipment, and the salaries of the teachers were all assumed by the Tema circuit of MCG. This generous support imbued the staff with a strong sense of appreciation and fostered discipline in the school. As an overtly Christian institution, students were exposed to Methodist worship services. This is an example of a local Methodist congregation recognizing a public need consistent with its religious impulses and responding boldly.

Wesley Secondary School, Kumasi

COSMOS. H. AHIABLE-ADDO, A LECTURER IN HISTORY AT KWAME Nkrumah University of Science and Technology, has compiled a historical account of all the educational institutions in the Kumasi District under MCG (Ahiable-Addo 1993, 134–47).[93] Between 1961 and 1992 the Kumasi District built 212 primary and middle schools. By 1992 there were 119 church-related kindergartens (though most are funded by the government of Ghana). Four of these, at Ejisu, Kwadaso, Asawase, Amakom, along with Ahinsan Methodist Preparatory, were totally managed and funded by MCG. By 1992 the Kumasi district of MCG also had 52 junior secondary schools of its own, and 6 others that it jointly operated with local government authorities. In October 1962, the Kumasi District of MCG transformed the Juaben Girls Boarding School into the Juaben Women's Training College, and ten years later it was converted into a coeducational secondary school.

One of the flagship institutions of the Kumasi district of MCG is Wesley Day Secondary School. In the late 1960s Methodists were bemoaning the fact that many parents could not afford to send their children to boarding schools. In 1974, under District chairman Joseph W. de Graft Johnson, the parents began considering alternative channels for their children's education. On November 1, 1979, Wesley Day Secondary School opened with 32 students and 8 teachers. By 1992 it had 770 students and 32 teachers. In spite of the fact that four headmasters have managed the school in its short history—the Reverends Joseph Kow Ghunney (who only assumed this role for two weeks), I. K. Quansah (1979–84), Titus Awotwi-Pratt (1984–86), and James Osei (1986–92)—the school has shown remarkable growth and progress.[94]

The chiefs and people of Asante greatly appreciate the MCG-sponsored educational opportunities, in addition to the other socio-economic benefits afforded by the presence and ministry of MCG. The Asantehene, Otumfuo Opoku-Ware II, (1910–99) sent the following greeting to the 1991 synod of the Kumasi District of MCG as it celebrated its thirtieth anniversary:

> From the very humble beginnings when the Rev. T. B. Freeman of blessed memory preached the first ever Christian sermon in Asante to my most revered ancestor, Otumfuo Kwaku Duah I, and his court in Kumasi, the seed of Methodism which was planted on that occasion, has sprouted and grown into the big tree that is now the Kumasi district of the Methodist Church of Ghana. The seed did not fall by the wayside or among brambles. It fell on a most fertile ground, and today, the Kumasi district proudly stands at the top of the League Table as the district with the largest number of circuits and the biggest representation on the Synod [Conference] of the Methodist Church of Ghana.
>
> We congratulate the Kumasi district for the tremendous success it has achieved in the church's missionary work, not only in winning souls for Christ, but also for bringing so much comfort and upliftment in the lives of many. The Kumasi district has a lot to show for its work in the fields of education and health-care delivery, and deserves the respect and admiration in which it is held for its contribution to the spiritual, social and material welfare of the people of our dear country. (Ahiable-Addo 1993, 168)

This diocesan level endeavor indicates the breadth of activities that can be undertaken with a unified vision and combined resources. Kumasi, which a century ago was the focus of Methodist missions, is now a self-supporting and vital part of the national body and a great initiator of missions through educational ventures.

Methodist University College, Ghana (Accra)[95]

THE FIRST PERSON PUBLICLY TO ADVOCATE ESTABLISHING A CHRISTIAN university was the Reverend Dr. John Kofi Agbeti. Agbeti, the first Ghanaian Methodist minister to earn a Ph.D.,[96] and the first non-Fante to be elected Chairman of the premier MCG district, Cape Coast, proposed the establishment of a university that would embrace all Christian traditions and not be sectarian but ecumenical in outlook. It would provide a "more conducive atmosphere . . . for a free, rational and divine development which may promote flexibility and equip the clergy to respond more meaningfully to . . . diversified problems" (Agbeti 1974, 34).[97]

Agbeti's vision took into account the fact that opportunities for higher education in the 1970s were rather limited. Many students completed their elementary and secondary education but were unable to go any further due to the limited capacity of the nation's universities. For instance, in 1973, of the 600 candidates who applied for admission to the University of Cape Coast only 6 gained admission, primarily due to this dilemma (ibid, 33). The situation prompted the central government to issue a call to non-governmental organizations to assist in expanding access to tertiary education.

Almost twenty-four years after Dr. Agbeti's recommendations, at the 1998 MCG Annual Conference, the presiding bishop, the Right Reverend Dr. Samuel Asante-Antwi,[98] led MCG in a plan to establish the Methodist University College, Ghana. The multicampus university quickly became a reality, receiving national accreditation and offering courses as of October 2000.

MUCG has set itself a seven-point objective: first, to provide educational programs and facilities to enable students to obtain the advantage of a liberal education, bearing in mind the manpower needs of the country. Second, to promote research and to advance knowledge and its practical application to social, cultural, economic, scientific, and technological problems. Third, to develop the ability of the students to think critically and to develop sound ethical and human values and aesthetic tastes. Fourth, to welcome all students irrespective of race, gender, and religion. Fifth, to provide students with the best academic professional and practical training, including the development of the spirit of entrepreneurship and innovation. Sixth, to encourage students to appreciate the importance of hard work and the dignity of labor, stimulating through teaching and research their interest in African culture and heritage. Seventh, to encourage students to yield their lives to God so as to reflect Christian principles, values, and ethics, including honesty, humility, and loyalty to their country (Sam 2000).

As part of the 1998 Annual Conference, MCG organized a symposium on the subject, "The Church and Tertiary Education in Ghana." The panelists included Professors Florence Dolphyne,[99] and K. A. Andam,[100] the Reverend Dr. E. K Marfo, and the Reverend John K. Bassaw, then the General Director of the Methodist Education Unit. The event prompted the pledging, over three years, of 236 million cedis (approximately $50,000—not an insubstantial amount in an economy with per capita income of $390).[101] The chiefs and people of Larteh, a mountainous city in the eastern region, gave by far the most significant gift toward the establishment of MUCG, a two-square-mile plot (1,280 acres) on which to build one of the campuses of this multicampus university.[102] The accompanying citation, which bears an imprint of one of Larteh's most distinguished members of the clergy, the Reverend Dr. Kwasi Ohene-Bekoe, sometime senior minister of the International Church of the Metroplex (Dallas, Texas), states that without the development of at least four more universities, only 5 percent of the nation's secondary school graduates will be able to gain access to a university education. The statement continues by declaring that MUCG has been "designed to ultimately function as a world-class center of intellectual excellence with a specific philosophical orientation, including the inculcation of ethical-moral values, and the provision of technical, professional, and entrepreneurial skills and techniques" (MCG Conference Agenda 1999; General Purposes Council 152–53).[103] Osabarima Asiedu Okoo Ababio III attested the proclamation.

At the time of the research the leadership of MUCG included

Professor Nathaniel Pecku, principal; the Reverend Dr. E. K. Marfo, vice-principal; and the Reverend Professor Joshua N. Kudadjie, dean of studies. Pecku was formerly principal of the University College of Education, Winneba; Marfo was formerly the chief executive of the Ghana Standards Board; and Kudadjie previously served as a lecturer at the University of Ghana, Department of the Study of Religions.

MCG has pledged to invest 10 percent of all annual harvest proceeds in the university. This, combined with a fundraising drive initiated by the MCG presiding bishop in MCG congregations outside Ghana, promises to establish the university on a firm footing (Odonkor 2000).

The establishment of MUCG was prompted, I believe, by a number of factors behind-the-scenes, different from those stated in the church records. First, there is the initiative of UMC in the United States in assisting the Zimbabwe United Methodist Church when it established Africa University in Mutare. Second, the best-organized private tertiary institution in Ghana today is Central University College of the International Central Gospel Church. The success this institution has garnered in its short history is remarkable. It has become the destination of choice for sabbatical leave for many European scholars of African Christianity. MCG, which heretofore has had the most enviable history of education in Ghana, had to act if it was to preserve its place of distinction in higher education (Larbi 2000).[104]

An important study by Paul Gifford on new developments in Ghanaian Christianity concludes by referring to the depletion of membership that the mainline churches have sustained as a result of the vibrancy of the newer Pentecostal and Charismatic churches (Gifford 1998, 111). The mainline churches, like MCG, have had to redefine themselves in the midst of a challenge that assumes that they cannot come up with any visionary thinking. An institution such as MUCG is a rebuttal to that challenge.

In providing educational facilities, MCG is underscoring a tradition which has been a part of its vision of outreach from the beginning.

MCG, Provider of Health Care

MEDICAL WORK HAS ALSO BEEN A SIGNIFICANT PART OF THE MISsionary thrust of MCG from its earliest stages of development. For over half a century MCG has provided health-care services to the people of Ghana, supplementing the efforts of the government. On the national level, the division of Health and Sanitation is under the MCG Board of Social Responsibility and Rural Development. According to Miriam Hornsby Odoi, MCG's involvement in the provision of health-care facilities stems from Jesus' affirmation of the disciples' role in healing diseases and curing people of unclean spirits. Odoi, who directs MCG's health programs, argues that the objective of the program is not merely to eliminate diseases but to provide a state of "complete physical, mental, and social well-being" (Odoi 1999, 8).

Some Methodist ministers have been known as healers. An example is found in the Reverend Jacob Arhin, who was so overwhelmed by those who traveled from near and far to receive his attention that he resigned from his pastoral position to devote full time to healing ministry (MCG Conference Minutes 1984, 33). As early as the 1930s MCG had intended to establish a clinic at the Lake Bosumtwi area, but the outbreak of World War II delayed their work. Finally, in the 1950s, a hospital was opened at Wenchi. In 1972, a clinic opened at Amakom, a town of about 2,000 inhabitants on the shores of Lake Bosumtwi, 34 miles from Kumasi. The Amakom clinic serves the health-care needs of 24 villages, each with an average population of 1,500. In the northern region, MCG operates a Lawra Mobile Clinic.

In December 1986, the Kumasi district Chairman, the Reverend Major (Ret) E. C. Bonney, formed the Methodist Medical Association (MMA), with the following objectives, (1) to provide public educational programs, including lectures and plays, to sensitize church members and the general public about health-related issues; (2) to establish primary health care posts; (3) to provide health-care for invalids in the church; (4) to provide first aid at church gatherings; (5) to operate mobile clinics in the rural areas, and (6) to build hospital complexes with full specialist facilities. In the period from 1986 to 1992 MMA established eight clinics in rural communities: Onwe, Aboraso, Nyameani, Pokukrom, Mpasatia, Asante-Wiawso, Pipiiso, and Brodekwano. Each of these has an outpatient department, emergency, labor, inpatient wards, and quarters for a resident nurse.

Ankaase Methodist Faith Healing Hospital

THE MCG FLAGSHIP MEDICAL ESTABLISHMENT IN THE KUMASI DIStrict is the Ankaase Methodist Faith Healing Hospital. Ankaase combines Western medical treatment with spiritual counseling, prayer, deliverance, and faith healing. Initially a community clinic, it has become a major facility. MCG member J. K. Manu singlehandedly constructed a two-story building with patient wards and outpatient facilities, a doctor's bungalow, and housing for seven nurses. For a time, these facilities lay idle, until Bonney visited Ankaase and persuaded the stakeholders to allow MCG to take over the facilities and the running of the hospital. The local chief added one-square mile to the hospital property, and Manu donated the buildings and facilities to MCG. Generous assistance, including the provision of an electric generator, came from the U.S.: The Mission Society for United Methodists (MSUM). Dr. Jean Young, a pediatric surgeon, and her husband, Robert, a hospital technician (both sponsored by MSUM), were the first missionaries on the hospital staff. The hospital was opened for service to the community at a public gathering, September 24, 1988. Present were the Reverend Dr. Jacob Stephens, president of the MCG Conference, Dr. J. S. Annan, MCG vice president; and the Rev. H. T. Maclin and Dr. Jeffrey Lester, representing MSUM. Later when the maternity facilities were completed, another ceremony was conducted, involving MCG president Kwesi Dickson (successor to Stephens), Vice-President Sophia Moore (successor to Annan), and MSUM's Dr. Roger Youmans (successor to Maclin). MCG has spent millions of Ghanaian cedis finishing the buildings as well as covering the ongoing operation of the hospital (Ahiable-Addo 1993).

In support of the healing ministry of the hospital, MCG provides ministers who serve as chaplains and counselors. Working alongside their partners in the curative method, MCG chaplains serve as facilitators helping patients combine spiritual, relational, as well as Western medical resources in attaining complete healing, thus following the Wesleyan heritage of care for the whole person. Once again, MCG was continuing traditions that have a direct bearing on the Ghanaian situation.

CHAPTER FOUR

Mission in Public Witness

IN POSTINDEPENDENCE AFRICA, THE CHRISTIAN CHURCHES, PARticularly the mainline churches, have wielded great influence in the African state. This has occurred when the abuses and failures of the African government have become more evident. According to a political scientist, Richard Joseph, the churches in Africa emerged as "the only tolerated countervailing power to that of the state in many countries" (Joseph 1993, 232). The churches' role was facilitated primarily by the Africanization of the clergy and by their position as providers of basic social services. In addition, the fact that African countries experienced totalitarian regimes meant that the Christian churches were, for the most part, a refuge for civil society, zones of associational liberty, and had the singular privilege of speaking to people across "tribal lines, class distinctions, racial groups, political ideology, and international boundaries" (238). As zones of liberty, they became repositories of the very idea itself of the entitlement to freedoms of conscience, association, assembly, and expression. The very multiplicity of denominations is an expression of societal pluralism.

The euphoria of independence in 1957 gave way to political instability through military interventions in the 1960s and 1970s, and then through the experience of the economic debacle of the 1980s. In the 1990s, in an ironic twist of fate, the collapse of communism was accompanied by a dramatic escalation of the crisis of governance and democratization in Africa. Africa never seems to attract headline attention except in its diseases and wars, and corruption and death. To witness to truth in such an environment is a very challenging calling.

MCG has distinguished itself not only in the fields of education and health-care delivery but also in the sociopolitical world of Ghana's tortuous political life. This was evident even in the decades prior to the gaining of autonomy in 1961.

MCG's Political Voice Prior to Independence

AS THE REVEREND DR PAUL KWABENA BOAFO STATES, "THE MISSION of the Methodist Church, Ghana, from the time of the missionaries, has been the Wesleyan objective to spread scriptural holiness throughout the land by the proclamation, demonstration, and teaching of the message of salvation in Christ. Its message is holistic, affecting body, mind and soul, and addressing the needs of humankind" (Boafo1999, 130). In this regard, Boafo contends, "MCG has established itself as a strong force for spiritual and socio-political reform in Ghana, a true reflection of the Wesleyan tradition. Generally the church did not divorce itself from the socio-political and economic concerns of Ghanaians" (130). The examples of such action span the precolonial, colonial and postindependence eras in Ghanaian politics. According to the Ghanaian theologian John S. Pobee,

> The Methodists produced some of the earliest newspapers which were committed to the defence of oppressed Africans, e.g. *The Christian Messenger and Examiner* (Cape Coast), produced

> by Rev. T. B. Freeman and Rev. H. Wharton in 1839; *The Christian Reporter: The Gold Coast Methodist,* edited interestingly by two Europeans, Rev. W. T. Coppin and Rev. W. M. Cannell, and which demanded African representatives on the Legislative Council; *The Gold Coast Methodist Times,* the editor of which was at one stage Rev. S. R. B. Solomon, who to indicate his Africanness, changed his name to Rev. S. R. B. Attoh-Ahumah. (Pobee 1991a, 57)

Using the medium of the church newspaper *The Gold Coast Methodist Times*, the editor Samuel Richard Brew Attoh-Ahumah fought the imposition of the 1897 Lands Bill, which was designed to vest lands in the British Crown. Attoh-Ahumah argued, "Our silence on matters political, so far as they traverse the fundamental principles of the Christian faith, will only synchronize with our absence from the editorial chair which position, of course, we occupy on sufferance" (Dickson 1991, 137–38). Such courageous advocacy is a worthy example of the role of Ghanaian Christians, especially Methodists, in the political evolution of their nation-state. The Methodist always seeks a public witness. David Kimble recognizes this fact when he writes,

> The nationalist movement could hardly have got underway had it not been for the remarkable work of the Missions in the field of education. Christianity also made a far more direct contribution, though one less readily acknowledged; this was through the liberation of the individual. E. W. Smith has summed up very well the revolutionary impact of the Christian teaching on African society, especially of the idea that every man is responsible to God for his own actions. The missionary, he points out, seeks individuals' conviction and conversion: for an African to respond means breaking in some degree from his group—an act which he has never before contemplated the possibility of doing. The preaching of moral autonomy of the person, of his right and duty to act according to Christian conscience, was one of the factors that led to the questioning of the authority of the chief under the older

> order. It was only a matter of time before this in turn led to a questioning of European authority and its moral basis.[105] (Kimble 1963, 166)

Clearly the churches of Ghana played a critical role in the nationalism movement before the days of political independence. The challenge was to bring a prophetic witness to the public after political independence. With its mission of public engagement and tradition of political concern, MCG attempted to meet the challenge.[106]

Pobee summarizes the role that the Christian churches in Africa should play in national political life: "The New Testament is united in counseling submission to the State," says Pobee. "Such submission may take the form of paying taxes, direct or indirect, praying for the State, especially that it may direct the affairs of the State in all godliness and righteousness, and in general supporting every measure of the State which makes for order as against chaos in society." Pobee further elaborates that such submission is urged for two reasons, namely, that the government is appointed by God (whether recognized or not), and that its mandate for governance is to be exercised under God. Furthermore, it is tasked by God to be a "bulwark against anarchy and through that bring peace, harmony, and security to the society." Finally, if the government fails in such a task, it is the calling of the church to "declare itself against particular anarchistic acts." Pobee concedes, "The problem is the delicate balance between submission and resistance" (Pobee 1974, 113).

Theologians in Africa have traditionally analyzed the engagement of African churches in national political issues along one of two lines, cultural or political. Sub Saharan African theologians have been charged with being preoccupied with issues of the cultural interpretation of Christianity; those from southern Africa have been portrayed as focused on issues of the political ramifications of the gospel in a part of the world where inequality was widely related to race. Most analyses run along the line posed by Desmond Tutu in his article "Black Theology/African Theology: Soul Mates or Antagonists?" (Tutu 1975; Young 1986). Current literature tries to show the inherent complementarity between the two foci of theology in Africa. One of Ghana's theologians, Emmanuel Martey, brings these themes together in the title of his book, *African Theology: Inculturation and Liberation* (1996).

According to Pobee, the church in Ghana is a "force with which to reckon." Given the precarious political history of Ghana in the period under review, 1961–2001; when there were four constitutionally elected governments and five military regimes, [107] the role of the church has been pivotal in preserving human rights and serving as a bulwark against the oppression of the ordinary citizen. Pobee asserts:

> For all the negative things that have been said about the church in Africa, she stands in Africa as a force with which to reckon. Partly because of her contribution to the social services, especially in the areas of education and health, the impact of the churches goes deeper and more widely than the statistics would suggest. Through their work in the social services, a strong Christian conscience about the worth of the individual was formed and generally, the Christian ethic became deeply implanted in Ghana. In addition to the avowed Christians, a sizeable proportion of the population represented "diffused Christianity" which was a useful asset to the Church. For it meant that there were several people in all walks of life who, even if they were not avowed Christians, were neither against the Church. It meant that there was a fund of goodwill towards the Church and Christianity, on the capital of which the Church could count. The combination of the avowed Christians and the diffused Christianity meant that Christianity and the Christian Churches were heavy weights with which to reckon in Ghanaian national life. (Pobee 1991a, 14–15)

Given the goodwill that Ghanaian Christianity enjoyed, church leaders were able to operate in this unstable political atmosphere. Their political engagement was never without cost as governments sought to divide their ranks and develop counter-poles of religious support. The witness of Ghanaian churches in the political arena is made more complex by the fact that in Ghanaian traditional thought authority is vested in a chief who is as much a political as a religious leader. Kofi Abrefa Busia (later prime minister of Ghana) in his studies on the chieftaincy institution wrote that "Chieftaincy in Ashanti is a sacred office. This has been shown by the rites of the chief's enstoolment and by his part in ceremonies. As long as he sits upon the stool of the ancestors, his person is sacred. As the successor of the ancestors he performed various rites for the welfare of the people. . . . If he abused his power, he was divested of it by having his special Connexion with his ancestors, established on his enstoolment, severed"[108] (Busia 1968, 36–37; Sarpong 1971).

Ghanaian traditional authority is therefore on the axis of a "double pivot"—that of a political and a religious leader. "By thus reckoning the authority of living rulers to be that of ancestors," Kwame Bediako argues, "African tradition appeared to make every challenge to political authority an attack upon the sacral authority of ancestors on whose goodwill and favor the community's continuance and prosperity are held to depend" (Bediako 2000, 111). Bediako further elaborates that Christ by his cross desacralized all worldly power and "relativizes its inherent tendency in a fallen universe to absolutize itself. . . . However, if Christianity desacralizes, it does not de-spiritualize. The African world continues a spiritual world; what changes is the configuration of forces. The human environment remains the same, but the answers to its puzzles are different" (2000, 104).

In any case, the traditional conception of power did not augur well for interventions by a group such as MCG, endeavoring to speak for those without an official outlet for their concerns. And yet, the Christian church in Ghana has never wavered in its calling to remind temporal authorities of the limits of their political power. In almost all cases of political engagement, the mainline Christian churches of Ghana, generally through the ecumenical Christian Council of Ghana,[109] have acted in concert with the Catholic Bishops Conference (CBC) and its Catholic Secretariat, thus unifying the voice of the Christian churches.

In the mid-twentieth century in Ghana, the Christian churches were a formidable presence.[110] At the same time, they were perceived as appendages of colonialism that needed radical reform. In 1944

Ebenezer Ako-Adjei, a classmate of Kwame Nkrumah at Lincoln University in Pennsylvania and the person who later persuaded the United Gold Coast Convention (UGCC) to appoint Nkrumah as its general secretary, wrote, "Spiritual or religious missions constitute one of the several agencies through which . . . a group of people or nation has been able to dominate another. Today many Africans look upon the Christian church as nothing more than an agent of European and American imperialism in Africa" (Ako-Adjei 1944, 190). Doubtless, since this was written at the height of the nationalist struggle, such an outlook is rather dated.

The Christian Churches and the Nkrumah Government

ONE OF THE EARLIEST ATTEMPTS IN THE SECOND PERIOD OF THE Nkrumah government (1961–66) to wrest power from the mission-related churches was to take control of education in the country. This was a role that had fallen to the local churches because of the pioneering work of missionaries in education. The government was keen on assuming control of the educational system in Ghana because Nkrumah felt that the Christian church, given its conservative stance, was an inappropriate body to be responsible for developing the mental and social capabilities of Ghanaian youths (Haynes 1996, 115).

Control of the education of youths became a battleground for the mind and hearts of the next generation. In the 1951 Accelerated Development Plan for Education, Nkrumah's government offered to pay 40 percent of the salaries of teachers through the local authorities, and it threatened to deny assistance to any school established by a religious organization unless the governing body at the local level approved. The churches' swift and uncompromising rejection ensured that the existing schools continued to enjoy the benefits of the central government while agreeing to submit any new educational ventures to these new measures (Pobee 1976, 123–24).

Nkrumah swept to power on the currents of nationalism that

had been initiated by the Ghanaian intelligentsia starting as far back in the days of the Fante Confederacy[111] and the West African Aborigines Rights Protection Society.[112] These nationalist groups were composed of Ghanaian elite who were all trained in Christian institutions (mainly Methodist); some held high positions in their separate churches. While the United Gold Coast Convention, arguably the early to mid-twentieth century successor organization to these movements, had advocated for self-government, the Nkrumah brand of nationalism added an urgent imperative: self-government *now*. When Nkrumah therefore withdrew from UGCC, he benefited from a mass movement that had been originally led and nurtured by an intelligentsia that had been educated in mission schools. Nkrumah adopted the political ideology of socialism.[113] Whether this was an actual system of government that Nkrumah passionately believed in, or whether it was merely a convenient way to express his anti-Westernism, this is a subject that has occupied analysts for some time.[114] In any case, Nkrumah promoted socialist policies that had baneful consequences for a country with such a large and active Christian population.

One of the earliest incidents in which the churches stood up to the government's desire to concentrate absolute powers was its stance against the Preventive Detention Act of July 18, 1958. By that law, the government gave itself the power to detain, without trial or charge, anyone considered dangerous to the security of Ghana for up to five years without a right of appeal to the courts. CCG sent a representation to Nkrumah and to Attorney General Geoffrey Bing on two different occasions, arguing that natural justice required that "any accused person should be given an opportunity to defend himself face to face with his accusers" (Pobee 1991a, 60).

When their appeals failed to turn the tide of authoritarianism in Ghana, the Christian churches appointed two of its leaders, Francis Chapman Ferguson Grant, president of MCG, and E. N. Odjidja, moderator of the Presbyterian Church, to visit detainees and to report on their plight. Even though the churches failed in their attempts to stop human rights abuses, MCG, acting in concert with CCG, did not fail in providing pastoral oversight to the voiceless and the falsely accused.[115]

Perhaps the most far-reaching aspect of Nkrumah's dictatorial tendencies was the quasi-deification and institutionalization of Kwame Nkrumah himself. Religious language was rampantly utilized in comparing Nkrumah to the founders and leaders of the great religions of the world.[116] Religious texts were recast in symbolism that depicted the central salvific role of Nkrumah in the liberation of Ghana from colonial power. The Lord's Prayer, the Apostles Creed, and Christian hymnody were all employed to show the divine origin and being of Nkrumah. One outstanding example is that of the statue of Nkrumah which adorned the Parliament Building in Accra. It bore the inscription, "Seek ye first the political kingdom and all other things shall be added to you." While the Ghanaian Methodist Kwesi Dickson sees this favorably as "an acknowledgement of the church's role in the development of the people's consciousness," he warns, "it does suggest a sacralisation of nationalism which could have the effect of giving the Christian faith a less than authentic character" (Dickson 1991, 142).

Pobee contends that CCG was misguided in its protests of these parodies and acts of the Nkrumah government. "Being a parody of a dominical saying does not make it blasphemous or idolatrous. . . . [CCG's objection] is an error of judgement" (Pobee 1976, 130). Nkrumah turned his birthplace into a shrine of pilgrimage and appropriated several honorifics[117] reserved for chiefs in the Ghanaian cultural system, even to the extent of allowing himself to be proclaimed as a chief in a part of the country where he had no blood connection.

But, according to Bediako, Nkrumah "became an ancestor-ruler in the old sacral sense" (Bediako 1995a, 242). By integrating in him the powers and privileges of altar and throne, Nkrumah ensured that all opposition to his rule would be construed in the Ghanaian context as inimical to the well-being of the society as a whole. In another sense he had twisted the understanding of the derivative power of all earthly power to suit his political ambitions.

Even though he concedes that Nkrumah did nothing to stop these acts of personality cult, Pobee shows dissatisfaction with the Christian churches, saying that they were not distinguishing between "the *esse* of Christianity and what was an *accident* of history" (Pobee

1976, 142; emphasis in the original). Pobee argues that the Christian churches took an unenlightened view of African tradition and failed to give moral leadership. Dickson offers a corrective analysis, in my opinion, when he writes, "That such compositions constituted an assault upon Christianity must be recognized. . . . Parodying religious language with a view to highlighting what is politically desirable could have the effect of devaluing religious sentiment" (Dickson 1991, 140). By highlighting motives, Dickson engaged the debate at the core. Ebenezer Obiri-Addo, I think, is incorrect when he states, "Dickson misses the overall context of Nkrumah's political leadership, particularly Nkrumah's quest to reorder Ghana's political culture through a synthesis of what is good in all available traditions, including Christianity" (Obiri-Addo 1997, 119). Nowhere in history can one say that a reordering of political culture through deification of its leaders has produced a salutary advantage for the ordinary citizen. The tale of woe that follows when a megalomaniac tyrant uses religious language and sentiment to enforce his self-delusion is every human-rights activist's nightmare.

Dickson argues, "Nkrumah emerged at a time when the Christian Churches in Ghana were tied in their theology and ethos, to the founding Churches in Europe and America." On matters of sociopolitical and economic substance CCG was virtually silent at its 1955 conference (Dickson 1991, 149). Therefore, without a locally developed and sufficiently clear understanding of the nexus binding religion and life, the church is prone to play a merely reactionary role instead of "working to create such public opinion as would make it difficult for such excesses as were objected to, to be perpetrated" (Dickson 1995, 261).

Dickson sees the church's interventions in the Nkrumah era as a failure. His criticism is threefold: Because the church was limited to an "inherited theology," it was not adequately aware of the sociopolitical climate of Ghana; the membership was not kept informed of the leaders' protestations on its behalf; and the church failed to create the conditions necessary to discourage the excesses of the regime (Dickson 1995, 261).[118] In my view, Dickson's critique is unnecessarily severe. Yes, certainly Ghanaians had received the gospel from the West, yet in the process they had appropriated it to their needs. Whatever the limitations of its theology, the Christian church was a heavyweight in Ghanaian society.[119] It is from the ranks of the churches that nationalism was spawned and colonialism terminated. When nationalist African governments took over from the colonial administration, they did not want to entertain any opposition, and therefore any organization that had a national character, even if it was apolitical, was considered an enemy of the state. Thus it should not be surprising that the churches "failed to create the conditions" for countering Nkrumah's excesses. The complexity of the situation lies in the fact that, although the MCG and the other historic churches had given the philosophical and practical motivation for self-government, the Nkrumah regime—with its blatant Communist leanings, whether deep-seated or merely perceived—was not their first choice to replace the colonial masters. In such an atmosphere, whatever the historic churches did or said was interpreted as part of that neocolonial conspiracy aimed at undermining the sovereignty of the new state. The church deserves commendation for speaking up as much as it did. Even secular analysts admit, "Nkrumah became a cult figure, a deity, and the sole decision maker in Ghana" (Pellow and Chazan 1986, 41). Offering prophetic witness in such an environment is dangerous if not outright impossible.

For the Christian an example is set in the life and ministry of Jesus Christ and supremely through his Cross. In Bediako's memorable words, worth repeating,

"By his Cross, Jesus desacralized all worldly power, relativizing its inherent tendency, in a fallen universe, to absolutize itself. . . . The Cross desacralizes *all* the powers, institutions and structures that rule human existence and history—family, nation, social class, race, law, politics, economy, religion, culture, tradition, custom, ancestors—stripping them all of any pretensions to ultimacy" (Bediako 1995a: 245; *emphasis in the original*).

The MCG and the National Liberation Council Government

ON FEBRUARY 24, 1966, NKRUMAH WAS OVERTHROWN IN A COUP d'état led by Lt. Col. Emmanuel Kwasi Kotoka and Maj. Akwasi A. Afrifa. (The public jubilation that followed somewhat justifies the leaders' self-designation as the National Liberation Council, NLC.) Barely a year later, there was an attempt made to overthrow NLC. On April 16 and 17, 1967, a military unit based in the eastern Ghanaian city of Ho entered Accra and took over the Broadcasting House. Kotoka, the leader of the coup against Nkrumah, was badly wounded and died on April 17. The mutineers were overpowered by NLC loyalists, then tried in a military tribunal and sentenced to death by firing squad. With the strong support of MCG as expressed in the 1967 Annual Conference agenda, CCG responded to the public executions of Lt. Samuel Arthur and Lt. Moses Yeboah as follows:

> The Council was deeply exercised by the subject of the holding of executions in public following the insurrection of April 17. While not questioning the rightness of the verdicts and sentences passed, the Executive [of CCG] agreed with the view that holding the executions in public encouraged crude demonstrations of hatred and excited morbid curiosity in the onlooker and in the public at large. Although no attempt whatever was made by any form of public address system to work upon the emotions of the crowd in any way, nevertheless in the event the behaviour of part of the crowd as reported in the local press could by any standard of judgment be of no credit to Ghana and its people. In view of the possibility of other executions, the Executive duly addressed a letter to the National Liberation Council in which these views were made known. The National Liberation Council most promptly replied giving the assurance that no future public executions were contemplated. (MCG Minutes 1967, 100)

In this intervention, CCG seems to agree with the government's decision to execute those who had used military means to overthrow it. Furthermore, the prompt response that NLC gave to CCG's letter showed a remarkable degree of respect by the government toward the church, respect that has often been lacking in Ghana's church-state relations.

MCG and the Busia Government

IN 1969 THE NLC CONDUCTED DEMOCRATIC ELECTIONS, AND KOFI Abrefa Busia was chosen as prime minister of the next government.[120] In his inaugural speech Busia stated, "We think the yardstick by which our success or failure should be judged must be the condition of the human being himself. We must judge our progress by the quality of the individual, by his knowledge, his skills, and his behaviour as a member of society, the standards of living he is able to enjoy and by the degree of co-operation, harmony and brotherliness in our community life as a nation. . . . Our goal is to enable every man and woman in our country to live a life of dignity in freedom" (Okyere 2000, 214).[121]

Before assuming political office, Busia had already distinguished himself as an intellectual. In that regard, Colin B. Essamuah records, "Methodist Puritanism permeated . . . his writings and the piety of his personal faith shone throughout his simple exposition of issues, no doubt due to his position as a Local Preacher. . . . The effectual vehicles of his scholastic expression were his affiliation to tradition, both intellectual and customary, and his deep Christian faith" (Colin B. Essamuah 1982, 10–11).

With one of its own distinguished members coming into the prime minister's office, MCG stood to have great influence.[122] Busia's political ideology was thoroughly suffused by his Christian convictions as evidenced by his foreign policy:

> It was his firm conviction that international relations should be based on the acceptance of two established facts: first, that all races are equally human, and second, that human cultures

> do not and cannot divide people because all people are capable of learning and mastering any culture to which they are given sufficient exposure and opportunity to learn. . . . He had been born into a royal family, raised by European missionaries who taught him the virtues of Christian humility and the ability to stand up to persecution with patient endurance. He was also taught to forgive and forget past wrongs. . . . One other quality, which he acquired from his missionary benefactors, and which stayed with him throughout his political leadership was prayer. His personal associates bear witness to the fact that every meeting or business at which Busia was present began with prayers. Even as Prime Minister, he would 'go upstairs' to say his prayers at anytime he was confronted with a difficult problem." (Danso-Boafo 1996, 131–32)

On the other hand, the US commentator Richard Wright remarks, "My personal impression was that Dr. Busia was not and could never be a politician, that he lacked that innate brutality of force and drive that makes a mass leader. He was too analytical, too reflective to even want to get down into the muck of life and organize them. I sensed too that maybe certain moral scruples would inhibit him acting" (Wright 1953, 90). This reflection is shared by another commentator who says, "The customary and intellectual attachment to tradition and his deep Methodist Puritanism, made it appear that the turbulent arena of politics was not his forte" (Colin B. Essamuah 1982, 46).

Given the Methodist roots of the Busia government, the inclusion of J. W. Abruquah, headmaster of the prime minister's alma mater, Mfantsipim, in the "Apollo 568" episode was surprising.[123] On February 21, 1970, Busia's government dismissed 568 civil servants, including Abruquah, for corruption, inefficiency, and ineptitude. Abruquah's dismissal prompted a ground swell of protests and petitions from the students, staff, board, and old boys of Mfantsipim. Eventually, the school board, led by T. Wallace Koomson, MCG president, met with the prime minister on March 7, 1970, to express its dismay. The prime minister refused to rescind his decision or divulge the reasons behind it. However, he promised to consider Abruquah for reposting (Boahen 1996, 452-56). Many analysts consider this mass dismissal as one of the factors that eventually distanced this government from the people, the underlying reason being that in a country such as Ghana, with such a network of extended family support, thousands of people were affected by the dismissal since they were primary breadwinners. Colin B. Essamuah records that in the Apollo 568 incident, "An examination of the facts . . . suggest[s] that Busia's deep Christian convictions and concern for the underprivileged reduced the projected 8-9,000 civil servants to be dismissed to 568" (Colin B. Essamuah 1982, 36).

This incident shows that MCG could not assume that having a Methodist overseeing the country meant that it could understand, let alone agree with, all the policies of the government. The Busia government was brought to an end by Col. (later Gen.) I. K. Acheampong in a coup d'état on January 13, 1972.[124]

The Christian Churches and the Acheampong Government

BY CALLING HIS GOVERNING BODY THE NATIONAL REDEMPTION Council, General Acheampong, like Kwame Nkrumah before him, sought to use religious terminology in engaging political issues. According to John S. Pobee, during Acheampong's government,

> The Christian Council of Ghana and the National Catholic Secretariat were superseded by the fringe groups of Christianity. This was so characteristic of General Acheampong's term that it could be suggested that the General felt more comfortable with the fringe groups than with the historic churches because the former addressed themselves to his psyche, his superstition, and somewhat base religion. And of course, the historic churches were not exactly [supportive] of the General because of their long standing critical attitude and their generally more sophisticated views on national issues." (Pobee 1987, 50–51)

This statement is especially noteworthy in light of the fact that Acheampong considered himself a Roman Catholic.[125]

Four examples of how Acheampong catered to religious minority and fringe groups are recounted here. As early as 1959, the government and CCG had cooperated in matters of formal national religious ceremonies and commemorations. Instead of following this time-tested procedure, Acheampong used leaders and organizations of new religious movements such as the Philadelphia Mission of Africa, led by the Reverend Abraham de Love, to organize a national week of repentance and other celebrations of national import.[126]

Another example is seen in Acheampong's response to demands for a return to civilian constitutional rule. He advocated a form of union government, which gained the support of various religious groups but which aroused resistance in the historic churches. The Unigov concept called for equal representation by civilians (mainly the student and professional bodies), soldiers, and the police. At a February 1978 press conference Alhaji Ramadan Ibrahim, secretary of the Islamic religious community, announced the Muslim chiefs' support for this form of government.[127] Ibrahim expressed the belief that, unlike party politics that divide the nation, Unigov sought to govern by a consensual process and thereby had the greater possibility of uniting Ghanaians. The chiefs declared, "We overwhelmingly embrace the proposed Union Government which is in line with the basic principles of the Islamic concept that all men are equal and united" (Pobee 1987, 52). Of course, one cannot maintain that Islam, though a minority religion in Ghana, can be ignored. But by deliberately courting Islamic leaders and various sectarian fringe groups, and by giving them political platforms to show their agreement with government policies, Acheampong blatantly used religious bodies for political advantage—to the disadvantage of mainline churches.

Another churchman given prominence during Acheampong's regime was the Reverend Brother Charles Yeboah Korie, founder and head of Eden Church, the only church at the time to belong both to CCG and the Pentecostal Association of Ghana. Acheampong stipulated that this church be featured at least once a month on the government radio. Korie was also named to serve on the

National Charter Committee to implement the General Charter of Redemption in Ghana.[128] Once when a delegation of CCG, including Korie, met with the government to express concern about the violent political atmosphere, and especially the victimization of the opponents of Unigov, Korie spoke passionately against the churches' stance and in favor of Acheampong's government.

The fourth example involves Elizabeth Clare Prophet, the "Mother Prophet" of Summit Lighthouse of the Keepers of the Flame Fraternity, based in southern California. This is a syncretistic religion combining elements of Christianity, Islam, Buddhism, Hinduism, Platonism, and Zoroastrianism. The Ghanaian *Weekly Mirror* of January 27, 1978, described it as "a fellowship of ascended Masters including Lord Jesus the Christ, Lord Buddha, Lord Krishna, Muhammed and Confucius." Father Patrick Ryan of the University of Ghana aptly described it as "a veritable Makola of the world's religious traditions"[129] (Pobee 1987, 55). According to *The Mirror*, January 17, 1978, Clare Prophet, in a public lecture, "redefined and expounded the cardinal Christian doctrine of the Trinity in terms of the Unigov: Unigov was to be accepted because it demonstrated the Christian doctrine of the Trinity. The armed forces represent God the Father; the professional bodies and the students represent the Son; the workers of Ghana represent the Holy Spirit. She even discovered 'a fourth person of the Trinity' in the Mother representing the women of Ghana" (57). The Ghana Bar Association expressed its dissatisfaction with this blatant attempt to mobilize spiritual language and sentiment in favor of a divisive political ideology:

> It is rather remarkable that at a time when Ghana is caught in a constitutional trauma, at a time when highly qualified and knowledgeable citizens of Ghana are denied the facilities and the freedom to discuss the issues and educate their countrymen, that an American citizen alien to our political, cultural and economic background, should appear on the scene to propagate the concept of Union Government not only as a political solution to our problems but as an institution ordained by Almighty God. Her so-called expert knowl-

> edge coincides with General Acheampong's own dictum. . . . In its desperation the government of the S. M. C. [Supreme Military Council] has considered it worthwhile not to limit the discussion of Union Government within the confines of intellectual common sense and objective appreciation but to launch out into the undefined misty and speculative fields of religion, occultism and mysticism. The aim whereof is to stupefy the gullible intellectually and becloud their vision. (57)

In a February 14, 1978, statement, CCG stated:

> The Christian Council wishes to express its disagreement with the religious and constitutional opinion of Mrs. Clare Prophet. . . . She was ill-advised to make a statement about Christian belief which has no basis in the Bible and in the tradition. . . . We deplore that whereas the place of the army and the police in any future government is a controversial issue, Mrs. Clare Prophet took the opportunity to claim on behalf of soldiers and police, among others, a "divine right" no less, to participate in government. The Christian Council wishes to declare that no individual or section of the public has any divine right or other right to participate in government except by the choice of the electorate freely expressed through the ballot box. (58)

But the church's work was not limited to countering governmental excesses. In what is called "their finest hour" (59), Pobee identified the churches as being the "credible reconciler of warring factions in society as evidenced by their mediatory role in the clash between the professionals and the government (Letters of June 17, 1977; July 4, 1977; July 14, 1977), the Nurses and the Government (Letters of April 13, 1978; April 21, 1978), the students and the Government (cf. Letters of June 2, 1977; June 6, 1977, June 10, 1977). They established themselves as the voice of the voiceless, pleading the cause of political detainees and in the process earning the wrath of General Acheampong" (Pobee 1987, 59).

In a March 15, 1978, memorandum CCG and CBC informed the public of the arbitrary detention of K. Addai-Mensah, the national secretary of the Ghana Bar Association. The memorandum expressed dissatisfaction with the uneven playing field made available for campaigning for and against the union government concept. Those on the government side were able to promote their cause, while those of the opposition were intimidated and threatened. In the discussion that followed, the government gave assurances of resolving the issue. But in actual fact, nothing changed. It was as if the churches' intervention had fallen on deaf ears.

MCG and the Akuffo Government

ON JULY 5, 1978, A RADIO ANNOUNCEMENT REVEALED THAT Acheampong had been retired from the army and that Gen. Fred Akuffo was the new head of state. Acheampong was accused of running a one-man show. Akuffo immediately released those who had been imprisoned because of their opposition to Unigov and disbanded the satellite organizations that formed the basis of Acheampong's support. However, Akuffo's government did not bring Acheampong to trial as was demanded by the vast majority of Ghanaians. Instead, after he was charged with acts of corruption and abuse of power, Acheampong was stripped of his military honors and confined to his hometown of Traboum in the Ashanti region (Ocquaye 180, 111–32).

The churches continued their campaign that encouraged the military regime to hand over power to a civilian constitutional government. When Akuffo placed a number of qualified civilians in charge of the economy, the churches had hopes that a genuine attempt was being made to return the country to a healthy state. But the events of June 4, 1979, determined otherwise.

The Christian Churches and the Rawlings Government

THE ARMED FORCES REVOLUTIONARY COUNCIL (AFRC), HEADED BY Jerry Rawlings,[130] came into office via a coup d'état on June 4, 1979, with three aims: eradication of all vestiges of corruption, malfeasance, ineptness, and exploitation; restoration of public accountability and awakening of Ghanaians to their rights and duties; and implementation of the return of civilian rule (Pellow and Chazan 1986, 60).[131] However, since the government was already on the path to a return to civilian constitutional regime, AFRC's time in office was a relatively short one.[132]

As a first step, Acheampong and former government official Maj. Gen. E. K. Utuka were executed on June 16, 1979. Ten days later, after a hastily assembled revolutionary trial, the death sentence was passed on Akuffo, Maj. Gen. R. E. A. Kotei, Air Vice Marshall George Yaw Boakye, Rear Adm. J. K. Amedume, Col. R. J. A. Felli, and Lt. Gen. Afrifa (head of state in 1969). All except Afrifa were leading military officers in the previous government. With the public's unhappiness over the military interventions that had derailed the democratic process and exacerbated the country's economic woes, it is not surprising that these executions were seen as "cathartic bloodletting" (Gifford 1998, 59). The mainline churches also were not happy with the spectacle of public executions, and they had the courage to say so. In a June 26, 1979, paper entitled "Memorandum on Revolutionary Courts and Summary Executions in Ghana," CCG and CBC wrote,

> We are all painfully aware of the mismanagement and corruption, which had rendered our dear country really bankrupt. We also believe that those who are responsible for this sorry state of affairs should be severely punished but we do not believe that the death penalty, especially after secret trials, is the only or even the most effective punishment that can be administered to those who are guilty. In the present situation, when tempers are high, certain citizens and groups may advise the AFRC to adopt unorthodox methods and shortcuts in punishing offenders. Such reaction is only normal but matters of life and death deserve to be handled dispassionately and not based on emotions. (Boafo 1999, 224)

This outcry from the more established bodies tempered the mood of the country, which had been greatly inflamed by the students' cries for more blood to flow. The ensuing years saw a gradual deterioration in the state of law and order in the country. The Provisional National Defense Council set up an alternative system of justice. Peoples' and Workers' Defense committees loomed over all aspects of Ghanaian life. Many people were threatened, beaten, or even secretly murdered.

In these dreadful times, verbal opposition to the government was gradually silenced. *Christian Messenger* (March 1982) reports that the Reverend Samuel B. Essamuah, president of MCG submitted a personal paper to a PNDC member, the Reverend Dr. Vincent Damuah, in which he called for the disbandment of the People's Defense and Workers Defense Committees because these quasi-political units had attracted the power-hungry. PNDC was called upon to lift the curfew imposed on the country and to withdraw soldiers from the streets, as their presence was intimidating people from going about their legitimate business. It is fair to conjecture that but for such interventions, private and public, there would have been worse breaches of human rights during the early days of PNDC.

In his now famous 1988 J. B. Danquah Memorial lectures, Albert Adu Boahen contested Rawlings's characterization of Ghanaians as passive,

> "I am afraid I do not agree with Rawlings's explanation of passivity of Ghanaians. We have not protested or staged riots not because we trust the PNDC but because we fear the PNDC! We are afraid of being detained, liquidated or dragged before the CVC [Citizens' Vetting Committee] and NIC [National Investigations Committee] or being subjected to all forms of molestation. And in any case have Ghanaians not been protesting at all, as the head of state thinks? They have been but in a very subtle and quiet way—hence the culture of silence." (Nugent 1995, 163).

This erudite historian in seeking to explain the silence of Ghanaians in the face of political and physical intimidation, suppression of rights, and a general atmosphere of living in a "cocoon of fear" resorted to the Bible (Amos 5:13 NIV) for an apt quotation: "Therefore the prudent man keeps quiet in such times, for the times are evil" (Boafo 1999, 225).

In October and November of 1990 the country as a whole debated the subject of democracy. Sunday, October 25, was designated the beginning of a week of prayer for the nation. CCG and CBC organized seminars across the length and breadth of Ghana.[133] In a December memorandum submitted to the government, CCG summarized its role as follows: "The Christian Council is aware that the Church in Ghana has a prophetic role to play, in witnessing to the truth in all matters affecting the welfare of our people, and a sacred responsibility to create a suitable climate for reconciliation and thereby promote understanding and forgiveness. It is in this way that bitter revenge may be avoided, and a calm and peaceful return to a Constitutional Democracy ensured, for the spiritual and moral well-being, and the material prosperity, of the Sovereign People of Ghana" (Ninsin, 1996, 32).

Over the last several years the church has addressed memoranda to particular sectors of government. In a June 17, 1992, paper, CCG and CBC encouraged the interim electoral commission to implement certain key policies desired by the people, as evidenced by their overwhelmingly positive vote in favor of the draft constitution on April 28, 1992. In the words of the memorandum, "The conception that should give birth to the Fourth republic took place on that day. What is required now is to ensure that the gestation period is not unduly disrupted, so that a healthy baby can be born to all of us" (162–163).

Dickson recalls the atmosphere surrounding the election that returned Rawlings to power in January 1993, an atmosphere pervaded by memories of abductions and extrajudicial executions under Rawlings's PNDC government.[134]

> The nervous anxiety was due to several causes, one of which was the rekindled dissatisfaction with the government during whose time there had been several executions, among the executed being former heads of state, and the abduction and murder of three judges and a retired army officer. The three

> judges were known to have given judgments not favorable to an earlier military government, the Armed Forces Revolutionary Council (AFRC), headed by Rawlings, now chairman of the PNDC . . . [Adding to the tension] was the suspicion that Rawlings might enter the race for [presidential] office in a new democratic government." (Dickson 1995, 263)

As a matter-of-fact, that is precisely what Rawlings did. He won, though the opposition contested the validity of the election.

In a joint memorandum entitled "From the Heads of the Member Churches of the Christian Council of Ghana and the Catholic Bishops' Conference on the 'Report on the Evolving Democratic Process,'" the churches asked the government to do four things: publish the government white paper on the report; set up an independent electoral body, with adequate resources, to supervise all elections; lift the ban on political parties; and take steps to generate the right atmosphere for healthy political activity in the country. Such steps, said the memorandum, should include the repeal of certain laws, particularly those dealing with executions for political reasons; the release of all political prisoners and detainees; and the granting of unconditional amnesty for all political exiles (265).

As Dickson notes, the government had come to look upon the churches as "being somewhat obstreperous" (265). In June 1989 the PNDC government announced Law 221, Religious Bodies (Registration) Law, which stipulated that all religious bodies must apply to the National Commission for Culture for approval. PNDC's decisions were to be final, with no recourse for consideration in the courts of the land.[135] Paul Nugent calls this "the greatest mistake of the Rawlings regime [because the mainline churches] were particularly well organized and wielded an influence over substantial sections of the population" (Nugent 1996, 187).[136] In the wake of meetings between CCG, CBC, and the government, in October 1989 the churches submitted a "pastoral letter" to the government, stating, "In its present form [the Religious Bodies (Registration) Law], constitutes an infringement on the fundamental rights of the freedom of worship. For this reason, we are of the view that our churches would be surrendering both for our present membership and for future generations, a fundamental and inalienable right, if we registered in accordance with the Law. . . . We cannot in conscience register under PNDC Law 221 as it stands" (189). However, the government took no remedial action. Finally, in August 1992, in anticipation of forthcoming elections, the churches submitted the following memorandum to the government:

> We do not question the right or the duty of government to check any activity, which goes against public decency and morality, promotes the financial exploitation of believers, endangers public peace or compromises national unity and honor. We would however like to affirm that government should, in all matters relating to freedom of worship, reflect restraint in the measures it takes. Where the due process of the law can be used to check misdemeanors and subversion of good order, it would appear to be always better to resort to the courts than to direct political or governmental intervention. . . . Further, the law pronounced recently tends to place in the hands of the government a tool by which the activities of all religious bodies and especially churches can easily be controlled. (Dickson 1995, 266)

The law was repealed following Rawlings's inauguration as president of the Fourth Republic, January 7, 1992. Boafo states that the churches' actions leading up to the 1992 election "became catalytic for more agitation that led to the return to Constitutional rule in 1992" (Boafo 1999, 226).

The opposition boycotted the second round of the 1992 elections and refused to take their seats in parliament because of allegations of fraud. Afterward CCG and CBC attempted to mediate to resolve the issue. Even though their intervention did not completely reverse the government's stance, the political leaders expressed their appreciation for the role of the churches. CCG and CBC, however, refused to participate in the national thanksgiving service called for by the Rawlings government. This was to indicate their sympathies with the opposition, which alleged that the elections amounted to a stolen verdict. In the vacuum created by the withdrawal of the opposition, the government turned favorably to the leaders of such new religious movements as Christian Action Faith Ministries, led by Duncan Williams. As Paul Gifford states, analysis shows "that the mainline churches studiously avoided sycophancy; it was Duncan Williams who did not" (Gifford 1998, 87).

A welcome development during the earlier years of the Rawlings era was the promulgation of the Intestate Succession Law, which concerned the property of the deceased. This law repealed Section 48 of the marriage ordinance and gave a specific portion of the estate of the intestate to the surviving spouse. PNDC Law 111 (1985) identified unambiguously what should belong to the children of the deceased and to the surviving spouse. For instance, members of the extended family could not take the family's house and household chattels from the widow and children; to do so was an offense punishable by fine and imprisonment. MCG was among the parties that advocated such clarity, especially in light of the predominantly matrilineal system of succession among the Akan.

Mainline churches of Ghana, though members of the World Council of Churches, (WCC) are more reflective of mainstream evangelical churches than their counterparts in the West. A number of the documents prepared by the working committees of these churches have been robust and effective in bringing a Christian witness to Ghanaian society. In Ghana's situation, not unlike several other African countries, the church has been one of the few national institutions that could be trusted by the people. The church's faithful presence in the midst of decaying social and political structures offered spiritual hope, and, on a more pragmatic level, a sense of the universality and solidarity of the Christian witness. MCG, as seen in the vignettes that have been recounted here, has stood as a testimony against tyranny and an active player in participatory democracy.

Mission churches, such as MCG, witnessed in an environment where they played a unique role as proto-democratic modernizing structures. The Methodists whose evangelical revival and public witness spared England the horrors of the French Revolution in these contexts acted as preservers of the social order amid the political upheaval and abuse of human rights.

MCG Members in the Employ of the Government

MCG, IN CONCERT WITH OTHER GHANAIAN CHURCHES, HAS FREquently attempted to confront the government of the day on issues of power and human rights. At the same time, it must be acknowledged that the government has often been able to capitalize on the services of church-trained personnel to help deflect the critique of religious leaders. From the days of Nkrumah, some of the government's allies have been Methodist ministers. They have served in Parliament, filled government positions at the ministerial and ambassadorial levels, and headed questionable political movements such as the Young Pioneers in the Nkrumah era. Understandably, some figures in MCG circles were "looked upon with suspicion and as traitors to the Christian cause" (143).

Conclusion

KWAME NKRUMAH WAS A CHAMPION FOR SELF-RULE. "WE PREFER self-government [with risk] than servitude in tranquility [for] it is far better to be free to govern, to misgovern yourself, than to be governed by anybody else" (Pobee 1976, 130).[137] The Ghanaian Methodist leadership, however, sought autonomy for different reasons. Summarized by President Grant, the goal of autonomy was to enable Ghanaian Methodists to be better Christians, to own the vision and mission of the church, and to spread scriptural holiness in Ghana. In doing this, they planted churches, established schools and hospitals, and gave an enduring, prophetic witness in the political arena during the years of decline and decay.

The 1982–83 prayer manual of the Methodist Church Overseas Division of the British Conference, *Going and Coming*, states, "Ghana has come through a political revolution aimed at releasing the nation from the grip of a corrupt elite. The economy is prostrate, national self-respect low, confidence almost gone. But the churches are crowded. In sound scriptural tradition and as a true priest, the Methodist Church President, the Rev. S. B. Essamuah, takes upon himself the sins of the nation and confesses them to God" (p. 9). The evangelistic and sociopolitical mission of the Methodist Church, Ghana, can only be comprehensively evaluated as it spans the entire spectrum of prayer and protest, all done as part of the holistic ministry of the church. That mission has seldom been better expressed than in this prayer of one of its presidents and my father:

> Lord Almighty, we adore you. God of present, past and future, you who created us earth-born beings still hold us safe in your everlasting arms. With shame we confess we have refused to listen to your bidding, our carelessness has encouraged our moral decay, we have allowed our fundamental rights to be eroded. We confess the misdeeds of our national life. Forgive our corruption, our incompetence, and our mismanagement; in deep repentance and faith, we turn to you, O God. Yet we thank you for the rapid expansion we see in your church, spiritual revival in so many of its parts, the palpable upsurge of the life of worship traceably hidden in the living God! Thank you for the sacred music that comes from the people's own life and tradition that consecrates the people's devotion. And raise up from among your people, we pray, political leaders of fidelity and skill, clear-thinking men and women of courage and grace, honest, impartial, dedicated leaders in Church and State. So, Lord, bless and save our nation.—Samuel B. Essamuah, 1979–84

CHAPTER FIVE

Barriers to Mission: A House Divided

"HISTORY IS A DELICATE ADMIXTURE OF FACTS AND INTERPRETAtion," writes the veteran Africanist Ivor Wilks.

> In researching and writing about the past we must observe the strongest possible commitment to truth. . . . even when it is not palatable. Few Germans now live comfortably with the knowledge of the extermination of the Jews, and few Americans with the knowledge that the expansion of their nation was achieved only by the virtual destruction of older societies. But these things happened and they cannot be suppressed. Different *interpretations* of what happened in the past are of course not only possible but are desirable, for thereby inquiry is advanced. But the facts, even when they are ugly facts have to be respected. (Wilks 1996, 42, 63, *emphasis original*)

MCG has experienced some house-dividing episodes in its exercise in self-government. Sometimes the facts have been "ugly," and those of us who are committed to the life and witness of MCG cannot "live comfortably" with every chapter in our history. But any portrayal of Methodist history in Ghana would be woefully incomplete without acknowledging some of the crises within the MCG family. They typically involved issues of ethnicity, style and system of government, and personal integrity and were all a challenge to MCG's mission.

In this way, one of the cardinal elements in their contextualization process, that is Akan culture, became a hindrance to the other two facets, specifically Methodist theology and Ghanaian identity. The perception that MCG was an Akan church was sorely tested.

Well before formal autonomy in 1961, the day-to-day administration of MCG was in Ghanaian hands. The fact that expatriate missionaries were a minority at the highest levels of the church hierarchy gave MCG a strong local flavor. In 1950 MCG had its first indigenous chairman in the person of the Reverend Gaddiel R. Acquaah, thus placing it well ahead of other mission-founded churches in Ghana.[138] The gaining of autonomy established that what had been enjoyed in fact would henceforth be acknowledged as lawful as well. It also meant that internal crises could not be blamed on expatriate missionaries.

Confronting Ethnic Dynamics and Style of Government

IN THE SEVERAL DECADES SINCE GAINING AUTONOMY, MCG HAS NOT presented a consistent Christian witness to the nation. Some observers are quick to trace MCG problems to ethnic competition. No less a person than John S. Pobee asserts, "The churches which claim to be committed to reconciliation are themselves tribal churches, and they fail to translate their rhetoric into action. For example, in the 1980s the Methodist Church of Ghana was in the throes of a struggle between the Fante and the Ga. The central issue was which tribe would the president of the conference come from?" (Pobee 1991c, 5). Many share Pobee's view.[139] While one can hardly doubt that ethnicity has been a factor in MCG history, there are deeper issues of interpersonal relationships and human culpability. To explain everything in terms of ethnicity—or governance—is simplistic.

Sad to say, MCG has had its share of church crises involving ethnicity, as the following episodes will show. Other issues were also confronted, including democratic versus hierarchical control of the church. The cases recounted here have been selected on the basis of their national impact on the denomination. Each situation was the subject of one or more annual conferences, and sometimes special, additional conferences had to be called. In the process, constitutional issues were raised and clarified. Some of these crises led to the suspension, dismissal, or resignation of MCG ministers. In each case the cohesion of MCG was threatened, and indeed, in one case a schism resulted. Issues of the style of governance often came into play, and issues of ethnicity were either raised openly or were implied as participants sought to understand the underlying causes of conflict.[140]

1965–73: The Calvary Experiment

RELATIVELY EARLY IN THE FIRST DECADE OF MCG'S AUTONOMY, the "Calvary Experiment" brought to the fore issues of ethnicity and church governance. The topics dealt with in connection with this rather drawn-out episode were to have continuing relevance for Ghanaian Methodists through the remainder of the century.[141]

In the 1920s there were three MCG congregations in Accra, the colonial capital of Ghana. The majority of members were from the Ga ethnic group centered in Southeast Ghana, and thus the Accra congregations were Ga-speaking. A number of Fante believers, while continuing to hold membership in these churches, formed a Fante Society. Most of the leadership were second, or third, generation Christians, having come from families that had been Christians for quite a while in the central and western coastal regions of Ghana. Language, culture, education, social class, and the fact that they were immigrants in the Accra area bound them together. The Fante members of the Accra churches soon decided to meet jointly for Sunday school, using Fante-Akan as the language. They met on Sunday evenings in Plange Memorial Hall of Wesley Church (also known as Wesley Central because of its location in Accra). The Reverend J. E. Allotey-Pappoe, a young Ga minister and an accomplished Ga musician, conducted their services. His commitment to outreach beyond his own ethnic group was indicated by the musical pieces he composed in Akan. In the early 1930s, the society grew under a young Ga preacher, Alec N. K. Sackeyfio, who later became an MCG minister. Following World War II there was a great deal of immigration into Accra from other parts of the country, especially from Fante communities in West and South-Central Ghana. This highlighted the need for Ga churches to accommodate themselves to Akan-speaking people. By the 1960s the Fante Society, at that time still affiliated with Wesley Society, was holding both morning and evening services in Lomoko House, the residence of the Accra superintendent.

The issue of the status and affiliation of the Fante Society became controversial in 1965 when the Fante group erected its own church building in Adabraka, a suburb of Accra, and therefore became more proximate to the Adabraka Circuit than to the Wesley Circuit.[142] A meeting of representatives from the Adabraka and Wesley circuits took place in March 1966 to decide on where the Fante congregation—which now called itself "Calvary Society"—should belong. Opinion was divided, and so the matter was forwarded to the Accra District Synod. The synod petitioned the 1966 MCG Annual Conference (which convened in August) to set up a commission to determine the boundaries of the Accra and Adabraka circuits, to decide on the appropriate affiliation for Calvary, and to consider suggestions for the creation of new circuits. Acting on behalf of the conference, the General Purposes Council (formerly Committee)[143] appointed a study commission. The commission took the name "Creedy Commission" after its chair and only missionary representative, Lawrence A. Creedy.[144] Other members of the commission were J. A. Hammond, Charles Awotwi-Pratt, I. K. Agyeman, and O. T. Agyeman.[145] The commission members were chosen to represent the major MCG ethnic groups, and the appointment of an expatriate missionary as chairman was designed to symbolize objectivity and evenhandedness. Meeting places also were chosen to signal neutrality.

The Creedy Commission delivered its report to the 1968 Annual Conference. It recommended that the Accra-Tema area circuits be reorganized to take account of the various separate-language congregations, and that Calvary affiliate with Adabraka Circuit, especially with a view to the opportunity to reach out to Akan speaking migrants flooding into the area to take urban jobs. These recommendations engendered such vigorous debate between the Accra and Adabraka representatives that the report was sent back to the GPC without decision. (It was later learned that the Adabraka Circuit's objection to the Creedy report was in reaction to the insinuation by some members of the Accra Circuit that Adabraka only wanted to gain Calvary's annual assessment, which was one of the largest in the denomination.)

GPC asked the Accra and Adabraka Quarterly meetings to consider this matter again, and when they did they came to the conclusion that the report from the Creedy Commission was the best way forward, and therefore the new affiliation of Calvary with Adabraka was effected. It must be noted that the Accra and Adabraka Quarterly meetings, as well as the Creedy Commission itself, had not invited the leaders of Calvary to participate in the deliberations. The members of Calvary took this as an affront to the dignity of the highly placed laity who were members of the society.

In a society-wide vote, conducted in March 1971, Calvary expressed the desire to become an autonomous circuit. Following the society vote, Calvary's leaders forwarded the petition to the Accra Circuit. The petition also indicated that the society wished to suspend its Accra-Circuit assessments beginning with the quarter ending May 31, 1971.

On June 8, 1972, a special Quarterly Meeting of the Accra Circuit was held to review Calvary's request for circuit status. It was agreed, "The petition of Calvary Society for elevation to circuit status might be forwarded [to the synod] but should *not* be recommended by the Quarterly Meeting" (emphasis in the original). In addition, the meeting stipulated that the circuit moneys should be paid up to date before the resolution would be forwarded.

Calvary responded to this rebuff by going directly to GPC. The leaders of Calvary felt that Accra's insistence that the circuit money should be paid before their request would be forwarded amounted to blackmail. It seemed to support what they had feared, that money and not the unity or the expansion of the church was the motive behind the Accra Circuit's noncooperation. The rebuff also seemed consistent with a pattern of the majority, who were Gas, who were using their numerical strength to turn aside the aspirations of the Fante members of Calvary. As expressed in its June 12, 1972, letter to GPC, Calvary's leaders felt that the action of the Accra Circuit reflected a lack of concern about those in the immigrant Akan community who were flocking to "spiritual churches."[146] Calvary pointed out that its membership included persons from ethnic groups other than Fantes, and that even though the society expected to cater primarily to Akan-speaking people, it was not advocating the creation of an Akan circuit.

This impasse ultimately led to the appointment of a new commission, named at the 1972 Annual Conference. The members were S. H. Amissah, K. J. A. Stedman, Samuel B. Essamuah, Kwesi A. Dickson, N. A. Mensah, A. N. K. Sackeyfio, N. T. Abraham, J. K. Essiem, J. A. K. Doughan, J. Adabie, and A. Quaison-Sackey. Amissah was named as convener and then was selected as chair,[147] while the lone missionary, the Reverend Stedman, was asked to serve as secretary.

The Amissah Commission dealt with seven issues. First, in answer to doubts that had been raised about the possibility of a single society being granted circuit status, the commission cited Standing Orders 401 and 402.1 to the effect that a circuit could consist of one or more societies. Second, as to the legitimacy of a society going directly to the conference and to GPC after being denied at the circuit level, the commission was divided. Some sought to interpret the standing orders as stated, while other members of the commission argued that no superintendent-minister or quarterly meeting should be able to frustrate the wishes of a society, or the nature of its democracy. Clearly, here was a debate about how democratic an institution MCG would be. In the end, Calvary was reprimanded for sending a petition directly to GPC. But it also noted that while the Accra Circuit Quarterly Meeting acted constitutionally by rejecting Calvary's petition, the rejection reflected more the letter than the spirit of the law.

Third, the commission unanimously faulted local ministers who had not kept the superintendent-minister informed of all business transacted at the society-level leaders meetings. The superintendent-minister, as required by the constitution, was to chair all meetings that considered major items, and this standing order had not been followed. Fourth, on the allegation that if this petition were granted the national church would be promoting the concept of a tribal circuit, the commission acknowledged that to stress tribal identity was provocative and separatist. However, when effective evangelistic outreach was the intent, it was warranted for a society to be formed among those having a particular language. Furthermore, it was agreed that the need to reach out to the immigrant Fante community in Ga-speaking areas would be better handled, administratively, if there were separate circuits instead of putting all under one administrative unit. In support of this stance, the commission quoted Allotey-Pappoe, who had said: "The Society—Calvary—came into being to meet a specific need. If by making a separate circuit, the church can better meet the needs, make the circuit. Meeting a need is more important than tribalism."

Fifth, the commission addressed itself to the fear that allowing this petition to go ahead would cause the "dismemberment of Ghana Methodism." On the contrary, the commission felt that loyalty to Christ and to his church would override tribal allegiances. Sixth, the commission, having investigated the issue of the financial arrangements between Calvary and the Accra Circuit, determined that in the past Calvary had been "over assessed." However, since Calvary's performance had always exceeded the targeted figures, the commission felt that the over assessment was not deliberate but rather was a positive anticipation of Calvary's Christian stewardship. Furthermore, the commission ruled that granting Calvary independent circuit status would not seriously affect the finances of Accra Circuit.

Seventh, the commission addressed a perception that Calvary Society was in a privileged position due to the fact that GPC included four of the members of Calvary's leaders meeting. It was also known that Calvary, with the approval of conference president T. Wallace Koomson, had changed the signatories to its bank accounts without prior consultation with the superintendent minister. Finally, the conference secretary, Isaac Asuamah-Thompson, had occasionally exercised pastoral oversight of Calvary. Despite these observations, the commission denied the view that Calvary enjoyed a privileged position.

In conclusion, the Amissah Commission recommended that Calvary Society should be allowed to become a circuit; that the possibility of other societies joining Calvary should be explored with the Accra and Adabraka circuits; and that the new circuit should not be called Calvary, nor should it be referred to as an Akan circuit, but rather it should be called North-Accra. The Amissah Commission concluded its assignment by praying that where there had been discord, there might be harmony, where there had been a breakdown of relationships, there might be reconciliation, and where there had been hurt or bitterness, there might be healing and forgiveness.

The issues in connection with the "Calvary Experiment" that were wrestled with in the late sixties and early seventies reappeared in the late nineties, as the Ghana Church dealt with its overseas branches made up of different language groups and having different expectations of the MCG office in Accra.

1983–84: Presidential Election Challenged

IN THE 1980S MCG BECAME A "HOUSE DIVIDED," SO MUCH SO THAT some members feared the outcome would bear out the words of Jesus: "If a house is divided against itself, that house will not stand" (Mark 3:25). For several years running it seemed that one crisis followed another.[148]

To what extent was ethnocentrism to blame? The Reverend Jacob S. A. Stephens, who was nominated in 1983 as MCG president-designate, and then served in that post from 1985 to 1990, declared in a retrospective interview that the problems of the 1980s had nothing to do with tribalism. He testified that as a Ga in a predominantly Fante church he was indebted to Fante mentors like the Reverends Gaddiel R. Acquaah and B. A. Markin. The problems of the 1980s he blamed on "ruffians" (interview with Methodist Historical Society, 1999).

As already indicated, it was at the 1983 Annual Conference that Stephens was chosen to be the next MCG president; his term of service would commence the ensuing year, in August 1984, assuming that his selection for the post would be confirmed by a 75 percent vote of the 1984 conference delegates.[149] His selection was especially significant in that it was the first time that MCG had chosen a non-Fante to be the top administrative official. He had completed, in 1982, an eight-year tenure as secretary of the conference, during which he served under Presidents Charles K. Yamoah, Charles Awotwi-Pratt, and Samuel B. Essamuah. Prior to that he was the Accra District Synod secretary and had on various occasions assisted the conference office. Earlier in his career he had served as rector of the Young Pioneer Movement, which was set up to advance the agenda of Nkrumah's Convention People's Party. With this background Stephens was a well-known public figure both within and outside the church.

Suddenly, in January 1984, five months after being named president-designate, Stephens's suitableness for the post was thrown into question by the circulation of an anonymous letter, sent to several MCG leaders, accusing Stephens of embezzling church funds when he was the secretary of conference. Since the underlying source of this information was contained in a 1982–83 audit report, and since circulation of the report had been restricted to President Essamuah and his closest MCG associates, it was concluded in a church investigation led by the Reverend J. E. Ebe-Arthur and by the veteran Ghanaian civil servant and intelligence chief Benjamin Forjoe that Essamuah was to be blamed for the anonymous letter.

Essamuah was already on a month-long leave on medical grounds. With six months remaining in his five-year term, he subsequently resigned effective March 1, 1984.[150] His early resignation meant that, in line with constitutional provision, the immediate past president, Awotwi-Pratt, stepped into office as acting president. In April, in response to the request of the Methodist laity association, Awotwi-Pratt appointed a committee to investigate the charges against Stephens. The committee members were Isaac K. Abban, chair,[151] Kingsley Nyinah; Benjamin Forjoe, the intelligence chief; Richard Asua-Sekyere; secretary, J. N. Okine; and Harry Dodoo. Okine and Dodoo were representatives of the Ga community in the Accra District, while the other four members were from the Akan and Nzima ethnic groups. After completing its investigation, the committee submitted two reports. The majority report found Stephens guilty of misappropriating church funds, while the minority report, submitted by Okine and Dodoo, exonerated Stephens from all charges. Awotwi-Pratt then suspended Stephens, thus preparing the way for the issue to come before a minor synod (in effect, a church court).

The Accra District, with its Ga majority, saw the charges against Stephens as a ruse to deny office to the first and only non-Fante to be elected as conference president. The real issue, as most Gas saw it, was Fante ethnocentrism. On the surface, at least, this seemed plausible, given the fact that all chairmen and secretaries of MCG districts, with the exception of Accra, were Akans. Church officials issued a denial of this interpretation, which the *Daily Graphic* reported in its issue of August 20, 1984: "The Methodist Church of Ghana has made it clear that the Church has never and would never be threatened by ethnicity as is being erroneously painted in the minds of the public. The Church, however, explained that it is fighting sin in high places of the Church and that if anything, the Church is rather threatened by sin and not tribalism."

In response, the Accra District rallied around Stephens. A meeting of leading Accra laity issued a statement calling for his reinstatement, or alternatively, the authors of the statement looked to Stephens to "unite the disintegrating District of Accra and govern its religious and other affairs." In effect, if the reinstatement of Stephens as MCG president was not forthcoming, it appeared that a separate Methodist movement would be formed.[152]

Soon after the Accra leaders issued their statement, a group of agitated members of the Accra District marched to the church office in Adabraka, where they attacked Acting President Awotwi-Pratt and the conference secretary, Joseph Tekyi-Ansah, with clubs. The attackers took Awotwi-Pratt and Tekyi-Ansah away in different vehicles, headed for Lomoko House, which served both as the residence of Stephens and headquarters of the MCG Accra District. En route to Lomoko House, Tekyi-Ansah managed to get the attention of the police, who released both of them; the police had them write down their accounts of the incident, and the next two weeks they provided protection.

With the minor synod scheduled for September, the August Annual Conference passed without the presence of Stephens and with the Accra laity still agitating for him to lead a seceding section of MCG. In the face of all these developments, Stephens declined to lead a secession, choosing instead to appear before the minor synod on September 28, 1984. The panel members were Charles Awotwi-Pratt; Victor B. T. Nartey Tokoli; Samuel Asante-Antwi; K. B. M. Edu-Buandoh; Seth Aryee; Noah Danquah; and a British missionary, Alec Jones. Edu-Buandoh and Aryee were appointed to serve as MCG prosecutors.

Stephens was asked to respond to five issues. First, what were the circumstances of his receiving a payment of 100,000 cedis from MCG? Second, why had a 5 percent tax been levied on vehicles bought for the use of MCG districts and circuits? Third, had church funds been used to pay for his children's education in Europe and in the United States? Fourth, what were the conditions surrounding loans to church workers and to a non church worker for their purchase of private vehicles? Fifth, how did vehicles earmarked for the Methodist Farms Company end up on his private farm?

In the end, Stephens's responses persuaded the minor synod to clear him of all charges. In regard to the payment of 100,000 cedis by MCG to Stephens, Awotwi-Pratt stated that he was satisfied with the explanation that it was reimbursement of a personal loan to MCG during a financially difficult period. The panel accepted the explanation that the 5 percent vehicle tax provided a welfare fund used for end-of-year bonuses to church workers. Stephens stated that he had no knowledge of any attempt to link payment of his children's overseas school fees with the church's foreign exchange. It turned out that the Christian Council of Ghana, and not Stephens, had provided the loans for the purchase of the private vehicles. The vehicles purported to have been intended for the Methodist Farms Company had been placed on church property and nobody knew who owned them. It was revealed that the vehicles were donated to Trinity Theological Seminary through the foreign contacts of one of its faculty.

The outcome of the minor synod did not clear the air. It appeared that either the church had not done its homework well (and should not have called for the minor synod), or that the panelists had decided, in the interest of peace and reconciliation in the church, that all the charges should be dropped. The panel's decision was given wide publicity in a letter dated October 2, 1984, with the conclusion that Stephens was reinstated and resumed his status as president-elect.

Still, doubts lingered. It was learned that Edu-Buandoh, strongly opposed the majority view. (The reader should keep this in mind as a possible factor in a later church crisis leading to schism, in which Edu-Buandoh was the central figure.) Tekyi-Ansah, upon his return from a course in Nairobi, also challenged the grounds for dismissal of the charges. In a letter addressed to GPC, dated November 13, 1984, he intimated that the minor synod had not considered all the relevant evidence. Although GPC sided with the minority opinion, the outcome of the minor synod paved the way for the confirmation of Stephens as the sixth president of MCG. This episode involving Stephens's leadership, and the underlying assumptions of ethnocentric prejudice, left MCG divided into opposing camps. It set the tone for some of the crises that followed.

1985–86: Cape Coast Schism

A MAJOR SCHISM WITHIN MCG OCCURRED IN 1986, TWENTY-FIVE years after the beginning of autonomy.[153] It involved the Reverend Edu-Buandoh, the lone member on the panel of the minor synod who had objected to the dismissal of the charges that had been brought against President-elect Stephens in 1984. Edu-Buandoh had entered the MCG ministry in 1959 and was first stationed at Cape Coast Wesley as second (assistant) minister. After a brief period of service at Essikadu, he moved on to the Saltpond Circuit for several years, where he also served as superintendent-minister. Then, upon receiving appointment as the MCG connexional youth minister, he spent 1974–75 at Emmanuel College, Ibadan, Nigeria, as part of his preparation for that assignment. However, after returning to Ghana and serving in the new post for two years, he was returned to pastoral ministry, first in the Akim Oda Circuit and later in the Anomabu Circuit. While at Akim Oda he served as secretary of the Winneba District Synod, and when he was posted at Anomabu he became secretary of the Cape Coast District Synod.

Trouble began to stir early in 1983. Edu-Buandoh learned that he was soon to be posted to Cape Coast Wesley as superintendent of the circuit and Chairman of the District. Even before he left Anomabu, he received the honor of being unanimously nominated to succeed the retiring chairman of the Cape Coast district. However, at the national office in Accra, GPC preferred that the post of chairman of the Cape Coast district be filled by the Reverend MacLean Kumi, and so the latter's name was submitted to the conference. Not to be denied, the supporters of Edu-Buandoh resubmitted Edu-Buandoh's name, and at the 1983 Annual Conference he was elected Chairman of Cape Coast District.[154]

In August 1985, two years after Edu-Buandoh's arrival in Cape Coast, trouble was signaled in a letter addressed to the conference president, Jacob Stephens, who was now just beginning his five-year term in the top office of MCG. B. K. Bondzi-Simpson, a prominent Cape Coast layperson and member of the Cape Coast leaders meeting, was the author. His letter enumerated a number of charges against Edu-Buandoh: dishonesty; withholding information from the quarterly meeting; making a false statement before the synod about Alec Jones, a missionary serving as chaplain to schools and colleges; attempting to tarnish the image of Jones; speaking ill of a fellow MCG minister; and so forth. Several of Bondzi-Simpson's concerns had to do with the welfare and reputation of Jones, who, as the lone missionary on the 1984 minor synod, had joined the majority in clearing Stephens of charges of wrongdoing.

From the perspective of Bondzi-Simpson, the crisis began in connection with Edu-Buandoh's request for a third minister to be stationed at Cape Coast. As to where the new minister would reside, it became apparent to Bondzi-Simpson and others that Edu-Buandoh had in mind the manse occupied by Jones. Bondzi-Simpson opposed the request for a third minister, in particular because it would bring hardship to the missionary. When Bondzi-Simpson's interventions failed to change Edu-Buandoh's mind, he wrote his letter to Stephens. Stephens responded by appointing a four-member investigative committee consisting of MCG vice president Alex Quaison-Sackey, the Reverends Kwaku Asamoah-Okyere, Kweku Abakah, and Sophia Moore. Quaison-Sackey, who was asked to chair the committee, was one of Ghana's most distinguished citizens, having served as the first African president of the UN General Assembly. The committee began its work on September 4, 1985, and rendered a report on March 10, 1986. Over the next six months the saga moved steadily to its schismatic climax.

The report confirmed that Edu-Buandoh intended to dislodge Jones without making suitable alternative arrangements for his accommodation. The committee also found that Edu-Buandoh was not democratic in his decision-making and failed to show sensitivity in his relations with other ministers; therefore the committee recommended that he be stationed somewhere other than Cape Coast. The accused responded by asserting that the committee had not called any of his witnesses but only those favorable to Bondzi-Simpson. President Stephens's response to the Quaison-Sackey report was to suspend Edu-Buandoh from his ministerial posts and for him to appear before a minor synod.

The Cape Coast District standing committee, made up of clergy and lay-people, promptly rejected the president's action and voted a unanimous show of support for Edu-Buandoh. In a letter to Stephens dated March 24, the standing committee called for a rehearing of the case on the grounds that the Quaison-Sackey committee had failed to conduct a comprehensive investigation. All sixty-four members present at the meeting of the premier Methodist Circuit in Ghana signed it. Eventually there was another extraordinary show of support involving all eleven circuits of the Cape Coast District, each of which convened emergency quarterly meetings that produced memoranda requesting the MCG head office to rehear the case at the level of an investigative committee rather than at the minor synod level.

Stephens's only response to Cape Coast was to question the legal standing of its March 24 action, since the Chairman, Edu-Buandoh, had been suspended and so could not legally have chaired the meeting that produced the letter. In the face of this rebuff, on April 17 the frustrated leaders filed a writ at the Cape Coast High Court seeking legal means to set aside the proceedings of the Quaison-Sackey committee and barring the MCG hierarchy from acting on the committee's report. The court's decision would be rendered in June.

In the interim, the delegates to the Cape Coast District Synod, having assembled for their May annual meeting, unanimously returned Edu-Buandoh to his seat as Chairman. This dramatic action not only underlined the widespread questioning of the Quaison-Sackey proceedings but also highlighted the growing lack of confidence in the leadership at the national headquarters in Accra.

The secular court's response to the Cape Coast leaders' petition was delivered on June 24. It ruled that the Quaison-Sackey committee erred in not seeking the counsel of the local Cape Coast leaders meeting. Furthermore, it barred Stephens from chairing any minor synod dealing with Edu-Buandoh, given the unavoidable bias he would carry as a result of the 1984 minor synod in which Edu-Buandoh voiced the only objection to clearing Stephens's name. But the court also ruled that Edu-Buandoh had to attend the minor synod if he wished to remain a minister of MCG.[155]

Frantic efforts were made by sympathizers on both sides to bring about reconciliation. On Friday, July 4, the superintendent ministers of all the circuits of the Cape Coast District met with Stephens in the spirit of Christian brotherhood and "helped" Edu-Buandoh apologize for the strain in his relationship with Stephens. The president informed the meeting that he would withdraw the letters of suspension and the invitation to the minor synod, and Edu-Buandoh promised to take the case out of the hands of the secular courts. The meeting ended with the leaders believing that the end of the Cape Coast crisis was in sight.

There are various accounts of the events of the following week. According to Edu-Buandoh, on July 6 the Reverend S. K. Acquah, the Sunyani District Chairman, was sent by the president to read a letter at the Cape Coast Wesley Sunday worship service, the purpose being to announce that Stephens had rescinded the suspension of Edu-Buandoh. It was believed by Edu-Buandoh supporters that the presence of Acquah was also designed to avert a threat from some members in Cape Coast to disrupt the service if they found Edu-Buandoh presiding. For reasons that remain unclear, Acquah declined to read the letter; and while Edu-Buandoh was conducting the service police officers in plain clothes arrested him and escorted him to the police station, walking in the rain because Edu-Buandoh refused to go by car. The service at the church continued under the leadership of Acquah. A few members, however, accompanied their minister on the march through town, which attracted a great deal of attention. It became known that the MCG lawyers Ewusie Wilson and Charles Cann had ordered the arrest, on the grounds that Edu-Buandoh had refused to obey church orders barring him from all ministerial duties. (Another Methodist lawyer, Amponsah Dadzie, was informed that Edu-Buandoh was arrested for refusing a new station ordered by the MCG hierarchy.)

Released on bail, Edu-Buandoh found the events of Sunday so traumatic that he fell ill on Monday. On Tuesday, July 8, he traveled to Accra to brief President Stephens on what had transpired. At MCG headquarters he learned that without his knowledge, senior MCG members had been summoned for a meeting dealing with the Cape Coast crisis. Questioned as to why he had not withdrawn the case from the court, Edu-Buandoh indicated that by the time he arrived home on Friday (Cape Coast is a three-hour journey from Accra), the judiciary offices were closed, Saturday was a non working day for government officials, and on Monday he had taken sick. No one (according to Edu-Buandoh) seemed prepared to believe him, with the result that the peaceful accord reached the previous

Friday was lost. His suspension was reinstated, and a fresh invitation was issued for him to appear before a minor synod. In addition, the Cape Coast leaders meeting was dissolved, and two ministers, the Reverends John K. Ampia-Addison and John Adubah, were posted to act as Chairman and secretary of the District, respectively.

Edu-Buandoh complied and attended the minor synod. He raised several objections regarding the process, focusing especially on the obvious fact that the participants were greatly overbalanced to represent the agenda of Stephens. Even the two church lawyers who had ordered Edu-Buandoh's arrest were present. Given Edu-Buandoh's vigorous objections, the meeting ended without resolution and the minor synod was delayed indefinitely.

When GPC held a meeting on August 4, it agreed that the membership of the minor synod should be reconstituted. On August 7, however, Stephens directed the conference secretary to write Edu-Buandoh ordering him to vacate his residence in Cape Coast. On Sunday, August 10, Stephens traveled to Cape Coast and convened a meeting of some of the leaders of the church at the Palace Hotel. On the following Tuesday, intruders forced their way into the manse, apparently with the intention of packing the belongings of Edu-Buandoh and setting them outside. Edu-Buandoh and his family fled from the house unharmed, though it was reported that some of the intruders threatened to "throw your dead body" into a nearby park (Edusa-Eyison 1994, 217). On August 13 Stephens chaired an emergency session of the Cape Coast Synod and demanded total compliance with the order for Edu-Buandoh to vacate his residence. After some hesitation, Edu-Buandoh complied.

A week later the *Ghanaian Times* carried an announcement that Edu-Buandoh had been expelled from the denomination. The item appeared on August 19, the day before the opening of the 1986 Annual Conference. Edu-Buandoh appeared at the conference, pleading to any who would listen that he be given an opportunity to tell his side of the story, but the conference leaders offered no opportunity for him to do so. In a letter dated September 8 and signed by the conference secretary, he was informed that the ministerial session of the conference had dismissed him from the ministry based on deficiencies in his "ministerial character and fidelity."[156] According to the letter, his expulsion was effective as of August 21. After mulling over his options, Edu-Buandoh established the Evangelical Methodist Church of Christ and several hundred former members of MCG joined him.[157]

The schism involving Cape Coast was a severe setback to MCG's mission. Inevitably it spotlighted issues of ethnicity; but personal ambitions, personality clashes, and age-old human stubbornness may well be suspected as the deeper causes.

1987–90:
WINNEBA CHARGES AND COUNTERCHARGES

WHILE THE CAPE COAST SCHISM WAS STILL FRESH IN THE MINDS OF Ghana's Methodist community, another trouble spot began to brew. First the Winneba society and then the entire Winneba District was at variance with the conference office, and in particular with Stephens. The first issue, involving financial accountability, came to light in 1988. An amount of 35,661 pounds sterling had been paid to the Fielder Gearing Associates, a British company based in London, for the purchase of a fifty-four-seat bus. This transaction, authorized by Stephens, had untoward consequences. The money was part of the grant given by the British Methodist Church Overseas Division. It was alleged that when this transaction was authorized, the British Methodist Church itself had already purchased from the manufacturer a similar bus for the MCG. Soon after the Accra office had placed its order, Fielder Gearing Associates filed for bankruptcy and MCG's money was lost. Kofi Acquaah-Harrison, a member of the Winneba society and also a member of GPC brought this information to light. He submitted his findings, which he claimed to have come from Scotland Yard sources, to the GPC for action. The administration was incensed and interpreted Acquaah-Harrison's action as an attempt to bring shame and disgrace to the president (MCG Conference Agenda 1989, 253). The president, in a letter dated July 12, 1988, dismissed Acquaah-Harrison from

GPC. The Winneba District standing committee, on whose behalf Acquaah-Harrison served on GPC, objected to his dismissal and called for an independent board to investigate the facts behind the loss of the money. The president refused to cooperate, maintaining that it was the purview of the finance subcommittee to deal with such matters and that the members of that committee had already done so (Winneba Standing Committee Minutes, August 5 1988).

About this time there began to circulate a letter with the signature of the president entitled "Personal Insights and Admonitions" (MCG MISC 99/CIC/88/2, 30 June 1988). In it, Stephens alleged that several leading churchmen, including members past and present of the Winneba leadership, had mistresses, had engaged in concubinage, had misappropriated funds, or had been guilty of a combination thereof. The letter asserted that the information had come to Stephens through Acquaah-Harrison (apparently acquired by Stephens in earlier days when the two men had a close personal friendship). It appeared that the intent of the letter was to paint Acquaah-Harrison in a bad light as a gossip and an evil person. But many who saw the letter wondered how the chief administrator of a denomination had time to write an eight-page letter insinuating immorality within the Winneba church community. Several of the accused were already dead, but living members of the families of those accused threatened to take this up in Ghana's secular courts. Some of Stephens's friends prevailed on him to apologize to the families that had been implicated in the letter.[158] There followed a series of family meetings at the Accra office at which the president showed appropriate remorse and gave assurances that his aim had not been to defame the families and that the letter itself had not been intended for public consumption.

The one person in this debacle who never received an apology was Acquaah-Harrison, who reacted by taking the matter to court. He did so because in the letter Stephens alleged that Acquaah-Harrison was part of a plot to overthrow the military government of the day, allegations that could have resulted in death or a life sentence for the accused. Acquaah-Harrison filed a writ on January

12, 1989, claiming damages from Stephens in the amount of half a billion cedis (1989 MCG Representative Conference Agenda, 1989, 235; also MCG Ministerial Conference Agenda 1989, 67).

GPC constituted a six-member panel consisting of Justice E. K. Wiredu, Lt. Gen. J. A. Ankrah, the Reverend J. E. Ebe-Arthur, Mrs. Alberta Ollenu, Mrs. Georgina Baiden, and the Reverend Dr. Benjamin W. Garbrah.[159] They were instructed to seek reconciliation between Acquaah-Harrison and Stephens and to do everything possible to prevail upon Acquaah-Harrison to withdraw his case. The president could not be persuaded to apologize, and the case went forward, capturing wide attention throughout Ghana. With the slow legal proceedings in Ghana, the Acquaah-Harrison/ Stephens court case was withdrawn after Stephens left office. No judgment was ever rendered.

While this sensational item played itself out on the public stage, new turmoil arose in regard to the appointment of the next president of the Conference. It was assumed by the delegates that Stephens would be completing the standard term of five years as president in August 1989, counting from his 1984 exoneration. However, this view of the chronology failed to take into account the fact that Stephens had been delayed in his accession to the presidency by one year; thus he began his five-year term in 1985, not in 1984. This element in Stephens's presidency, lurking in the background, confused and complicated MCG procedures.

Stephens himself had not recognized the implications of the delay of one year in his assumption of the post of presidency. Therefore, at the 1988 Annual Conference, knowing that the constitution allowed for an extension of his term if he received a 75 percent majority vote, he submitted his name for reelection. After three rounds of voting at which he failed to garner the required level of votes, Stephens announced that he was stepping down to make room for fresh elections without his name. It was at this point that conference designated the Reverend Professor Kwesi A. Dickson to be the next president. (That is, he would assume office in one year's time, assuming that at the 1989 conference, to be held in August a year hence, he would receive confirmation by a 75 percent majority vote.)

Two new situations developed soon after the 1988 conference that complicated the picture. First, the Kumasi District, in a letter dated March 10, 1989, pointed out that because Stephens had not yet presided over five consecutive annual conferences, the 1988 conference had erred in holding the election for president; the election ought not to have been held until the 1989 Annual Conference. Second, when Dickson, currently a visiting professor in Swaziland, learned of his election, he wrote to inform MCG that since he was on a two-year contract in Swaziland, any attempt at terminating it ahead of time in order to assume the office of MCG president would be professionally and financially unwise. When Dickson's concern was shared at GPC, some members of the committee reacted rather negatively and threatened to apply the constitutional rule that ministers who declined station assignments should consider themselves dismissed from the ministry of the MCG.

In the course of this turmoil, the Winneba District objected to an extension of Stephens's term, seeing in this nothing more than an attempt at entrenching an administration with which it was already at odds. (The Winneba district also happened to be Dickson's home area.) At its April 25 and May 25 meetings, GPC struggled to deal with this stew of ill will and miscommunication. Ultimately it remitted the Kumasi letter to the districts for discussion; at the same time it proposed an emergency conference, to be held July 4, 1989, at which time this issue would be debated and also with the view that the 1988 decision regarding the nomination of Dickson might be rescinded, thereby allowing Stephens one more year as president (August 1989 to August 1990).

In retrospect, if GPC had been a bit more charitable toward Dickson, it might have built a reasonable case for granting Stephens his fifth year, by which time (August 1990) Dickson was scheduled to return from Swaziland, enabling him to take up the post of MCG president without complicating his professional career. Instead, in the spring of 1989 GPC virtually ordered Dickson to wind up his activities and to return home. Dickson dutifully returned to Ghana and was posted as superintendent minister of the North Accra Circuit (Calvary Society) as he waited to assume the reins of the MCG presidency.

Given all the uncertainty, members of the Winneba District standing committee initiated a restraining order in the secular courts (dated June 27) to prevent the July 4 emergency conference from debating or overturning the election of Dickson as president-designate. The plaintiffs included S. H. Amissah, vice president of MCG in 1977–79, and Alex Quaison-Sackey, the immediate past MCG vice president. It was in this rather unpleasant atmosphere, a month after the July 4 meeting circumscribed by court order, that the 1989 Annual Conference was held at Sunyani. The conference was unique in the annals of MCG. A bus carrying delegates from the head office and from the Accra District had an accident on the road to Sunyani; when the delegates from Accra finally appeared, they were sporting assorted bandages. The delegates who happened to be lawyers constituted themselves into a group and met to give legal counsel to Stephens so that nothing would occur that might draw the displeasure of the courts.[160]

In the end, the desire of the Kumasi District to extend Stephens's tenure until the 1990 conference was achieved; this was simply because those who were against him were not of a mind to withdraw from the court their case that was designed to preserve the nomination of Dickson. Finally, on January 18, 1990, the Winneba District felt it could withdraw the court case without risking Dickson's status as president-designate. Eventually, the conference convened in special session, April 18, 1990, and decided that Dickson should be inducted into office at the regularly scheduled Annual Conference to be held in Koforidua in August. To help safeguard the induction of Dickson, the special session repealed the standing order requiring that a president-designate garner 75 percent of the vote of the conference delegates to be confirmed. Instead it ruled that a simple majority standing vote would suffice.

Difficult as it may be to imagine, the turmoil of the last two years of Stephens's presidency was still not over. At each annual conference MCG appoints one minister and one layperson to be its representatives at the British conference. As fraternal delegates with voting rights, their presence and participation in the British conference served to convey the warmth of international fellowship that exists. MCOD also organizes special events around the visit of MCG delegates, which enable the delegates to meet former missionaries and others who have shown interest in MCG over the years.

At the 1988 conference the Chairman of the Winneba District, the Reverend Kodjo Haizel, was appointed as MCG representative for that year. But, later the same year, Stephens changed that decision in favor of the Reverend E. J. Bonney, Chairman of the Kumasi District. Given the fact that the two districts were embroiled in a constitutional battle to interpret the duration of service of the president, this could hardly be seen as other than a coarse political move. The Winneba District provided an air ticket for Haizel to go to the British conference, and the Accra headquarters office paid for Bonney to attend the conference. Upon his return, Haizel was summoned to a minor synod for defying authority and to answer charges of doctrinal infidelity (MCG Ministerial Session Conference Agenda, 1989, 260).[161] Haizel was eventually found guilty of the charges of doctrinal infidelity and retired early from the active Methodist ministry.

Each annual conference also provides affirmation for those who have been nominated by their synods to serve as synod chairmen. For the most part, those who are nominated as chairmen of their district synods are confirmed without question at the Annual Conference; out of respect for the integrity of the district leaders, the conference votes are largely formalities. Only in rare instances would GPC or the Annual Conference put forward competing names to serve as synod chairmen. In May 1989, by a vote of 70 for the Reverend Kwaku Abakah and only 10 for the runner-up, the Winneba district nominated Abakah as its next chairman. But GPC set this aside in favor of the Reverend J. Yedu Bannerman. (Bannerman is the veteran Ghanaian expert on Akan culture and proverbs.) When the Winneba standing committee learned that their candidate had been rejected, they decided that they would take the matter to the floor of the Conference so as to reverse the GPC nomination in favor of their own synod's choice. President Stephens, having learned of this, suspended all the ministerial members of the Winneba District who were delegated to attend the Annual Conference; thereby he ensured that the motion would not be entertained at the conference. The immediate consequence was that the affected ministers—Kodjo Haizel, Kwaku Abakah, Charles Ekuban, and Esther Hagan—had to vacate the manses they occupied and get along on greatly reduced stipends.[162] As might be expected, at one point or another each of these suspended ministers had been perceived as not having been loyal to Stephens.

With their suspension, the ministers could not act as Methodist representatives in the Winneba District and so the lay leadership constituted themselves into a seven member committee composed of Alex Quaison-Sackey, K. Ghartey-Sam, Kofi Acquaah-Harrison, J. E. K. Awotwi-Pratt, I. K. Idan, Efua Mills-Robertson, and Rebecca Tagoe. The Reverend Edusa-Eyison, then serving as chaplain at the Winneba Secondary School, was invited to administer the Lord's Supper and preach on first Sundays of the month. But in July 1990 a letter from the MCG administrative office mandated Edusa-Eyison to stop providing these services. In April 1990, GPC met and ratified letters, which had been written on March 5, 15, and 22, suspending thirteen lay members of Winneba Methodist churches. The charges ranged from taking the church to court to abusing leadership status. In the interim, Chairman of the District Bannerman had to reside in different stations and manage the affairs of Winneba District from afar. It was only after the 1990 conference, when Dickson had been confirmed as president, that matters gradually subsided and Bannerman was able to return to Winneba for a proper induction service.

The three-year-long Winneba crisis resulted in a tragic waste of resources. Time, attention, and financial resources were expended in a direction that ultimately benefited no one. The lack of accountability on the part of MCG leadership, and the refusal to be transparent on church finances, cost MCG dearly. The effect on its mission was devastating, and the human cost in personal stress, humiliation, and loss of Christian fellowship cannot be quantified.

1996–98:

THE RESIGNATION OF CONFERENCE SECRETARY KUMI

AT THE 1996 ANNUAL CONFERENCE, HELD AT WINNEBA IN AUGUST, two names were placed before the delegates for president-designate: Samuel Asante-Antwi and MacLean A. Kumi. Asante-Antwi was serving as Chairman of the Kumasi District, while the Reverend Kumi was serving as MCG conference secretary. The delegates at the 1996 conference gave the nomination to Asante-Antwi by a seven-vote margin. In his acceptance speech as president-designate, Asante-Antwi stressed, "My vision is to seek unity and reconciliation so that all can translate dreams and visions for action towards the 21st century. . . . There should be an open expression of regrets and we must not be seen to be glossing over the mistakes of the past" (Asante-Antwi 1996, 1, 3).

At the next Annual Conference, in August of the following year, Asante-Antwi was confirmed as president by the required 75 percent vote. Then, barely five months after the Asante-Antwi administration was in place, the MCG community was taken aback to learn that Kumi had resigned from his post as conference secretary. His resignation occupied the attention of the press for some time,[163] and Asante-Antwi was compelled to issue a pastoral letter to all Methodist churches. He assured his readers that since he and Kumi were confirmed in their respective positions as president and secretary, "The two of us have worked harmoniously until now. There has never been an occasion when the two of us have exchanged words or disagreed strongly on any issue."[164] (In subsequent months, information divulged by various staff members would raise serious doubts about this claim.)

A review of developments in the early 1990s illuminates the dynamics underlying Kumi's resignation. Prior to his service as MCG conference secretary (from August 1993), Kumi had been serving as the Chairman of the Koforidua District. The fact that he had served as a district Chairman was significant, for that made him the first person in MCG history to bring to the post of Conference secretary the experience and maturity of district chairmanship. Furthermore, his performance as secretary was such that Dickson determined that the day-to-day details of the administration could be left in Kumi's hands, freeing him (Dickson) from being overly concerned with in-house office management. In effect, under Dickson, Kumi as conference secretary more or less functioned as de facto head of administration.

Thus, in the weeks leading up to the August 1996 elections, it was widely felt that Kumi's performance as secretary and his previous responsibilities as a district Chairman made him especially suited as a front runner to succeed Dickson. Articles appeared in the Ghanaian press lauding Kumi's achievements, thus reflecting the perception of many Methodists that the work of MCG had been significantly advanced under Kumi's stewardship. Published assessments of the relative strengths and weaknesses of the two contenders favored Kumi.[165] Such was the interest in the forthcoming election that the *Methodist Times* carried an article educating the public on the process of choosing a president for MCG. But, as has already been stated, by the narrow margin of seven votes, the 1996 conference delegates elected as president-designate, Asante-Antwi over Kumi.

Barely three months after the election—that is, many months in advance of the day when the president-designate would be confirmed as president at the 1997 Conference—Asante-Antwi made an unprecedented move: He requested auditing of moneys received from the (U.S.) United Methodist Board of Global Ministries from 1983 forward. This included the period of Kumi's secretaryship, that is, from August 1993.[166] For a president-designate to request such an audit was unprecedented. First, president-designates typically maintain very low profiles so as not to disturb the retiring president's last year in office. Second, the individual's year as president-designate is typically given to reflection and preparation for office, not in interjecting himself into the institutional operations of an organization he has yet to oversee.

Meanwhile in May-June 1997, on the authority of President Dickson, and following Kumi's attendance at the World Methodist

Evangelism Conference at Emory University in Atlanta, Georgia, Kumi returned home by way of Toronto to settle a dispute between two factions of an emerging Ghanaian Methodist church. On his return to Ghana, he submitted a report to the 1997 conference advising that two ministers be sent to care for the groups (one for each group), since in his judgment, the split could not be solved by fiat from the MCG office in Ghana. Kumi encouraged both groups in Toronto to seek affiliation with the United Church of Canada, the only Methodist-related family in Canada. One of the factions followed that advice; the other did not.

After Asante-Antwi took office in August 1997, it was not long before staff members at the national office in Accra were given to understand that they were to work directly with him, not with Kumi as they were accustomed to doing. Thus, staff workers in the accounting office stopped presenting checks to the conference secretary for his signature. Control of the fleet of cars was taken away from the secretary and placed in the hands of the drivers themselves. Drivers were instructed not to hand over a vehicle to the secretary without first consulting the president. In October 1997, Asante-Antwi wrote to the Toronto Ghanaian Methodists demanding that both groups come together. He discounted Kumi's counsel submitted two months earlier to the Annual Conference. It seemed that the tensions experienced by the Toronto-based Ghanaian Methodists were reverberating in the MCG office in Ghana.[167]

About this time Kumi received an invitation from the United Church of Canada Ethnic Ministries Division to celebrate the reception of the group that had decided to join this Church and then to remain to give them pastoral help. This presented Kumi with a dilemma. He could not represent MCG without the president's authorization, which he thought he was unlikely to receive. But since one of the groups had affiliated with the United Church of Canada as he had counseled, a decline of the invitation would be difficult for the Ghanaian congregation to understand. After first having a personal discussion with Asante-Antwi, Kumi wrote to him on March 5, 1998, to formally request leave to spend some time with his children in the United States and to visit the Toronto Ghanaians who had associated with the United Church of Canada.

(Kumi later reported to his friends that the president had verbally agreed with this proposal.) But when GPC met to discuss Kumi's letter, the hierarchy responded by directing him to accept stationing at Bechem, a small Methodist congregation that would normally not be the appropriate place for a person with such wide experience in the ministry. It seems difficult to see this directive as anything other than a punitive action. Furthermore, GPC may have expected Kumi to refuse the assignment, which would lead to his resignation/dismissal from the ministry. In any case, that is precisely what happened, and it was as a suspended MCG member that Kumi left for North America.

About a month after Kumi arrived in Toronto, President Asante-Antwi paid a pastoral visit to the Ghanaian Methodist congregation in Toronto, seeking to bring the unaffiliated group under the jurisdiction of MCG and to ensure that the church that had affiliated with the United Church of Canada did not accept Kumi as its pastor. According to Kumi, some of his Toronto friends told him that Asante-Antwi, during his visit, alleged that Kumi had embezzled funds from MCG, but when told to write it down so that appropriate action could be taken, he did not comply.

In October 1998 a leading Ghanaian woman who is a charismatic Methodist minister, visited Toronto with a note from Asante-Antwi introducing herself as a traveling evangelist. She visited with both groups, consulting with the leaders and guiding them in writing to Asante-Antwi seeking affiliation with MCG. The outcome was that Kumi was barred from serving as a pastor in the Toronto area, and the Ghanaian churches experienced further division. In May 1999 Asante-Antwi again visited Toronto, and urged the United Church congregation to join the MCG branch he had inaugurated the previous year. Yet earlier they had been assured that a minister from Ghana would be sent as pastor for them.

The upshot of this turmoil was that in the late 1990s no less than four congregations of Ghanaian Methodists operated in the metropolis of Toronto, and only one affiliated with MCG. There are also several MCG ministers in the Toronto area, and only one is accredited by MCG to offer pastoral care. A similar situation subsequently arose in the Atlanta area, with divided congregations and only one Ghanaian minister accredited to serve them even though there are other Ghanaian ministers in the area who could offer pastoral oversight. That such a crisis should occur suggests that a power contest rooted in Ghana itself was being played out in the Diaspora, using the Diaspora communities as pawns.

One of the striking elements in the Toronto debacle is that ethnic rivalry involving the Fantes cannot be offered as an explanation, for the two ethnic groups in the Toronto Ghanaian community are Asantes and Akuapem-Guans. This supports my contention that reference to ethnic differences is an inadequate, one-dimensional explanation for a much more complex web of causes. Ultimately, Christian communities experiencing intergroup and interpersonal conflict must consider the more sinister root cause common to all humanity: sin. Human sinfulness manifests itself in pride, greed, and lack of charity towards those who have offended or who are perceived to have stood in one's way. It leads to the labeling of colleagues as friends or enemies. It exhibits itself by empire building and the creation of a system of awards and punishments as a way of manipulating underlings. One of the lamentable dimensions of MCG's sorry record is the timidity of lay leaders who support the more influential among the clergy, thus reinforcing traditional notions that the chief does no wrong. This tendency flies in the face of modern egalitarian tenets and breeds resentments that prepare the ground work for the next crisis.

There have been some worthy constitutional changes prompted by MCG's crises. Now there has been put in place a more suitable procedure for the election of Chairmen (called bishops in MCG's newer episcopal system). Candidates are expected to submit their curriculum vitae and be vetted by a committee made up equally of representatives from the particular synod and the GPC. Out of this preliminary stage, three finalists are presented to the district synods and the election at that level is final. This eliminates the opportunity for the central authority, GPC, to set aside those who are nominated by the district synods.

Furthermore, at the time of the research for this book, MCG was considering the stipulation that should a conference secretary standing as a candidate for the post of president/presiding bishop lose the election, the individual is to be transferred to a different station to allow the incoming president/presiding bishop to choose their own team. This new regulation is designed to ensure that MCG does not experience a repeat of the events surrounding the resignation of conference secretary Kumi.

Should these troubles be traced simply to ethnocentrism? The subject of ethnocentrism has received attention in Ghanaian intellectual circles. Kwame Gyekye, the erudite philosophy professor at the University of Ghana, Legon, distinguishes between attitudes of appropriate ethnic pride and destructive ethnocentrism. He affirms a group's pride in its own culture but draws the line at "raising the values and achievements of one's culture to the status of an apotheosis." Ethnocentrism typically fails "to recognize the weakness and defects of one's own culture, while pointing up those of other cultures, [and fails] to appreciate the worth of other cultures" (Gyekye 2000, 38–40).

The Christian Council of Ghana likewise has addressed the issue of ethnicity and ethnocentrism in its seminar series (Dartey 1994). Robert K. Aboagye-Mensah writes that ethnocentric people "become strongly attached to their own cultural identity, values, symbols and ideologies, almost to the point of worshipping them . . . [But] we were made in the image and likeness of God [and] our unity with one another in God is deeper than the bonds of biological or geographical or political union" (Aboagye-Mensah 1994, 22, 25)

The Ghanaian scholar Florence Abena Dolphyne has written, "As long as some sections of the population feel that particular ethnic groups are being favored . . . to the neglect of others, people will use ethnic sentiments to create dissent and resentment among those who see themselves as disadvantaged" (1994, 41). Dolphyne refers to the example in Great Britain involving the Scots and Welsh vis-à-vis the English. Ethnic tensions have simmered for a long time, but because development in the modern era is evenly distributed, it has not reached the pitch of rebellion. In sharp contrast, Somalia presents a society that is mono ethnic, mono linguistic, and monoreligious; yet uneven distribution of national development has thrown the people of Somalia into an unending war cycle. Ethnicity, per se, does not lead to ethnic tensions and war. It is rather a pretext when deeper issues fester below the surface. In all the cases of conflict within MCG recorded in this chapter, the ultimate issue was human sin. In Ghanaian Methodist history, church leaders, like politicians, have tended to use their power and the institutions they control to advance their own personal interests over and above that of the church. These disputes over power have damaged the outreach of MCG in many areas, one of which is the numerical decline in membership.

MCG's Numerical Decline

METHODISM IN GHANA HAS LOST ITS CENTRAL ROLE AS THE LARGEST Protestant church. A great deal of the blame needs to be attributed to the crises that have sapped the spiritual energy, motivational drive, and missional focus of MCG in the last two decades of the twentieth century (Ter Haar 1994; Gifford 1998; Foli 2001a). At best it can be said that Methodism in Ghana is not growing but struggling to keep up with the population growth.[168]

MCG conferences set time aside for a minister or layperson who does not usually occupy a formal position in the church's hierarchy to address it on a topic of their own choice under the general rubric of "Conversation on the State of the Work of God." It has been an opportunity for voices that are usually not heard to speak on issues that the vast majority of members would want addressed. One such useful discussion was led by Emmanuel A. B. Bortey, who argued at the 1986 conference that the statistics showed the church's growth rate, which averaged 3.9% over 25 years, was lower than the national growth rate of 4.3%. In actual terms, by 1986, there were more non Methodist Ghanaians in Ghana than in 1961. The church, he concluded, had been growing as a result of an increase in the number of births among Methodists than by conversions and evangelistic outreach (Bortey 1986).

At the time of autonomy, MCG was the largest Protestant denomination in Ghana (Hastings 1979, 45), with an adult dues-paying membership of about 70,000 and a total constituency (including children and irregular visitors) approaching 200,000. This position was maintained for up to about ten years afterwards, at which time it was reported that membership had risen to 80,590 with a total constituency of almost 225,000. MCG had 1,600 congregations and preaching places, with more than a 1,000 schools (Moss 1974). Yet, at the end of the twentieth century MCG was no longer in a position of numerical superiority as far as Ghanaian Christianity was concerned. The Ghana Evangelism Committee conducted two surveys, in 1986–87 and again in 1991–93. These surveys were designed to identify the "unfinished task" of the Christian churches in Ghana. It recorded the actual attendance record at services nationwide on a particular Sunday, rather than relying on statistics provided by denominational offices.

The survey revealed that Pentecostals were far outgrowing the traditional AICs as well as the mainline Protestant churches. Admittedly the survey instrument was flawed in that AICs and Pentecostals were lumped together. In fact, in the ten years surveyed, AICs opened 3,500 new churches, while Pentecostals opened 25,000, with the mainline Protestant churches opening only 1,400. When the figures from the two surveys are compared, MCG is the mainline church in Ghana with the lowest growth rate of 2%. Those in the lead are the Evangelical Lutheran, 206%, and the Baptist (Convention) 72%. The closest ally of MCG, both theologically and ecclesiologically, the Presbyterian Church of Ghana, had a 17% growth rate (National Church Survey 1989). It bears repeating that this decline was experienced at the height of the church's internal conflict.

Between 1996 and the end of 1999 MCG increased membership by 30,054, bringing the overall membership to about 1.5 million (MCG Fact Sheets 2001/2002). The ministerial pool offering pastoral oversight in 2000 was 573, with 3 full-time catechists, 112 lay evangelists and indigenous missionaries, as well as 26,725 voluntary lay preachers and class leaders. The *Daily Record* for the MCG Conference in 2000 held at Koforidua bemoaned the low returns of the numerical strength as compared to the 3 million professed Methodists reported in the population census. What accounts for this discrepancy? That the church's roll would miss half the number of people who consider themselves Methodists in Ghana? Several factors can be adduced. One is the fact that the figure of 3 million might include thousands who had been educated in Methodist schools and who consider themselves Methodists even though they are not active in MCG any more. It is also possible that some of these professed Methodists also frequently attend AICs but were not bold enough to say so. On the other hand, since in the MCG the financial assessment of societies is based on the numerical strength as reported by the leadership, it is not unusual for ministers to underreport since some of their members might have relocated and may not be reached in order to discharge their financial responsibilities. For whatever reasons, some ministers also do not reveal all the names on the books. But no matter what, the discrepancy between the census figures and church records reveals a fundamental issue at stake here. MCG does not occupy the central place it did in the imagination of Ghanaian Christians. One cannot but concede that in their pioneer years, the mainline denominations operated more like movements and could therefore exhibit flexibility in their work; such flexibility has eluded the more traditional missions churches over the years.

Statistics on the whole are to be cautiously interpreted. Various categories could have been lumped together to arrive at these conclusions. Several are worth noting. Comparing members on the rolls with those in attendance on any given Sunday is not the best means of arriving at these conclusions. None of the categories reflect the thousands of Ghanaians, many of them Methodists, living in the Diaspora.

One discernible result of the attention on positions and power was that MCG has not been able to sustain its former position of numerical ascendancy among Ghanaian Protestants.

CHAPTER SIX

Self-Theologizing: The Process of Contextualization

THIS CHAPTER EXAMINES FOUR AREAS OF CONTEMPORARY GHANAian Methodism that illustrates how MCG, in the process of adapting to Ghanaian culture, has redefined the Methodism inherited from Britain. These areas are worship and liturgy, especially the singing of *ebibindwom*; polygamy and church membership; church union; and, finally, church structure. Initiatives in these areas indicate that MCG has matured into a different self-understanding from that which was inherited from the British. These post independence efforts at contextualization connected MCG's mission focus with Akan culture and Ghanaian identity.

Primary Means of Self-Theologizing:

WORSHIP

WORSHIP GENERALLY PRECEDES A COMMUNITY'S ARTICULATION of its theology. Dogmatics and apologetics come later as a reflective rationalization of a set of religious beliefs. A community's formal theology, therefore, may not be the most authentic or immediate source for inquiry about a church's self-understanding. It is the church at worship that exhibits what the worshipers believe and hold dear.

In evaluating Christian worship, one needs to allow room for flexibility, since not all will agree on its essential parts. This helpful commentary by J. Christopher Thomas summarizes the situation:

> There is always tension for the Christian between the Word which he believes has been revealed to him by God and the assumptions of the society in which this word has to be made intelligible. God's word, whether it is in the Eucharist or anywhere else must be interpreted in terms of the culture in which it is to be ministered—always assuming that the beliefs adopted from any given culture do not radically alter the content of God's revelation. It is of course difficult to judge where and when the gospel has been irrevocably changed to something which is not the gospel: and Christians are sure to differ about this as much as they do about the meaning of the Bible itself. (Thomas 1974, 15)

Analyzing the liturgies in some of the mainline churches in Ghana, Thomas showed how the churches had blindly adopted worship styles and practices that were culturally relevant only in the context of their Western origins.

It is widely (though falsely) believed that Ghanaian Christians have wholeheartedly adopted the Christianity of missionaries without any serious contextualization. Sidney. G. Williamson, a missionary of the British Methodist Conference, asserts, "The Christian faith as historically implanted by western missionary enterprise among the Akan has proved unable to sympathize with or relate its message spiritually to Akan spiritual outlook. . . . It has launched a frontal attack on Akan traditional beliefs and practices, and sought to emancipate the Akan from his traditional outlook. [This] had the effect of calling the Akan out of his traditional environment, not of redeeming him within it. The Christian missionary impact constituted a denial of the Akan worldview" (Williamson 1965, 175). The

Akan educated elite have been critical of the brand of Christianity preached and practiced by the expatriate missionaries, charging that the message of the missionaries failed to connect with the worldview of the Akan.

I contend, on the contrary, that such an assessment underestimates the resiliency of the Akan and their ability to pick and choose, reject, and/or combine. The fact is, the Akan, with great ingenuity, have appropriated Christianity and made it their own.[169]

If there is one area in which the contextualization of the gospel or lack thereof of is evident, it is in worship forms and content.[170] The Reverend Samuel B. Essamuah, who served a term as MCG president, was a leading figure in assuring the integration of Christian worship with the Akan worldview.[171] The appropriation of Christianity within the context of Akan culture can be observed particularly in MCG's liturgical innovations, centered on the singing of what is known as ebibindwom.

Ebibindwom as the Definitive Characteristic of Ghanaian Methodists

IT IS A WELL-KNOWN FACT THAT SINGING AND DANCING PLAY AN important role in African life. These two activities mark both joyful and sorrowful times. If the church and the Christian faith are to encompass all of life, then it cannot fail but engage these two activities in its worship and liturgy. In Ghanaian Methodist church life the role of singing and dancing is evident in the emphasis on *ebibindwom* (sacred lyrics). In fact, it can be said that the singing of *ebibindwom* is MCG's most definitive characteristic as a popular movement.[172] *Ebibindwom* is the indigenous musical form that Ghanaian Methodists have bequeathed to the Christian traditions in Ghana (Turkson 1995, 160). Most of them are unwritten. Eighteen pieces of this musical form can be found at the back of the Fante Methodist hymnal, the *Christian Asor Ndwom*.[173]

The *ebibindwom* genre is similar to African-American gospel music in that there is a significant level of audience participation, the repetition of song verses, and constant improvisation during performance in the pattern of its calls and responses. Kwesi Dickson emphasizes that the cantor must not only be familiar with the biblical passage being preached on but must also be "theologically aware so as to fit that spontaneous music piece in the whole counsel of God. . . . The language is concrete and expresses the thought of a God who cares for the person in all life's situations, both spiritual and physical: he saves not only from sin but also from the dangers of childbirth" (Dickson 1984, 109). Williamson observes, "A competent singer . . . can fasten upon an aspect of Christian truth or experience which is immediately relevant [to the preacher's words] . . . and express and expound this in the recitative with great skill. The congregation, apparently with equal facility, joins in the required chorus" (Williamson, 1958, 126; also see Mensah 1960 and Turkson 1995).

Robert T. Parsons quotes an unidentified church leader as saying, "The preservation and the Christianization of the lyrics has been one of the best things that Methodism has done for our country. This is indeed the silencing of our mouth from profanity and filling it with songs of praise to God" (Parsons 1963, 114).[174]

In 1962 the Reverend Essamuah was asked by the MCG Conference to preserve for posterity all the Ghanaian Methodist *ebibindwom* (MCG Conference Minutes 1963, 150). To this end, over the next several months lyric festivals were held in five of the six districts of MCG—Accra, Cape Coast, Kumasi, Sekondi, and Winneba. A national lyric festival was held on November 11, 1973, at Besease in the Ajumako Circuit.[175] The enthusiastic participation of Ghanaian Methodists illustrate the fact that *ebibindwom* accompanied by drums and other musical instruments, greatly enhanced the process of the indigenization of Christianity in Ghana.

Atta Annan Mensah states that the use of *ebibindwom* in Christian worship originated during the ministry of Thomas Birch Freeman (Mensah 1960, 183). The importance of *ebibindwom* for nourishing and sustaining piety among members of MCG rivals Western hymnody, especially among rural congregations. What makes this musical genre missiologically important is its entirely indigenous heritage. It attracts non-Christians to the church's message in a manner that a straightforward sermon might not be able to accomplish.

The *ebibindwom* musical heritage has been traced to several sources of Akan tradition. One stream is the Anansesem, the "spider stories." As these Akan folktales are recounted and recited, members of the audience interject interruptions. A listener may stop the narrator to offer an explanation, a commentary, or an approving gesture. The Anansesem are important sources of entertainment, moral values, and sometimes religious beliefs. Often reflecting Akan social structure, perhaps even revealing some weakness in a particular authority figure, Anansesem are one of the most significant conveyors of the Akan value-system. (The typical practice of spontaneous interruption, offering affirmation to the preacher, helps explain the boldness with which Christian lyricists interrupt sermons with their music.)[176]

The second source for understanding the heritage of *ebibindwom* among members of MCG are the songs of the traditional military companies, the Asafo, which are used in war, disasters, and emergencies, as well as on joyous occasions such as the enstoolment of chiefs.[177] These are typically songs of invocation, incitement, or exultation as they invoke the ancestral spirits to aid a military campaign.

The third tradition underlying the *ebibindwom* heritage is the *adenkum* (calabash) festival music. At Akan traditional festivals, which mark the New Year, rites of passage, harvests, planting, and reaping, and so forth, the people give thanks to the divinities and spirits for success in life. Most people, especially from rural areas, try to return home at least once a year to participate in the rituals, whether they believe in them or not. By rooting *ebibindwom* in these traditions of Akan culture, Ghanaian Methodists have created a fundamentally new genre from inherited materials. Adolphus R. Turkson recalls:

> In about 1940, the Methodist Church in Ghana permitted its congregation to dance in a procession during revival or camp meetings organized to commemorate some historic event such as a centenary of the birth of John Wesley or during the

> annual celebration of the Church. The dancing was discontinued but it was revived again in about 1980 with renewed spirit. It was to be performed in the nave and in a more reverent manner as expected of the faithful; no form of lewd dancing was to be allowed in the church. In this way, the African dance has been transformed, and its music modified to give it a proper spiritual meaning. (Turkson 1995, 165)

There is an obvious benefit in MCG's use of *ebibindwom* related to the fact that in Africa, as in many societies with low literacy rates, ordinary people internalize the Christian faith not via doctrines and official church statements but via music. Through the medium of *ebibindwom*, many people who would be considered formally illiterate became biblically literate. After people came to know the content of the stories, the refrain provided homiletic exhortation. MCG's use of *ebibindwom* in its outreach and mission mirrored the historic Wesleyan tradition in which Methodism was seen as a singing movement.

What Walter J. Hollenweger asserts for Pentecostals is equally true of the membership of MCG: "Proclamation took place not in doctrinal statements but in songs, not in theses but in dances, not in definitions but in descriptions. . . . What held believers together was not expressed by a systematic account of faith or creed, but by the fellowship that was experienced, by songs and prayers, by active participation in liturgy and diaconia" (Hollenweger 1996, 4). William H. Willimon writes, "Some believe the Wesleys reached the common folk . . . more through their music than by any other means. . . . Most of our really important ideas about God [were] sung before they [were] thought [of]" (Willimon 1990, 61).

Ebibindwom also provided an outlet for ministry by women long before their formal role was recognized in official circles. Leadership in *ebibindwom* singing from time immemorial has been the preserve of women: "In the Methodist Church, Ghana, a tradition of lyrical rendering of the gospel stories grew out of the Fante primal worship and became the women's response to preaching. From the start, the majority of the preachers and exhorters were men; so were the few who could read. The women absorbed the stories, committing to memory chapter and verse of what they heard, read, or were told through preaching. This provided the repertoire from which they wove the lyrics they sang" (Oduyoye 1988, 35–53; cf. 1986, 100). It is possible that the relative ease with which MCG accepted the ordination of women was a result of their singular leadership role in *ebibindwom* singing. In a society with a predominantly oral orientation to life, for women, it was "the songs and cries, their celebrations and tears and the totality of their being [that was brought] to understand that message, to interpret it, to institutionalize it, to celebrate it and weave it into their daily life" (Mbiti 1986, 19–20). *Ebibindwom* therefore, proved to be instrumental not only in developing and forming the spirituality of MCG, but also in paving the way for the formal acceptance of women as ordained ministers in MCG.[178]

In the 1980s President Essamuah combined *ebibindwom* with a special healing ministry. According to J. Kwabena Asamoah-Gyadu, Essamuah "undertook a countrywide, olive oil aided healing tour," for which he composed the following theme song:

> Oduyefo kese, fa wo nsa boto mo do. Besa me yare ma me na menya ahoodzen dze asom wo o. Yare nketse nketse rehaw me wo sunsum mu; nsem nketse nketse rehaw me wo sunsum mu. Mekyinkyin, ekyinekyin, ekyinkyin, me nnya ano edur koraa, Egya, e, besa me yare ma me, na menya ahoodzen na m'asom wo o.
>
> *(Great Healer, come and touch me. Heal my ailments that my strength may be renewed for your service. Lord, I am deeply troubled, deeply troubled by spiritual sicknesses, anxieties and worries. I have been to many places in search of healing, but none has been of help. Come, Lord, release me from these spiritual ailments and troubles; that I may enjoy the health, strength and vitality needed to serve you.)*

In the wake of Essamuah's tour, many Methodist ministers felt empowered to use olive oil in their faith-healing activities (as some had been doing secretly), knowing that they would not be disciplined or accused of non-Methodist ritual practices (Asamoah-Gyadu 2000, 97–99).[179] Essamuah's *ebibindwom* composition paved the way for this wider ministry of healing. As confirmed by Dana L. Robert, healing is a major motif in the mission outreach of African mission churches today (Robert 2003).

As Willimon says, the church "exists to worship a God, who according to Psalm 150, loves to be listened to, prayed to, sung for, and glorified" (Willimon 1990, 57). Surely, "Religion is a matter of both words and music, and the music is more important than the words. . . . The music of religion is its life of love; and it is the latter which wins men" (McCutchan 1947, 160). Clearly, this medium of gospel communication has stood the test of time, nourishing generations of MCG members in the towns and villages of southern Ghana. From church growth, to cultural transformation, to theologizing and healing, MCG's use of *ebibindwom* has been an effective missiological tool.

Polygamy and Church Membership

IF THERE IS ONE AREA OF THE CHRISTIAN ENTERPRISE IN AFRICA that met with resistance and reluctant acceptance, it is the reconfiguring of marriage along Christian patterns. Given the fact that African marriages unite not two individuals but two families, the discussion of marriage, and especially of polygamy, affected the vast majority of Christian believers. The Methodist synod of 1871 described polygamy[180] as "the prevailing sin of Africa . . . the great obstacle in the way of many giving thanks to God" (Gocking 1999, 89). The 1910 Missionary Conference in Edinburgh called polygamy "one of the gross evils of heathen society, which like habitual murder or slavery must at all costs be ended" (Kisembo 1977, 104).[181]

Under the tutelage of missionaries, the MCG response was to create two categories of membership, one for those who could live up to the ideal of Christian monogamy, and another for those who for whatever reason could not do so.[182] The latter were categorized as less than full members and were barred from the Lord's Supper and from holding church office. "Monogamy was [seen as] an open door to civilization and closer to Christianity. No one thought that it was necessary for salvation. However, to most Africans, to whom a sense of belonging was more important than doctrinal acquiescence, by depriving polygamists access to the Lord's supper, it is as if one was endorsing a two-tier membership structure" (Webster [in reference to Yoruba land] in Baeta 1968, 230).

Among other things, what this policy meant was that when a polygamous member of MCG died, the funeral service could not be conducted within the church. Over the years many deceased polygamous members had been taken round the chapel property but never inside the sanctuary. It was an especially awkward situation if the dead were benefactors of the church who had contributed generously to the building fund or to recurring ministry needs.

Finally, two decades after gaining autonomy in 1961, a number of MCG leaders felt they had to deal with the polygamy issue without missionaries looking over their shoulders. This process was an important stage of contextualization and self-theologizing. In 1985 the Accra District requested a Connexion-wide re-examination of MCG's policy regarding polygamous members. In typical Ghanaian Methodist fashion, the conference referred the issue to the various districts for debate, and they were invited to bring their findings to a general conference. As the months passed, it became clear that there was a wide divergence in opinion and limited enthusiasm for the subject.

In 1986, in response to the conference's call for debate and study, the Accra District synod appointed a committee of five, headed by Dickson, and asked it to submit a report by November of the same year. The other members of the committee were the Reverends E. A. B. Bortey, and Rachel Tetteh, Regina Adu, and Joshua Kudadjie. Although the committee invited reports from Methodist congregations and members throughout the denomination, the input was so limited that it was considered inconsequential (MCG Minutes 1987, 97). Within the Accra synod area, only the Adabraka circuit reported. (Adabraka's position was that there was no theological justification for the present practice of excluding polygamists from the sacraments of the Lord's Supper and baptism.)

The committee began its discussions by explicitly distinguishing between polygamy and concubinage, and between polygamy and cohabiting without benefit of marriage. Concubinage and cohabitation they categorically disallowed. In the view of the committee, polygamy was a marriage contracted with two or more wives according to traditional cultural norms. The committee highlighted the fact that in traditional society the acquisition of a second wife usually occurs only after the first wife has been consulted and "pacified." This usually took the form of ceremonial gifts.

Examining the basis for the exclusion of polygamists from full church membership, the committee reasoned that the church's attitude might have been shaped by the following presuppositions: first, that polygamy is inherently sinful, and that therefore all polygamists are sinful; and second that a polygamist, despite claims to the contrary, cannot be sincerely committed to Christ.

The committee identified a number of situations that lead to polygamy. The first cause cited was infertility or barrenness. In Africa barrenness is not accepted with equanimity but is considered a curse and a threat to society. It is felt to be a disgrace to the man who would be leaving no one behind to perpetuate his line and memory. Hence people go to great lengths to avoid or circumvent infertility.[183] This attitude is given religious sanction by the fact that all libations poured invoke the blessings of children. If a woman believes that barrenness and childlessness amount to extinction of her family line, she may consent to her husband having a second wife instead of divorcing her. For after all, she can call her husband's children by another woman her own children. John S. Mbiti comments, "Adding another wife removes the shame and anxiety of unproductivity" (Mbiti 1965, 142). (In circumstances where the man is the cause of the infertility, the woman is usually free to leave the marriage.)

Again, the committee weighed the fact that in some traditional societies, a nursing mother could not return to her marital home until at least three months, and in some instances twelve months after the delivery of the baby. This was a natural and traditional method of birth spacing. In anticipation of such a situation, some men chose to have a second wife. The committee noted that some polygamous marriages are contracted as status symbols. People of wealth, chiefs, and other elders may choose to contract polygamous marriages as a mark of their standing in society. It was also observed that some men take several wives, and consequently have several children, in order to have more farm hands for greater agricultural production. Thus, there may be a socio economic dimension to polygamy. Lastly, where a wife suffers from a protracted illness, some men have seen the need for another woman to take care of the home and family. And finally, the committee saw as a motivation for polygamy the obsession for a son to preserve the family line. This led some men to take another wife in order to increase the chances for a male heir.

Over against these considerations are the dangers of polygamy, as reflected in Akan traditional proverbs. Awar dodow ma banyin ne tekyerema ye nta. [Polygamy makes a husband a double-tongued man]. That is, polygamy affects one's trustworthiness. Mbaa dodow kun yare a, okom na okum no. [If a polygamist is taken ill, he starves to death because each thinks the other wife, or wives, will cook for him. In other words, everybody's business is nobody's business] (Pobee 1979, 134). Although traditional wisdom revealed the inherent dangers in polygamous marriages, it did not necessarily indicate outright disapproval.

In providing this list of factors motivating polygamy in Ghanaian society, the committee made it clear that it neither claimed to have exhausted the causes of polygamy nor necessarily agreed with the justifications given for these marriages.[184] From the perspective of those involved, every polygamous marriage is contracted on the basis of some "compelling needs," wrote the committee, and should be examined on its own merits.

The committee's report to the 1987 Annual Conference noted that there is no biblical evidence for the view that polygamists are living in sin and cannot therefore love God. On the basis of the Old Testament, the committee members argued that although polygamy was not the normal form of marriage, it was an acceptable one, as witnessed in the epistle of Hebrews, chapter 11. Abraham, Jacob, and David, though polygamous, are considered to be worth emulating. Of course, it is the totality of their sincere belief and absolute dependence on God that is being held up for emulation, not their marital practice. The committee's report duly noted the negative consequences of these polygamous arrangements, including Abraham's expulsion of Hagar, the maltreatment of Joseph by his step siblings, and the assassination of Amnon by his stepbrother Absalom—not to mention the example of King Solomon whose foreign wives led him into idolatry. In the Old Testament polygamy is portrayed as being inimical to the maintenance of good order in the home, and its baneful effect can be implied as even affecting one's Christian faith. The committee submitted that the Old Testament says nothing more than this implied criticism against polygamy.

The committee pointed out that even the New Testament is not explicitly and incontrovertibly against polygamy. The classic passages cited in favor of monogamy—Mark 10:1–8, Matthew 19: 5, 6, Ephesians 5:31, 1 Corinthians. 7: 3, 4, and 1 Timothy 3:2—all focus on the church as the bride of Christ. The committee pointed out that the issue of what kind of marriage God desires for humanity is not the point at stake. Just as in the Old Testament, Israel is referred to as God's bride (e.g., Hosea), the New Testament passages call the church to be faithful to, and worthy of, its bride, the Lord. These latter passages do not in and of themselves address the issue of monogamy or polygamy.

The committee, in its report, then spent some time analyzing some of the other critical passages in light of the polygamy issue. Passages such as Ephesians 5:21–33, 1 Corinthians 7:3–4, Mark 10, and Matthew 19 all deal with the general subject of marriage, the marital relationship, and divorce. There is only one set of passages that explicitly commends monogamy: 1 Timothy 3:2 and Titus 1:6. What is clear is that an elder of the church needs to be able to manage his household well as an example to the flock, and the assumption is that monogamy is the ideal for setting that example. It can be said that the entire church is admonished to follow the example of the elders and to be monogamous. That being the case, the committee summarized its biblical survey by stating that polygamy was not the normal form of marriage in biblical times; however it was an acceptable form of marriage; it was likely to produce situations prejudicial to good order and faith; polygamists were deemed capable of love for God. The committee therefore concluded that there is no reason why polygamists should be excluded from the Lord's Table.

The committee then probed the churches' understanding of the meaning of the Lord's Supper. Did the practice of excluding polygamists imply that the Lord's Table is meant only for those Christians who are without fault? Protestant theology generally affirms that Holy Communion is a means of grace, that it is a channel or avenue by which God's free, unmerited favor reaches men and women (1 Corinthians 11:23–26). Through the symbols of bread and wine, the Lord Jesus freely offers us his self-giving love and satisfies our spiritual hunger so that we are strengthened in faith. It also offers us an opportunity to assess the sincerity of our love for the Lord and for one another (1 Corinthians 11:27–32).

If the Lord's Supper is a means of grace, then the question arises whether the practice of excluding some from the table who profess faith in Christ can be justified. What about prayer, Bible reading, worship services, and other means of grace? Is it conceivable that persons could be considered unworthy of participating in these activities because they are members of a polygamous family? Should the church refuse to baptize a person who publicly confesses faith in Christ and who willingly applies himself to learning about him?

The committee noted the fact that in the only scriptural caution about partaking of the Lord's Supper, 1 Corinthians 11: 28, the onus is placed on the individual to examine himself (implying that surely, there is a limit to the extent to which one mortal can judge another person's worthiness) before partaking of the Holy Communion. The committee reached the conclusion that whether an individual's polygamous state preceded or followed conversion to Christ, such persons should not be denied access to the Lord's Table. At the same time, the committee explicitly noted, that *monogamy is clearly the acceptable practice for Christians*. The church should teach that monogamy is the norm.

If polygamists can be admitted as full members, then the question arises whether they can serve as leaders in the church. Following the lead of the Apostle Paul, the committee stated that Christian leaders would want to avoid a relationship that could undermine faithfulness to God and the good order of the home; since the individuals may end up setting a poor example for those under their charge (1

Tim. 3:2–5). That being the case, the committee considered it inadvisable to permit a polygamist to serve in any leadership position in the church; furthermore, any leader who turns polygamous should relinquish his position but in all other matters polygamists should have equal rights.

The most difficult aspect of the committee's assignment was engaging the general membership in the discussion and eliciting their approval. In most instances, the rank and file of MCG thought that any relaxation of the earlier stance would either encourage polygamists or send the wrong signal to the other Christian communities in Ghana.[185] So it could be said that monogamy is an identity marker of the mainline African church. In the end, the treatment of the issue of polygamy sometimes resembled an academic debate more than a vital issue that affected a large proportion of the church's membership. Whatever the reasons for the lukewarm reception of the committee's recommendations, it must be said that MCG showed considerable courage in opening a debate that other mainline churches in Ghana have consistently avoided.[186]

A Failed Quest for Church Union

BEGINNING IN 1957, MCG, WITH OTHER MAINLINE CHURCHES IN Ghana, invested nearly three decades exploring the possibility of church union. The efforts, notwithstanding the duration and intensity of the discussions, failed to achieve the desired results. This phase of MCG history is missiologically significant because it was an attempt at redefining Ghanaian Christianity away from the denominational and ethnic shells with which it had been birthed. Ghanaian Christians hoped to become a truly national body, to be authentically Ghanaian by overcoming their denominationally divided missionary heritage. The negotiations, and the reasons for failure, illumine Ghanaian thinking on the Church Universal, and they expose the problems inherent in the different church structures inherited from the West.[187]

The chair of the Ghana Church Union Committee, (GCUC) was Christian Goncalves Baeta, the veteran ecumenist. Serving as committee secretary was Laurence Creedy, the veteran Methodist missionary. In 1960 the committee set forth the aims and principles of church union in a brochure entitled *Our Approach to Church Unity*. This was followed up in 1963 with *Proposals for Church Union in Ghana: The Inauguration and Constitution of the United Church.* This booklet was revised in 1965 after the committee had received responses from the negotiating churches. In 1972 the committee published an English-language pamphlet entitled *Church Union in Ghana: Questions and Answers*, which was translated into all the major languages of southern Ghana—Fante, Ga, Twi, and Ewe. About a hundred thousand copies of this brochure were sold. The committee had issued the following declaration to be attested to by the various congregations:

> We, the congregation [NAME TO BE INSERTED], solemnly declare that when our synod/conference has decided, after full consultation throughout the church, that the Constitution of the United church and arrangements for its inauguration are acceptable, we, for our part, will GLADLY GO INTO UNION, and that accordingly during the period before union we will in every possible way CO-OPERATE WITH OUR BRETHREN IN THE CHURCHES CONCERNED.[188]

By late 1972 most of the congregations of three major churches—the Presbyterian Church of Ghana, the Evangelical Presbyterian Church, Ghana, along with MCG—had signed the declaration. On December 6, 1973, a formal worship service was organized at the Presbyterian Church of the Resurrection, Accra, to receive the proposals and to initiate the final phase.

As part of its work, C.G. Baeta's team traveled the length and breadth of the country and was warmly received by all. The heads of the negotiating churches toured the country together in 1977, addressing various forums to answer questions related to the union concept. These church representatives emphasized at each location the need for neighboring congregations to plan and work together on activities of mutual concern. The churches finally approved the following resolution: "The Church agrees to unite with all the other churches which also agree on Union, in accordance with the proposals contained in the book entitled *Proposals for Church Union in Ghana: The Inauguration and Constitution of the United Church*."

The synod of the Presbyterian Church of Ghana affirmed this resolution with a 96% affirmative vote. In 1978 the Conference of the Methodist Church, Ghana, passed the same resolution, and confirmed it in 1979 with a 94% affirmative vote in the representative session and by 90% in the ministerial session.[189] In 1979 the synod of the Evangelical Presbyterian Church, Ghana, passed the same resolution unanimously.

The committee set out to make preparations for the inauguration. However, there had been opponents from the beginning. The first serious setback was the sudden withdrawal of the Anglican Church. Incredibly, it occurred soon after the Church Union Committee obtained from the Anglican Consultative Council of the United Kingdom assurance of their full consent for the proposals. Nevertheless, the representatives of the diocese of Accra, seat of the then only Anglican bishop in Ghana, refused to have any further discussions with the committee.

Despite this turn of events, an attempt was made to fix a date for the inauguration. This seemed to lead to new episodes of hesitation and stalling. The deathblow to the entire effort came in 1983, when both the Presbyterian Church of Ghana and the Evangelical Presbyterian Church, Ghana, signaled their decision not to participate any longer. This left MCG as the only church to affirm its continuing commitment to the cause of the church union in Ghana.

Baeta provides historical insight that helps to explain the action of the Presbyterian Church. In 1927, when the Christian Council of Ghana first came into being, one of the main objectives was to put an end to "sheep stealing," whereby members of one denomination leave their own church and are promptly admitted to a church of another denomination. The churches accepted a "comity" policy that assigned various areas of influence within a country to the respective mission churches on the understanding that they would restrict their operations to the areas assigned to them. However, the policy proved to be impractical. For example, when members of the Evangelical Presbyterian Church, Ghana, came from its predominant base in the Volta Region and moved westward to take employment as civil servants, teachers, itinerant farmers, and so forth, they rarely sought church association, leaving many people without a church fellowship. Those who persevered and joined a new church often chose one from a denomination different from the denomination they had been part of at home.[190] Thus the comity principle began to break down. Many churches found it impossible to follow their members to their new places of residence or to recognize any territorial restrictions whatsoever.

John S. Pobee offers insight into the withdrawal of the Anglican Church from church union negotiations. Although the Anglican missionary bishop, Reginald Roseveare, was a prominent exponent of ecumenism (in the early years of post independence he served as the first chair of the Christian Council of Ghana), as soon as he left Ghana the local leaders withdrew from the council. According to Pobee, they "felt that to go into Union in Ghana was to fall out of communion with the mother Church in England. Crudely put, the African Anglicans were afraid to lose access to the resources of SPG" (Pobee 2000, 420).

Joseph M. Y. Edusa-Eyison attributes the failure of the church union movement in Ghana to personal ambitions for positions of authority and to an unwillingness to yield to other church leaders. He believes that church union was perceived by the general Christian community as a top-down venture that would primarily serve the personal interests of the leaders. "Every head of a church," writes Edusa-Eyison, "wanted to head the United Church when formed" (Edusa-Eyison 1994, 100, 103).

MCG experienced its own internal wrangling. Some MCG members questioned the constitutionality of the process and threatened to go to court to stop it. The cause was not advanced when the proponents of church union were asked to meet together with those who were opposed, to form a subcommittee to resolve their differences. Lacking an impartial arbiter, the committee was never able to meet.

The mere fact that church union discussions spanned twenty-eight years undermined their success. During this passage of time, within each of the denominations several different administrations were involved. MCG, for instance, had five different presidents from the late 1950s to the mid-1980s, and five different conference secretaries. Not all came into office equally supportive of church union. Even those fully committed to the cause were limited by their relatively brief terms. If they were to affect the process, let alone hasten it, they really needed to remain in office over a longer period. In the later years in MCG, other issues arose to take priority, such as the creation of more districts.

Throughout the period, the key administrative members of the Church Union Committee remained unchanged. While they professed to discern advances in acceptance, the recurring turnover in leadership from the denominations meant that the process was perpetually returning to an elementary stage.[191]

One also has to wonder if having an expatriate missionary (Creedy) as the committee secretary might have given the impression that the push for church union was a residue of the missionary era. No doubt Creedy was selected for his organizational abilities and administrative skills. During his long tenure in Ghana, he had gained experience well beyond the confines of MCG. Yet one wonders why such an important duty had not been assigned to an indigenous leader.

In its final report to the MCG conference in 1985, the Church Union Committee had little choice but to acknowledge that its mission was unattainable at the present (MCG Minutes 1985, 188–92). Baeta noted that the churches had set out with a vision of a progressive restoration of the visible unity of the church in Ghana. He emphasized positive outcomes from the venture. Over the course of the committee's work, he wrote, the churches had developed more efficient and professional organizations, resulting in a strengthening and furtherance of Christ's mission in Ghana.

Baeta rejoiced that ecumenical relations in Ghana had improved immeasurably. He cited the founding of Trinity College (now Trinity Theological Seminary), the primary theological seminary for the Protestant denominations in Ghana; the annual joint procession of Christian witness during Passiontide; the establishment of ministerial fraternals; increased friendliness in local relationships; and more frequent cooperative undertakings including pulpit exchanges. These and other less tangible but very positive features of church life would have been unthinkable in the 1920s and 1930s.

The church union concept has been left in abeyance ever since.[192] The churches have become passionate about other subjects—the establishment of universities and/or structural changes such as episcopacy. It is to the latter subject that we will devote our attention.

A New Church Structure:
EPISCOPACY

A NUMBER OF CHANGES WERE MADE IN THE FIRST THIRTY-NINE years of MCG autonomy involving church structure and operations. In the preface to the revised constitution of 1988, the MCG president Jacob S. A. Stephens wrote that "the former structures were overburdened by the stresses and strains of the growth (in membership) of the church [which impeded] . . . the implementation of conference decisions" (reproduced in MCG 2000 Constitution, preface, 5). Stephens noted the need to bring provisions for discipline of clergy and laity into line with contemporary social, cultural, and legal practices. The revised constitution was designed to incorporate into a single document the resolutions that had been passed at various conferences.

An important step had been taken in 1983 when a committee was established to review the constitutional changes that had been made up to that point. After the committee had gathered the necessary materials, a joint consultative session was held in 1985 with a team from the British Methodist Conference, led by the Reverend Dr. Albert W. Mosley, general secretary of the British Methodist Church Overseas Division, in November 1985 in Accra.[193]

A number of changes implemented in 1985 focused on the administrative structures at the denominational office in Accra. To lessen the load on the conference secretary as the sole implementor of conference decisions, various boards and divisions were established. Other significant administrative and structural procedures implemented in prior years had to do with the election and tenure of MCG's top officers. At the time of autonomy, 1961, MCG placed no limit on the number of years one could serve as chairman of a district. Until the constitutional changes of the year 2000, the elections of denominational executives were conducted by secret ballot without prior nominations. Typically, there were three ballots until one candidate received a simple majority of the votes cast. Presidents of the conference, who had not reached the mandatory retirement age, could serve two additional years beyond the initial five years if they received 75 percent or more of the votes for extending their tenure.[194]

Closely related to this was the process for nominating general superintendents and District Chairmen. In the 1960s when there were not many qualified candidates, GPC recommended names of possible candidates to synods for election as Chairmen of district, and the nominees were typically confirmed at the conference level. By the 1980s the districts were selecting their own nominees, and GPC would typically endorse the district's choice (although the names submitted to GPC were not binding on the GPC).

The revised constitution of 2000 has brought in a number of changes to the procedures just described. Now a committee made up equally of diocesan synod and GPC appointees screens all possible candidates for the diocesan bishop's office and recommends several names to GPC, which submits three names to the synods for election. In the case of the Conference secretary (now known as the administrative bishop, per the 2000 constitution), GPC nominates candidates, and from these the Conference selects one. The new system allows for more participation and input from a wider selection of people from within and outside a particular diocese. It is not unusual for several individuals to find their names on more than one synod list.

Some of the constitutional changes have been motivated by the need to cut down on administrative costs. The conference now meets biennially and not annually as it did from 1961 to 1999. But along with this change have come the loss of certain advantages associated with the former system. For example, the convening of MCG, on an annual schedule, at a particular district station brought some level of revival to the local societies as they responded to the national attention focused on them. Under the pre-2000 arrangement the conferences ensured that ministers and laypeople had opportunities where they could foster friendships among leadership throughout the year. A desirable side effect of annual meetings is that, in an environment where travel is difficult and sometimes rumors and half-truths are hard to refute, timely opportunity is created for correcting misinformation.

The current practice of governing MCG by an expanded GPC of 100 members, meeting twice a year for a day or two, has not cut down costs when compared with 200 people meeting for five to seven days once a year. Indeed it adds to the financial outlay if the cost of transportation is considered. Having the conference meet only biennially means that fewer people have input into decision-making and power sharing within the church. Decision making is now centralized and consolidated in the head office—a far cry from the intended participatory democracy. This centralization of power has been aggravated by the fact that the 1998 conference made the decision not to read reports from the districts but rather to give more time to read summaries submitted from the boards, which tend to reflect the agenda of the central office. The vitality of the grassroots church has been somewhat subverted by the head office.

By far, the most far-reaching change has been the decision in 2000 to adopt the ecclesial structure of episcopacy.

Proclamation Sunday

PROCLAMATION SUNDAY, HELD JANUARY 23, 2000, HAD ALL THE elements of a grand finale service at the MCG Annual Conference, and then some. The proceedings were led by the Reverend Dr. Samuel Asante-Antwi, then president of the conference (about to be consecrated presiding bishop),[195] and the visiting primate of the Nigerian Methodist Conference, His Eminence Dr. Sunday Mbang.[196] Several political and religious leaders attended the special service, with some playing leading participatory roles.

The service began with a long procession led by the past presidents and vice presidents of MCG. They were followed by a number of clergy who were to be appointed as new bishops, led by the current conference secretary, Albert Ofoe-Wright (about to be recognized as administrative bishop). The Reverend Comfort Quartey-Papafio (about to be named as assistant to the administrative bishop) accompanied Dr. Mbang. Finally, the Reverend Dr. Ohene-Bekoe, sometime administrator of the Methodist University College, Ghana, and the Reverend Dr. Emmanuel Asante, president of the Trinity Theological Seminary, Legon, escorted Dr. Asante-Antwi. After the singing of the traditional opening hymn, "Head of Thy Church Triumphant," Mbang read the objectives of the service as follows:

> (a) To solemnly make an official announcement to the Church Universal, and the world that the Methodist church, Ghana, has adopted A BIBLICAL PATTERN OF EPISCOPACY OR LEADERSHIP OF THE CHURCH BY BISHOPS;
>
> (b) and to formally and ceremonially place the national head of the Methodist Church, Ghana and each of the Chairmen and General Superintendents, and the Conference Secretary in the official positions of Presiding Bishop, Diocesan Bishops, and Administrative Bishops respectively; and to finally
>
> (c) ask for God's continual guidance as the congregations, the lay leadership, the deacons and the bishops work together to mark out a fresh spiritual and a continued developmental route for the Church.

After this declaration and another hymn, Mbang addressed Asante-Antwi, recognizing him as the presiding bishop, and the congregation silently prayed for the new presiding bishop. Mbang then asked Asante-Antwi to publicly confess his faith. After this, Mbang presented the connexional Bible, pastoral staff, and stole to the new presiding bishop.

Then came the reading of the Proclamation by His Lordship Justice George Lamptey of the Supreme Court of Ghana, after which Asante-Antwi and the lay president of MCG, Naomi Okine, along with the two living past presidents, affixed their signatures to the document as officially witnessing the event.[197] (See appendix E for the text.) Bishop Asante-Antwi then called forward the bishops, and after asking questions that elicited their public confession of faith, called for silent prayer on their behalf by the congregation.[197] The vice president of the Republic of Ghana, Professor John Atta-Mills, and the national chairman of the opposition party, Odoi-Sykes (both Methodists), delivered messages of goodwill. The Catholic primate Peter Turkson delivered the sermon.

It had been a full day and even though the ceremony started on time at 8:30 a.m., an hour earlier than usual, and ended before 12:30 p.m., it was as if the leadership of the MCG wanted to leave no doubt about the unanimity of agreement underlying the new dispensation.

History of Episcopacy Discussion

THERE HAD LONG BEEN INTIMATIONS FOR ADOPTING EPISCOPACY, even predating the granting of the autonomy in 1961. In 1957, with the Protestant churches (including the Anglicans) forming a task force to explore church union, MCG had implicitly agreed that bishops would administer all the churches. At the 1961 conference MCG declared its continuing interest in unity negotiations by affirming the following:

> The negotiating churches agree in accepting the following outline of the office of bishops in the United Church: The bishop will be the chief shepherd under Christ of His flock in a diocese and their father in God. Under the guidance of the Holy Spirit and in Christ's name he will have a concern for all who live in the diocese whether Christians or not; and within the Christian community he will care particularly for the other ministers in the diocese. He will strive, both personally and in the name of the diocesan synod, to ensure that the worship, teaching, and preaching of the church are pure, that its fellowship is maintained, that its evangelism is zealous and effective, and that discipline is administered with a view to the welfare of both the whole body and the member who becomes subject to it. Bishops will be elected by both the Church in the dio-

> cese concerned and by constitutional representatives of the Church as a whole having an effective voice in their appointment. (GCUC 1961, 20)[198]

The negotiating churches further agreed that the bishop would maintain the unity of the church in the diocese, represent the diocese to the outside world, and consult with a duly constituted body in the discharge of his duties. It was understood that the churches would endeavor to work out an appropriate balance between the personal responsibility of the bishop in the Anglican tradition and the corporate oversight that existed in the Methodist and Presbyterians churches.

For a good number of years the typical member of MCG did not hear very much about the subject. But the debate was re-energized during the presidency of Jacob S.A. Stephens. First of all, he restructured the MCG administrative system, making it more American than British, by introducing boards. He also hoped to make the formal transition to episcopacy, but due to the controversies of his presidency (1985–90), this was something he could not accomplish.

In 1991 a resolution came from Kumasi Synod, then chaired by Asante-Antwi, requesting the conference to grant meaningful autonomy with Episcopal leadership to all the Districts. The conference's response was to appoint a study committee; the committee subsequently assigned the task of writing a report to a subcommittee. The responsibility of chairing the smaller committee fell to the Reverend Dr. John K. Agbeti, the Chairman of the Cape Coast District. In its interim report to the 1992 Annual Conference at Tarkwa, the Agbeti committee wrote:

> From the history and analysis of the episcopacy . . . the Protestant Reformers had good reasons for rejecting the term Bishop. But the reformers retained the functions of the bishop in the ordained ministry whose roles continue to be 1) Administrative, coordinating of societies, circuits and synods; 2) Teaching, supervision and oversight of societies, circuits, synods and districts; 3) Presiding over the Eucharist, marriage, baptism, burial etc. That is, what the bishop had abandoned,

> the current ordained ministry had assumed in addition to the other roles: the Christological or Eucharistic role of the ordained ministry has been preserved. (Cited in Yalley 1992, 128–29)

The Agbeti report concluded by saying, "Hitherto, these functions have been and are being performed by our present system" (129). Having said that the adoption of episcopacy was functionally redundant in MCG, it nevertheless conceded that, given developments in ecumenism and current trends within the world Methodist family, MCG should conform to contemporary trends by adopting episcopacy.[199]

Undercurrents of division over this issue were not put to rest by the report. While it seemed that there would always be a group of people convinced of the necessity of adopting episcopacy, there were also many who either objected outright, or who had not studied the subject in any detail, or who simply did not consider it to be a very important issue.

The conference now forwarded the Agbeti report to the district synods. Three districts—Sekondi, Winneba and Northern Ghana—failed to provide any response at all. Three other districts—Kumasi, Sunyani, and Tarkwa—favored the adoption of episcopacy. The Koforidua and Accra districts gave conditional acceptance, commenting that (1) the current administrative structure needed to be maintained; and (2) the present time, 1992, was not ripe for the adoption of episcopacy. Both Akim Oda and Cape Coast districts concluded that since the present system focused on the functional gains of the proposed episcopal system, there was no need to adopt the new system.[200]

One might have thought that with such an inconclusive outcome, the idea would have been shelved. But the advocates of episcopacy felt that the uncommitted districts could be won over. In response, conference established yet another task force to collate ideas and present proposals. After a two-year study period, a document was produced that raised the following questions: What form of Episcopal systems should the Methodist Church adopt? Does MCG need to have the same understanding of the historic episcopate as the

Roman Catholics and Anglicans? Does adopting the historic episcopate mean that we are ceasing to be Methodist and becoming Anglican or Roman Catholic in our church's life?

When the study material was sent for the consideration of the district synods, Accra, Sekondi, Winneba, Koforidua, and Tarkwa districts stated they were not in support of the adoption of episcopacy. Sunyani called for more education. The remaining four districts, Cape Coast, Kumasi, Northern Ghana, and Akim Oda, did not respond at all.

Adoption of Episcopacy

BUT BETWEEN 1996 AND1999 THE PICTURE SEEMED TO CHANGE. After Asante-Antwi began his term as conference president in 1997, the leadership at the denominational headquarters reported that there was sufficient support to warrant the adoption of episcopacy. Those in the districts that were not supportive observed that the individuals who had kept alive the embers of the debate for many years were now in the ascendancy as district chairmen and conference president. The supporters, it was felt, were reinterpreting past discussions, selectively giving the greatest weight to that which favored episcopacy. The negative repercussions of adopting episcopacy were swept aside, and the benefit of conforming to others was highlighted.

A last battle had to be waged over the principle of the priesthood of all believers enshrined in the Deed of Foundation of the Methodist Church, Ghana. It is presented in distinctly Wesleyan terms:

> The Methodist Church holds the doctrine of the priesthood of all believers and consequently believes that no priesthood exists which belongs exclusively to a particular order of class of men [and women], but in the exercise of its corporate life and worship special qualifications for the discharge of special duties are required and thus the principle of representative selection is recognized. . . . For the sake of Church order and

> not because of any inherent virtue in the office, ministers of the Methodist Church are set apart by ordination to the Ministry of Word and Sacraments. (MCG Deed of Foundation, July 28, 1961)

In addition, the deed states, "Christ's ministers in the church are stewards in the household of God and shepherds of His flock. Some are called and ordained to this sole occupation and have a principal and directing part in these great duties, but they hold no priesthood differing in kind from that which is common to the Lord's people and they have no exclusive title to the preaching of the gospel or care of souls. These ministries are shared with them by others to whom also the Spirit divided His gifts as He wills." Accommodating a hierarchy of bishops to the priesthood of all believers presented quite a challenge. The proposed episcopacy needed to affirm a shared ministry that empowered the laity and that would not concentrate ministerial powers and responsibilities only in the bishop or in a bishops' council. Another provision allowed the title of bishop to be retained by the individual after leaving office, but there would be no provision for holding the office of bishop for life. Tenure in office would be determined by conference vote in the same manner as it had been done prior to episcopacy. (This followed the pattern and practice of the United Methodist Church in the United States.) Finally, it was underscored that the proposed episcopal leadership would not substantially change the existing administrative structures of the church; rather it would assist in its development along the following lines: (1) the ecumenical community would better understand the existing structures; (2) the adoption of episcopacy would bring the Methodist Church, Ghana, closer to the world Methodist family, especially the churches that have adopted episcopacy; (3) there would be a clear distinction between the church's structures and secular organizations (the church would avoid secular nomenclature such as "term," "chairman," and "boards," ; and (4) the use of the title "bishop" would provide gender-neutral designation for church office.

One of the reasons lurking in the background for MCG's adoption of the episcopacy system was surely the resurgence of charismatic and Pentecostal churches. Just as in the previous decade when MCG accommodated itself to the use of drums and the singing of choruses in church services to stem the tide of those leaving for AICs, one cannot help but feel that ultimately, the adoption of the episcopacy and the founding of the Methodist University College reflected concern about competition from the new charismatic churches. These new religious movements exercised great freedom in appropriating the historic designations of church leadership, with several of them taking on titles of bishops and archbishops even when they had only one congregation.

The adoption of episcopacy also reflects the fact that the leadership most in favor came from a part of the country that had a much more pronounced system of chieftaincy, where historically chiefs and elders were deeply involved as figures of power and authority in all aspects of Akan society. Thus, sociologically speaking, church leadership in the Ghanaian milieu may be seen as an aspect of chieftaincy.[201] In its authority patterns, sacralization of office, and the predominance of consensus in the decision making process, MCG's adoption of episcopacy has great potential for contextual appropriation.

Episcopacy with a Servant Spirit

PREACHING THE SERMON ON PROCLAMATION SUNDAY, JANUARY 23, 2000, Archbishop Peter Turkson concluded with a reflection on the ministry of Moses:

> [Moses displays] the childlike disposition of being excited about new things; and that is an admission in Moses that he does not know it all and he has not seen it all yet. This capacity for wonderment, curiosity and self-interrogation in Moses is an admission of ignorance, but at the same time it indicates the presence of a spirit of openness: two attributes which are indispensable for all who walk with God. . . . The admission of ignorance before God about his designs in our lives and in his Church, and the attendant openness to his Spirit and to

> his ever-newly fashioned presence in the world are episcopal virtues we need to acquire. For, as in the case of Moses, we need to remind ourselves always that the people who are the occasion of our appointment to this office are God's people, not ours. God must always have his way with them; and that means that we must constantly seek the face of God and discern his will for his people. . . . For us, there should be only one aim in life, and it is to be called servants of God on the basis of our deeds and ministries. For, as Gregory of Nyssa says, the end of spiritual life is to be called servants of God.[202]

The mantle then falls on the Most Reverend Dr. Robert Aboagye-Mensah, appointed in 2002 to succeed Asante-Antwi as presiding bishop, and his successors to reflect these sentiments. Right at the heart of the service inaugurating a new system of church governance was this call for a servant spirit approach to leadership.

Conclusion

BY DELIBERATELY ENGAGING ISSUES OF WORSHIP AND CHURCH POLity, MCG entered a process of contextualization that has marked it significantly as a Ghanaian church. MCG's attempts at intentional contextualization utilizing Methodist theology, Ghanaian identity, and Akan culture have had a far-reaching impact on Ghanaian Christianity beyond the boundaries of the denomination.

MCG has continued its indigenous ethos by encouraging the use of *ebibindwom* in the worship. By so doing, MCG taps into the visceral aspects of Akan tradition. The active engagement of redefining worship through the improvisatory means of the *ebibindwom* is a vital aspect of self-theologizing. MCG guidelines for church membership tested the limits of inherited theology and traditional practice; yet MCG leadership successfully incorporated polygamists into the church. Perhaps that attempt could have included a more in-depth treatment of Ghanaian Methodist understanding of Christian marriage, recognizing the fact that the Akan society has a tradition of matrilineal inheritance. MCG is the only mainline church in Ghana that has treated this subject in such detail, and it indicates its boldness in questioning the inherited theology and seeking to refashion it for the future.[205] Even though the attempts at church union would have significantly altered MCG church order, the cordial relations that MCG enjoys with other mainline churches is a result of the long years of church union negotiations. The identity of mainline Christianity was under siege when these discussions were going on, and yet other reasons must be adduced for the failure to achieve in Ghana a united church. Finally, on the question of the episcopacy, MCG has shown its ability to change and adapt to contemporary trends while at the same time responding to the traditional concepts of power and authority. These facets of self-theologizing indicate that MCG as an African institution has come of age. MCG's process of contextualization touched on issues of worship, marriage, identity, and ministry.

CHAPTER SEVEN

CONCLUSION

IN THE WORDS OF ONE OF METHODISM'S OUTSTANDING HISTORIANS, "It is the Wesleyan spirit that we must pray and hope for once again: that strange miracle that turned a censorious zealot into a herald of grace, that fusion of mind and heart and muscle in joyful service, that move from passion to compassion, that linkage of revival and reform, that stress on local initiative within a connexional system—that actual willingness to live in and to be led by the Spirit of God in faith and hope and love" (Outler 1971, 33). In the forty-eight years since it obtained autonomy from British Methodism, MCG has provided a contemporary example of that spirit. It has challenged the perception that the churches of Africa were relics of colonialism that would soon diminish in influence, if not completely die out.

African churches are said to be either strong or weak in proportion to the depth of their vernacular roots.[206] In the admittedly ambiguous political and religious climate of mid-twentieth-century Africa, Christian communities were challenged to prove their relevance in the socio cultural and political context of postcolonialism. The battle cry was "indigenization"; churches did not wish to be seen as mere branches of their corporate head office in Rome, Canterbury, and elsewhere. Measures had to be taken to ensure that the national loyalty of the Christian community was to the African state and not to the countries from where the missionaries had originated.

The challenge of demonstrating its indigenous and national character faced the MCG as it attained autonomy in 1961. In its commitment to be a contextualized church, MCG employed three cardinal elements, namely, Methodist theology, Akan culture, and Ghanaian identity.

MCG was built on the foundation of indigenous initiative, beginning with the leadership of the Fante Bible band. Early on, Wesleyan Christians successfully challenged the major religious institution of the Fante people, Nananom Mpow. The Wesleyan community grew exponentially in the early twentieth century as a result of mass conversions associated with the ministries of the West African prophets William Wadé Harris and Samson Oppong. MCG took root in circumstances in which the Christian gospel was mediated with an understanding of the spiritual quests and needs of the Akan people, thereby giving MCG an undeniable Akan flavor.

Having gained autonomy with the express purpose of carrying out its mission endeavors without the overlay of British Methodist supervision, MCG continued an evangelistic and outreach ministry in the northern regions of Ghana. In the 1960s and 1970s MCG grew dramatically in urban areas and in the Ghanaian Diaspora, largely due to the initiative of the laity. Undergirded by a holistic Methodist theology, MCG advanced its mission outreach by establishing schools and hospitals as a means of providing Christian education and social uplift and by supporting Ghanaian forms of holistic health care. Mission through evangelism, church planting, education, and health-care delivery were in continuation of the missionary heritage bequeathed to MCG.

MCG's self-identity as Ghanaian was dramatically exhibited in the years when the church, along with other mainline churches in Ghana, challenged the conduct and policies of arbitrary military governments. Serving as watchdogs of democracy and advocates of human rights, MCG provided a prophetic witness in Ghanaian politics. John Wesley's motto "the world is my parish" emboldened Methodists not only to work outside of the established church but to be seen and heard in the public square.

Issues of ethnicity that beset MCG in the 1980s underscored the fact that ethnic identity can play an inimical role in the well-being of the church. At the same time, it cannot be denied that deeper issues of power politics and personal aggrandizement played a major role. When ethnicity predominated at the expense of Ghanaian and Wesleyan identity (with its emphasis on unity in Christ), the church's missionary outreach suffered. Although the elements of ethnicity, nationalism, and Christian (Methodist) identity sometimes got out of balance, MCG's overall record demonstrates its commitment to all three.

A particularly prominent expression of an Akan cultural hallmark is MCG's appropriation of the musical genre of *ebibindwom*, which has proved to be a most effective tool of evangelism and discipleship. It has been the vehicle of imparting biblical knowledge and Christian teaching even to Ghanaians with limited literacy skills. Leadership by women in *ebibindwom* may well have paved the way for the inclusion of women in the ordained ministry of MCG.

MCG's conscious engagement with Akan culture prompted it to reexamine the practice of a two-tier system of church membership—one for those in monogamous marriages and another for those in polygamous marriages. MCG boldly reexamined polygamy in the light of the Bible's teaching and Akan cultural tradition. MCG study committee concluded by recommending that polygamists be accepted as full members, including the privilege of partaking of the Lord's Supper. At the same time it acknowledged monogamy as the Christian ideal and for that reason barred polygamists from holding church leadership positions.

Self-conscious, Ghanaian national identity in the context of post independence Africa also motivated MCG to explore the possibility of union with other mainline Ghanaian churches. It was prepared to move ahead with a union Ghanaian church, even as its mainline partners withdrew from the process. Finally, by changing its church structure from a British Wesleyan model to one closer to an American episcopacy style of governance, MCG has carved out an identity distinct from its missionary inheritance.

Methodism in its earliest form was a missionary movement. This was no less the case when MCG claimed its autonomy in 1961 in the context of independence-era Africa. It maintained its mission focus while intensifying the process of contextualization that embraced Akan cultural identity, Ghanaian nationality, and Wesleyan holistic mission theology. On occasions when one or another of these elements threatened to distort the church's image, discussions at the district level and conference hearings at the national level helped MCG return to a proper balance and to renew its commitment to its Christian mission. That mission has guided MCG in its first forty-eight years of independence as a distinctly Ghanaian church.

EPILOGUE

ALMOST A DECADE HAS PASSED SINCE THE INITIAL RESEARCH UNDERgirding this book was started. In the meantime, several incidents in the history of MCG have confirmed the relevance of the original objectives of this work. As I sign off I would like to offer a brief reflection on some of the significant recurring themes

MCG among the Ghanaian Diaspora is growing and thriving. As stated earlier, the Concordat agreements that have governed the relationship of MCG Diaspora with the mother church and UMC needs to be revisited and reviewed in light of current needs. A dispassionate and non-partisan resolution would mirror what other Ghanaian churches are doing—viewing their Diaspora branches as both a mission field and a mission force. The potential for growth is unprecedented when such an approach is reached. Thankfully there is now more literature on the subject of African immigrant churches through the works of such authors as Jacob Olupona, Jehu Hanciles, Kwabena Asamoah Gyadu, and Afe Adogame. The need for a more formal structure that oversees the Diaspora churches is now even more imperative than ever. On the positive side, in the last ten years, MCG has intentionally planted churches in neighboring Burkina Faso, a French-speaking, and majority-Muslim country. This is an outstanding achievement given its prior history of rather ineffective outreach in northern Ghana.

The Methodist University College, Ghana, is the second largest private university with well over three thousand students. MCG needs to ramp up its support as it is a direct investment in the future of Ghana.

MCG has introduced a new liturgy book, to be used side by side and to eventually supplant the older one. Though long overdue, it is commendable. However, it fails to capture the practical areas of pastoral use, such as those enumerated by the 1978 Fellowship of the Kingdom Committee, i.e. that the liturgy should deal with (1) fear and insecurity due to sickness, death, darkness, hatred, lorry accidents, lightning, enemies, witchcraft, poisoning, and so forth; (2) distress over the isolation of ethnic group from ethnic group, clan from clan, and village from village; (3) anxiety regarding the disintegration of traditional culture, the generation gap, and Western materialism; (4) apprehension over the perceived presence of the dead and dependence upon the ancestors. In addition to the usual services conducted at churches, the committee had also suggested that liturgies for the following occasions be drawn up: naming/christening of infants, widowhood rites, consecration of a burial ground, dedication of a tombstone, laying of the foundation stone of a private house, traditional festivals (e.g., puberty rites; and the deer hunt), and installation of a chief.

Most ministers who often officiate in such settings would appreciate more guidelines from a committee that is theologically qualified as well as contextually astute.

But by far the most controversial development within MCG in the last decade has been the adoption of the episcopacy. The debate has shifted from its doctrinal and ecclesiastical usefulness to its practice. There are no more arguments about whether MCG episcopacy should be monarchal or biblical, instead recurring issues center around what should become of the dozens of ex-bishops in active service, and what are the appropriate perks for the office of a bishop. While there are several good minds on both sides of the issue, the fact that in the last two instances after the adoption of episcopacy, MCG conferences have selected qualified non-bishops as the presiding bishop is telling. On another constitutional note, MCG continues to experience the pangs of growth and in the last couple of years witnessed a constitutional crisis concerning one person who was duly nominated for two dioceses as bishop. Appropriate steps are needed to ensure that such occurrences are not repeated. Ethnocentrism continues to be reflected in the elections of bishops. One wonders if MCG will ever elect a bishop who might not originally come from that particular diocese.

This book has had to be limited in many respects. There are several ministers and lay leaders who have served MCG in spectacular ways who are not mentioned here at all. If one were to recall all the ministries and stories, the vibrancy of MCG will be even more evident. Earlier on I had indicated that a glaring lacuna is a focused treatment on the role of women, and especially of MCG's flagship female institution, the Wesley Girls High School (WGHS), Cape Coast. In order to do adequate and justifiable justice to the history of this stellar institution more time and space would have been needed, and yet that is not to diminish the role of WGHS, which has produced, in the last decade alone, the first women to serve as chief justice of Ghana, the inspector general of police, and the vice-chancellor of a leading university among other national luminaries. In the larger sense, more scholarly attention is called for, as I said earlier, on the role of women within MCG and Ghanaian society in general; the religious and liturgical traffic between MCG, AICs, and now Pentecostal/Charismatics; the unique features of MCG sermons; biographies of leading women and men in MCG; histories of church organizations, schools, and military and police chaplaincies and a comparison of *ebibindwom* and American gospel music. These elements of church life all point to the indigeneity of the church and are areas that call for further research. If this work provokes more studies on these subjects, the objective would have been sustained.

All in all, as witnessed during the 2005 celebrations of the 170th anniversary, MCG is a vibrant organization that is poised for greater works in future. Its better days are ahead. The best is yet to be.

Ad majorem Dei gloriam Et aedificationem ecclesiae

APPENDIX A

MAP OF GHANA

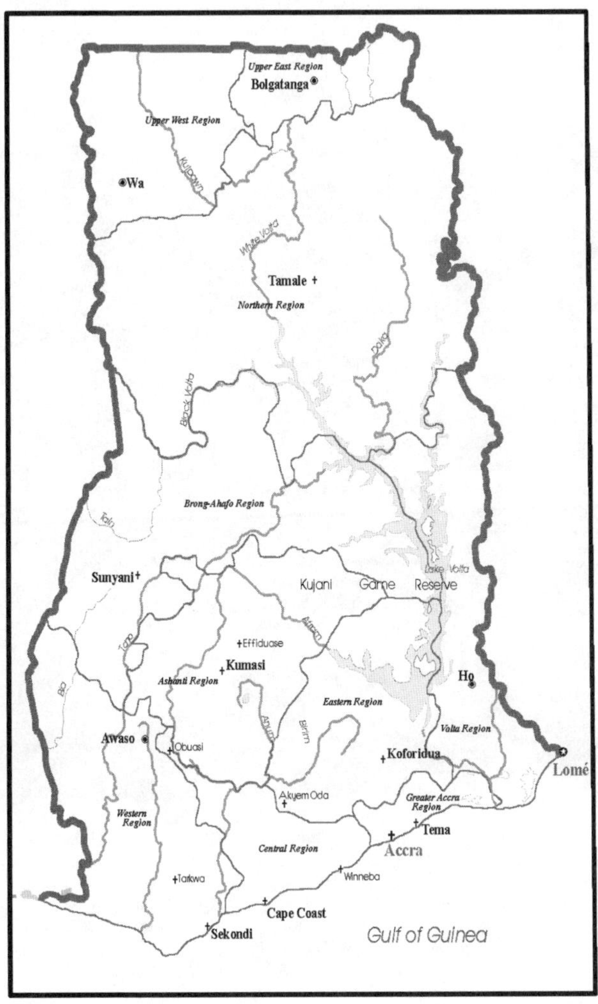

† Seats of Bishops

APPENDIX B

The Methodist Church Ghana Deed of Foundation

THIS DEED OF FOUNDATION is made on the 28th day of July, 1961 by the persons appointed to represent the Methodist Church and to represent the Synod of the Ghana District of the Methodist Church, being the persons whose names are set out in the First Schedule to this Deed.

Whereas

1. The Methodist Church is the Church in which since 1932 have been united the three Churches known before their union as the Wesleyan Methodist Church, the Primitive Methodist Church, and the United Methodist Church.
2. To assist in the establishment of Churches overseas which shall maintain and spread the Faith in their own countries and among their own kindred is one of the declared aims of the Methodist Church.
3. In the year 1835 a mission was inaugurated in Ghana, then Gold Coast, by Missionary Society of the Wesleyan Methodist Church and from that mission has grown the present Church in Ghana, which is part of the Methodist Church.
4. The administration of that Church (which is hereinafter referred to as the Existing Ghana Church) is now carried on under the ultimate authority of the Conference of the Methodist Church exercised through the Methodist Missionary Society, which is the overseas department of the Methodist Church.
5. The Synod of the Ghana District of the Methodist Church is the organization in Ghana by which the work of the Existing Ghana Church is immediately administered and which advises the Conference of the Methodist Church on all matters connected with that work and with the well-being of the members of the Methodist Church in Ghana.
6. The Synod has petitioned the Conference of the Methodist Church that there should now be established an autonomous Methodist Church, Ghana, in place of but in natural succession to the Existing Ghana Church and the Conference has willingly resolved to accede to that request.

7. For that purpose the Methodist Church has by resolution of the Conference dated 5th of July 1960 appointed the persons whose names appear in Part I of the First Schedule hereto as its representatives, and the Synod has by resolution dated the 20th of January 1961 appointed the persons whose names appear in Part II of the First Schedule hereto as its representatives, to execute this Deed of Foundation; and each resolution provides that execution by two-thirds of the representatives shall be sufficient and binding.

NOW therefore THIS DEED WITNESSETH that the Methodist Church and the Synod by their representatives DECLARE as follows:

1. The Methodist Church, Ghana is hereby constituted and recognized as an equal and autonomous community of Christian Believers, in no way subordinate to the Methodist Church, though joining with the Methodist Church in their common faith and heritage.
2. The doctrinal standards of The Methodist Church Ghana as of the Methodist Church, are: The Methodist church claims and cherishes its place in the Holy Catholic Church, which is the Body of Christ. It rejoices in the inheritance of the Apostolic Faith and loyally accepts the fundamental principles of the historic creeds and of the Protestant Reformation. It ever remembers that in the Providence of God Methodism was raised up to spread Scriptural Holiness through the land by the proclamation of the Evangelical Faith and declares its unfaltering resolve to be true to its divinely appointed mission.

   The Doctrine of the Evangelical Faith that Methodism has held from the beginning and still holds are based upon the divine revelation recorded in the Holy Scriptures. The Methodist Church acknowledges this revelation as the supreme rule of faith and practice. These Evangelical doctrines to which the Preachers of the Methodist Church both Ministers and Laymen are pledged are contained in Wesley's Notes on the New Testament and the first four volumes of his sermons.

   The Notes on the New Testament and the 44 Sermons are not intended to impose a system of formal or speculative theology on Methodist Preachers, but to set up standards of preaching and belief which should secure loyalty to the fundamental truths of the Gospel of Redemption and ensure the continued witness of the Church to the realities of the Christian experience of salvation.

   Christ's Ministers in the Church are Stewards in the household of God and Shepherds of His flock. Some are called and ordained to this sole occupation and have a principal and directing part in these great duties but they hold no priesthood differing in kind from that which is common to Lord's people and they have no exclusive title to the preaching of the gospel or the care of souls. These ministries are shared with them by others to whom also the spirit divides His gifts severally as He wills.

   It is the universal conviction of the Methodist people that the office of the Christian Ministries depends upon the call of God who bestows the gifts of the

Spirit, the grace, and the fruit that indicates those whom He has chosen.

Those whom the Methodist Church recognizes as called of God and therefore receives into its Ministry shall be ordained by the imposition of hands as expressive of the Church's recognition of the Minister's personal call.

The Methodist Church holds the doctrine of the priesthood of all believers and consequently believes that no priesthood exists which belongs exclusively to a particular order or class of men, but in the exercise of its corporate life and worship special qualifications for the discharge of special duties are required and thus the principle of representative selection is recognized. The Preachers—itinerant and lay preachers—are examined, tested, and approved before they are authorized to minister in holy things. For the sake of Church order and not because of any priestly virtue inherent in the office the ministers of the Methodist Church are set apart by ordination to the ministry of the Word and Sacraments.

The Methodist Church recognizes two sacraments namely Baptism and the Lord's Supper as a Divine Appointment and of perpetual obligation of which it is the privilege and duty of Members of the Methodist Church to avail themselves.

3. In order to secure the full co-operation between the Methodist Church and The Methodist Church, Ghana, which both desire, the two Churches shall as soon as possible after the assembly of the second Conference of The Methodist Church Ghana being the first to be held under the Deed of Church Order referred to below, negotiate arrangements for ensuring their mutual co-operation in Church matters.
4. A Conference to be known as the Foundation Conference shall be held for the purpose of setting and adopting a Deed of Church Order, which shall be the Constitution of The Methodist Church Ghana. The Foundation Conference shall be the first Conference of The Methodist Church Ghana. The members of the Foundation Conference shall be:
   (a) The representatives of the Methodist Church and the Synod whose names appear in the First Schedule hereto:
   (b) Such other persons if any as are appointed by the Synod to be members being (1) persons already so appointed by the Synod in anticipation of the execution of this Deed or (2) persons appointed by the execution of this Deed but before the meeting of the Foundation Conference;
   (c) The constitution of an annual Conference consisting of a Representative Session and Ministerial Session which shall be the supreme authority of The Methodist Church, Ghana.
5. The Deed of Church Order shall contain such provisions relating to the organizations and government of The Methodist Church, Ghana as the Foundation Conference shall think fit and shall provide for the following, among other matters:
   (a) The appointment of such committees, departments and local bodies as may be desirable.

(b) The appointment of such Officers of the Church as are to be appointed by the Conference.

(c) The making by the Conference of Standing Orders for the regulation (subject to the Deed of Church Order) of any matters it is desirable that the Conference should have power to regulate.

(d) Provision that the Conference may revoke, alter, or add to any of the provisions of the Deed of the Church Order (save the doctrinal standards) but that such revocations, alterations, or additions shall require:

(i) (In all cases) a resolution passed by the Representative Session by the votes of not less than three fourths of the members of the session present and entitled to vote and confirmed in the next following year by a similar resolution similarly passed; and also

(ii) (In the case of a revocation, alteration or addition which affects the continuance of the Ministerial Sessions as a separate body or the respective powers of the Representative and Ministerial Sessions or the union of The Methodist Church, Ghana, with another Church or religious organization) a resolution passed by the Ministerial Session meeting separately by the votes of not less than three-fourths of the members of that session present and entitled to vote and confirmed in the next following year by a similar resolution similarly passed.

(e) A statement of the doctrinal standards in the terms herein before contained and a provision that the standards shall not be capable of being altered.

(f) A provision that the Conference of The Methodist Church, Ghana shall be the final authority within that Church for deciding all questions concerning the interpretation of its doctrines.

(g) Notwithstanding anything contained in this Deed it shall be within the powers of The Methodist Church, Ghana, to join or merge itself in union with any other Christian Church or religious organization. Provided that this power shall not be exercisable unless:

(a) Any provisions regarding the procedure for affecting such union which may be contained in the Deed of Church Order as for the time being in force shall have been complied with; and

(b) The proposals for the union shall (notwithstanding any provision of the Deeds of Church orders as for the time being in force) have been approved by a resolution of The Conference or other governing assembly for the time being of The Methodist Church, Ghana, passed by a majority of not less than three-fourths of the members of the Conference or governing assembly present and entitled to vote and confirmed in the next following year by a similar resolution similarly passed; and so that as long as the Conference or other governing assembly consists of both a Representative and a Ministerial session separate resolutions of each session, each passed by the majority aforesaid, shall be requisite for approving and confirming proposals for union.

6. This deed shall not itself operate to transfer to The Methodist Church, Ghana, any property now held by or on behalf of the Methodist Church or any contract or liability entered into by the Methodist Church but arrangements shall be agreed between the Methodist Church and The Methodist Church, Ghana. Whereby:

(a) Property of the Methodist Church held in Ghana in connection with the existing Ghana Church shall (so as law allows) be transferred to The Methodist Church Ghana by vesting the property in such persons or bodies as may by or pursuant to the Deed of Church Order be designated for the purpose of holding the property of The Methodist Church, Ghana.

(b) The Methodist Church Ghana will take over from the Methodist Church contracts and liabilities in respect of the said property or otherwise in connection with carrying on of the Existing Ghana Church.

(c) Officers in Ghana of the Existing Ghana Church and other persons employed in Ghana in connection with the Existing Ghana Church shall (subject to any necessary consent by them) become officers or employees of the Methodist Church. Pending the agreement and carrying out of the arrangements mentioned in the preceding clause, the Methodist Church will allow The Methodist Church, Ghana to use and enjoy the property of the Existing Ghana Church and the services of its Officers and employees to the intent that the work of the Church may be carried on in Ghana without interruption.

7. Until the assembly of the second Conference of The Methodist Church, Ghana, (being the first to be convened pursuant to the Deed of the Church Order) the Foundation Conference (and until assembly of the foundation Conference, the Synod) shall exercise in relation to The Methodist Church, Ghana, all powers and authority which have heretofore been exercised in relation to the Existing Ghana Church by or on behalf of the Conference of the Methodist Church, other than powers and authorities relating to the disposal of property of the Methodist Church.

8. Subject to the provisions of this Deed the present constitution and powers of the Synod and any other regulation or matter relating to the Existing Ghana Church shall be deemed to continue in force so far as may be necessary to enable the Synod to perform its functions under this Deed and generally so far as may be necessary to enable the transition from the Existing Ghana Church to the Methodist Church to be carried out and completed in Ghana without interruption during the period of transition.

9. This Deed shall come into operation on the 28th July, 1961.

The Deed was signed by the following persons:

Maldwyn L. Edwards (President of the Conference of the Methodist Church)
Marjorie W Lonsdale (Vice President of the Conference of the Methodist Church)
G. Thackray Eddy
R. Wilfred Pile
T. Allen Beetham
J. Kingsley Sanders
R. A. Lockhart
E. Benson Perkins
Ernest Sawyer
Arthur L. Dixon
Eleanor M. Edwards
L. B. Greaves
C. Irene Mason
F. C. F. Grant (Chairman of the Synod of the Ghana District of the Methodist Church)
C. Awotwi Pratt (Secretary of the Synod of the Ghana District of the Methodist Church)
J. T. Clegg
J. E. Allotey-Pappoe
Solomon Butler
E. W. Obarmey-Tetteh
W. Quartelai Quartey
Henry W. Dennis
G. A. Apatu
Kwasi Benjamin Ellis
Hugh E. Thomas
J. Osam Tawiah
W. G. M. Brandful
J. C. Koomson
Joseph K. Baiden
Robert J. Figures
Peter Howard
A. Osei Asibey
J. F. Bart-Addison
Thomas W. Koomson
Charles K. Yamoah
J. K. Clegg
J. Emmanuel Yarquah
J. W. deGraft Johnson
J. Appiah-Yankson
J. K. Andoh
L. H. S. Osae-Addo
A. N. K. Sackeyfio
John K. Owusu
Joseph Yedu Bannerman
J. H. Nyame
E. A. Ebonyi

J. K. Agbeti
Kwesi A. Dickson
J. K. Kyereboah
S. K. Debrah
J. Glad Williams
C. C. Andoh
D. B. Ofori Rockson
H. B. Abruquah
J. B. Affainie
A. S. K Aidoo
S. H. Amissah
J. Abram Annobil
J. O. Appiah
G. E. Asumah
K. B. Banful
F. L. Bartels
B. K. Bondzi-Simpson
J. R.W. Buaful
L. A. Creedy
Benjamin Eshun
Clarice Garnett
Benjamin A. Markin
J. E. Wi-Afedzi
Joseph Wilson
M. K. Debrah
S. Y. Brew
W. C. Cudjoe
S. B. Essamuah
S. T. Ofei
Paul Adu
Charles D. Kittoe
Y. Adu Badu
Robert E. Akaah
Noel L. Wàrman
I. K. Asuamah Thompson
E. L. Adjetey-Adjei
A. E. K. Orgen
F. M. Akyea
Leslie Holmes
D. Famiye Yankey
W. E. D. Acquah
I. K. Agyeman
Margaret Amissah
A. Anno
James Apatu
K. E. Asamoah
George N. Baffoe
J. Scott Bennin
A. Wilson Brown
A. E. Chinbuah
K. John A. Stedman
J. K. Acquah
R. R. Agbettor
S. Y. Aidoo
B. Asare Amponsem
R. I. Anom
J. B. Arhin
J. P. Baddoo
E. A. Bannerman
J. T. Bedu-Addo
George A. Botsio
Mary Carlis-Paittoo
Gladys Dagadu
Charles Eshun
A. B. Ghunney
J. E. Addo
C. C. Ohene
H. V. Acquaye-Baddoo
F. E. Kwesi Ekuban
J. A. Hammond
Jane E. Gaisie
Louie L. Harvey
Kenneth H. Holgate
A. S. Kwaw
G. A. Mante
Jane O. Noom
E. D. Okyere
Comfort L. Peregrino-Aryee
J. E. Tufuoh
I. F. Konadu
E. N. Kwei
I. Ackom Mensah
E. O. Nsiah
J. K. Odoom
Philip Kwesi Panford
M. A. Quarshie
C. W. Tachie-Menson
Robert C. Korley
E. O. Lindsay
Irene Morrow
J. Beau Nunoo
J. E. Okaah
P. E. Pentsil
Charlotte Quarshie-Idun
Robert Dodoo
Grace Bart-Addison

SOURCE: The Constitution and Standing Orders of MCG (2000).

APPENDIX C

Methodist Church Ghana
Origins and Beliefs

1. INTRODUCTION

The beliefs of The Methodist Church Ghana are the same as those of the parent Methodist Church in Great Britain and the sister Methodist Churches in West Africa.

2. ORIGIN

(1) In the year 1835 a mission was inaugurated in the Gold Coast by the missionary society of the Wesleyan Methodist Church, and from that mission there developed a Methodist Church in Ghana. Prior to 1961 this church was administered by a District Synod under the authority of Methodist Church of Great Britain, but by the signing of the Deed of Foundation of the Methodist Church, at Cape Coast on 28th July, 1961, The Methodist Church, Ghana was established as an equal and autonomous community of Christian Believers, in no way subordinate to the parent Methodist Church (though joining with her in their common faith and heritage). Comprising all Methodist Circuits, Missions, Societies, and Institutions formerly under the Jurisdiction of the Ghana District Synod.

(2) The Methodist Church, Ghana claims and cherishes its place in the Holy Catholic Church, which is the Body of Christ. It rejoices in the inheritance of the Apostolic Faith and loyally accepts the fundamental principles of the historic creeds and of the Protestant Reformation. It ever remembers that in the Providence of God, Methodism was raised up to spread scriptural Holiness through the land by the proclamation of the Evangelical Faith and declares its unfaltering resolve to be to its Divinely appointed mission.

3. DOCTRINE

(1) Doctrines of the Evangelical Faith, which Methodism has held from the beginning and holds, are based upon the Divine revelation recorded in the

Holy Scriptures. The Methodist Church acknowledges this revelation as the supreme rule of faith and practice. These Evangelical Doctrines to which the Preachers of the Methodist Church, both ministers and Laypersons, pledged are contained in Wesley's Notes on the New Testament and the first four volumes of Sermons.

(2) The Notes on the New Testament and forty-four sermons are not intended to impose a system of formal or speculative theology on Methodist Preachers, but to set up standards of preaching and belief which should ensure loyalty to the fundamental truths of the Gospel of Redemption and secure the continued witness of the Church to the realities of the Christian experience of salvation.

(3) In accordance with the terms of the Deed of Foundation and the Deed of Church the doctrinal standards of the Church stated in these Deeds are unalterable.

(4) The Conference shall be the final authority within The Methodist Church, Ghana for interpretation of the doctrinal standards of the Church.

4. THE MINISTRY

(1) Christ's Ministers in the Church are stewards in the household of God and shepherds of the flock. Some are called and ordained to this sole occupation and have a principal and directing in these duties, but they hold no priesthood differing in kind from that which is common to the people and they have no exclusive title to the preaching of the gospel or the care of the souls. Others, to whom also the Spirit divides His gifts as He wills, share these ministries with them.

(2) It is the universal conviction of the Methodist people that the office of the Christian ministry depends upon the call of God who bestows the gift(s) of the Spirit, the grace, and fruit, which indicate those whom He has chosen.

(3) Those whom the Methodist Church recognizes as called of God, and therefore receive its ministry, shall be ordained by the imposition of hands, as expressive of the Church's recognition of the Minister's personal call.

(4) The Methodist Church holds the doctrine of priesthood of all believers, and consequently believes that no priesthood exists which belongs exclusively to a particular order or class of persons; but in the exercise of its corporate life and worship special qualifications for the discharge of special duties are required, and thus the principle of representative selection is recognized.

(5) The preachers, ordained and lay, are examined, tested, and approved before they are authorized to minister in holy things. For the sake of Church Order and not because of any priestly virtue inherent in the office, the Ministers of the Methodist Church are set apart by ordination to the Ministry of the Word and Sacraments.

5. THE SACRAMENTS

(1) The Methodist Church recognizes two sacraments, namely Baptism and the Lord's Supper, as of Divine appointment and of perpetual obligation, of which it is the privilege and duty of members of the Methodist Church to avail themselves.

(2) Baptism is the Sacrament signifying entry into the visible community of Christ's Church. Our Lord Jesus gave commandments to His disciples to baptize in the name of the Father and of the Son and of the Holy Spirit. The Sacrament of baptism is administered to:

a. Young people and Adults who, not having been baptized as children, are received into the Church upon profession of faith in the Lord Jesus Christ, after a suitable period of instruction;

b. Children for whom promises are made by responsible persons, usually the parents, that they will be brought up in the Christian faith.

(3) The Sacrament of the Lord's Supper, or Holy Communion, is that central act of Christian Worship instituted by our Lord Jesus Christ when, in the same night He was betrayed, He took bread, and when He had given thanks, He broke it and gave it to His disciples, saying "Take, eat; this is My Body which is given to you: Do this in remembrance of Me." Likewise after supper He took the cup; and when He had given thanks, He gave it to them saying, "Drink ye all of this, for this is My Blood of the New Covenant, which is shed for you and for many for the remission of sins: Do this as often as ye shall drink it in remembrance of Me."

6. MEMBERSHIP

(1) All persons are welcome into the membership of The Methodist Church, Ghana, who sincerely desire to be saved from their sins through faith in the Lord Jesus Christ, and evidence the same in life and conduct, and who seek to have fellowship with Christ Himself and His people and take up the duties and privileges of membership.

(2) It is the privilege and duty of members to present their children for the Sacrament of Holy Baptism, and full members should avail themselves regularly of the Sacrament of the Lord's Supper.

(3) It is expected of all members that they use, as regularly as possible, all the means of grace, public and private. As membership involves fellowship, it is the duty of all members to seek and to cultivate this in every possible way. The weekly Class Meeting has from the beginning proved to be the most effective means of maintaining among Methodists true fellowship in Christian experience. All members shall have their names entered into a Class Book, and shall be placed under the care of a Class Leader.

(4) All members are expected to engage in evangelism and other forms of Christian service, and to contribute to the funds of the Church in proportion to their means.

(5) If any question shall arise whether a particular person is a member of The

Methodist Church, Ghana, the entry of his name in a current Class Book shall be the accepted evidence of membership.

7. CHURCH UNION

(1) The Methodist Church, Ghana shares with the Universal Church the apostolic belief that the Church is one. It is deeply grieved that the expression of this unity is impaired by differences, which prevent Christians from uniting, particularly at the Table of the Lord, in worship and service. It rejoices at every evidence that the Holy Spirit is at work healing such wounds in the Body of Christ.

(2) The Methodist Church desires to undertake co-operative work with members of other Christian communions.

(3) It will work for the consummation of Church Union in Ghana.

(4) It looks forward to and will work for the worldwide unity of the Church.

(5) As it seeks to forge closer links between the Christian communions The Methodist Church, Ghana will welcome the advice of the Council of the Methodist Church in West Africa and the Conference of the Methodist Church.

(6) The procedure for entering into a Church Union is laid down in the Deed of Church Order

Source: The Constitution and Standing Orders of MCG (2000).

APPENDIX D

Methodist Church, Ghana
Ministers in the Connexion 2000 and their Year of Commissioning

1939	S	Koomson, Wallace T., K.G.B., G.M.
1951	S	Andoh, Joseph K., B.A.
	S	Stephens, Jacob S.A., B.A., M.A., S.T.M., D.Min. M.Sc.
1952	S	Ayerakwa, Henry G.
1954	S	Bannerman, Yedu J.
	S	Dickson, Kwesi A., B.D., B.Litt.
1955	S	Debrah, Solomon K.
	S	Williams, Joseph G.
1957	S	Akyea, F. Mensah
	S	Rockson, D. B. Ofori
	S	Agbeti, John K., B.A., S.T.M., Ph.D.
1958	S	Baiden, Ebenezer K. S.T.B., M.A.
1959	S	Ewoodzie, Isaac C.
	S	Okwaisie, Daniel K.M.
	S	Quarm, Samuel E.A., B.D., S.T.M.
1960		Dadson, Ebenezer K., E.D., S.T.M.
	S	Hazel, Kodjo, B.D.
1961	S	Ackeifi, John E.
	S	Acquaah, Jonathan L.
1962		Ampia-Addison, John K.
1963	S	Barnes, Isaac
	S	Danquah, Noah K.
1964	S	Acquah, Samuel K.
1965	S	Asamoah, Samuel K.
		Ashitey, Emmanuel A.
		Etsibah, Alphonse, B.A.
		Hodasi, Samuel K.
	S	Mensah, Peter K.
	S	Obeng, Walter G.
	S	Wilson, Joseph
1966	S	Affranie, Stephens B.
		Ansah, Justice K. N.

		Bonney, E. Christian
		Gordon, Albert A.
1967		Asiedu, Nathan K.
		Asua-Sekyere, Richard, B.D.
		Doni-Kwame, Felix
		Pappoe, Charles R. A.
1968		Blankson, William R. A., B.A., S.T.M.
		Dodd, Nathaniel D.
	S	Ebe-Arthur, Joseph E., B.D.
		Tekyi-Ansah, Joseph K., B.A., M.Th.
1969		Asante-Antwi, Samuel, B.A., M.A., Ph.D.
		Ashon, John F. K.
		Dadzie, Samuel W.
		Entsua-Mensah, Hawl
		Jonfia, William
		Kanetey-Essel, J.
		Odoom, Daniel B.
1970		Efa-Quayson, Thomas A., M.Div., M.A.
	S	Eshun, John A.
	S	Odum, Kodwo E.
	S	Quarcoo, Alfred K., B.Sc., M.A., Ph.D.
		Tagoe, Abraham A., B.A.
1971		Bakpanla, Peter D.
		Dadson, Justice K. A., B.A., M.Th.
		Edmund, Joseph K.
		Ghartey-Tagoe, David B., M.Div., S.T.M., Ph.D.
		Mensah, David C.
	S	Yawson, Albert K. A.
1972	S	Eku, Isaiah E. K.
	S	Oduro, Solomon F.
	S	Ofori, William
		Peters, Emmanuel J.
		Sarfo, Jacob O.
1973		Abakah, Kweku A.
		Aboagye-Mensah, Robert, B.Th., M.A.C.E., Ph.D.
		Aryee, Seth A., M.A., M.Phil., Ph.D.
		Banson, John K., B.A., Dip.Ed.
		Buabin, John F.
		Egyir, Kow B., B.A.
		Eshun, Peter K. Y.
		Harvey-Ewusie, John
		Quainoo, Albert O. M.Div., Th.M., D.Min
		Tinsari, Edison K., B.D.
1974		Asare, Kweku B.
	S	Brew-Riverson, E. H., B.A., M.A.R, D.Min.
	S	Nartey-Tokoli, Victor B. T., BA., M.A.
1975		Asare, Benjamin K., M.A.
		Amoah, James
		Ansah, Stephen O.
		Baffoe, Samuel K. K.

		Boateng, Emmanuel A.
	S	Enim, Herbert N.
		Sagoe, Kweku F., B.A.
1976		Addai, Isaac K.
	S	Adjei-Turton, Emmanuel
		Akassi, John K.
		Amponsah-Donkor, Edward
		Appiah-Thompson, Peter
		Asiedu-Mensah, J.
		Baah, Samuel
		Bentil, Isaiah O. B.
		Crentsil, John A.
		Donkor, Joseph M.
		Fosu, Emmanuel, K.
	S	Kesson, Samuel K.
		Kyeremeh, Emmanuel K.
	S	Mensah-Attah, Samuel R.
		Mponponsuoh, Samuel
		Obeng-Dompim, Joseph P.
	S	Odoi, E. Hudson
	S	Onumah, George K.
	S	Pobee, Joseph B.
		Quansah, Isaac K., B.A., M.A.
		Tetteh, Daniel O.
1977		Acquah, Jacob E.
		Addo-Beatson, Kingsley K.
		Arhinful, John W. K.
		Asamoah-Okyere, Kwaku, B.A., M.A.
		Asare-Bediako, John
		Ashitey, Edmund A.
		Atto Brown, J. K., B.A.
		Amoah, Peter K.
		Ansah-Arkorful, John
		Appiah-Acheampong, John K.
		Dennis, Ebenezer B.
		Gyamfi, Isaac Y. (Lt. Col.)
	S	Hutchful, Joseph S.
		Incoom, Samuel
		Owusu, Sampson K.
		Panford, Michael E.
		Pratt, Titus K. A., B.A.
		Sam, Christian A.
		Sarpong-Danquah, Emmanuel K., M.Ed., Ph.D.
1978		Ackon, Emmaunel E.
		Bortey, Emmanuel A. B., B.A., M.A., M.B.A.
		Botchway, Paul K. K.
		Ghunney, Joseph K., M.Div., M.Sc.
		Hammond, John E.
		Himil, George
		Koranteng, John K.

		Kyireh, Noah B. B. K.
		Lartey, Emmanuel Y., B.A., Ph.D.
	S	Obeng-Asiamah, K.
		Omanano, Daniel P.
		Osei, Joseph, B.A., M.A., Ph.D.
	S	Sappor, Solomon D.
	S	Tetteh, Emmanuel W. M.
		Thompson, Andrew
	S	Woolley, John B. L.
		Yamoah, Sampson
1979		Adjei-Tutu, Samuel
		Adubah, John A. Y., B. A.
		Amponsah, Kofi, B.Sc.
		Assabil, James K.
		Bassaw, John K., B.A.
		Diuri, Edward H.
	S	Garbrah, Benjamin W., Ph.D.
		Nyarko, Edward F., BA.
		Ofoe, Benjamin T.
		Osae-Addo, Benjamin
	S	Tettey-Enyo, Abraham A.
1980		Abban, Albert E. K
		Achamfuo-Yeboah, Samuel O., B.Sc. M.A.R.
		Adiekor, Daniel K.
		Agyei-Mensah, Samuel N., M.A.
		Agyeman-Kwakye, Samuel
		Ametefe, Winfred H. Y., B.A., M.A.
		Andam, Alfred S.
		Antwi, Moses O., B.A.
		Antwi-Boateng, Samuel, B.A.
		Asamoah, Samuel Y.
		Asante-Nnuroh, Samuel
		Baffour-Awuah, James, B.Ed.
		Dadzie, Samuel A.
		Gaisie, George A.
		Mensah, George
		Osabutey, Marslad A.
	S	Osei-Wireko, Samuel K.
		Otoo, Abraham A.
		Sarpong, Kwasi A., B.A.
1981		Addo, Raymond
		Ampiah-Bonney, George A.
		Annan, Emmanuel E.
		Annan, Francis Kwamena
		Antwi-Amoo, Samuel
		Arthur, Samuel K.
		Asare, David K.
		Boampong, George K.
	S	Bonney, George A.

Year		Name
		Bosomtwi-Ayensu, Stephen R., B.A.
		Danquah, Jubilant B., M.Div.
	S	Dartey, John A.
		Davies, Walter K.
		Ekuban, Charles A.
		Ekwam, Matthew S.
		Esuon, Philip K. K.
		Impraim, Joseph B.
		Morrison, Jeremiah A., B.A., M.A.
		Nkrumah, I. K.
		Nyankom-Ababio, Michael
		Omane-Achamfuor, K., B.Sc.
		Osei-Tutu, David
		Otabil, Peter E.
		Owusu-Acheampong, Alexander K.
		Quarshie, James K.
		Sey, Ebenezer
		Walters, Emmanuel E., B.A.
		Woode, Charles
1982		Abakah, Stephen G. Y., B.A., M.Phil.
		Aboagye, Francis A.
		Agyepong, Samuel O., B.A.
		Aidoo-Bervell, Samuel
		Asane, Nicholas K., B.A.
		Baidoo, Emmanuel K.
		Boateng, Frank Opoku
		Brobbey-Kyeremateng, K.
		Danso-Sintim, Daniel
		Donkor, David D., B.A
		Dwomo-Mensah, P.
		Ephraim, Ebo D.
		Kusi, Samuel
		Mensah, Isaac K.
		Ntiappiah, Enoch O.
		Oduro, Kwabena M., B.A., B.L.
		Opare, Emmanuel K.
		Otoo, John L.
		Owusu, Kwame J., BA., Dip. Ed.
		Quansah, Benjamin D., B.A.
		Sackey, Eric A.
		Sackey, John T.
		Sagoe, James K.
1983		Abubekr, Nuh B. Jr, B.A.
		Acquaah-Arhin, Samuel, M.Div.
		Amachie, Joseph B.
		Andoh, Francis
		Appianing, Alfred K.
		Aryeetey, Alfred N. O.
		Asante, Emmanuel K.,

	Awuku, Juliana, B.D.S.
	Barfoe, Thomas C.
	Boakye, Oswald S. K.
	Brewu, Paul A. (Maj.)
	Ennin, George O., B.A.
	Eshun, Ebenezer
	Essandoh, Daniel K., B.A
	Forson, Thomas H.
	Nnuro, Grace
	Nunoo, Daniel D.
	Owusu-Ansah, Albert
	Roberts, Conrad
	Walton, James K., B.Sc., M.Div.
1984	Akesse, Elizabeth
	Anderson, Theophilus K.
	Anderson, Victor
	Appianyah, Joseph
	Arko-Boham, Kojo, B.Ed.
	Baffour, K. Kyei
	Bennin, Kwasi A.
	Churcher, Emmanuel K., B.A., M.E.D.
	Foli, Richard, B.A., M.Phil.
	Forson, James E.
	Hagan, Esther G., M.Div.
	Kusi-Appiah, Samuel, B.A., M.Ed.
	Kwakye-Nuako, F., M.A.
	Mensah-Bonsu, Emmanuel
	Obeng, Yaw
	Quainoo, Samuel A.
	Sackey, Michael P.
	Sam, Isaac K., B.A.
	Twum-Baah, Emmanuel G. L., M.A.
1985	Akushie, Conforter, B.A., M.Th.
	Amankwa, Richard K., B.A.
	Baidoo, Joseph K.
	Buabeng-Odoom, John K.
	Brace, Daniel deGraft, B.A.
	Ekem, John D. K., B.A., M.Phil., D.Th.
	Fynn, Isaac T.
	Iddi, Philip Musa
	Kittoe, Albert K., B.A.
	Kyere, Amos H.
	Manso-Afriyie, Daniel D.
	Orgen, Joshua K. A.
	Osabutey, Samuel K., M.A.
	Quarcoo, Asford N. Y., M.A.
	Samwini, Nathan I., M. A.
1986	Abakah-Wilson, Ebenezer K.
	Akushie, Isaac S.

		Arthur-Mensah, Kwesi
		Asamoah-Gyadu, Johnson, B.A., M.Phil.
		Baiden, John W.
		Boafo, Paul K., B.A.
		Donkor, Addo S.L.
		Donkor, Edward O.
		Edusa-Eyison, Joseph M. Y., B.A., M.Phil.
		Gyabeng, Sampson K.
		Tweneboah Koduah, Abraham
	S	Larbi, Ebenezer
		Mensah, James K.
		Obeng, Robert K.
		Osei, James, B.A.
		Osei-Kuffour, Janet
		Owusu, James K.
1987		Ababio, Quophie A.
		Acheampong, Peter Y., B.A.
		Acquah, Isaac K.
		Addai-Antwi, Jonah
		Asiedu, Kofi B.
		Atuahene-Nsowaah, Jacob A., B.A., M.Th.
		Baffoe, John M.
		Bessa-Simons, Samuel K.
		Egyir, Gordon A.
		Eshun, Robert O., B.A.
		Jackson, Moses K.
		Morris-Mensah, John K.
		Nnuroh, Frederick, B.A.
		Ofori-Akyea, Samuel
		Oppong, Robert K.
		Osei-Owusu, K.
		Quarm, George K.
1988		Abakah, Emmanuel P.
		Abassah, Peter N.
		Aidoo, Isaac J.
		Amoah, Isaac S.
		Ampofo, Grace
		Ato-Smith, Franklin
		Bassaw, Nana E. K., M.Div.
		Boadu-Ayeboafo, Samuel
		Boamah, Isaac Y.
		Bossman, Michael A., B.A., M.A.
		Brew, James E. K.
		Cronze, Isaac B.
		Foli, Patricia
		Essamuah, Casely B., B.A., M.Div.
		French, Jacob William
		Grant-Essilfie, Solomon P., B.A.
		Gyimah, John B.

	Konadu, Charles K., B.Ed., M.A.
	Laryea-Adjei, Samson N. A. M.
	Monney, Comfort E. K.
	Nketsia, Samuel E.
	Odoom, Jane
	Owusu, Peter B. K.
	Quayson, Moses, B.A.
	Kantanka, Osei S., B.Sc., M.Sc., Ph.D.
	Wie-Addo, Kow A., B.Sc.
	Wright, Albert O.
1989	Abeka, Isaac N.
	Adjei-Boafo, Samuel
	Akromah, Philip K. D.
	Anaman, Esther
	Apau, Kusi B., B.Sc.
	Aryee, Emmanuel K., B.A.
	Boateng-Enninful, Ebenezer, B.Sc., M.Sc.
	Cudjoe-Mensah, John
	Dadzie, Dominic S., B.A.
	Essiamah, Banasco
	Kudadjie, Joshua N., B.A., M.A.
	Mensah, Joseph C., B.A.
	Obiri, DeGraft S.
	Odum-Baidoo, Nicholas
	Ossei, Joseph M., B.A
	Pimpong, Walter A., M.Div.
	Quartey-Papafio, Comfort H., M.T.S., Th.M.
	Quartey, Samuel K.
	Tetteh, Nicholas
	Yalley, Ebenezer A., B.A
	Yankey, Emmanuel I.
1990	Adu, Paul, Jr.
	Anim, Mercy A.
	Ansah, Emmanuel
	Antwi, Mary D.
	Antwi-Boasiako, Clarence
	Arhin, Emmanuel K.
	Armah, Benjamin K.
	Arthur, Ebenezer O.
	Asare-Kusi, Emmanuel K., B.A.
	Bediako, Asare K.
	Boamah, Alfred Y.
	Boyetey, Victor B. B.
	Dapaah, Kenneth O.
	Glover, Robert T.
	Grahl, Helena H. A., B.A., M.A.
	Kroan, Ezekiel K.
	Mpere-Gyekye. William A., B.A., M.A.R.
	Onwona, John

	Opoku-Sarkodie, Helena A. S., M.A., S.T.M.
	Orlan-Hackman, Joseph
	Oseku-Afful, Thomas, W. A.
	Priddy, de-Graft J.
	Sackey, Anthony K. A.
	Sarpong, Ohene Kwasi
	Tannor, Daniel K.
	Taylor, William
	Turkson, Emmanuel E. K.
	Twum, Isaac K.
	Van-Dyck, James E. B., B.A.
	William, Jacob O.
	Woolley, Emmanuel O. (Capt.)
	Wuver, Isaac N. K.
1991	Abedu, Eric M.
	Addae, Alexander
	Addae, Bediako K.
	Adjekumhene, Richmond S.
	Adjei, D. K.
	Afriyie, Emmanuel M.
	Aggrey-Ogoe, Emmanuel
	Anaman, Winifred
	Andoh, Joshua A. O.
	Ansah, Peter S.
	Ansuh, Samuel F.
	Ayensu, Amos F.
	Bassaw, Robert B.
	Blankson, Isaac A.
	Boahen, Jacob K.
	Buabeng, Joseph I.
	Dadson, Christopher K.
	Danquah, Daniel K.
	Darko, George A.
	Darko-Yawson, Samuel K.
	Donkor, Sampson Y.
	Essel, Moses K.
	French, Daniel K.
	Gaisie-Amoah, A.
	Konadu, Yanchira K.
	Kwotie, John B.
	Magnus, John O., B.A.
	Morrison, Victor E.
	Nkansah, Samuel A.
	Obresi, Kobina K.
	Obuo-Dadzie, K. M.
	Odame, Kwame
	Owusu, Stephen K.
	Peprah, Yeboah S., B.Sc.
	Quansah, John K. B.

	Quayson, John E.
	Quarshie, Abedu, B.A.
	Sackey, Albert O., B.A.
	Sackey, Seth A.
	Yawson, Samuel K. D.
1992	Ackom, Forson A.
	Acquah, Francis K., B.A
	Adjabeng-Asenso, James
	Amankwa, Samuel A.
	Ameyaw, Boateng K.
	Ampaw, Asiedu K.
	Andam, Christopher N.
	Annan, Ralph E. O.
	Arko-Mensah, Emmanuel T.
	Arthur, Isaac I.
	Asema, Boadi Joseph
	Badu Bota, Emmanuel K.
	Bart-Plange, Nana K.
	Berchie, Patricia
	Blay-Baidoo, Kwame
	Boateng, Ransford P.
	Boatey, Diana
	Bonna, Stephen M.
	Cudjoe, Richard
	Dadson, Albert K
	Dadzie, James B.
	Dakwa, Joseph
	Davis, William E.
	Donkor, Thomas
	Dzima, Albert A. E.
	Ekuafo, James
	Gyang, Diana
	Koampa, James Y. A.
	Koranteng, Charles
	Kyei, Kwakye S. K.
	Mensah, Georgina
	Ofori, Emmanuel K.
	Osafo-Parry, Joseph, B.A.
	Quarshie-Wood, Oheneba
	Salia, James M.
	Sekyere, Daniel K.
	Sobeng, Solomon
	Techie, Moses M.
	Twum-Baah, Frank D.
1993	Acquah, Francis I.
	Adomako, Sophia
	Adu-Gyamfi, Paul
	Afful, Mark W. Y., B.A., M.A.
	Amo-Ayesu, Samuel

	Ampadu-Bonsu, Kofi
	Ankrah, Emmanuel K.
	Arthur, Joseph
	Asamoah, John A. O.
	Baffour, Kwame K.
	Boateng, Samuel A.
	Bortey, John G.
	Botchey, Symonds A. M.Sc., Ph.D.
	Eshun, Solomon
	Ennin, Saint F.
	Frimpong, Noah A.
	Gyimah, Valentine
	Harrison, Stephen E. K.
	Kankam, Samuel
	Mbea-Baiden, Andrew
	Mbiah, James K.
	Marfo, Emmanuel K., B.Sc., M.Sc., Ph.D.
	Mpereh, Samuel K., B.A.
	Opoku, Samuel K., B.A.
	Palm, Alfred K.
	Tenakwa, George A.
	Tweneboah-Kodua, Maxwell
1994	Agyam, Moses K.
	Amoateng, Kofi
	Annan, Dominic K.
	Archer, Emmanuel A.
	Baidoo, John
	Baidoo, Joseph
	Boateng, Alexander Y.
	Donkor, Joseph G.
	Ennuson, Francis, B.A.
	Fynn-Aikins, James, B.A., Dip.Ed.
	Ghansah, Ishmael N., B.Sc., M.Sc.
	Mensah, Samuel
	Norgbordzi, Philip T.
	Quansah, Samuel B. K.
1995	Adusei-Poku, Hayford
	Adutwum-Nkrumah, Ebenezer
	Amankwa-Amponsah, Godson
	Ampah, Charlotte R.
	Antwi-Asenso, John
	Annan, Eugene A.
	Bamfo, Edward C.
	Dadzie, Samuel K.
	Esar, Paulina
	Gorman, Benjamin
	Gyimah, Frimpong S. G.
	Hagan, Crowther S.
	Hagan, Mary

	Kwarteng, Kwaku
	Kyeremeh, Isaac K.
	Mensah, Ernest
	Mintah, Philip K.
	Noble-Yorke, Timothy D.
	Nyarko, Laurene
	Osei, Grace D. Afranie
	Oteng-Poku, Philip H.
	Pobee, Amos J.
	Sarpong, Kingsley K.
	Yawson, James F.
1996	Ackom, John K.
	Acquaah, Ishmael K.
	Adjei, Ebenezer P.
	Agyemang, Badu E.
	Afrofie, Paul
	Amponsah-Donkor, Thomas
	Andam, Richardson A.
	Annan, Marian A.
	Anyimah Samuel
	Arthur, Stephen
	Aryee, Maxwell
	Ashun-Yorke, Isaac J.
	DesBordes, J. K. K.
	Dickson, Kweku A.
	Gyasi, Boateng S.
	Gyekye-Fosu, Kwaku
	Gyimah, Joseph Kwesi
	Mensah, Charles
	Ofori-Sampong, Samuel
	Ollenu, Nii Nmai S.
	Osei, Mercy E.
	Owusu-Fordjour, A.
	Siaw, John K.
1997	Acheaw, Kwasi O.
	Addae, Magnus E.
	Addo-Nartey, Nathan
	Adjei, Boatey
	Afful, Alex K.
	Ameyaw, James Takyi
	Amo Baiden, Humphrey
	Appiah, Broni Nancy
	Arthur, Emmanuel Kwesi
	Asamoah-Agyei, Baffour
	Asenso, Emmanuel Boatey
	Bentum, Ignatius Nana M.
	Brown, Anthony
	Frimpong-Manu, Adjei
	Gyawu, Ofori Arko

	King, Charles Emmanuel
	Manu-Yeboah, Bernard
	Peregrino-Braimah, Emmanuel
	Quaye, Godfrey Amatey
1998	Adjaotor, Margaret R.
	Aidoo, Mark S.
	Ampofo-Twumasi, William
	Ansah-Eshun, Peter K.
	Ansong, John K.
	Atuahene, Joseph O.
	Baiden, Rebecca
	Boadu, Dennis J.
	Dapaah, R. B.
	Duah, Gordon K.
	Essien, Emmanuel E.
	Laryea, Florence
	Mensah, Awuah Paul
	Sackey, John Prince
1999	Aboagye, Jonas S.
	Amartey, Lawrence K. L.
	Amoako-Baah, Benjamin
	Amoo, Emmanuel K.
	Amponsah, Hannah A.
	Annan, David J.
	Antwi, Moses
	Asher, Stephen
	Darkwa, Elvis R.
	Donkoh, Benjamin
	French, John K.
	Oppong, Samuel
	Sackey, John P.
	Sarpong, Helena
	Tetteh, J. E.
	Twumasi, Ampofo
2000	Amponsah, Samuel
	Appau-Gyekye, Nana
	Appiah, Samuel Nick
	Boateng, George
	Boateng, Kwadwo Agyekum
	Frimpong, Isaac Kofi
	Fynn, Isaac Y.
	Mensah-Bonsu, Okontomene
	Obeng-Mensah, Charles
	Opare, Beatrice
	Owusu-Asamoah, Collins K.
	Sakyi, Daniel K.
	Wiafe, Frimpong

SOURCE: MCG Conference Ministerial Agenda (2000).

APPENDIX E

Proclamation
By the Methodist Church, Ghana
Adopting
A Biblical Pattern of Episcopacy

To the Church Universal,
The Nation,
and The World,

The Grace of the Lord Jesus Christ, and the Love of God, and Fellowship in the Holy Spirit, be with you all (2 Corinthians 13:14).

WHEREAS the Deed of foundation of The Methodist Church, Ghana promulgated on the 28th day of July, 1961, states that ministry involves the entire Church; and

(1) Every individual believer has a particular ministry to carry out in the Church; and
(2) Ministry is not the exclusive preserve of the ordained; and
(3) The ordained ministry exists to ensure Church order, facilitate the preaching and teaching of the Word, administer the sacraments, and to provide leadership in the Church and the wider community; and
(4) The Church realises the need to conform to a biblical pattern of episcopacy; and
(5) For the purpose of effecting the changes stated in this Proclamation the Constitution and Standing Orders will be amended accordingly; and
(6) The 38th Annual Conference discussed the proposals at both its Ministerial and Representative Sessions and unanimously adopted the proposals resolving that the proposals herein stated be implemented forthwith pending the amendment of the Constitution;

NOW THEREFORE, This Proclamation witnesseth that the Conference of The Methodist Church, Ghana at its 38th Annual Conference held in Koforidua from 18th to 25th August, 1999 in a spirit of humility proclaims:

1. THE PRESIDING BISHOP OF THE METHODIST CHURCH, GHANA

1.1 That the President of the Conference, the chief servant-pastor, overseer, and teacher of our Church, by the power of the Holy Spirit, shall be known as The Presiding Bishop of The Methodist Church, Ghana and referred to as "The Most Reverend . . ."

1.2 That upon ceasing to hold office, a Presiding Bishop will assume the title: "Past Presiding Bishop," and retain the designation "The Most Reverend

2. THE LAY PRESIDENT

2.1 That the Vice President of the Conference shall be known as The Lay President of The Methodist Church, Ghana.

2.2 That upon ceasing to hold office, a Lay President will assume the title: "Past Lay President."

3. THE ADMINISTRATIVE BISHOP

3.1 That the Secretary of Conference shall be known as The Administrative Bishop of The Methodist Church, Ghana with responsibility for the administrative affairs of the Church and shall be referred to as "The Right Reverend . . ."

3.2 That upon ceasing to hold office The Administrative Bishop shall have the title "Past Administrative Bishop," and shall retain the designation "The Right Reverend . . ."

3.3 That where a Diocesan Bishop becomes The Administrative Bishop the Diocesan Bishop shall have the designation of The Administrative Bishop only.

4. DOCESE AND DIOCESAN BISHOPS

4.1 That the Administrative Divisions of the Church known as Districts shall be known as Methodist Dioceses.

4.2 That the Chairmen and General Superintendents of existing Districts shall be known as Diocesan Bishops and referred to as "The Right Reverend . . . ."

4.3 That upon ceasing to hold office, a Diocesan Bishop shall have the title of "Past Bishop" and shall continue to be referred to as "The Right Reverend . . ."

5. DIOCESAN SYNOD SECRETARY

5.1 That an ordained minister on being appointed a Synod Secretary shall be known as "The Very Reverend."

6. SUPERINTENDENT MINISTER

6.1 That an ordained Minister on being appointed a Superintendent Minister shall be referred to as "The Very Reverend . . ."

7. OTHER CHURCH OFFICIALS

7.1 That the following categories of ordained Ministers shall be referred to as "The Very Reverend."

(i) The Assistant to Administrative Bishop (Assistant Secretary of Conference). All Methodist Ministers in Methodist Related Institutions who are Heads/deputies or are of the rank of Senior Lecturer and above.

(ii) The General Manager of Schools if a Minister.

(iii) The General Director.

(iv) Methodist Chaplain Generals and the General Secretary of CCG if an ordained minister of The Methodist Church, Ghana.

8. ELDERS

8.1 That all Ordained Ministers shall be considered as Elders and shall be referred to as "The Reverend . . ."

9. DEACONS

9.1 That all Probationers or Ministers-On-Trial shall be considered as Deacons and shall be referred to as "The Reverend . . ."

10. OFFICIAL ATTIRE/VESTMENTS

10.1 That the details of official ministerial attire/vestments shall be a part of the particulars specified in the Schedule to this Proclamation.

SCHEDULE

Signed for, and on behalf of, The Methodist Church Ghana, at The Proclamation Service held in the name of the Father, the Son and the Holy Spirit, on this 23rd day of January, 2000 in The Year of The Lord at The Wesley Methodist Church, Asafoatse Nettey Road, Accra.

The Most Reverend Dr. Samuel Asante-Antwi, B.A., M.A., Ph.D.
presiding bishop

Mrs. Naomi E. Okine
lay president

The Most Reverend Thomas Wallace Koomson
past president of conference

The Most Reverend Dr. J. S. Adama Stephens
past president of conference

Source: The Constitution and Standing Orders of MCG (2000).

OFFICIAL MINISTERIAL ATTIRE/VESTMENTS

I. GARMENTS

The following are for The Presiding Bishop, Diocesan Bishops, and The Administrative Bishop.

PRESIDING BISHOP

Maroon/Purple Cassock with Stole. Mauve/Purple Shirt. The Presiding Bishop may, however, wear any ministerial outfit during any liturgical season.

ADMINISTRATIVE BISHOP

Same for Bishops.

BISHOP

Black, Grey, Maroon/Purple, or White Cassock and Stole, plus Bands with a maroon band on the sleeve of the Cassock and button holes. Mauve Shirt. Gowns may be worn over the cassocks.

Ministers for whom special colours have been prescribed can wear Shirts of other colours approved to be worn by Methodist Ministers on informal occasions. Superintendent Ministers, General Directors who are ministers will wear Green Shirt. A minister who does not hold or has never held any position for which special colours are prescribed should not wear those colours.

II. STOLE

PRESIDING BISHOP

(i) The Methodist Logo
(ii) An emblem distinct from that of the Diocesan Bishops that reflects the Connexion

ADMINISTRATIVE BISHOP

(i) The Methodist Logo
(ii) An emblem depicting the function of the office

DIOCESAN BISHOPS

(i) The Methodist Logo
ii) An emblem distinctive of the particular Diocese

The colours of Stoles, if worn, should be reflective of the occasion or Church Season.
The liturgical colours are WHITE/GOLD; GREEN; RED; PURPLE/VIOLET/BLUE.
The TIPPET comes in one colour only: BLACK

APPENDIX F

Administrative Institutions of the Conference

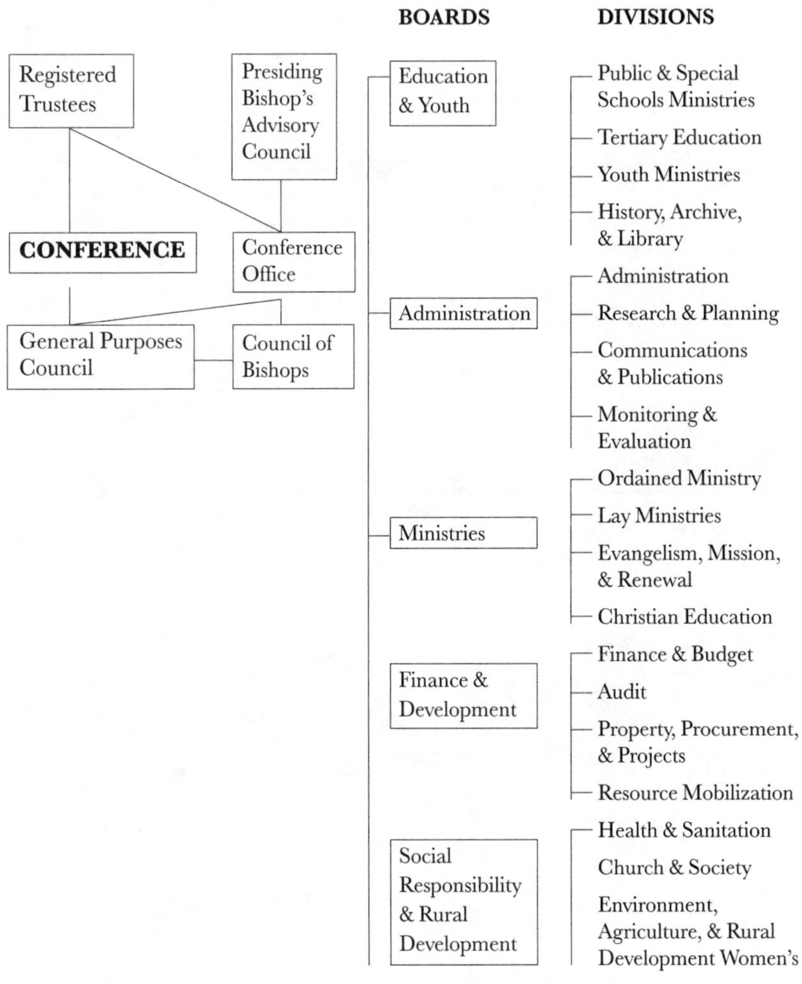

Source: The Constitution and Standing Orders of MCG (2000).

APPENDIX G

Office Holders and Years of Service, 1961–2000

A. PRESIDENT/PRESIDING BISHOPS:

1.	Most Rev. Dr. F. C. F. Grant	1961-66
2.	Most Rev. T. Wallace Koomson	1966-73
3.	Most Rev. Charles K. Yamoah	1973-77
4.	Most Rev. C. Awotwi-Pratt	1977-79
5.	Most Rev. Samuel B. Essamuah	1979-84
6.	Most Rev. C. Awotwi Pratt	1984-85
7.	Most Rev. Dr. Jacob S. A. Stephens	1985-90
8.	Most Rev. Prof. Emeritus Kwesi A. Dickson	1990-97
9.	Most Rev. Dr. Samuel Asante-Antwi	1997-2003

B. VICE PRESIDENT/LAY PRESIDENTS:

1.	Bro. S. H. Amissah	1977-79
2.	Bro. Crakye Denteh	1979-81
3.	Bro. Isaac K. Agyeman	1981-83
4.	Bro. Joseph. B. Odunton	1983-85
5.	Bro. Dr. Alex Quaison-Sackey	1985-87
6.	Bro. Nana Dr. J. S. Annan	1987-89
7.	Sis. Sophia Moore	1989-91
8.	Bro. Dr. Augustus. A. Armah	1991-93
9.	Bro. Jacob. A. Boateng	1993-95
10.	Sis. Georgina Baiden	1995-97
11.	Bro. Timothy E. Osam-Duodu	1997-99
12.	Sis. Naomi Elizabeth Okine	1999-2002

C. CONFERENCE SECRETARY/ADMINISTRATIVE BISHOPS:

1.	Rt. Rev. W. C. Cudjoe	1961-68
2.	Rt. Rev. Isaac. K. Asuamah-Thompson	1968-74
3.	Rt. Rev. Jacob S. A. Stephens	1974-82
4.	Rt. Rev. Joseph K. Tekyi-Ansah	1982-86
5.	Rt. Rev. Ebenezer H. Brew-Riverson	1986-93
6.	Rt. Rev. Maclean A. Kumi	1993-98
7.	Rt. Rev. Albert Ofoe-Wright	1998-2004

APPENDIX H

Act of Covenant between the United Methodist Church and MCG

PREAMBLE

Covenants have been an integral part in the history of God's relationships with the People of God. Indeed, as the General Conference on 1968 stated ("On the Ecumenical Road," A Statement on the Cause of Christian Unity): ". . . the profoundest imperative to Christian unity springs from God's own design and providence for His covenant people." In the preamble to the Constitution of the United Methodist Church we are alerted to the dangers of all dividedness: "The Church of Jesus Christ exists in and for the world, and its very dividedness is a hindrance to its mission in that world." In recent decades we have received clearer understanding of the relationship between Christian unity and our covenant with God. At the same time we have new insight into the nature of the Christian Church and a new sense of common global mission. Geographical and political boundaries do not limit the Body of Christ.

The United Methodist Church has a stake in the faithful discipleship of other communions. Other communions have a stake in the faithful discipleship of the United Methodist Church. Thus, the United Methodist Church now seeks a new form of acceptance of God's gift of unity. We seek to engage in covenant with other Christian churches wherever more visible Christian unity can increase effective mission in the modern world. This covenant is a symbol of the search for deeper relationships with churches that are a part of the whole Covenant People of God.

In the Act of Covenanting, the emphasis is on our roots in the Apostolic Faith and in our contemporary experience of God's love and will. It is aimed at encouraging a new sense of global common cause, mutual support, mutual spiritual growth, common study of scripture and culture, creative interaction as ministers in the mission of God's Church, cross-fertilization of ideas about ways to be in that mission, sharing of resources, and exploring new forms of service directed at old and emerging needs.

In this covenant, The Methodist Church, Ghana and the United Methodist Church acknowledge the centrality of the Sovereignty of Jesus Christ, as basic to all relationships. Our links with the Apostolic Faith through Scripture, Tradition,

Experience, and Reason lead us now solemnly to affirm to each other that "all who are baptized into Christ are members of Christ's ministry through the people of the One God, Father, Son and the Holy Spirit." (Commission on Christian Unity Digest, 1974, p.335; Official Record, XII, 1974).

COVENANT:

(a) We, therefore, recognize our respective baptisms as different facets of the one baptism and mutually recognize the members of The Methodist Church, Ghana and those of the United Methodist Church are members one of the other.

(b) We, therefore, recognize each other as authentic expression of the One, Holy, Catholic, and Apostolic Church of Jesus Christ.

(c) We, therefore, recognize the ordained ministries of our churches and pledge our mutual efforts at effecting forms of reconciliation of those ministries, including the exchange or transfer of ordained ministers between properly constituted bodies where the approval and consent of the appropriate authorities involved is given. The assumption of pastoral care of members visiting or residing in each other's countries is another instance of this aspect of the act of Covenanting.

(d) We are committed to a systematic participation in full Eucharistic fellowship as a symbol of transcendence over manifestation of human divisions.

(e) We expect that the various agencies of our two churches will function in new ways of partnership in mission and evangelism, in education and implementation of the Gospel. Mutual sharing of principles and methods can improve our functioning in our separate contexts and especially in continuance of new developments of joint projects in mission between The Methodist Church, Ghana and the United Methodist Church.

(f) We expect that an expanded and focused international linkage of visitations and partnerships will take place. The bishops or presidents of the church will arrange for mutually agreeable visitations and exchanges that will provide contact with and some knowledge of the social, political, economic, moral, and religious contexts in which the people of the world struggle for existence, meaning, and purpose. Mutual visitations may include occasional presence at each other's assemblies.

(g) External partnerships might be possible between, for example a covenanting church or its part and a particular congregation, Annual Conference or Episcopal Area of the United Methodist Church. Such participation in this covenant will be by special action subsequent to adoption of the covenant. Such an extended partnership, perhaps in consultation with specific United Methodist agencies as well, might be for a defined period to enable a mutual flow of persons, interest, and commitment. The partnership can be extended or ended by mutual agreement. Such extended partnerships will make palpable the global stake we have in each other in various parts of the world. These focused partnerships will be integrated with visitations by leaders, and the sharing by agencies of time, ability, and funding resources.

(h) Our covenant assumes the continuing independence and autonomy of the covenanting churches in their structure, traditions, styles of implementation of ministry, existing partnerships, agreements and explorations, forms of worship, and program. But we look forward to knowing each other in love, to losing our fear of difference and our fear of differences for the same, of more effective participation in the mission of God's church. We make bold to anticipate that out of our experience we will be led by the spirit to new forms of covenant and to new relationships for the global Christian community.

(i) A brief liturgical celebration of the Act of Covenant shall be prepared by representatives of the two churches and shall be celebrated at the chief legislative bodies of both covenanting churches.

NOW THEREFORE, BE IT RESOLVED, that the undersigned do hereby covenant and agree to the ACT OF COVENANT as heretofore set forth, and hereunto set their hands and seals for and on behalf of their respective churches the day and year of our Lord set after their names.

THE UNITED METHODIST CHURCH
By:

President, Council of Bishops

Joseph H. Yeakel
(Name Printed)

DATE 11 May 1992

Carolyn M. Marshall
Secretary, General Conference

DATE 11 May 1992

THE METHODIST CHURCH, GHANA
By:

President of Conference

Rt. Rev. Prof. Kwesi Abotsia Dickson
(Name Printed)

DATE 4 October 1990

Dr. Ebenezer Henry Brew Riverson
Secretary, General Conference

DATE 4 October 1990

SOURCE: MCG Conference Representative Agenda (2000).

APPENDIX I

Proclamation Presented to
THE METHODIST CHURCH, GHANA
Through
The Rt. Reverend Dr. Samuel Asante-Antwi, B.A., M.A.
The President of Conference
By
THE PEOPLE OF LARTEH, AKUAPEM-GUAN, EASTERN REGION

Whereas the Central Government has always been the sole provider of university education; and

Whereas His Excellency Flt. Lt. Jerry John Rawlings, The President of the Republic of Ghana, and his Government, are to be commended for the exceptional strides they have made in the practice of constitutional democracy, and in the transformation of the structures of society, particularly in the field of education; and

Whereas quantitative projections indicate that without the development of at least four more universities within the next two to four years, only 5% of the nation's secondary school graduates will be able to gain access to university education by the year 2005; and

Whereas the urgency of the situation has prompted the Government to sound a clarion call to philanthropists and non-governmental organizations to pitch in by endowing the existing five universities and/or by founding new ones; and

Whereas The Methodist Church, Ghana has thoughtfully resolved to establish an accredited five campus university in response to the Government's call, and in keeping with the spirit of the Great Commission of Matthew 28 verses 19-20; and

Whereas the Methodist Church, Ghana is nationally respected for its rock solid accomplishments in the building and management of excellent first, second, and third cycle institutions, and other widely known centres for teaching, and learning, including Mfantsipim, Wesley Girls, Wesley College, Komenda, Wesley Grammar, Offinso, Osei Tutu, Breman, and Wenchi, as well as Juaben, Mmofraturo, Methodist High, Mamfe and Methodist Agricultural Secondary/Technical, Oyoko, Kwadaso, and the School for the Blind at Wa; and

Whereas it is a well-known fact that The Methodist Church, Ghana is a major national ecclesial body with an eminently good, if not a unique, "can-do-spirit" and

Whereas it is largely this very aspect of the Methodist heritage—the can-do-spirit—that moulded scores of luminaries such as Professor John Atta Mills, the outstandingly well-qualified Vice-President of President Rawlings' world-renowned N.D.C. Government; Dr. Kofi Annan, the Secretary General of the United Nations (U.N.); The Reverend Dr. John K. Agbeti, the first Ghanaian Methodist Minister to earn a doctorate; Professor Florence Dolphyne, formerly Pro-Vice Chancellor of the University of Ghana; Mr. S.C. Appenteng, a noted industrialist; Professor Dr. Amba Ewudziwa, [Mercy Oduyoye] an internationally respected Systematic Theologian and formerly Deputy General Secretary of the World Council of Churches; Dr. Kofi Abrefa Busia, a former don of Oxford University and the Prime Minister of Ghana's Second Parliament; and

Whereas these luminaries include, but are not limited to Dr. Alex Quayson Sackey, a one-time President of the Security Council of the U.N.; The Honourable Solomon K. Sarfo, an Engineer of the highest rank and an N.P.P. Member of Parliament; Mrs. Rose Coker, an accomplished College Principal, Ministry of Education; The Reverend Dr. S. G. Nimako, the first citizen of New Juaben to earn a doctoral degree, and one of Ghana's pioneer ambassadors during the first Parliament of Osagyefo Dr. Kwame Nkrumah's Government; Dr. E. M. Debrah, a retired Senior Ambassador, and an international civil servant; Mr. Timothy Ewudzi Osam-Duodu, the Vice President of the Methodist Conference, and a graduate of Massachusetts Institute of Technology (M.I.T.), one of the world's most respected universities and finally, The Reverend Dr. Francis C. F. Grant, a truehearted man of the cloth, the first President of the Methodist Church Ghana, and a scholar in his own right; and

Whereas his performance to date, and reasoned prognostications, indicate that The Reverend Dr. Samuel Asante Antwi will steadily continue to give new life to Ghana Methodism, and also will continue to distinguish himself both on the domestic and international scene as an upstanding ecclesiastic, an unassuming scholar, and a man of ideas and action, who clearly knows how to make things happen; and

Whereas the town of Letteh (Larteh) has contributed significantly to the growth of Ghanaian civilization by producing more than its share of educators, intellectuals, and ministers, public officials; and other reliable professional women and men of character, who have given and continue to give themselves unselfishly to the service of the church and society; and

Whereas the Methodist Church and school at Larteh are counted among premier Methodist schools and churches in the nation; and

Whereas the weather, the lush greeneries, and the beautiful mountains of Larteh are so refreshingly conducive to the processes of serious concentration such as teaching, research, and learning; and

Whereas the Larteh campus of the University will serve as the Headquarters of the administrative centre for the various campuses; and

Whereas the overall University has been designed to ultimately function as a world-class centre of intellectual excellence with a specific philosophical orientation, including the inculcation of ethical-moral values, and the provision of technical, professional, and entrepreneurial skills and techniques; and

Whereas the establishment of such a top-notch diversified educational institution augurs well for the enrichment of the quality of life in the Larteh area; and

Whereas the central traditional authoritative body of the Akuapem Guanman is handing over momentarily to The Reverend President—without conditions and without demur, and at no cost to the Church—approximately two-square miles (3218.688 meters) of prime mountaintop landscape for the development of the University; and

Whereas the people of Larteh and their friends have resolved to maintain a doxological attitude by always praising God, from whom all blessings flow, for the singular honour done them by The Methodist Church, Ghana;

Now, therefore, in appreciation of the overall educational program of the Ghana Government, in the interest of Higher and Relevant Education, and in honour of The Church Universal, particularly the distinctive paradigm called the Methodist Church; and on behalf of the entire Akuapem Guanman, I do hereby proclaim today, Saturday, the Tenth Day of July, AD 1999 as Ghana Methodist University Day at Lartch, and urge all Letteh-esse (Larterians) and their well-wishers to individually and jointly celebrate this day every year; and also respectfully ask The Methodist Church, Ghana to enter this date in its connexional calendar and in other appropriate yearly publications.

Signed By
Osabarima Asiedu Okoo Ababio III
Akuapem Guanmanhene

Attested By

The Reverend Dr. K. Ohene-Bekoe, B.D., M.A. (Pol Sc.), M.Th, D.Min.
Public Theologian & Methodist Minister, University Contact Person at Larteh,
Senior Minister Emeritus of The International Church of The Metroplex,
Ex-President & Chief Executive Officer, The International Center, Dallas, Texas, USA.

SOURCE: MCG Conference Representative Agenda (2000).

APPENDIX J

PASTORAL LETTER FROM THE PRESIDENT OF THE CONFERENCE, 12TH FEBRUARY, 1998

Grace to you and Peace from our Lord and Saviour Jesus Christ.

A recent publication in the *Daily Graphic* on Friday, 6th February, 1998, No. 14667 about the resignation of the Secretary of Conference has caused a great stir in the minds of the general membership of our Church, The Methodist Church, Ghana.

The questions people have raised since the said publication, include whether or not there is "a feud rocking the Methodist Church," as alleged by the *Daily Graphic*; whether or not the Secretary of Conference has indeed resigned and if he has resigned, what is the church doing about it?

As the President of Conference, I wish to respond to these concerns by means of this pastoral letter.

1. Is there a feud rocking the Methodist Church as alleged by the *Daily Graphic*?

I wish to assure you all there is no feud or crisis in the Methodist Church, Ghana at the moment. As you are all aware, the 36the Annual Conference held at Cape Coast confirmed my designation as President of Conference and that of the Rev. Maclean A. Kumi as the Secretary of Conference. Since then, the two of us have worked harmoniously until now. There has never been an occasion when the two of us have exchanged words or disagreed strongly on any issue. Therefore the impression given by the publication in the *Daily Graphic* that there is a feud between the two of us is unfounded and very regrettable. While we affirm our commitment to the freedom of the press (and we shall continue to pray for them) it is our wish that our members will not be led astray by its sensationalism.

2. Has the Secretary of Conference resigned and if so what is the Church doing about it?

By a letter dated 3rd February, 1998, addressed to the General Purposes Council, the Secretary tended in his resignation on personal grounds with immediate effect. An emergency meeting of the General Purposes Council was subsequently called on Wednesday, 11th February, 1998 to meet the Secretary of Conference and to respond to his letter of resignation. At this meeting, the Secretary was given the opportunity to either withdraw or to confirm his letter of resignation and he chose not to withdraw but to confirm it. After further deliberation on the issue, the General Purposes Council painfully accepted the letter of resignation effective March 1998 GPC meeting. The GPC also took due note of the Secretary's dedicated services to the Church in his capacity as Secretary of Conference with much appreciation and wished him all the best in the new area that he will be serving the Church.

In the meantime, the Assistant Secretary, the Rev. Albert Ofoe Wright has been authorised by the GPC to take over from the Secretary who has resigned, as the Acting Secretary until a substantive Secretary is appointed.

As your President of Conference, I wish to assure you that we will not do anything unconstitutional that will jeopardise the good image and the peace and unity of The Methodist Church, Ghana. The Church as the mission of God on earth must continue to bear witness to the saving grace of God through our Lord Jesus Christ through all the changing scenes of life.

To this end, we implore all of you to remain prayerful, faithful to the Church, steadfast in your commitment to the Lord and not to be distressed by any speculative publication or media sensationalism.

Finally "be careful—watch out for attacks from Satan, your great enemy. He prowls around like a hungry, roaring lion, looking for some victim to tear apart. Stand firm when he attacks. Trust the Lord; and remember that other Christians all around the world are going through these sufferings too." (I Peter 5:8-9)

May God bless you all.

(Rt. Rev. Dr. Samuel Asante-Antwi)
12th February, 1998

APPENDIX K

Ebibindwom—The Bible in Song[1]

While *ebibindwom* lyrics span the whole gamut of scripture, the vast majority have to do with Jesus' Passion. The events of Palm Sunday through Easter account for almost half of the lyrics that I identified in my research. This emphasis agrees with the central theme of Christianity, but it is also the case that there is strong resonance here with the central place that death plays in the life of the typical Ghanaian.

It will be seen in the following lyrics below that most are the Bible in song format and need little interpretation or adaptation. In Ghanaian culture, where story-telling is a significant aspect of the informal educational process, *ebibindwom* lyrics become for illiterate Methodists the source of Bible knowledge and a means for recalling outstanding sermons on these subjects.

Palm Sunday

1

Hosanna e, Oreba o,	Hosanna, He is coming
Onam Ewuradze dzin mu o,	He comes in the Lord's name
Hosanna e, Oreba o,	Hosanna, He is coming
Onam Ewuradze dzin mu.	He comes in the Lord's name
Nkenkanee	*Cantor*
(a) Ohen Jesus oroko	King Jesus goes to the
Jerusalem afahye no ase	Jerusalem festival
Womfa merenkonson	Follow Him with
ndzi N'ekyir o	palm branches

1 See Samuel B. Essamuah (1965), the translations are by Casely B. Essamuah.

(b) Osiarfo Jesus oroko
Jerusalem Afahye no ase
Wombubu ndubaa
ndzi N'ekyir

Blessed Jesus goes to the
Jerusalem festival
Follow Him with
palm branches

(c) Agyenkwa Jesus oroko
Jerusalem Afahye,
Womfa adwontow
ndze N'ekyir

Savior Jesus goes to the
Jerusalem festival
Follow Him with
praise-songs

(d) Hen Hen Jesus,
Orupue ne Hen nde
Womfa mberenkonsun
Nhyia No o

Our King Jesus outdoors His
kingship today
Greet Him with
palm branches

2

Dede pii yi ase nye den,
Emidze metse Kwan nkyen
Reseresere adze

Why this commotion?
I am a blind man sitting by the
wayside, begging

Nkenkanee
Oye nokwar e,
Meye ofurafo
Tse Kwan nkyen
Reseresere adze o.

Cantor
It is true
I am a blind man
by the way side begging

Good Friday and Passion Week (Amandzehu dapen nye Fida Pa)

1

Ma onye ntsem,
Fa sekan no hye boha no mu,
Peter e

Hasten
Put the sword in its sheath
Peter

Ma onye ntsem,
Fa sekan no hye boha no mu,
Mo nua e

Hasten
Put the sword in its sheath
My brother (or sister)

Nkenkanee
Mo nuanom,
Afei awerehow dodow nye de
Aber a wokyir No n'
Wohyee ase boboo no asotor

Cantor
My brothers and sisters
Sadly
When they came for him
Some started slapping him

Wobinom boboo no mpotsibaa	Some lashed him with whips
Ho ara naa Peter oyee no awerehow	Then Peter was saddened and angered
Ma Otwee sekan wo no boha mu	He removed the sword from its sheath and
Twaa ambrado-panyin akowaa n'asowa	slashed the servant's ears off
Ma otoo daadze	till it fell to the ground
Ewuradze Jesus kaa kyere Peter de	Lord Jesus said to Peter
'Mma nnye dem,	Do not do that
Hon a wotwe asekan na	Those who use the sword on others
Wobowu asekan ano	get killed by the sword
2	
Bogya dehye mennkeka megu,	I will not spill royal blood
Bogya dehye menkedzi ho so	I will not be responsible for spilling royal blood
Nkenkanee	*Cantor*
Ambrado Pilate oahohor ne nsaha o	Governor Pilate has washed his hands
3	
Bon ben na Oaye na munku	What sin has He committed
No mema hom yi?	That I should crucify Him for you?
Nkenkanee	*Cantor*
M'Egya Nyame	My heavenly Father
Oama akatafo abo esu	He cleanses lepers
Ohen nye Nyame	God is King
Oama eyifo aserew	He makes mourners rejoice
4	
Wobema me eben,	What would you pay me
ma minyi Agyenkwa maa hom?	For betraying the Savior to you?
Judas ribisa o?	Judas is asking
Nkenkanee	*Cantor*
Na iyi na Jewfo mpanyimfo nye	Then the Jewish leaders
No dzii ano	bargained with him and
Obaa dwetebona eduasa	it came to thirty pieces of silver
Wotuaa no kaw.	They paid him
Wodze ekitsa ne nsamu	They have given it to him

Wokaa kyere Judas de
Yetua wo kaw, ibesi den ma nsa aaka No?

They then asked Judas
We have paid you, how can we get hold of Him?

5

Sua da, onye ko da nnse,

Konyim fir Nyame,
Sua da, onye ko da nnse

Day of promise is different from day of fulfillment
Victory comes from God
Day of promise is different from day
Of fulfillment

Nkenkanee
Iyi na nkyii abanyimbasiaba bi baa bio,
Ber yi nna adze rekye koraa
Ohwee Peter n'enyim dzinn
N'asem nye de:
'Obarimba yi a ogyina
guamu na worotoatoa
No yi, eka Noho,
Peter kaa ntam de onnyim No
Ho ara na akoko bonee
Nkyii na enyim retsewtsew koraa
Jesus dan N'enyiwa hwee Peter de otse ho,
Onye N'enyiwa yee anan
Mewuo, afei naa Peter oakaa
Ebei Peter, Ebei Peter,
Sua da, onye ko da nnse.

Cantor
Then a young man appeared
When it was getting to dawn
Gazing quietly at Peter's face
He said:
You are one of those who belong
to this man suffering persecution in public
Peter vowed that he never knew him
Immediately the cock crew
Then it was dawn
Jesus turned and looked at Peter
Jesus had eye-to-eye contact with Peter
(Gee), then Peter remembered
Oh Peter, Oh Peter
Day of promise is different from
Day of fulfillment

6

Eguambaa Siarfo e,
Wo bogyaa agye hen nkwa o

Blessed Lamb
Your blood has saved me

Nkenkanee
Odzebonyeyi nana nye me,
Obusuanyi
Adam na Eve nana nye me
Owerehonyi a
Wo bogyaa no ahor me oe

Cantor
I am a child of sinful people
I am a wretched sinner
I am a child of Adam and Eve
Miserable man, Without any hope
Your blood has cleansed me

7

Hom nsan no
Na womfa no mbre Me
Wobisa hom a hom nse de
Ewuradze wo no ho hia e

Untie it
And bring it to me
When questioned answer that
The Lord needs it

Nkenkanee
Aber no Jesus rukopue
Ne hen wo Jerusalem no o
Osomaa esuafo beenu bi de
Hom nko ekuraba a
Oda hom enyim no mu
Hom bohu asoasaba a
Obi ntsenaa do da
Hom nsan no mbra
Se wobisa hom a,
Hom nka de
Ewuradze wo no ho hia o

Cantor
When Jesus was inaugurating his
kingship in Jerusalem
He sent two of his disciples
to a nearby village
ahead of them
You will find a donkey
which has never been ridden
Untie it and bring it to me
When questioned
You should answer that
The Lord needs it

8

Egya fakye hon,
Wonnyim dza woreye
Wonnyim dza woreye

Father forgive them
For they do not know [understand]
What they're doing [to me] *repeat*

Nkenkanee
Wonnyim dza woreye
Bon ahye hon ma
Wonnyim dza woreye
Enyitan ahye hon ma
Wonnyim dza woreye
Akohwi ahye hon ma
Wonnyim dza woreye
Ebufuw ahye hon ma

Cantor
They don't know what they're doing
They are full of sin
They don't know what they're doing
They are full of envy
They don't know what they're doing
They are full of deceit
They don't know what they're doing
they are full of anger

Eastertide (Wusoer)

1

Onnyi ha, Oasoer o, Kyerewsem reka—
Woboo no mbeamudua mu,
Oasoer efi ewufo m'

He is not here, he is risen—
He was crucified
He is risen from the dead

Nkenkanee
Mary, Owerehonyi, oye den na
'rohwehe Tseasefo wo ewufo mu yi?

Cantor
Mournful Mary, why do you
Look for the Living among the dead?

Onyame N'asomfo, woye no den na
Hom 'rohwehe Gyefo wo ewufo mu yi?

God's worshippers, why do you
Look for the Savior among the dead?

2
Mma mmfa woho nnka
Medze Moho rekekyere M'Egya

Do not touch Me?
I am going to see my Father

Nkenkanee
Nyame a Osomaa Me no,
Onnhun Me o
M'Egya a Osomaa Me no
Medze Moho rekekyere No

Cantor
God Who sent me
Has not seen me
God Who sent me
I am going to see Him

Whitsuntide (Sunsum Kronkron)

1
Yeregye wo sunsum
Yedze aye edwuma

We await your Spirit
To enable us to work

Nkenkanee
Noah a opaam hen
David a odzii ako
Stephen a ogyee abo
Paul a okaa asem
Na wo sunsum
Na odze no paa
Na wo sunsum
Na odze no dzi
Na wo sunsum
Na odze no gye
Na wo sunsum
Na odze no ka

Cantor
It enabled Noah to build an ark
It enabled David to fight
It enabled Stephen to endure stoning.
It enabled Paul to preach
It is Your spirit
Who enabled him to build
It is Your Spirit
Who enabled him to fight
It is your Spirit
Who enabled him to receive
It is your Spirit
Who enabled him to preach

Praise (Ntonton nye Ayeyi)

1

Ewuradzee,	Lord
Agyenkwa,	Savior
Otu apo e	
Ao Agyenkwa, Ao Agyenkwa	O Savior, O Savior
Yegya Wo ekyir a, onnye o	If we leave you we perish
Nkenkanee	*Cantor*
Hen Wura, Onye hen nam	Our Lord walks with us
Enye hen nam a,	You Lord walk with us
Abonsam nnkotum esi hen enyim	The devil cannot stand us
Osian hen ntsi,	Because of us
Obeseen mbeamudua no do yi	He hung on the tree
Ope hen nkwa,	he desires us to have life
Ommpe hen Wu mprenu	And not die two times
Gye no dzi,	Believe/Trust in him
Obema sunsum abehye hen ma	He'll send his Spirit to fill us
Twe w'afowa, Osabarimba	Unsheath your sword, great warrior
Twe w'afowa ma dom yi ngu	Unsheath your sword to defeat this opposition

Christian Experience, Hope and Endeavor
(Christian Bra, Enyidado nye Mbodzenbo)

1

Menye kronkron rekasa o	I speak with the Holy One
Emi a menye kronkron rekasa	Even I speak with the Holy One
Adam detse na nso besiaba	1, Adam's dust and yet
Emi a menye knronkron rekasa o	I speak with the Holy One
Nkenkanee	*Cantor*
Ewuradze Nyankopon	Lord God,
Kronkron, Kronkron, Kronkron,	Holy, Holy, Holy,
Kronkron hen o! Onyame a	O Holy God, O God
Oama onnse bi mase bi e	Who has made the insignificant significant
Oama Emi dem yi	Even I
Menye Kronkron rekasa o	I speak with the Holy One
Menye kronkron rekasa	I speak with the Holy One

New Testament Parables (Ahyemu Fofor mu Mbe bi)

1

Dua bi onnsow aba,	The tree has no fruit
Wontwa nkyen	Cut it down
Woyee no den	How come it has
Na woasow ebun twerede yi?	No fruit
Nkenkanee	*Cantor*
Jesus kor ase	When Jesus went there
Woanya biribi wo do o	He didn't find any fruit
Hen so yebeye den	What shall we do
Na yeasow aba	To produce fruit?
John na Peter, wosoow aba	John and Peter—they produced fruit
Mary na Martha wosoow aba	Mary and Martha—they produced fruit

2

Okuafo no opee	The Sower went to sow
aba oafona no ho	his seed in the land
Okwan nkyen aba nye yi	Some fell on the wayside
Mfaso biara nnyi ho	They brought no profit
No ndwow no sisi abotan do	The roots were on rocks
Asaase pa mu aba	The seed that fell on good soil
Na mfaso wo ho	That was profitable

Life Hereafter (Owu Ekyir Nkwa)

Se yesom yie a obefa hen aketsena	If we worship aright,
Onyame man mu afeboo	we will be taken to God's land
	to live forever.
Onyame man mu afeboo, afeboo,	God's land forever and ever
Ndaamba yebehiya mu o	One day we will meet
Onyame man mu afeboo	In God's land for ever
Nkenkanee	*Cantor*
Se yetum som a	If we worship aright
Ndaamba yebehyia mu	One day we will meet
Onyame man mu afeboo	In God's land for ever

NOTES

Introduction

1. For example, G.W. Johnson Bond, writing of mission churches, asserts, "These preserve essentially the same form and content in Africa that they have in Europe" (Bond 1979).
2. The fact that the missionized ultimately were able to separate Christianity from the culture of the missionaries, embracing Christ without denying their own culture, shows an element of local agency that is usually missing in this debate.
3. The Methodist Church Ghana is a British Methodist-instituted denomination in Ghana. It is distinguished from the Ghana branch of the African Methodist Episcopal and African Methodist Episcopal Zion churches, both of which are still under the jurisdiction of their American churches. The Evangelical Methodist Church, an offshoot of the MCG is discussed in chapter 6.
4. The British established the Gold Coast Colony after the defeat of the Asante in the Anglo-Asante War of 1873–1874. (This conflict was known locally as "Sagrenti War," after the commander of the English forces, Sir Garnet Wolseley, a conflation of his title and name.) The colony covered the broad expanse between the Asante kingdom and the Atlantic Ocean. For administrative purposes it was divided into two spheres: the colony and the protectorate, the colony being the coastal enclave which had had contact with Europeans since the fifteenth century, and the protectorate being the interior region between the coastal belt and Asante (Boahen in Ajayi and Crowder 1973, 167–205).
5. AICs are churches founded in Africa by Africans and primarily for Africans. Typically, they do not have any formal connection with churches in the West, even though some of them are now establishing branches in the Western world for the benefit of African immigrants. AICs are also called African Independent Churches or African Indigenous Churches. In this study I use the term African Initiated Churches. For a useful work on the various typologies, see Harold Turner 1967.
6. Elaborating this point, Dana Robert argues that scholars have assumed that "historic mission churches were mere clones of their western founders. Studies of mission initiatives within mainline churches focused on how Christians in mission churches left them to start independent movements or else were forced

out by colonialists and European traditionalists. The flowering of AIC studies has left historians of historic mission churches in a defensive posture, caught between the need to decolonize mission history on the one hand, and to defend themselves against charges of inauthenticity vis-à-vis AICs on the other" (Robert 2003, 5). In a similar affirmation of mainline churches, Obeng adds, "It is not only the independent churches that have taken the initiative to foster the incarnation of the Christian message" (Obeng 1996, 6).

7. See, for example, John Baur's discussion on the crisis in the Democratic Republic of Congo (formerly Zaire) between the government and the Catholic Church on the issue of Africanness and authenticity. For the philosophical discussions, see Jacob Golomb's analysis of the notions of authenticity offered by Kierkegaard and others (Golomb 1995).
8. As a noun, Akan is both singular and plural.
9. "If You Are a Devil, You Are a Witch and, If You Are a Witch, You Are a Devil" (Meyer 1992). A more in-depth treatment appears in her book *Translating the Devil: Religion and Modernity among the Ewe in Ghana* (1999).

CHAPTER ONE | Foundations of Ghana Methodism

10. The literal meaning of Nananom Mpow is "ancestral grove." Some scholars, including Thomas C. McCaskie, use the form Nanaam Mpow, a colloquial spelling. I will use Nananom Mpow unless citing sources that use the colloquial form.
11. In the text I am using Andrew F. Walls's spelling of Samson Oppong in the Biographical Dictionary of Christian Missions (BDCM). In citations, where the spelling sometimes varies, I will retain the spelling found in the original sources.
12. Technically, the country of Ghana came into being on March 6, 1957. Its immediate predecessor, the Gold Coast, was a combination of three separate territories under British colonial rule, namely, the Colony, Asante, and the Northern Territories. The British called the three areas as a group Gold Coast. For the sake of consistency in this study, I will use "Ghana" and "Ghanaian" retrospectively throughout all the different phases of its history. The Gold Coast, Asante, and the Northern Territories will be used when needed in specific instances. In the past, most authors used "Ashanti" when referring to the Asante kingdom, region or people. In this book, I will use Asante, the more accurate terminology for all three.
13. There is ample evidence to suggest that Europeans on the coast intentionally frustrated the efforts of the Ghanaians who had become Christian ministers. Isaac Tufuoh refers to one such incident when he records that the governor used every conceivable excuse to cancel church services in the castle during Quaque's time. See "Relations between Christian Missions, European Administrations, and Traders in the Gold Coast, 1828–74" (Tufuoh 1968, 34–58). Tufuoh concludes, "A constant source of frustration for those who had attempted evangelization in these parts before the Wesleyans had been the indifference, sometimes hostility, displayed by the merchants toward an activity

which all too often stood as a silent reproach to their manner of life" (55).

14. "Cape Coast" is an English corruption of the Portuguese Cabo Corso, meaning, "short cape." It was a name given in the mid-fifteenth century to the rocky promontory on which two centuries later a trading post was built (Hinderink and Sterkenburg 1975, 29).
15. Though the culpability of Africans in the slave trade is still a hotly debated issue in African and African-American studies in the United States, there is no gainsaying the fact that the slave trade was aided and abetted by the Africans who sold their fellow Africans, usually of a different ethnic group who were taken captive as a result of warfare and raids. In recent years, Henry Louis Gates Jr., of Harvard University, has accused Africans of committing a Holocaust-type crime by selling other blacks to whites. See his documentary series *The Wonders of the African World*, and in particular, "Slave Kingdoms, Episode 2, Elmina Slave Fortress." This series engendered such a robust rebuttal, especially from African intellectuals in the Diaspora that Lansine Kaba's 2000 presidential address to the African Studies Association was devoted to the subject. In the rebuttal, Kaba suggests that perhaps Gates allows the personal circumstances of his family's ordeal to overwhelm him so that he pays scant attention to the European initiation and participation in the slave trade. Kaba admits that the African elite participated in, and benefited from, the slave trade, but he rejects any assertion of an equal culpability between white slave traders and black middlemen. He writes, "Unlike the investors, the insurers, the shipbuilders, the dealers, and especially the mariners from abroad, the local African providers had little knowledge of the whole Atlantic system. Moreover at a time when Africa was lagging technologically behind Europe, the slave trade, with its capital intensive nature, could function only with the advanced technology then available in the West." Additionally, Kaba argues that to equate the trans-Atlantic slave trade with the Holocaust is to infer that the African participants had a program to annihilate neighboring tribes, in this case, captives from raids and prisoners of wars, when, in fact, they bartered slaves for guns in order to survive the onslaught of European firearms. This last point of the need by Africans to favorably compete in the militarization of the period is given credence by Basil Davidson: "Huge quantities of firearms were poured into West Africa during the period of the slave trade, and the state of Dahomey, increasingly a militarized autocracy, was among those that had the doubtful benefit. At the height of the eighteenth-century commerce, gunsmiths in Birmingham alone were exporting muskets to Africa at a rate of between 100,000 and 150,000 a year and it was common talk that one Birmingham gun rated one Negro slave. This last was Birmingham sales talk rather than a statement of fact . . . yet the spirit of the saying was true enough." (Davidson 1980, 242)
16. Isichei's statement, though helpful, rather obscures the fact that the slave trade and the arrival of Methodism in Ghana falls outside the traditional definition of Middle Ages being 500–1500 A.D.
17. William Wilberforce derived his inspiration for his abolitionist views from John Wesley, in particular from his letter of February 1791 (Cormack 1983, 70).

18. Without in any way diminishing the influence wielded by Wilberforce and other activists, one needs to acknowledge that the slave economy of the southern American plantation was no economic match for the fast growing age of machine technology (Fyfe 1985, 30–57).
19. In its barrier-breaking, women-empowering, unmediated and expressive spirituality, and explosive global spread, Methodism of the nineteenth century interestingly set the pattern for Pentecostalism of the last decades of the twentieth century (Hollenweger 1972; Cox 1995; especially Martin 2002, 7–9).
20. I will be using the form "de Graft" in line with Walls in BDCM, but when citing others I will keep their rendition intact.
21. Kwame Bediako states that MCG is a church begun by Africans who read the Bible and felt they needed more Bibles. The founders are not Joseph Dunwell and the Methodist Mission in Britain, great people that they were. The beginning, the foundation of MCG, was de Graft and friends in Cape Coast. It is an African church. It is very much an educated, a learned people's church. The founders of Mfantsipim [MCG's leading educational institution], as well as Mensah Sarbah, Gaddiel Acquaah, and all these—they were authentically African, but Africans who were global. As early as the eighteenth century, they were global people. And therefore, to be African does not mean ethnic, provincial, or racial. We [Akan] have no words for race—black race, white race, etc. To be African is to be global. (Interview with author January 17, 2000).
22. Arthur C. Southon compares this Bible Band to the one that the Wesley brothers had at Oxford. He notes, "Wesley and his companions were striving to find fellowship with God and personal holiness in an age of religious indifference and much open evil living. De Graft and his friends sought precisely the same ends in all the darkness of superstition and savage cruelty of vicious Europeans and fierce Ashantis . . . They followed a prepared course of reading, and entered in a book a 'minute' of each day's proceedings in a manner wholly foreign to Africa at that period. The first 'minute' reveals their high purpose, and gives a vivid picture of these remarkable African youths" (Southon 1935, 27).
23. It is possible that Southon is romanticizing an inquirer's movement into an advanced hermeneutics class. To credit them with "breaking with all their inherited beliefs and customs," is to devalue what must have been their innate educational principle of learning from the known to the unknown.
24. The phenomenon of name-change is as ancient as biblical literature. Abraham, father of the three Fertile Crescent's monotheistic religions, Judaism, Christianity, and Islam, had a name-change in Genesis 17:5 to indicate his new covenant-relationship with Yahweh. A New Testament example is the disciple Simon, who was renamed Cephas or Peter by Jesus reflecting Jesus' statement in Matthew 16:18 that his church would be built on the rock of Peter and his confession.
25. John Petersen makes a similar argument when he cautions against a wholesale labeling of nineteenth-century Creole society in Sierra Leone as a "mirror image of that upper class life led by the successful oligarchy" (Petersen 1968, 101–126).

26. Was MCG indigenously rooted by accident or design? Although the "accidental" factor might appear to be obvious, one cannot but be impressed by the fact that the local Fante were equal to the task of sustaining their Christian faith and initiating growth and expansion. Thus, it can be argued that the enterprise was intentionally designed to be indigenous. At the same time, it cannot be said that the Fante became Methodists by design, since the Bible band had not heard of the Methodists prior to de Graft's contact with Potter. If Captain Potter himself had not had Methodist sympathies, the Fante Bible band would in all likelihood have associated with the Church Missionary Society or the SPG, thus making the church Anglican.
27. In Methodist parlance a "local preacher" is a layperson licensed to preach within a circuit, but not ordained to administer the sacraments.
28. George Wrigley's singular achievement is recorded by Francis L. Bartels thus: "He made history when after only eight months in the country; he read the Ten Commandments in Fante on Sunday 28 May, preached in Fante on 20 August and used Fante for baptism on 3 September 1837" (Bartels 1965, 22).
29. Regrettably not unlike many histories of the age, the first name of Mrs. Harrop is not found in any of the sources.
30. It is remarkable to note that while fifteen missionaries died between 1834 and 1844, no missionaries died in the following twenty-four years. No great discoveries had then been made in tropical medicine or hygiene to explain this phenomenon. During the following fifty years, forty more expatriate missionaries were sent to Ghana. And yet, MCG grew faster during the first decade than at any other time. Southon offers many possibilities for understanding this occurrence, but it seems that MCG grew best when the indigenous leaders had limited recourse to an expatriate staff. Had the ratio between the expatriate and national staffs been more balanced from the outset, the local people might have associated Methodism with the foreigners and not with their own kith and kin (Southon 1934, 81-82).
31. The Basel Mission, operating northeast of Cape Coast, in the Accra and Akwapim areas of Ghana, had experimented with sending missionaries from the West Indies, where the climate was similar to that of coastal Ghana, and yet they had not fared any better (Williamson 1965, 3–16).
32. Harrison M. Wright writes that Thomas Birch Freeman displayed considerable sympathy and understanding toward his African brethren. Even though Freeman disliked many African ways, he was always amiable and outgoing in his personal relationships (Freeman 1968, xxiv–xxvi). In *Freeman's Journal of Various Visits to the Kingdoms of Ashanti, Aku, and Dahomi in Western Africa*, he often cites the collaboration and assistance he received from Africans. "Had not the people exerted themselves exceedingly, it could not have been so forward; but I am glad to say they assisted nobly, both in labour and contributions" (74).
33. The fact that Joseph Smith accompanied the Freemans in coming to Cape Coast highlights the initiative of the local leadership and points to the indigenous role in the growth of MCG.

34. The quarterly meeting is the highest decision-making body of a number of Methodist societies grouped as a circuit.
35. One of the most significant results of Joseph Rhodes Dunwell's short ministry was the reconciliation of the two Bible bands; at this time de Graft and his group were part of the Cape Coast group.
36. The Watchnight service is usually held on the last night of the year. It features several sermons, musical pieces, testimonies, and prayers.
37. It is possible that this mass wedding ceremony was to reduce costs as well as to Christianize this all important social contract.
38. This was a British practice. In the nineteenth century, such meetings were held in places such as Exeter Hall on the anniversary of charities.
39. The fact that the king presided over Christian worship in his palace calls into question some of the fearful tales of Asante cruelty. From a missiological standpoint, it is obvious that the Asante mission followed a top-down approach with royal sponsorship as a key feature.
40. Freeman's visit captured the attention of the political establishment as well. N. Allen Birtwhistle records that the Select Committee of the House of Commons in session in 1842, receiving reports relative to West Africa, stated, "We would here acknowledge the great services rendered to religion and civilization on this coast by the Wesleyan body; they have even established a friendly communication with the barbarous court of the Ashantee; which promises results important in every way; and, indeed, little in the way of instruction would have been done without them" (Birtwhistle 1983, 62).
41. Freeman seems to have overspent his budget not in careless extravagance but with an unflinching determination not to limit God's work. According to Birtwhistle, Freeman's passion for the spread of the gospel made him unmindful of "what the world calls the main thing in these matters" (Birtwhistle 1960, 100). WMMS sent men, William West to be the financial secretary on the Gold Coast, and Daniel West to report on the state of the work. Unfortunately, Daniel died before reaching home. In the meantime, he had sent ahead a report, which states inter alia, "God has, by means of his servants, wrought a great work. We have good chapels and schools and houses, and large attentive congregations. . . . The whole country is open to us. In many villages and towns through which I passed, one uniform state of feeling was evident—one desire earnestly expressed: 'Send us teachers and missionaries' . . . Oh, that we had the means" (67).
42. I am aware that the term "mulatto" may sound awkward in modern ears, but for purposes of historical consistency I have decided to retain it to show how Freeman's biracial background affected his work on the West African coast. Sundkler's work (2000, 208–09) also retains this terminology.
43. The Fante word Nana refers to elders, chiefs, grandfathers, and ancestors; the plural is Nananom.
44. Similarities abound between the oracular nationalistic directives from Nananom Mpow and the Shona's Mwari cult (Daneel 1970). It needs to be pointed out, however, that the Fantes did not consider the Nananom Mpow

to be the abode of a Supreme Being as in the case of the Shona view of the Matapo Hills.

45. On March 6, 1844, eight African leaders and the British lieutenant governor signed an agreement defining British jurisdiction in the area, which came to be known as the Protectorate. Technically, the British were allowed to administer justice in this area when capital punishment was involved, but their actual influence was the molding of Fante customs to the general principles of English Law (Owusu-Ansah and McFarland 1995, 60).
46. Nana Kuma, who had been persuaded to participate in the court case by other Fante chiefs, reneged on his promise to pay damages and so a second hearing was called at which he eventually acquiesced to the dictates of the court.
47. One gets a sense that this transformation in Fante society involved more than the ascendancy of the Christian faith over the traditional Fante religion. The very heart of the Christian message was being redefined within the Fante spiritual and political landscape. A Fante historian J. B. Crayner has written a number of books on Nananom Mpow in the Fante language. In one of these he reconstructs the evangelistic dialogue between Akweesi and Kweesiar Ata: "Akweesi inquired, 'what are you trading?' The hunter Kweesiar Ata responded, 'The gospel is my trade.' Akweesi further inquired, 'What is the medium of exchange?' Ata replied, 'Good life, patience, forgiveness, and love—these are the medium of exchange in my trade,' Akweesi then asked to be given this treasure. In response, Kweesiar Ata began telling him about Joseph's tribulations, Job's trials, the difficulties that the children of Israel encountered in the wilderness, the fiery furnace into which the three Hebrew men were thrown, Daniel in the lion's den, and finally Jesus' life, from his birth to his death" (Crayner 1967, 68, my translation).
48. This is probably a justifiable propagandist hyperbole, but to state that no Fante consulted the national gods is to be taken with a grain of salt.
49. David B. Barrett records that AICs saw the missionaries were mounting an attack against African institutions like polygyny, witchcraft, and the ancestors. This "failure in love" primarily referred to insensitivity to African culture, missionary paternalism, and an inability to distinguish between the good and bad elements in African tradition and especially failure to explore how traditional aspects of culture could be utilized in African Christianity (A. Anderson 2001b, 278–79).
50. There is an account that bears witness to the phenomenal impact of William Wade Harris's ministry on MCG. "The previous minister at Axim had warned the members to keep away from 'that false prophet' or they would run the risk of being put out of membership. Ernest Bruce (a Ghanaian Methodist minister) however, was less hasty in his judgment, and waited until he had met Harris himself. When Harris came to greet him, he demanded to see his Bible. He saw that the book Harris placed in his hands was the Authorised Version, so he warmly welcomed him. He offered him the use of the school and the chapel. When the time for service drew near, people from far and near poured in, bearing their loads of charms. After preaching to them, Harris called forth those

professing salvation, and began baptizing them. This went on for hour after hour, to a thousand a day. Still the people continued to come. Harris had time neither to rest nor to eat. As he baptized people he urged them to join the local church. After baptizing ten thousand people in Axim, Harris left. But his converts remained to fill the Methodist churches through the Nzima district. Some fell away, but the majority remained and grew into Christian manhood" (MCG Inaugural Conference Program 1961, 26–27).

51. Sebewie means the one who ends life by the power of magic. Sebetutu means the one who burns amulets and charms. These are two sobriquets that Samson Oppong acquired in his two opposing professions—first as a traditional magician and then as a Christian prophet and evangelist.
52. Hans W. Debrunner says that about 110,000 might have been converted, of which about 50,000 relapsed into their old ways.
53. My attention has been drawn to similar developments in other mission churches in Ghana, in particular. Paul Jenkins studied four Anglican churches and concluded that three out of the four were initiated and maintained by indigenous leadership. The three churches were a result of Harris's work in the western part of Ghana, through migration of Nigerian Yoruba Anglicans and through local Asante people returning to their hometown after converting to Anglicanism elsewhere. He concluded that in all these cases expatriates tended to exercise rather spasmodic leadership and that the expatriate influence was reduced in direct proportion to their distance from the urban centers. Comparing his findings with that of MCG, he writes, "The Wesleyan Methodist Missionary Society had considerably fewer missionaries compared with the size of the Methodist Church community in Ghana; indeed, the Methodist Church was often being referred to as an 'African Church' in this period because missionary control was so weak" In conclusion, he writes, "On the whole, therefore, the evidence suggests that missionaries must have played a relatively small role in the leadership of Ghanaian Anglicanism in this period. All rural congregations must have been left mainly to their own devices. Where communication had to be in the vernacular, missionaries would have been able to exercise little influence in detail; even among the English-speaking congregations in towns, there would have been periods with no resident missionaries. Thus, the day-to-day life of the Anglican Church in Ghana between 1905 and 1924 must have depended largely on local leadership; this would have been true to differing extents in differing localities, but nowhere was local leadership unimportant (Jenkins 1974, 23–39, 30-31).

CHAPTER TWO | **Mission Through Church Planting**

54. Here, too, Dana Robert's assessment of the Zimbabwean situation is applicatioble to Ghana.
55. There is a fascination account of a meeting between representatives of the Conference of Missionary Societies in Great Britain and Ireland on October 29, 1947, and Kwame Nkrumah and Awoonor Renner representing the West African National Secretariat. According to Charles Weber, "The minutes indi-

cate that at this meeting Nkrumah insisted his group 'had one aim and one aim only, to free the whole of West Africa from European suzerainty and make it a self-governing and independent empire. His committee wanted to know whether the missionaries would keep out of this political struggle and allow the African to carry on his struggle with the imperial governments concerned.' The missionaries pledged to use their collective influence to inspire friendship, goodwill and honesty on both sides but stopped short of offering any active political role to further this principle of self-government" (Weber 1997).

56. Francis C. F. Grant's paternal grandfather was Francis Chapman, who donated the land that served as the head office and home of the Methodist mission in Ghana, Standfast Hill, Cape Coast, from 1835 to 1922. Educated at Mfantsipim and Wesley College, Grant served on the staff at these educational institutions and participated in the itinerant ministry of MCG. By the time he was elected Chairman of MCG District and subsequently president of its conference in 1961, he was already known as an authority in the Fante language, having translated large portions of the Scriptures and Methodist hymns into Fante. As president of the conference, he consolidated MCG's autonomy by advocating for the further training of MCG ministers. He served the larger ecumenical community as chair of the Ghana Christian Council, 1961–65 and was awarded an honorary doctor of divinity by the University of Cape Coast and a Grand Medal, Ghana's highest civilian award. His first wife, Lily Amonoo, predeceased him in 1926 and he married Victoria Duncan in 1933. His first marriage produced a son and a daughter, and his second wife already had three daughters (culled from funeral program, November 22, 1986).

57. Grant is alluding to a request made by the MCG Synod of 1915 to the British conference that in the light of the wartime needs of the mother church, no more remittances should be given to MCG for the support of its Ghanaian staff. All moneys that came from the mother church were limited to the support of the expatriate staff and to various projects. To this extent, then, MCG has been self-supporting since World War 1 (Bartels 1965, 173). Thomas A. Beetham, a British missionary who served in Ghana (1928–48), reveals that "in 1928 the pastoral ministry—as distinct from the educational—was exercised by 30 Ghanaian ministers and three Europeans, [and] the 30 were entirely locally supported" (Beetham 1990).

58. The record of debate leading to the foundation of MCG as an autonomous body is well documented in Bartels. (Bartels 1965, 297-302. The extant record may indicate that several other issues were at play in the negotiations).

59. The Wesleyan Methodist Church, with its mission society, was united with the Methodist Church of Great Britain in 1932. Thus, the work of WMMS in Ghana came under the auspices of the Methodist Missionary Society.

60. The initial five districts were constituted of the following circuits: Cape Coast District: Abaasa, Abura, Ajumako, Anomabu, Assin, Cape Coast, Elmina, and Saltpond; Accra District: Aburi and Mampong, Accra, Adabraka, Dodowa and Prampram, Koforidua, Larteh, Nkawkaw, Nsawam, and Volta; Sekondi District: Axim and Nzima, Dixcove, Dunkwa, Sefwi Mission, Sekondi, Shama,

Wassaw, and Western Frontier Mission; Kumasi District: Ahafo, Asante-Akim, Bekwai, Berekum and Wenchi, Effiduase, Kumasi, Mponua, Obuasi, Sunyani, and Dormaa; Winneba District: Agona, Akim Oda, Akim Swedru, Apam, Arkra, Asikuma, and Winneba (FCB 1961). They were also graded into A, B, and C status, meaning self-supporting, aided, and mission circuits. The total MCG trained and paid personnel numbered forty-seven men and twenty-two women (Edusa-Eyison 1999, 48).

61. One example is that with autonomy, property held in the name of MMS would revert to MCG, and MMS would no longer serve as collateral for the loans negotiated by MCG. As far as MMS was concerned, granting autonomy to the MCG meant relinquishing the role of serving as collateral in banking arrangements (Bartels 1965, 296).

62. The cultural differences in the process of decision making in the Akan and British systems were evident in these discussions. Bartels's analysis of the differences is worth repeating: "This timetable [the British missionaries' proposal to form a West African Union], with the written material behind it, was too neatly packaged for a people with an oral tradition, who were used to teasing out the problems of a situation by interminable discussions. Often when they were led along by masses of material on paper, they would have their doubts but be hesitant to say so in case they appeared to be impolite or even unintelligent. Few of the educated Africans who took part on the debates on autonomy would admit that they were not bilingual. They were hardly conscious of the fact that they had been educated in two different linguistic worlds, that they were not equally at home in both of them and that they were trying to live in two worlds simultaneously with varying degrees of success, [and therefore it was difficult] to think in an indigenous language essentially agglutinative in formation, and in English which is inflexional in character, each language being expressive of different thought processes and therefore of different social behavior. They had the inescapable difficulty of having to select experiences in two linguistic worlds, to achieve harmony within their thoughts and then endeavor to communicate them to their European colleagues whose reactions derived from one language world, and who, try as they would, understood the processes of thought confined to that world only" (298).

63. Kofi Abrefa Busia, at that time the leader of the opposition in Ghana Parliament, was a staunch Methodist. In 1969 he became the second prime minister of Ghana.

64. Several church dignitaries sent messages of congratulations. From the U.S. Methodist Church, the chair of the council of bishops, Gerald Kennedy, stated, "This is a great day to be in the spiritual tradition of John Wesley. I believe with all my heart that his witness in the eighteenth century is very much needed in the twentieth century" (FCB 1961, 43); the Reverend Robert McVeigh, president of the Methodist Church in Ireland, wrote, "Christian work in Ghana has been in the thoughts and prayers of Irish Methodism for many years, and our people have always felt it to be a great privilege to share in that work, and to know that the labors of our missionaries have been so greatly appreciated" (43).

Other messages came from the president of the World Methodist Council, Dr. Harold Roberts; the chairman of the Council of Methodist Churches in West Africa, Reverend James Jackson; the chairman of the Christian Council of Ghana, Dr. Christian Baeta; the president-general of the Methodist Church of Australasia, Reverend Professor H. H. Trigge; Bishop H. Sumitra, Church of South India, and the Right Reverend Hugh McLeod, moderator of the United Church of Canada.

65. The nature of MCG's mission in the North has always included agricultural development, health care delivery, and educational opportunities for the youth. For instance, there is a mobile clinic at Lawra, a 125-acre agricultural project at Wa, and a school for the blind which already has produced one Ph.D.

66. A generation earlier, as Sundkler notes, "The Methodists and Presbyterians [in 1936] co-operated in providing a pastor for the Akan Diaspora population at Tamale," the capital of northern Ghana (Sundkler 2000, 728–29).

67. This policy was reiterated in 1981 when MCG vice president Crakye Denteh proposed that northern churches be "twinned" with southern congregations. As a result, the Anomabu Circuit adopted Wa, Accra (Wesley Society) adopted Viera, Swedru adopted Kpongu, and so forth (MCG Conference Minutes 1981, 60).

68. The 1993 population survey of Ghana reported Christians 62%, 20% traditional religious practitioners, and 16% others. The 2000 census reports the Christian population at 69%, with Muslims at 15.6% (Azumah 2000, 23–26). The majority of the Muslim population is in the North, though not in as large numbers as the traditionalists.

69. This state of cordial relations between Christians and Muslims is not unique. Until recently, there was a very high level of tolerance of religious diversity in Ghana. C. G. Baeta records, "The fetish priest and the chief malam of a locality would often support a Church Harvest Thanksgiving festival or contribute to the cost of building a Christian school or even a church. Relatives and friends of deceased persons would attend memorial services for them with religious groups different from their own; Christian festivals such as Christmas and Easter are occasions of celebration and rejoicing for many beyond the folds of the churches, while some Christians would pour libation to the ancestral spirits or be present at strictly animist ceremonies and customary rituals, especially on tribal or family occasions" (Baeta 1967).

70. John Collins, a Ghanaian musicologist, reports that during the government's quasi-Marxist-Socialist "cultural revolution" instructions were given to the Ghana Broadcasting Corporation to reduce the amount of airtime given to gospel music (Collins 2002). A range of items pertaining to church/state relations in Ghana is treated in chapter 5.

71. In spite of this, the leadership of the moderate elements on both sides—Christians and Muslims—has cooperated on a number of issues dealing with national matters. For instance, in 1992 during the period of the general elections, as tensions increased between the ruling party and the opposition political parties, the Ahmadiyya Muslim Mission joined the Christian Council of

Ghana, the National Catholic Secretariat, and the Ghana Pentecostal Council to call for restraint from the leadership of the political parties. Similarly, in 1994, as fighting in northern Ghana broke out between two ethnic groups, these same religious bodies called on the warring factions "in the name of God and in the name of Allah" to stop fighting and to give peace a chance. Lastly, on December 7, 1994, these same religious bodies called on Ghanaians to eschew all hatred, ethnic exclusivism, and religious extremism, adding that as "religious leaders we remain united in our continuing search under God's guidance for peace and justice" (Azumah 2000, 25).

72. For a report of the Presbyterian efforts, see John Azumah "Northern Outreach Program." Also see "NOP Hits Ten Years: A Decade of Achievement," where Azumah states, "The main achievement of the NOP in the last ten years is that the Presbyterian Church of Ghana now has more Builsa, Frafra and Kasena members in the south than the north. In other words, the NOP has in ten years achieved what the Presbyterian Church in the North failed to do in about half a century."
73. In a message by Superintendent William R. A. Blankson we read, "In the 25 years of your existence. . . . Mt. Olivet Society has had 3 daughters [planted churches] and 6 grand daughters. For over 10 years in succession you have been the highest single congregation contributor in the whole of Ghana to the financial fund of the Bible Society of Ghana during the latter's annual Bible week Observance" (Mount Olivet Society 1999).
74. Also see "Tidbits" (MCG 1994, 5).
75. See Michael P. Sackey 1999, 7. In my view the eight fold award system devalued the program, since more than half of the thirteen districts were awarded one thing or another.
76. *Methodist Times*, June 1999, 6. MPRP is the operational arm of EMR.
77. Dansoman Mount Olivet musicians have provided music leadership at national events, for interdenominational as well as Methodist programs. The Mount Olivet Church and Kumasi Wesley are two of the better-known MCG congregations that have outreach programs to help people from the northern regions residing in Accra and Kumasi.
78. In 2000 MCG listed the following Diaspora churches: in the United States: Ebenezer MC in Washington, D.C., Calvary Redeeming in Maryland; Gaddiel Acquaah Memorial MC in Virginia; Ghana Methodist churches in the Bronx, Brooklyn and New Jersey; and Ghana Community Church, Atlanta; in Canada: Ghana MC of Toronto; in Europe: the Dusseldorf MC, the Hamburg Ebenezer MC: the London Ghanaian Methodist Fellowship, Amsterdam Wesley MC; and The Hague Wesley MC; and in Israel: the Methodist/ Presbyterian Church. Also noted was a request for pastoral care for Ghanaian immigrants in Italy (MCG Fact Sheet 2001, 5).
79. There is an emerging literature with regard to both the Ghanaian Diaspora and the wider African Christian Diaspora. Unfortunately, all deal with Europe and none, to my knowledge in 2003, with the United States. Thankfully, now

there are other works on the African immigrant churches in the United States in the first decade of the twenty-first century. See Roswith Gerloff, 1997; Gerrie ter Haar 1998a; 1998b; and Emmanuel K. Akyeampong 2000. The July 2000 edition of the *International Review of Mission* was devoted entirely to this topic: Open Space: The African Christian Diaspora in Europe and the Quest for Human Community (IRM 84, no. 354). For more current work, see for instance Jacob Olupona, Jehu Hanciles, J. Kwabena Asamoah-Gyadu and Frieder Ludwig, and Afe Adogame.

80. The historical facts in this case study are from a letter, dated January 28, 2002, from Acquaah-Arhin to the author. I have supplemented this information with details from conference agenda as well as from the profile provided in the *Methodist Times* 7 (December 1993), p. 4. The first leaders of the church were as follows: Acquaah-Arhin, pastor; Lydia Akesson, secretary; and the following members of the Leaders Meeting: Charles Kumah, Nana Kwame Appiagyei, Akwasi Kankam, Ofosuhene Darko, Rebecca Kumah, Ernestina Boateng, Adjoa Acquaah-Arhin, and Mary Adom. Later others joined them, including Esi Akyeampong (nee Esi Baidoo), Ernestina Sarkwa-Darko, Jessie Acquaah-Arhin, Josephine Gwira, Kwabena Adom, Afua Mansah Baddoo, Robertson Darko, Grace Darko, Kwadwo Boateng, and Comfort Serwah.
81. The mission statement of the Ghana United Methodist Church, Brooklyn, states among other things that it will preach the Good News of Jesus Christ in a compassionate and loving manner to the people who live and work in Brooklyn and surrounding areas. The church seeks to serve the community by first preaching the good news to all people regardless of age, sex, race, creed, nationality, or disability, with a specific outreach to the Ghanaian community; second, enabling Bible teaching and encouraging the experience of the Kingdom of God among them; third, working with the connexional church (UMC) in spreading the Good News of Jesus locally and globally; fourth, supporting in whatever way possible the Methodist Church of Ghana; and fifth, covenanting with each other socially, financially, and spiritually until all grow to the stature of Christ.
82. Even though a Diaspora congregation, the Ghana United Methodist Church, Brooklyn, follows a liturgy that is very close to that which pertains in Ghana (Acquaah-Arhin 1998).
83. Ministers serving Diaspora churches who have been dismissed from the MCG ministry by one president have sometimes been accepted back into the fold by the next presiding bishop. Without a consistent policy, given the pattern over the years, all the pastor needs to do is to wait for another presiding bishop to restore him or her to full ministerial status within the MCG.
84. See appendix H for the Act of Covenant. Given the spread of MCG in the American states, and the semi autonomous state of each diocese, the Concordat as signed is not binding on all states. Furthermore, the changing times call for a thorough review of the Concordat for the mutual benefit of MCG and UMC.

CHAPTER THREE | MCG and Social Uplift

85. In 1961 MCG had four secondary schools: Mfantsipim and Wesley Girls High School, both at Cape Coast; Prempeh College, jointly run with the Presbyterian Church, Ghana, Kumasi; and Wesley Grammar School in Accra. MCG also had four teacher training colleges: Wesley College, Kumasi, Komenda Training College, Komenda, Aburi Training College, Aburi, and Osei Tutu Training College in Kumasi (Edusa-Eyison 1994, 44; MCG Conference Minutes 1962, 28).
86. In 1842 the Reverend Samuel Shipman established the "Akrah Theological Institution," aimed at training local Ghanaians to become agents of the church, including ministers, catechists, evangelists, and teachers. Through the thick and thin of political, economic, and ecclesiastical fortunes, the institution evolved into the Kumasi-based Wesley College in 1924. From 1924 to 1942 Wesley College served as the training center for Ghanaian Methodist ministers. David Kimble, a social scientist who analyzed the rapid spread of Methodism among the coastal Fante, writes: "After the establishment of the native ministry in 1852, the society spread very quickly especially among the Fante on the Coast, its popularity being no doubt due, in some measure, to the democratic nature of its institutions and system of Church Government" (Kimble 1963, 162). (That is, local laypeople shared authority in many church affairs.)
87. Albert Adu Boahen, the renowned Ghanaian historian, has written a fascinating account of the story of *Mfantsipim* (Adu Boahen 1996). For important reviews, see Colin B. Essamuah (1996). In 1960, three years after political independence, out of the sixteen administrative heads of the civil service, eleven were products of Mfantsipim; in the same year the University of Cambridge offered four scholarships to Ghanaians for further studies, and all four nominees came from Mfantsipim; under the military regimes of the late 1960s and 1970s, the four secretaries to the cabinet and heads of the Ghana Civil Service—Francis Apaloo, Quist-Therson, David Awotwi, and Ebenezer M. Debrah—were all "old boys" of Mfantsipim.
88. The preferred term for graduates of Mfantsipim is "old boys."
89. Kofi Atta Annan has received several awards in addition to the Nobel Peace Prize for 2001. In an honorary doctor of civil law conferred by Oxford University, he was lauded as "a far-sighted partisan of justice and a tireless advocate of peace. . . . Annan is not a man to shirk problems which are either arduous or dangerous, and he is conspicuous also for his readiness, if something goes wrong, not to take refuge in the all-too-familiar pattern of bureaucratic obfuscation, of evading responsibility, and of leaving any criticism to be faced by the subordinates" (Akpata-Ohohe 2001, 22). The Sept. 4, 2002, issue of *Time* magazine featured Annan on the cover and discussed the "Five Virtues of Annan" as *Enyimnyam* (Dignity), *Awerehyemu* (Confidence), *Akokodur* (Courage), *Ehumbòbor* (Compassion), and *Gyedzi* (Faith). These Fante traits were honed in a Methodist mission school in Ghana (Ramo 2002).

90. I am grateful to the late Reverend John Bassaw, who was the headmaster of St. Paul's Secondary School for ten years, sometime general manager of schools, Methodist Education Unit, for information corroborating the church records. (Interview with author, Feb. 10, 2002)
91. Aidoo's wife's name is not given in the records. Regrettably in this section I am unable to provide several of the first names from all available sources.
92. The various geographic divisions in Tema are called communities, hence MCG churches (with number of congregations) are said to be the following: Calvary Community 3, Bethel Community 8, Immanuel Community 11, Middle East-Ashiaman, St. Peter-Ashiaman, Aldersgate, Lebanon, Charles Wesley- Ashiaman, Adjei Kojo, West Ashiaman, and St. John-Manhean. Several soldiers who had returned from international peacekeeping operations under the auspices of the United Nations founded the communities called Middle East-Ashiaman and Lebanon.
93. The Kumasi District MCG operates vocational/technical/commercial institutes at Adwumakese-kese, Asokore, Wiamoase, and Bantama.
94. In 1993, for instance, 39 of the 40 candidates successfully completed their exams and were awarded the General Certificate of Education Ordinary Level and moved on to further studies.
95. The Methodist University is one of the many positive contributions that MCG has made in this decade. Its website www.mucg.edu.gh tells its story very well. At the moment it is the second largest private university in Ghana with a student population of well over three thousand and with campuses in Dansoman, Tema, and Wenchi.
96. S. G. Nimako was in fact the first Ghanaian Methodist minister to gain a doctoral degree, but on his return to Ghana he served mainly outside MCG.
97. Dr. John Agbeti proposed the following steps: first, establish a course in practical theology at one of the departments of religious studies at any of three universities, namely; University of Ghana, Legon; Kwame Nkrumah University of Science and Technology, Kumasi; or the University of Cape Coast; second, Trinity College should be made into a religious university with power to award its own degrees; with a two year fundraising campaign to establish the university. It is interesting to note that Dr. Agbeti has seen all these proposals come about, though in different forms. For instance, Trinity College is now a theological seminary, an independent degree-awarding institution; the University of Ghana's Department for the Study of Religions conducts more contemporary and locally relevant courses. My attention has been drawn to others who earlier on proposed similar educational structures; unfortunately I have not been able to get verification and so will have to leave the material as is for the meantime.
98. About two years before the adoption of episcopacy, the presidents of the conference were given the title "Right Reverend." When episcopacy was adopted in 1999 and implemented in 2000, the District Chairmen were designated as bishops and the presiding bishop was designated as "Most Reverend."
99. Professor Florence Abena Dolphyne was then the pro vice-chancellor of the

University of Ghana, the first woman to hold that position. Professor Dolphyne is a daughter of an MCG minister, Samuel Akesson. She went to Wesley Girls' High School and also took a sixth-form course at the all-boys Mfantsipim School at a time when WGHS did not have a sixth form. In 1965 she completed her Ph.D. in linguistics from the University of London. She spent her career at the University of Ghana, where she taught and served in various administrative positions. She was also a visiting professor at several overseas universities (Dolphyne 2000, 77–86).

100. At the time of my research, Professor K. A. Andam was serving as vice chancellor of Kwame Nkrumah University of Science and Technology.

101. Following the example of King David (1 Chron. 29:3), the MCG presiding bishop pledged an amount of $2,000. Pledges were received from individuals, districts, and church organizations.

102. In the land tenure system of Ghana, all lands are vested in traditional authorities and technically are never sold, but rather leased for 99 years at a time. That being the case, a 1999 MUCG report states that a payment of "5 million cedis was paid to the Omanhene" (approximately $500 at that time). This is to register the church's claim to the land even though it was given as a gift.

103. The citation extols MCG for providing sterling education in its institutions and lauds the professional achievements of some of the products of MCG institutions, including the vice president of Ghana, John Atta Mills, and Secretary-General Annan of the UN. Among those who have served in church-related institutions, it cites "Dr. John K. Agbeti, the first Ghanaian Methodist minister to earn a doctorate . . . and Dr. Amba Ewudziwa [Mercy Oduyoye] . . . former deputy General Secretary of the World Council of Churches" (MCG Conference Agenda 1999, GPC, 153).

104. I am grateful to Dr. E. Kingsley Larbi, the then president of Central University for a copy of this history. Central University bought its current buildings from the family of the late MCG benefactor, C. K.K. Baah. Almost all its current faculty belong to mainline churches.

CHAPTER FOUR | **Mission in Public Witness**

105. There are similar sentiments expressed by other African nationalists all over the continent. The Zimbabwean Ndabaningi Sithole wrote: "The Christian church has created in Africa . . . a strong Christian consciousness that transcends the usual barriers of race and color, and this Christian consciousness is based on the love of God and the love of our fellow men. It is based on a strong sense of human justice. The story of African nationalism would be incomplete if this Christian awareness was ignored, since it is this awareness that is an integral part of the creativeness of African nationalism. . . . The Christian faith may be regarded in one sense as its spiritual father and in another as its guardian angel, whether or not the Church recognizes these roles." He concludes, "The Christian Church by sending religious, educational, and industrial missionaries to Africa broadened the outlook of many an African.

It provided opportunities for many Africans to develop their latent qualities; it has discouraged tribal hatred and encouraged universal brotherhood instead. Incidentally, tribalism was also discouraged by African nationalism when it emerged so that, in this respect, the Christian Church paved the way of the universalism—that is, the nontribalness—inherent in the African nationalism that was to come. The present enlightened political leadership would be next to impossible but for the Christian Church that spread literacy to many parts of Africa" (Sithole 1977, 88–89, 94). In Ghana, for instance, the Convention Peoples Party used the Christian hymn "Lead, Kindly Light" as part of its political musical tradition. The party later adopted a hostile stance towards the mainline Christian churches.

106. Ghana's rather fluctuating postindependence political history has been aptly likened to a swinging pendulum. Nkrumah's socialist regime was replaced by moderate army officers, followed by Western-oriented democracy, followed by a spell of military dictatorship. In 1979 Rawlings appeared on the scene, first as a revolutionary; then after a brief constitutional government, Flight Lieutenant Jerry John Rawlings assumed power again, as a military ruler and then as the first president of the Fourth Republic (Pellow and Chazan 1986).

107. A 1951–66, Kwame Nkrumah, CPP; elected president of the First Republic, 1960.

B 1966–69, Emmanuel Kwasi Kotoka and Akwasi A. Afrifa led the coup d'état, and established NLC (National Liberation Council); Kotoka was assassinated in a failed coup; Afrifa takes over, then honors the election of Busia;

C 1969–72, Kofi Abrefa Busia elected prime minister of the Second Republic, August. 22, 1969;

D 1972–75, I. Kutu Acheampong, NRC (National Redemption Council), assumes control in coup d'état, January 13, 1972, constitution suspended;

E 1975–78, Kutu Acheampong, SMC (Supreme Military Council), continues as head of government, followed in 1978–79 by Fred Akuffo (also SMC); 1979 Jerry John Rawlings, AFRC (Armed Forces Revolutionary Council), takes power (for four months only); Acheampong and Akuffo executed; then Rawlings hands over power to Limann;

F 1979–81, Hilla Limann, PNP (Peoples National Party; revival of Nkrumah's CPP), elected president of Third Republic; 1981–92, Rawlings, PNDC (Provisional National Defense Council) resumes power; June 1982, three judges abducted and murdered; June 1989, Religious Bodies (Registration) Law 221 promulgated (mainline churches resist);

G 1992, elections return Rawlings to power as president of the Fourth Republic;

In November.–December 1996 he wins another four years;

H 2000–, John Kufuor, NPP (New Patriotic Party), elected president.

108. The stool is the traditional symbol of authority. It symbolizes group solidarity,

embodies the spirit of ancestors, and signifies their presence. The stool represents the continuity between the living and the dead. Chiefs are therefore said to be "enstooled" or "destooled." Unlike southern and eastern societies in Ghana, Togo, and Nigeria where the stool is used, in the northern parts of Togo, Nigeria, Benin, and Ghana an animal skin is sometimes used as the symbol of the chief or king, and the skin represents the throne or stool. The most important aspect of Ashanti chieftaincy was undoubtedly the religious one. "An Ashanti chief filled a sacral role. . . . [His stool] represented the community, their solidarity, their permanence, their continuity. The chief was the link between the living and the dead, and his highest role was when he officiated in their public religious rites, which gave expression to the community values. He then acted as the representative of the community. . . . The sacred aspect of the chief's role was a powerful sanction of his authority" (Busia, 1967, 26).

109. CCG was founded on October 30, 1929, by the AME Zion, The English Church Mission (Anglican, later the Church of the Province of West Africa), Ewe (later Evangelical Presbyterian Church-Bremen Mission), Presbyterian Church of Ghana-Basel Mission, and Wesleyan Methodist Church. In 1932 the Salvation Army joined and during the 1950s and 1960s the following churches also joined CCG: African Methodist Episcopal, Baptist Church, Society of Friends, Mennonites, Christian Methodist Episcopal Church, and Evangelical Lutheran Church. The Young Men's Christian Association and the Young Women's Christian Association are associate members. The first non-mainline church to be admitted was F'Eden Church in 1970, (see Pobee 1991a, 50). During the years under review, 1961–2000, the following MCG presidents served as chairmen of CCG: F. C. F. Grant (1963–65), T. W. Koomson (1968–69), C. K. Yamoah (1975–76), C. A. Pratt (1979), S. B. Essamuah (1984), J. S. A. Stephens (1988), and K. A. Dickson (1991–1993). The following served as general secretaries: Peter K. Dagadu (1952–58), W. G. M. Brandful (1965–76), and the Reverend Dr. Robert Aboagye-Mensah (1998–2003). For a biographical treatment of Dagadu, see Peter Barker (1983).

110. In 1948 there were 641,427 Christians in Ghana distributed as follows: Colony 18.5%, Ashanti 13.7%, Togoland 20.5%, and Upper Region 3.6% (Williamson 1965, 11). In 1966, 42.8% of the population claimed to be Christians (Pobee 1976, 122).

111. Fante chiefs wanting to defend themselves against the Asante and certain Europeans, specifically the Dutch, who had great political and economic power, established the Fante Confederacy in 1863. The confederacy was also established because of the declining interest of the British in protecting coastal tribes against Asante invasion. The confederacy also recognized that the abolition of slavery meant that there needed to be an economic replacement. Its stated objectives were to promote friendly relations among the Fante; improve the country at large; and improve agriculture, education, and the mining industry (Ward 1967, 251–64; Hayford 1903, 327).

112. This was primarily established by chiefs and the middle-class merchants and intelligentsia as a nationalist body (Ward 1967, 357).

113. There is considerable literature on the evolution of this political ideology over the years. I have found B. D. G. Folson (1977) very useful in delineating the various strands of ideologies within Nkrumah's party apparatus. Folson quotes Nkrumah's foremost political opponent, Dr. J. B. Danquah, as responding in derision when asked whether Nkrumah was a Communist: "No, he knows nothing about communism. He calls himself a Marxist socialist, but he has not read even ten pages of Karl Marx." Folson refers to Basil Davidson, *Black Star: A View of the Life and Times of Kwame Nkrumah* and to Robin McKown, *Nkrumah: A Biography* as two sympathetic treatments that give little credence to Nkrumah's assertion that he was a socialist.

114. John S. Pobee considers Nkrumah to have been a thoroughbred socialist who only acquiesced to Western demands and expectations of "colonial overlords," and so spoke of democracy (Pobee 1976, 125). Deborah Pellow and Naomi Chazan argue that "as an ideology, Nkrumahism was inconsistent: it drew haphazardly from Marxism and Leninism, from Fabian socialism and British libertarianism, from a mystification of the African past, and from a variety of Christian sources. Far removed from Ghanaian realities, it became an abstract vision which could not provide the concrete guidelines needed to help Ghana overcome the economic and political difficulties it confronted at the outset of independence" (Pellow and Chazan 1986, 42).

115. The Anglican Bishop Reginald Roseveare, then chairman of the CCG, epitomized the church's condemnation of the Young Pioneers. When he railed against its godless nature, Nkrumah deported him but ultimately acquiesced to the enormous pressure from the Christian community and invited him back into the country. Obiri-Addo cites Pobee referring to Nkrumah's capitulation as indicating that the churches in Ghana were "heavy weights with which to reckon" (See Obiri-Addo 1997 and Pobee 1991a).

116. An example may be seen in an editorial of the Nkrumah party paper, the *Evening News*, February 4, 1960, which states, "All day, all night, we are reinforced in our belief that the whole phenomena of Nkrumah's emergence is second to none in the history of the world's Messiahs from Buddha and Muhammad to Christ." Ten years earlier the Beatitudes had been parodied in the same paper (Dickson 1991, 139).

117. Eight of such honorifics are provided by Pobee and underlined by Kwesi Dickson as well: "Asomdweehene"-Prince of Peace, "Osagyefo" - one who saves in battle, "Oyeadeeyie" - one who rights wrongs, "Kasapreko" - one who speaks once and for all, "Kukuroduroni" - brave or valiant one, "Osuodumgya" - water that extinguishes fire, and "Abrofusuro" - the one who instills fear in Europeans. Akan-speaking Christians in referring to God in extempore prayers regularly use all the honorifics except the last one. John S. Pobee is also right in reminding us that these honorifics are also used in referring to the Akan chiefs, but he fails to show that given the religious role of the chiefs these honorifics are not applied to their persons but to their office, a distinction that the Nkrumah party refused to make (Pobee 1976, 136; Dickson 1991, 145).

118. The Christian churches in Ghana mounted a very broad-based civic education program in 1988, organizing lectures, symposia, and seminars on the democratization process, (see Boafo 1999, 233).
119. Kimble states, "The training for leadership given to African ministers . . . may be regarded as a positive stimulus to the development of the nationalist movement. . . . Church organizations did not take a definite part in nationalist agitation, but prominent members were often outspoken on political issues. Most educated Africans were the product of Missions Schools, and accepted their teaching as a guide to the new, western ways of life, and a background to political thinking" (Kimble 1963, 161).
120. Busia was born July 11, 1913, to the royal house of Wenchi. In his youth, he was raised and received his education in the home of Methodist missionaries, the Reverend and Mrs. William Whittle. Educated at Mfantsipim and Wesley College, he served the University of Ghana in several capacities before plunging into politics. Whittle officiated at his funeral in Oxford, September 5, 1978.
121. These and other sentiments revealed the heart of the man, a great scholar of sociology and a devout Methodist. The policies that the Busia administration put in place, especially with regard to its setting up of the Ministry of Social and Rural Development (the first of its kind in Ghana), were to serve as blueprints for subsequent regimes that sought to improve the lot of Ghanaians. Elsewhere Okyere notes, "Under [Busia's] administration, no one was arbitrarily arrested or detained on any spurious reasons or tortured under any pretext. There was freedom of the press, association, religion and speech" (Okyere 2000, 218).
122. Adu Boahen's words on the composition of this government by Mfantsipim-trained people bears repeating here: "It was during the civilian regime of the second Republic, that followed the short military interlude in September 1969 that the School made its greatest contribution to the political life of this country. At that time, not only the Prime Minister, K. A. Busia, and his two deputies, J. Kwesi Lamptey and William Ofori-Atta, but also the Leader of the Opposition, Madjitey, and his deputy, B. K. Agama, were all Old Boys of *Kwabotwe* [Mfantsipim]" (Boahen 1996, 492).

    On another intriguing point, Robert Aboagye-Mensah remarks that we have yet to assess "the missiological significance of a Methodist soldier, Akwasi A. Afrifa, who overthrows a dictatorial government and at the end hands over to a Methodist civilian, Kofi Abrefa Busia" (interview with author 2000).
123. The "Apollo 568" political episode took place at the time of the time of the Apollo space flight.
124. Okyere states, "It could be judged from later developments that the coup was staged to serve the selfish interests of the conspirators as the cut in the defense budget for the military was not cited as having sufficiently affected the operations of the Ghana Army. More importantly, the fact that [Acheampong] is believed to have stated that he started planning the coup only six (6) months

after Busia had assumed office is an indication that he tried to rationalize an unjustifiable act" (Okyere 2000, 222).

125. Ghana's population at this time was divided into the following religious categories: African traditional 21.61%, Christian 52.65%, and Muslims 13.92%. Those who registered no religion or other religions totaled 11.82%.
126. Among Reverend Abraham de Love's credentials was the fact that he was the head of relatively unknown organizations such as the Christian Brotherhood Council, the National Union of Christian Youth, Christian Association of Businessmen, and Pioneer of the Christian Youth Jamboree (Pobee 1987, 50).
127. Pobee lists the following: Alhaji Salihu Maikankan, adviser to Muslim chiefs in Ghana and chairman of the National Mosque Building Committee; Alhaji Amida Perigrino Briamah, chief of the Yoruba Muslim community; Ibrahim Dagomba, chief of the Dagomba community; Alhaji Alhassan Chokosi, chief of the Chokosi community; Alhaji Shamoi Gimailah, chief of the Wangara community; Alhaji Ali Bawa Kadri English, chief of the Hausa community; Alhaji Salifu Mahama, chief of the Gonja community; and Alhaji Barimah Shadow, chief of the Nupe community (Pobee 1987, 51–52).
128. The Charter of Redemption featured seven tenets: (1) One Nation, One People, One Destiny; (2) Total manpower development and deployment; (3) Revolutionary discipline; (4) Self-Reliance; (5) Service to the People; (6) Patriotism and International Brotherhood; and (7) Mobilization of the Spiritual, Intellectual and Will Power of the People.
129. Makola is the biggest market in Ghana's capital Accra, where practically anything can be procured.
130. Rawlings has occupied a large space in Ghana's political history. He came to power as a Marxist revolutionary on June 4, 1979, handed over power after a four-month period, and then returned to power on December 31, 1981. In November.–December 1992, he won the presidential elections and his party, the National Democratic Congress (NDC), won parliamentary elections. In 1996, he won reelection for his last term. In November-December 2000 his party lost power to John Kuffour and his New Patriotic Party (NPP).
131. For a revelation of the extent of human rights abuses during the 1980s, see Adjei 1994.
132. Robert K. Aboagye-Mensah reports (1991, 89) that during the 1979 elections to usher in the Third Republic, the former political party of Kofi A. Busia "had a sharp disagreement which split the party into two—the United National Convention (UNC) led by William Ofori-Atta (a devout evangelical, popularly known as Paa Willie), and the Popular Front Party (PFP) under the leadership of Victor Owusu. The CCG and the Catholic Secretariat urged the two parties to come together against Dr. Hilla Limann, candidate of the PNP (PNP—Peoples National Party was the new name for Nkrumah's Convention People's Party)." Aboagye-Mensah fails to note the factional character of this initiative on behalf of the churches. It reflected the CCG and the

Catholic Secretariat's intellectual and ideological predilection for the liberal democratic ideals espoused and practiced by what in Ghana is known as the Danquah-Busia faction (Aboagye-Mensah 1991, 89).

133. Publications from such meetings included "The Catholic Church and Ghana's Search for a New Democratic System" (February 20, 1991) and *The Nation, the Church and Democracy* (Accra, Christian Council, 1992). The latter came out of the July 23-24, 1991 seminar.
134. The victims were Justices Cecilia Koranteng-Addo, K. A. Agyepong, F. P. Sarkodee, and Maj. Sam Acquah. They were abducted on the night of June 30, 1982, and their bodies were later found on military property.
135. The PNDC's intent in promulgating the law was to prevent a situation in which misguided people could wreck havoc in Ghanaian society through religious institutions. It may have been aimed in particular at certain little-known religious bodies that had been implicated in possibly treasonable acts. In a meeting with PNDC representative Daniel Francis Annan, requested by CCG and CBC, the churches were assured that the new law sought to regulate rather than control the activities of religious bodies. In response, CCG and CBC argued that they already had in place provisions to ensure that they lived by the laws of Ghana, and furthermore, they did not want to be lumped together with new religious movements, some of which had proved to be a disguise for immoral practices.
136. Later, in his treatment of this episode, Paul Nugent modifies his assessment somewhat when he acknowledges that the churches and professional bodies, despite their steady barrage of criticism, were unable to mount a direct challenge to the Rawlings regime. However, the fact remains that the church's role constituted internal opposition, and when this was supplemented by pressure from the Western world, Rawlings was ultimately forced, reluctantly, to agree to multiparty politics (Nugent 1996, 270).
137. Adu Boahen argues in *African Perspectives on Colonialism* that in assessing the nature and significance of the legacy of colonialism, "The debit side far outweighs the credit side. Indeed, my charge against colonialism is not that it did not do anything for Africa, but that it did so little and that little so accidentally and indirectly; not that the economy of Africa under colonialism did not grow but that it grew more to the advantage of the colonial powers and the expatriate owners and shareholders of the companies operating in Africa than to the Africans; not that improvements did not take place in the lives of the African peoples, but that such improvements were so limited and largely confined to the urban areas; not that education was not provided but that what was provided was so inadequate and so irrelevant to the needs of the African themselves; not that there were no upward social mobility but that such a relatively small number of Africans did get to the top. In short, given the opportunities, the resources, and the power and influence of the colonial rulers, they could and should have done far more than they did for Africa. And it is for this failure that the colonial era will go down in history as a period of wasted opportunities, of ruthless exploitation of the resources of Africa,

and on the balance of the underdevelopment and humiliation of the peoples of Africa" (Boahen, 1987).

CHAPTER FIVE | **Barriers to Mission: A House Divided**

138. It was 1958 before the Catholic Church consecrated its first Ghanaian bishop (Brandewie 2000, 338). The Anglican Church consecrated its first indigenous bishop ten years later. For the Anglican record in Ghana, see Pobee (2000, 409–21).
139. A senior colleague of mine within MCG intimated to me in an exchange of correspondence that in the 1980s the denomination was forced to come to grips with its ethnocentric outlook.
140. Problems occurred in the Tarkwa, Cape Coast, Winneba, and Kumasi districts that are not covered in this study. They have been omitted primarily because their impact was largely confined to the local area. It is also possible to argue that the way in which they were handled was very different from what is depicted in the following accounts.
141. This saga is contained in a twelve page report submitted by the Conference Commission on Calvary Society to the 1973 conference, which for our purposes we have designated the Amissah Commission Report. The report contained 8 appendixes bringing the total pages to eighty-five.
142. Methodist churches are called "societies" and a number of these in a geographic area constitute a "circuit." Usually the name of the circuit is derived from the name of the society where the superintendent-minister, as head of the circuit resides.
143. GPC functions as the MCG executive committee on the national level.
144. At his death in 1986, Creedy was the longest-serving missionary in Ghana. He was a principal at training colleges, helped establish the accreditation boards for teachers, and also worked for the Boys Brigade of Ghana. His services to the country were acknowledged by the Ghanaian government, which honored him with its highest civilian award. His name is associated with the proposed (but never realized) interdenominational church union in Ghana, since he served as secretary of the church union committee.
145. The Reverend Awotwi-Pratt would later serve as the fourth president of MCG Conference, and I. K. Agyeman served as the third vice president of conference.
146. In Ghanaian Christian parlance, spiritual churches are the preferred terminology for AICs (see Baeta, 1960).
147. S.H. Amissah was for many years the principal of MCG's premier teacher training college, Wesley College in Kumasi. Later he served as the second general-secretary of the All-Africa Conference of Churches, 1964–71. He also was the first vice president of MCG, 1977–79. Other commission members were equally significant. The most senior clergy members, Essamuah and Dickson, respectively, were the fifth and eighth presidents of the conference; N. A. Mensah went on to have an illustrious career at the office of the

All Africa Conference of Churches in Nairobi; Sackeyfio became chairman of the Accra District; among the lay members, Alex Quaison-Sackey, the former foreign minister of Ghana under Nkrumah, had served earlier as the first black African president of the General Assembly of the UN, he was the fifth vice president of MCG.

148. In order to reconstruct the history of internal conflicts in MCG during the 1980s, I have consulted denominational minutes and other national and district-level documents. However, MCG records, including GPC minutes, tend to provide minimal information and use euphemistic language. Additional information was made available to me through the research, completed in 1994, of the Reverend Joseph. M. Y. Edusa-Eyison and I gratefully express appreciation for his assistance. Edusa-Eyison is a professor of church history at the Trinity Theological Seminary, Accra. The cited research was part of a graduate degree program at the University of Ghana, Legon, conducted under the supervision of the Reverend Professors Joshua N. Kudadjie and John Kofi Agbeti.

149. Under the system in the late 1980s, the president of the conference is elected on the vote of a simple majority at the close of one conference, and confirmed by a vote of 75 percent at the beginning of the following year's conference. As long as no other candidate gains more than 25 percent of the second vote, the individual may serve for a total of five years without having to stand for reelection.

150. On the surface, Essamuah's resignation suggests that he was either distressed by the (false) accusation that he had leaked the information about Stephens, or that by removing himself he was tacitly acknowledging responsibility. Despite making inquiries of Essamuah's family members and colleagues, I could find no confirmation one way or the other, and regrettably, I must leave the matter unresolved.

151. Isaac K. Abban was a distinguished jurist. During the 1975 referendum conducted by the Acheampong military government, he served as electoral commissioner, attracting threats on his life that sent him briefly into hiding. At the time of his death, in 2001, Abban was serving as chief justice of Ghana.

152. See "Submission of Definitive Statement" (MCG Archives, 1984).

153. Three other defections had occurred in earlier years. In 1862, members of a Temperance Society (Akonomsufo, literally "water-drinkers"), based at Anomabu, challenged the church to take a stand against alcoholism (Bartels 1965, 82). In the early twentieth century, a small Methodist community in the Saltpond Circuit led by Benjamin Sam converted en masse to Islam, and the Musama Disco Christo Church also resulted from a breakaway (Debrunner 1967, 241; Baeta 1962). Neither defection had the same significance as the Cape Coast schism. This was because the communities involved in the earlier defections had a much lower profile in Ghana Methodism than the churches of the premier Cape Coast MCG District, and their leaders were not highly placed figures like K.B.M. Edu-Buandoh.

154. On the surface this may seem capricious but there has been similar practice in

the past where the district synods' choice for Chairmen has been voted down at the national level. New guidelines put in place will minimize such occurrences in the future.

155. See the Superior Court of Judicature: In the High Court of Justice, Central Region, held at Cape Coast on Tuesday the 24 of June, 1986 Coram: A. W. Dove J: Suit No. M 44/6.
156. Letter of expulsion (MCG Archive, 1986).
157. Attempts were made during the 1990–97 presidency of Kwesi Dickson to engage Edu-Buandoh and negotiate his return to the church. Two of the three MCG ministers who originally joined him have been readmitted to MCG. After Stephens's presidency concluded in 1990, several former members of MCG who had joined Edu-Buandoh's new church, returned to MCG. It is believed that one of the reasons why Edu-Buandoh has not returned is because his church adopted an episcopal system of government that recognizes him as bishop, a standing he would lose if he returned to MCG. Recently, MCG has adopted episcopacy; this action may make a healing of the schism possible.
158. In a rather circuitous way of conflict resolution, GPC, meeting on January 26, 1989, asked Acquaah-Harrison and the Winneba District to apologize to Stephens for reading and publicly discussing the letter he had written. When they refused to apologize, other intermediaries prevailed on Stephens to be the one to issue apologies rather than vice versa (MCG Representative Session Conference Agenda, 1989, 235; also MCG Ministerial Session Conference Agenda 1989, 67).
159. At the time of research Justice E.K. Wiredu was the chief justice of Ghana and the late Ankrah was a former head of state of Ghana.
160. At the end of his tenure, in 1997, Dickson had this to say about the Sunyani conference: "[It was] unforgettable because it was one of a kind: disorderly, bad-tempered and fractious, a conference whose disunity was palpable, and whose dignity was at stake" (1996, 4).
161. The Reverend Kodjo Haizel had been known for holding to some elements of mysticism that could well be unorthodox. These views were known before his election as Chairman of Winneba District. Bringing up these charges at this time seemed to serve a different purpose than to ensure doctrinal fidelity.
162. The constitution stipulates that when minister are under suspension, they are to receive only half the usual stipend.
163. See, for example, *Daily Graphic*, February 6, 1998.
164. See Appendix J for the pastoral letter.
165. *Daily Graphic*, August 1, 6, 9, and 10, 1996.
166. At the time, observers wondered if this action represented a concern for the transparency of MCG fiscal operations, or if it was a "fishing expedition" that might reveal inadequacies in Kumi's management of the headquarters office and thereby ensure that Maclean A. Kumi would not reappear on the 1997 ballot for the post of conference president. When the audit report finally came out in January 1998 it was revealed that an amount of $145,000 had

been misappropriated. This ensued in the dismissal of Regina Adu, the head of the Women's Division (MCG Representatives Session Conference Minutes, 1998).

167. When the Ghanaian press reported, on February 5, 1998, that Conference Secretary Kumi had resigned, the report cited the cause as disagreement over payment of the disembarkment fees of a Ghanaian minister who had returned from theological training in the United States. However, the minister in question, the Reverend Kow Ghunney, states that this had nothing to do with the relationship between Asante-Antwi and Kumi, since the matter had been settled by President Dickson before Asante-Antwi assumed office (Ghunney 1998, 1).

168. Some may argue that church crisis can sometimes motivate growth instead of decline but in this case all the statistics point to a numerical decline.

CHAPTER SIX | **Self-Theologizing: The Process of Contextualization**

169. Bediako goes so far as to say that Christianity in Africa is the renewal of a non Western religion (Bediako 1995, especially chapters 4 and 10).

170. MCG has evidenced a consistent desire to contextualize its liturgy and worship. Consider, for example, the recommendations of an MCG worship committee regarding liturgy. (I summarize here key items included in materials for the 1978 Annual Conference.) Sharing highlights from a meeting of the Ghana Fellowship of the Kingdom, the committee recommended that worship liturgy should deal with (1) fear and insecurity due to sickness, death, darkness, hatred, lorry accidents, lightning, enemies, witchcraft, poisoning, and so forth; (2) distress over the isolation of ethnic group from ethnic group, clan from clan, and village from village; (3) anxiety regarding the disintegration of traditional culture, the generation gap, and Western materialism; and (4) apprehension over the perceived presence of the dead and dependence upon the ancestors. In addition to the usual services conducted at churches, the memorandum suggested that liturgies for the following occasions be drawn up: naming/christening of infants, widowhood rites, consecration of a burial ground, dedication of a tombstone, laying of the foundation stone of a private house, traditional festivals (e.g., puberty rites; and the deer hunt), and installation of a chief. In the 1970s and early 1980s liturgical reform was seen as especially important in order to make the MCG liturgy more contextual and thereby stem the tide of Methodists joining the newly founded independent churches, where they felt more culturally "at home."

171. Samuel B. Essamuah (March 10, 1916–January 27, 1987) was MCG's fifth president (1979–84). Born into a family of a Methodist catechist, he spent almost half his active ministerial career in the mission field of the Asante region, serving in Kumasi, Bekwai, and Konongo. He interspersed his career with educational courses in England, Zambia, Zimbabwe, and Ghana. An outline for worship, included in the preparatory materials for the 1978

Annual Conference, was typical of his sensitivity to Akan culture. Worship, he wrote, should include the following: (1) **Adoration**: to adore God as the God of our fathers, to acknowledge the universality of God, to recognize him as the Provider, the Guardian against evil, the Reconciler, and the Lord of all human relationships; (2) **Confession**: for resorting to idols and talismans, for resistance to God's fatherly guidance, for lacking love in personal and family relations, and for thoughts of evil against one's enemies; (3) **Thanksgiving**: for deliverance from evil spirits, sin, natural disasters, and power of enemies; and for God's providence; (4) **Intercession**: for the world church, neighboring congregations, non-Christians, and for doctors, nurses, and pregnant women; (5) **Petition**: for deliverance from clannishness, infidelity, drought, and so forth. He was a foremost expositor of *ebibindwom*, and over the course of his pastoral career he composed and compiled more than three thousand *ebibindwom* lyrics, spanning the whole gamut of the liturgical calendar. When Rawlings assumed power as president in the 1980s, Essamuah was the face of valor. At great personal risk, he delivered stirring addresses and timely denunciations of the abuse of human rights.

172. A friend recalled how this was brought home to him afresh on New Year's Eve, December 31, 1999. On this occasion he had accompanied other Ghanaian Methodists who had decided to join their compatriots, Ghanaian Presbyterians, at a traditional Ghanaian Watchnight Service in Worcester, Massachusetts. The Presbyterians offered a warm welcome and introduced them by saying, "Now that the Ghanaian Methodists are here, we expect they can lead us in singing *ebibindwom*." Sometimes, as in this instance, it is when one is placed in a cross-cultural setting that one's identity as perceived by others becomes crystal clear.

    Most African societies exhibit through their music a sensibility with which its people relate to life and the world around them (Chernoff 1979, 154). The centrality of *ebibindwom* in MCG's development is reflected by Hoyini H.K. Bhila when he writes, "Methodism thrived through its class meetings and local-preacher system, which permitted rapid development of local Ghanaian leadership through the popularity of its singing and in its early provision of schools" (Bhila 2000). Robert Parsons adds, "The Fante people evangelized by the Methodists have shown a greater interest in the development of the local music and they had a marked influence upon other ethnic groups by the spread of their Christian songs to all churches" (Parsons 1963, 113). Asamoah-Gyadu, a Ghanaian Methodist theologian, refers to the use of the *ebibindwom* among the AICs as a form of oral theologizing (Asamoah-Gyadu 2000, 74).

173. Appendix K contains several examples of *ebibindwom* that span the liturgical calendar.

174. The source of Parsons's statement includes a reference to a "cathedral" and to African elements in an installation service. This leads me to speculate that the quotation is from Bishop Peter Sarpong, the Catholic Bishop of Kumasi,

one of the foremost advocates of the Africanization of Christianity in Africa.

175. Between 1962 and 1973, Essamuah carried on his itinerant ministry in five different stations and with two overseas study leaves and appointments. This schedule coupled with the minimal financial support from the denominational office for this music project undoubtedly affected the pace of the work.

176. This interjection could be interpreted as a means of negotiating the differences between men and women, lay and clergy, and illiterate and literate as well as an aversion to ordered liturgy as opposed to spontaneous worship.

177. Akan chiefs are placed on sacred stools as symbols of state authority. When they take office, the event is known as an enstoolment ceremony; conversely, if they are relieved of their office, they are said to have been destooled.

178. Curiously, *ebibindwom* does not occupy a central place in the theological reflections of leading Ghanaian Methodists. In their work, they have privileged the written sources against the oral tradition (reflecting their Western academic training). Doing so, they ignore the general experiences of Ghanaian Methodists, especially of rural Methodists, for whom *ebibindwom* may be the only source of liturgical music and biblical instruction.

179. Asamoah-Gyadu's work has been published as *African Charismatics: Current Developments within Independent Indigenous Pentecostalism in Ghana* (Brill, 2005).

180. Technically, polygyny is a more accurate description of the phenomenon of plural unions. Polygyny refers to men having more than one wife, while polyandry refers to women with more than a single husband. However, the word that is most used in the literature and common parlance is polygamy, and I will follow that convention.

181. This is not always the case elsewhere in Africa, see J. B. Webster, "Attitudes and Policies of the Yoruba African Churches towards Polygamy" (Baeta 1968, 224–47). After Henry Venn's 1857 memorandum stating that polygamists should not be accepted into the church, the third Lambeth Conference (1888) laid down three principles, namely, that baptized converts who took a second wife had to be excommunicated, that polygamists would not be accepted into membership, and that wives of polygamists might be baptized only under certain conditions. But there was never unanimity among the missionaries on this subject. Some like Pinnock, felt that if the missionaries could not use moral suasion then they should refrain from using the "big stick" also. When his views contradicted that of church policy, Pinnock chose to resign.

182. Theological argument played a minor role in determining the missionaries' attitude. Rather, their restrictive policy reflected a feeling of superiority rooted in the Victorian bourgeois society of England. Playing upon Africans' desire for the material benefits of Europe, missionaries pointed out in long, dreary recitals of world history that monogamist peoples were the conquerors, the civilized, and the inventors—in short, the master races. Polygamous people were the conquered, the savage, and the imitators; in short "the lesser breeds without the law" (Webster in Baeta 1968, 228).

183. For theological reflections on a personal basis on the subject of childlessness in Africa, see Oduyoye (1999).

184. There are instances where menstruating women were prohibited to enter the houses of a chief, family head or traditional priest. Thus some chiefs chose to have second or even third wives in order to take care of household chores, including cooking.
185. With increased attention given to the subject of polygamy by African feminist theologians, MCG will have to revisit the issue in the near future (see Nasimiyu-Wasike in Oduyoye, 1992: 101–18).
186. At the 1987 conference, it was reported that the Sunyani and Oda districts were "definitely against any change in favour of polygamous converts" (MCG Minutes 1987, 77).
187. Church Union discussions in Nigeria and East Africa failed because of various factors. In the case of East Africa, the Presbyterians and Lutherans could not agree on the nature of the episcopal leadership. The fact that there were three churches, with varying number of followers in three different countries, was a major factor. "Those who found it most difficult were the Anglicans. The Methodists and Presbyterians were in Kenya only, while Anglicans were in Kenya and Tanzania. A union of Anglican, Methodist and Presbyterians would have meant little to Tanzanian Anglicans, to whom Presbyterians and Methodists were virtually unknown . . . They would have had to change their constitution, for the sake of people they did not know and had not even seen in the flesh" (Macpherson 1970, 143–44, see also Kalu 1978).
188. This statement was endorsed by the leaders of the various congregational organizations (MCG Conference Minutes 1985, 189).
189. The Deed of Foundation of the Methodist Church, Ghana, requires that any such resolution must be passed by a majority of seventy-five percent at two consecutive conferences. It is truly remarkable that both votes garnered 90 percent approval or more.
190. V. J. R. Richter, son of a Presbyterian minister, for example, served for many years as the connexional treasurer of MCG; yet on his deathbed he was claimed by the Presbyterians and re-baptized. Clergy from the Presbyterian Church conducted his funeral service.
191. Hans-Werner Gensichen, writing in the *Dictionary of Mission*, says that the Ghana Church union project failed because "the decentralized process of preparation for the union through union committees in each of the proposed union dioceses proved to be so demanding and time-consuming that the central committee had to postpone the date again and again" (Gensichen in Muller 1997, 468).
192. The committee in winding up its affairs decided to hand over all its documents to the Methodist Church, Ghana for safe keeping in the hope that they would be brought into use again. So far no such efforts have been mounted.
193. This was one of three consultations held between British Conference representatives invited by MCOD, and Sierra Leone (1984), Ghana (1985), and Nigeria (1986). I am indebted to John Pritchard for the fact that the MCG constitution was only part of the agenda and not the main reason for the consultation. It is significant that MCG involved the mother church in evolving

the new changes. Another significant but less noticed change is the practice of sending one minister and one layperson as representatives, with full voting rights, to the annual British Conference. Currently a layperson goes one year and a minister goes the next. This alternating system was adopted as an economy measure (these are all-expenses-paid trips) until the mid 90s.

194. In the history of the church, only two people have served for seven years, T. Wallace Koomson and Kwesi A. Dickson.

195. Samuel Kwame Asante-Antwi, the eighth and last president and first presiding bishop of the Conference (1997–2003), was born May 27, 1937, in Moseaso, Akim Abuakwa. He studied at Komenda College, Trinity College, Asbury Theological Seminary, and Yale Divinity School. He crowned his academic career with a Ph.D. in social anthropology at the University of Aberdeen, Scotland. He pastored several churches in the Kumasi, Pinanko, Calvary, Ridge, Suhum, and St. John societies. While serving as principal of MCG's Trinity Theological Seminary, he developed a special B.A. program linked with the University of Ghana, Legon. He served WCC as a member of an observer team to express solidarity with the South Africa frontline states during the apartheid regime. He also went to Latin America on behalf of the All Africa Conference of Churches to observe, analyze, and make recommendations on economic, political, and social issues for action by international bodies. Several projects were developed under his leadership during his tenure as Kumasi district Chairman (1989–96), bringing him to national attention: the renovation of Wesley and Freeman colleges, the establishment of vocational and technical institutes, the creation of the Kumasi, Obuasi, and Effiduase districts (replacing the former single district of Kumasi), and the construction of the Osofokrom Methodist Shopping Centre near Kejetia, the central market. He also formed the Christian Chiefs and Queen mothers' Association (See Asante-Antwi, 1997, 4-6).

196. Mbang was the President of the Christian Association of Nigeria, the association that embraces all Protestant and Catholic churches, and even some Pentecostal churches, in Nigeria. This group has been very influential in the area of church-and-state relationships (a sharp issue in Nigeria due to the desire of the Muslim community to declare the entire country a Muslim nation). In 2003 Mbang also served as Chair of the World Methodist Council. Though the matter was little noticed in the publicity for the occasion, his presence reminded some that it had been Ghanaian Methodists who started the Methodist Church, Nigeria, in collaboration with Thomas Birch Freeman, in the mid-nineteenth century(see chapter 2).

197. Kwesi A. Dickson, the other past president living and active did not attend the ceremony for personal reasons.

198. They were lined up as follows: Rt. Rev. Albert Ofoe-Wright, Connexional Administration, Wesley House, Accra; Rt. Rev. Justice K. A. Dadson B.A., M.Th.–Cape Coast; Rt. Rev. Kwaku Asamoah-Okyere B.A. M.A.–Kumasi; Rt. Rev. Kow B. Egyir B.A. –Sekondi; Rt. Rev. William Jonfia (Col. Ret.) –Winneba; Rt. Rev. Joseph K. Ato-Brown B.A.–Koforidua; Rt. Rev. K.

Omane Achamfuor, B.Sc.–Sunyani; Rt. Rev. Sampson Yamoah–Tarkwa; Rt. Rev. Joseph K. Tekyi-Ansah, B.A. M.Th.–Northern Ghana; Rt. Rev. Benjamin A. Asare, M.A.–Akim Oda; Rt. Rev. Moses O. Antwi, BA-Effiduase; Rt. Rev. Samuel N. Agyei-Mensah, M.A.–Obuasi; and Rt. Rev. Seth A. Aryee, M.A., M.Phil., Ph.D. –Tema.

199. This is the Ghana Church Union Committee Section of Draft Basis of Unions Submitted to Negotiating Churches in July 1961 (GCUC 1961).

200. In the *Methodist Times*, Agbeti opined that MCG should suspend its enthusiasm for episcopacy. His main argument was that the money needed to purchase expensive vestments could be better utilized in preparing Christian education materials for the church so that they could spearhead evangelistic outreach campaigns (Agbeti 1994).

201. In the early 1990s, the present author was a member of a subcommittee appointed by the Cape Coast District Standing Committee to review the issue of the adoption of episcopacy. All three members, the Reverend Kweku Abakah, Nana C. M. Cann, and the author, concluded that the reason given by those who supported episcopacy, namely, that it conformed to contemporary trends, was not sufficient grounds for making the change. The subcommittee proposed that the attention and energy of MCG leadership would be more fruitfully focused on safeguarding church property, improving MCG resources, and consolidating the Donewell Insurance Scheme, then a newly founded MCG-owned insurance company in Ghana.

202. Compare *The Spirituality of African Peoples: The Search for a Common Moral Discourse*, in which Peter J. Paris compares the traditional African understanding of chieftaincy to that of the nature of ministry in the Christian Church. What he says of the African-American Church is applicable to MCG, as well: "Whenever a person is elected to the episcopacy of African-American Methodism . . . that person's family gains a status within the denomination analogous to that of royal families in traditional Africa. With few exceptions, similar analogies can be seen in the magnificent way congregations treat virtually all African American clergy and their families" (Paris 1995, 61).

203. Author's videotape of Episcopacy Sunday, January 23, 2000.

204. Dr. Robert Kwasi Aboagye-Mensah came to this position after serving as general secretary of the Christian Council of Ghana. His leadership in CCG has been evaluated as "one of the most impressive in sub-Saharan Africa" (Gifford 1992, 72). Born at Asuokwaa, near Chiraa in the Brong Ahafo region of Ghana, he became a Christian through the ministry of Nigel Sylvester, traveling secretary of Ghana's Scripture Union. During missionary service in Gambia he came into contact with the Reverend Dr. John Stott and was enabled to do a degree program at St. John's College, Nottingham University, in England. He then completed a doctoral program at the University of Aberdeen, Scotland. Upon returning to Ghana, he taught for ten years at Trinity Theological Seminary while pastoring Trinity United Church and Police Church in the Tema and Dansoman circuits. Through his writings he has articulated the theological stance of mainline churches vis-à-vis the new

Pentecostal and charismatic movement.

205. See similar reflections by the Tanzanian Anglican bishop, Simon Chiwanga (2001, 297–317).

206. The Anglican Communion has ruled that though monogamy is the preferred goal, members in polygamous marriages would not be excluded from the church.

CHAPTER SEVEN | **Conclusion**

207. Lamin Sanneh has dramatically highlighted the role of scriptural translation in enabling indigenization and contextualization (Sanneh 1993).

REFERENCES

PRIMARY SOURCES

ARCHIVES

1. Methodist Church, Gold Coast Synod. 1948. I Will Build My Church. Report of a Commission to Consider the Life of the Church.
2. Methodist Missionary Society. 1951. Report of a Secretarial Visit to West Africa.
3. Methodist Church, Gold Coast Synod. 1953. Report of the Commission on the Finances of the Gold Coast Methodist Church.
4. Methodist Missionary Society. 1954. Report of a Secretarial Visit.
5. Methodist Missionary Society. 1957. Report of the West African Conference, African Committee (February).
6. Methodist Church, Ghana. 1961. Inaugural Conference Program. Mfantsiman Press, Cape Coast.
7. Methodist Church, Ghana. 1961–2000. Annual Reports and/or Fact Sheets.
8. Methodist Church, Ghana. 1961–2000. Conference Minutes and/or Tidbits.[1]
9. Methodist Church, Ghana. 1961–2000. Ministerial Session, Conference Agenda[2]
10. Methodist Church, Ghana. 1961–2000. Representative Session, Conference Agenda.
11. Methodist Church, Cape Coast. 1963. Report of the Council (March).
12. Methodist Church, Ghana. 1966. Women's Fellowship Handbook.
13. Methodist Church, Ghana. 1971. 10th Annual Conference Handbook.
14. The Christian Sentinel. 1971–2000 (gaps).[3]
15. Wesley College. 1977. Golden Jubilee Anniversary Program.
16. Methodist Church, Ghana. 1981. Women's Fellowship Jubilee Program.

1 Minutes of MCG Annual Conferences were produced up to 1970. Thereafter the denominational head office issued "Conference Tidbits."

2 Agenda refers to printed reports from various dioceses and organizations distributed before and used during conference.

3 Publications have been inconsistent. In some years there were 2 issues, and in others only 1.

17. Submission of Definitive Statement, Resolutions, and Supporting Document of the Laity of Accra District of the Methodist Church on the Future of the District. September 13, 1984.
18. Methodist Church, Ghana. 1986. Christ's Little Band Centenary Celebration Program.
19. Letter of expulsion. 1986. From the Methodist Church, Ghana to the Reverend Edu-Buandoh, signed by the Reverend Tekyi-Ansah, September. 8. Ref. no. MISC 95/MDGC/36/6.
20. Ghana Evangelism Committee. 1989. National Church Survey: Finishing the Unfinished Task of the Church in Ghana. Accra.
21. Mount Olivet Society. 1990. A Short History of Mount Olivet Society, Dansoman, Accra. Souvenir Program for the Inauguration of Circuit and induction of the Reverend Isaac Bonful as the first superintendent minister (March 31) 24–28.
22. Wesley College. 1992. 70th Anniversary Program.
23. Ghana Evangelism Committee. 1993. National Church Survey: Finishing the Unfinished Task of the Church in Ghana: Update 1993. Accra
24. Christian Council of Ghana. 1999. 70th Anniversary Program.
25. Methodist Church. 1999. Report to World Methodist Evangelist Meeting for West Africa, Nigeria (June 30–July 4).
26. Mount Olivet Society. 1999. Silver Jubilee Souvenir Brochure.
27. Methodist Church, Ghana. 2001–2002. Fact Sheets.
28. Open Space: The African Christian Diaspora in Europe and the Quest for Human Community. 2000. International Review of Mission, (July 2000: 84, no. 354).

REFERENCES

SECONDARY RESOURCES

Books & Articles

Aboagye-Mensah, Robert K. 1998. The Protestant Experience in Ghana. *Journal of African Christian Thought* 1 (2): 42–50.

———1994. *Mission and Democracy in Africa: The Role of the Church*. Accra, Ghana: Asempa.

———1993. Mission and Democracy in Africa: The Problem of Ethnocentrism. *International Bulletin of Missionary Research* 17 (3): 130–33.

——— 1991. Socio-Political Mission of the Church in Ghana. In *AD 2000 and Beyond: a Mission Agenda*. A Festschrift for John Stott's 70th Birthday, ed., Vinay Samuel and Chris Sugden, 82–96. Oxford: Regnum Books.

Abruquah, Joseph. 1971. *The Catechist*. Accra, Ghana: Ghana Publishing.

Ackah, C.A. 1988. *Akan Ethics: A Study of the Moral Ideas and the Moral Behaviour of the Akan Tribes of Ghana*. Accra, Ghana: Ghana Universities Press.

Acquaah-Arhin, Samuel. 1998. Ghanaian-American Worship Practices. In *Worship Across Cultures: A Handbook*, ed. Kathy Black, 90–99. Nashville: Abingdon Press.

Addo-Fening, Robert. 2000. Doing Local Christian History. *Journal of African Christian Thought* 3 (1): 37–40.

Adeyemo, Tokumboh. 1979. *Salvation in African Tradition*. Nairobi: Evangel.

Adjei, Ebenezer Ako. 1944. Imperialism and Spiritual Freedom: An African View. *American Journal of Sociology*. Vol. 50, No. 3 (Nov., 1944), pp. 189-198

Adjei, Mike. 1994. *Death and Pain in Rawlings' Ghana: The Inside Story*. London: Blackline.

Adogame, Afe, Roswith Gerloff, and Klaus Hock. 2008. *Christianity in Africa and the African Diaspora: The Appropriation of a Scattered Heritage*. New York: Continuum.

Agbeti, John Kofi. 1994. Suspend Episcopate Issue: Urges Rev. Dr. Agbeti. *Methodist Times* 8 (May-June).

———1986. *West African Church History: Christian Missions and Church Foundations, 1482–1919*. Leiden, Netherlands: E.J. Brill.

———1974. New Perspectives in Theological Education with Special Reference to Ghana. *Ghana Bulletin of Theology* 4 (6): 19–36.

———1971. Theological Education in Ghana. *Ghana Bulletin of Theology* 3 (10): 23–34.

Agyekum, Kofi. 1997. The Unmentionability of Death among the Akan of Ghana. *Legon Journal of the Humanities* 10:43–61.

Ahiable-Addo, Cosmos. H. 1998. Methodism in Asante 1843–1900: An Existence in Tenuity. *Trinity Journal of Church and Theology* 8 (July): 44–59.

———1997. The Introduction of Methodism among the Asante of Ghana and Their Responses, 1839–1844. *Trinity Journal of Church and Theology* 7 (July): 28–43.

———1996. Focus on the Early Methodist Church in Ghana: 1835–1838. *Trinity Journal of Church and Theology* 6 (December): 1–25.

________1993. A Concise History of the Methodist Church in Asante, Ghana. 1835–1992. (Manuscript)

Aidoo, Samuel Yorke. 1999. Ghana Methodism Joins Episcopal Family—Rejoinder. *Methodist Times* 13 (November–December): 2.

Ajayi, J.F.A. 1965. *Christian Missions in Nigeria, 1841-1891: The Making of a New Elite.* London: Longman.

Akpata-Ohohe, Bunmi. 2001. People: Appointments and Awards. *Africa Today* (August).

Akyeampong, Emmanuel. 2000. Africans in the Diaspora: the Diaspora and Africa. *African Affairs* 99 (395): 183–215.

Akyeampong, H. K. n.d. *Ghana's Struggle for Democracy and Freedom: Speeches 1957-69 by Dr. Kofi Abrefa Busia.* Accra, Ghana: Danquah Memorial Publishing.

———n.d. *Busia—A Symbol of Democracy*. Accra, Ghana: Danquah Memorial.

Akrong, Abraham. 2001. Salvation in African Christianity. *Legon Journal of the Humanities* (University of Ghana) 12:1–29.

———1998. The Historic Mission of the African Independent Churches. *Research Review* (University of Ghana) 2: 58–68.

Allen, Roland. 1995. *Missionary Methods: St. Paul's or Ours?* Grand Rapids: Eerdmans. Reprinted: World Dominion Press, 1962.

Amoah, Elizabeth, ed. 1997. *Where God Reigns: Reflections on Women in God's World.* Accra, Ghana: Sam-Woode.

———1990. Women and Rituals in Akan Society. *Dialogue & Alliance* 4:85–95.

Anderson, Allan. 2002. Diversity in the Definition of "Pentecostal/Charismatic" and Its Ecumenical Implications. *Missions Studies* 19:40–55.

———2001a. *African Initiated Christianity in the Twentieth Century.* Laurenceville, N.J.: Africa World Press.

———2001b. "Failure in Love"? Western Missions and the Emergence of African Initiated Churches in the Twentieth Century. *Missiology: An International Review* 29 (July 3): 275–86.

Anderson, Gerald H., ed. 1998. *Biographical Dictionary of Christian Missions*. New York: Simon & Schuster Macmillan.

———1961. *The Theology of the Christian Mission.* New York: McGraw-Hill.

Anderson, Gerald H., Robert T. Coote, Norman A. Horner, and James M. Phillips, eds. 1994. *Mission Legacies: Biographical Studies of the Leaders of the Modern Missionary Movement*. Maryknoll, N.Y.: Orbis Books.

Anderson, Gerald H., and Thomas F. Stransky, eds. 1974. *Third World Theologies*. New York: Paulist Press and Grand Rapids: Eerdmans.

Annan, Kofi A. 1998. U.N. Press Release (November 17).

Anquandah, James. 1979. *Together We Sow—The First Fifty Years of the Christian Council of Ghana, 1929–1979*. Accra, Ghana: Asempa.

———1974. Christian Torn between the World and His Faith. In *God's Mission in Ghana,* ed. W. G. M. Brandful. Accra, Ghana: Asempa .

Antwi, Daniel, and Paul Jenkins. 2002. The Moravians, the Basel Mission and the Akuapem State in the Early Nineteenth Century. In *Christian Missionaries and the State in the Third World,* eds. Holger B. Hansen and Michael Twaddle, 39–51. Oxford: James Currey.

Appiah, Joseph. 1990. *Joe Appiah: The Autobiography of an African Patriot*. Accra: Asempa.

Appiah-Kubi, Kofi. 1981. *Man Cures, God Heals: Religion and Medical Practice among the Akans of Ghana.* Totowa, N.J.: Allanheld, Osman & Co.

Appiah-Kubi, K., and S. Torres, eds. 1979. *African Theology en Route*. Maryknoll, N.Y.: Orbis Books.

Appiah, Kwame. 1992. *My Father's House: Africa and the Philosophy of Culture.* New York: Oxford University Press.

Appiah, Kwame Anthony, and V. Y. Mudimbe. 1993. The Impact of African Studies on Philosophy. In *Africa and the Disciplines: The Contributions of Research in Africa to the Social Sciences and Humanities,* eds. Robert H. Bates, V.Y. Mudimbe, J. O'Barr. Chicago and London: University of Chicago Press.

Arhin, Kwame, ed. 1991. *The Life and Work of Kwame Nkrumah.* Papers presented at a symposium by the Institute of African Studies, University of Ghana, Legon. Accra: Sedco.

Apter, D. E. 1972. *Ghana in Transition.* Princeton, N.J.: Princeton University Press.

Asamoah, E. A. 1962. The Christian Church and African Heritage. *Christianity as Seen by the Africans,* ed. Ram Desai, 60–67. Denver: Alan Swalow.

Asamoah-Gyadu, J. Kwabena. 2005. *African Charismatics: Current Developments within Independent Indigenous Pentecostalism*. Leiden, Netherlands: Brill.

———2002a. Pentecostalism and the Missiological Significance of Religious Experience: The Case of Ghana's "Church of Pentecost." *Trinity Journal of Church and Theology* 7 (July-December): 30–57.

———2002b. Pentecostalism in Africa and the Changing Face of Christian Mission: Pentecostal/Charismatic Renewal Movements in Ghana. *Missions Studies* 19:14–39.

———1994. Meeting the Challenges of the Ordained Ministry in a Needy World. Paper presented at the Methodist Church, Ghana, Annual All-Ministers Retreat. Wesley College, Kumasi, Ghana (January).

________. 1993. Spiritual Burnout: The Bane of Christian Leadership. *Trinity Journal of Church and Theology* 3 (June): 61–72.

________. 1992. Salvation in African Independent Churches and Charismatic Ministries in Ghana. *Trinity Journal of Church and Theology* 2 (December): 84–98.

Asante, Emmanuel K. 2001. The Gospel in Context: An African Perspective. *Interpretation,* 55:44, 355-366.

———. 2000 The Distinctive Episcopacy of the Methodist Church, Ghana. Paper presented at the All Ministers Retreat at Prempeh College, Kumasi. (January 2–7).

———. 1995. *Toward an African Christian Theology of the Kingdom of God: The Kingship of Onyame.* Lewiston, N.Y.: Edwin Mellen.

Asante-Antwi, Samuel Kwame. 1996. How It All Happened. *Methodist Times* (September. 4): 1.

Assimeng, Max. 1989. *Religion and Social Change in West Africa.* Accra, Ghana: Ghana Universities Press.

Atiemo, Abamfo O. 1993. *The Rise of the Charismatic Movement in the Mainline Churches of Ghana.* Accra, Ghana: Asempa.

Austin, Dennis. 1964. *Politics in Ghana, 1946–1960.* London: Oxford University Press.

Awoonor, Kofi N. 1990. *Ghana: A Political History from Pre-European to Modern Times.* Accra, Ghana: Sedco.

Ayittey, George B. N. 1998. *Africa in Chaos.* New York: St. Martin's Press.

———1992. *Africa Betrayed.* New York: St. Martin's Press.

Azumah, John. 2000. Controversy and Restraint in Ghana. *Transformation* 17 (1): 23–26.

——— n.d. Northern Outreach Program: A Decade of Achievement. *Christian Messenger* 12 (4): 7.

——— n.d. NOP Hits Ten Years. *Voice of Missions* 3, no. 2.

Baeta, C. G. 1988. My Pilgrimage in Mission. *International Bulletin of Missionary Research* 14 (3): 116–20.

———1974. The Mission of the Church Is Christ's Mission. In *God's Mission in Ghana*, ed. W. G. M. Brandful, 2–19. Accra, Ghana: Asempa.

———1971a. Some Aspects of Religious Change in Ghana. *Ghana Bulletin of Theology* 3 (10): 9–22.

———1971b. *The Relationships of Christians with Men of Other Living Faiths.* Accra, Ghana: Ghana Universities Press.

———1968. *Christianity in Tropical Africa.* Studies presented and discussed at the Seventh International African Seminar, University of Ghana, April 1965. International African Institute, London: Oxford University Press.

———1967. Aspects of Religion. *A Study of Contemporary Ghana: Some Aspects of Social Structure*, eds. Walter Birmingham, E.N. Omaboe, I. Neustadt. Pp. 240–50. Evanston, Ill: Northwestern University Press.

———1962. *Prophetism in Ghana: A Study of Some "Spiritual" Churches.* London: SCM Press.

———1955. The Challenge of African Culture to the Church and the Message of the Church to African Culture. In *Christianity and African Culture*, ed. S. G. Williamson, 51–61. Accra, Ghana: Christian Council.

Bannerman, J. Yedu. 1999. *Roots and Fruits of the Methodist Church, Tema*. Tema, Ghana: Methodist Church Tema Circuit.

Barker, Peter. 1983. *Peter Dagadu: Man of God.* Accra, Ghana: Asempa.

Barrett, David B. 1968. *Schism and Renewal in Africa: An Analysis of Six Thousand Contemporary Religious Movements*. Nairobi: Oxford University Press.

Bartels, Francis. L. 1965. *The Roots of Ghana Methodism.* London: Cambridge University Press.

Bartle, Philip F.W. 1983. The Universe Has Three Souls: Notes on Translating Akan Culture. *Journal of Religion in Africa* 14 (2): 85–114.

Bates, R. H., and V. Y. Mudimbe, J.O'Barr. 1993. *Africa and the Disciplines. The Contributions of Research in Africa to the Social Sciences and Humanities,* Chicago, Ill.: University of Chicago Press.

Baur, John. 1994. *Two Thousand Years of Christianity in Africa: An African History, 62–1992,* Nairobi: Paulines.

Bayart, Jean-Francois. 1993. *The State in Africa: The Politics of the Belly*. London: Longman.

Bediako, Kwame. 2000. *Jesus in Africa: The Christian Gospel in African History and Experience*. Akropong, Ghana: Regnum Africa.

———1996. African Theology. In *The Modern Theologians* 2nd ed., ed. David Ford, 426-44. Oxford: Basil Blackwell.

———1996. How Is Jesus Christ Lord? Aspects of an Evangelical Christian Apologetics in the Context of African Religious Pluralism. *Exchange* 25 (1): 27–42.

———. 1995a. *Christianity in Africa: The Renewal of a Non-Western Religion.* Maryknoll, NY: Orbis Books.

———1995b. The Significance of Modern African Christianity—A Manifesto. *Studies in World Christianity* 1 (1): 51–67.

———1994. Christ Lord: How Is Jesus Christ Unique in the Midst of Other Religious Faiths? *Trinity Journal of Church and Theology* 4 (2): 50–61.

———1991. *Theology and Identity: The Impact of Culture upon Christian Thought in the Second Century and Modern Africa*. Oxford: Regnum Books.

———1990. *Jesus in African Culture: A Ghanaian Perspective*. Accra, Ghana: Asempa.

_______. 1989. World Evangelization, Institutional Evangelicalism, and the Future of the Christian World Mission. In *Proclaiming Christ in Christ's Way: Studies in Integral Evangelism,* eds. Vinay Samuel, Albrecht Hauser and W. Arnold. Oxford: Regnum Books.

Beetham, Thomas. A. 1990. My Pilgrimage in Mission. *International Bulletin of Missionary Research* 14 (October): 167–71.

——— 1967. *Christianity and the New Africa.* London: Pall Mall Press.

Berinyuu, Abraham, ed. 1997. *History of the Presbyterian Church in Northern Ghana.* Accra, Ghana: Asempa.

Bhila, Hoyini H. K. 2000. The Work of Christian Missions in Africa before the Colonial Period (1850-1880). In *Methodism and Education: From Roots to Fulfillment,* ed. Sharon Hels. Nashville: General Board of Higher Education and Ministry, The United Methodist Church.

Birtwhistle, N. Allen. 1983. Methodist Missions. *A History of the Methodist Church in Great Britain,* eds. Rupert Davies and E.G. Rupp. 3:1–116. London: Epworth Press.

——— 1950. *Thomas Birch Freeman*. London: Cargate Press.

Bissell, Richard E., and Michael S. Radu. 1984. *Africa in the Post-Decolonization Era*. New Brunswick, N.J.: Transaction Books.

Boahen, Adu. 1996. *Mfantsipim and the Making of Ghana: A Centenary History 1876-1976*. Accra, Ghana: Sankofa.

———1987. *African Perspectives on Colonialism.* Baltimore: Johns Hopkins University Press.

———1975. *Topics in West African History*. London: Longmans.

———1970. *History of West Africa: The Revolutionary Years, 1815 to Independence*. New York: Praeger.

Bond, G. W. Johnson, and S. S. Walker, eds. 1979. *African Christianity: Patterns of Religious Continuity.* New York: Academic Press.

Booth, Newell, ed. 1977. *African Religions: A Symposium*. New York: Nok.

Bortey, Emmanuel A. B. 1986. Conversation on the State of Work of God in Ghana. Methodist Church, Ghana Conference.

Bosch, David J. 1991. *Transforming Mission: Paradigm Shifts in Theology of Mission.* Maryknoll, N.Y.: Orbis Books.

———1985. *Witness to the World: The Christian Mission in Theological Perspective*. London: Marshall, Morgan & Scott, Atlanta, Ga: John Knox Press.

———1981. Church Unity amidst Cultural Diversity. *Missionalia* 10 (January): 21.

Bowditch, Nathaniel. 1999. *The Last Emerging Market: From Asian Tigers to Africa's Lions? The Ghana File*. Westport, Conn.: Praeger.

Bowie, Fiona. 1999. The Inculturation Debate in Africa. In *Studies in World Christianity* 5: 67–91.

Brandewie, Ernest. 2000. *In the Light of the Word: Divine Word Missionaries of North America.* Maryknoll, N.Y.: Orbis Books.

Bujo, Benezet. 1992. *African Theology in Its Social Context,* trans. John O'Donohue. Maryknoll, N.Y.: Orbis Books.

Busia, Kofi Abrefa. 1968. *The Position of the Chief in the Modern Political System of Ashanti*. London: Frank Cass.

——— 1967. *In Search of Democracy*. New York: Praeger.

———1955. The African Worldview. In *Christianity and African Culture,* ed. S. G. Williamson, 1–6. Accra: Christian Council.

———1954. The Ashanti of the Gold Coast. In *African Worlds*, ed. Darryl Forde, 191–209. London: Oxford University Press.

———1950. *A Report on a Social Survey of Sekondi-Takoradi*. London: Crown Agents.

Chernoff, John M. 1979. *African Rhythm and African Sensibility: Aesthetics and Social Action in African Music Idioms*. Chicago: University of Chicago Press.

Chiwanga, Simon. 2001. Beyond the Monarch/Chief: Reconsidering the Episcopacy in Africa, pp. 297-317 in *Beyond Colonial Anglicanism: The Anglican Communion in the Twenty-First Century*, eds. Ian T. Douglas and Kwok Pui-Lan. New York: Church Publishing.

Christian Council of Ghana. 1970. *The Rise of Independent Churches in Ghana*. Accra, Ghana: Asempa.

Christensen, J. B. 1970. The Adaptive Functions of the Fanti Priesthood. In *Continuity and Change in African Cultures,* eds. W. R. Bascom and M. J. Herskovits, 257–78. London: University of Chicago Press.

———1954. *Double Descent among the Fanti.* New Haven, Conn.: Human Relations Area Files.

Collins, John. 2002. Gospel Boom. *West Africa* no. 4339 (August 19–25): 12–13.

———1996. *Highlife Time: The Story of the Ghanaian Concert Party, West African Highlife and Related Popular Music Styles*. Accra, Ghana: Anansesem.

Coleman, Robert E. 1990. *Nothing to Do but to Save Souls.* Wilmore, KY.: Wesley Heritage Press.

Conn, Harvie M. 1984. *Eternal Word and Changing Worlds: Theology, Anthropology and Mission in Trialogue*. Grand Rapids, Mich.: Zondervan.

Conn, Harvie M., and Samuel F. Rowen. 1984. *Missions and Theological Education in World Perspective*. Palatine, Ill.: Associates of Urbanus.

Cook, Jerry O., ed. 1989. *Roots and Branches: Historical Essays on Methodism in Southern New England*. Boston: New England Methodist Historical Society.

Coppedge, Allan. 1991. How Wesleyans Do Theology. In *Doing Theology in Today's World: Essays in Honor of Kenneth S. Kantzer*, eds. John D. Woodbridge and Thomas Edward McComiskey, 267–89. Grand Rapids: Zondervan.

Cormack, P. 1983. *Wilberforce, the Nation's Conscience*. London: Pickering.

Costas, Orlando, E. 1974. *The Church and Its Mission: A Shattering Critique from the Third World.* Wheaton, Ill.: Tyndale House.

Cox, Harvey. 1995. *Fire from Heaven: The Rise of Pentecostal Spirituality and the Reshaping of Religion in the Twenty-first Century*. Reading, Mass.: Addison-Wesley.

Crayner, J. B. 1967. *Akweesi Egu Nananom Mpow.* Accra, Ghana: Bureau of Ghana Languages.

Crawley, Winston. 2001. *World Christianity 1970–2000: Toward a New Millennium.* Pasadena, Calif.: William Carey Library.

Daneel, M. L. 1970. *The God of the Matopo Hills.* The Hague: Mouton.

———1987. *Quest for Belonging: Introduction to a Study of African Independent Churches*. Gweru, Zimbabwe: Mambo Press.

Danquah, J. B. 1968. *The Akan Doctrine of God: A Fragment of Gold Coast Ethics and Religion.* London: Frank Cass. (Reprinted with a new introduction by Kwesi A. Dickson, 1944.)

———1945. *The Akan of the Gold Coast*. London: Lutterworth.

Danso-Boafo, K. 1996. *Political Biography of Dr. Kofi Busia*. Accra, Ghana: Ghana Universities Press.

Dartey, David A., and Vesta Nyarko-Mensah, eds. 1994. *The Church, Ethnicity and Democracy*. Mid-year Seminar Report. Accra, Ghana: The Christian Council of Ghana.

Davey, Cyril. 1985. *John Wesley and the Methodists.* London: Marshall Pickering.

Davis, R. E and E.G. Rupp. 1966. *A History of the Methodist Church in Great Britain*. London: Epworth.

Davidson, Basil. 2007. *Black Star: A View of the Life and Times of Kwame Nkrumah.* London: James Currey.

———.1980. *Black Mother-Africa and the Atlantic Slave Trade.* Harmondsworth, U.K.: Penguin Books.

———1976. *Ghana: An African Portrait.* London: Gordon Eraser.

Debrunner, Hans W. 1967. *A History of Christianity in Ghana.* Accra, Ghana: Waterville.

——— 1965. *The Story of Sampson Opong.* Accra, Ghana: Waterville.

———1961. *Witchcraft in Ghana: A Study of the Belief in Destructive Witches and Its Effects on the Akan Tribes.* Accra, Ghana: Presbyterian Book Depot.

Der, Benedict. 1974. Church-State Relations in Northern Ghana, 1906–1940. *Transactions of the Historical Society of Ghana* 15 (June 1974): 41–61.

Desai, Ram A., ed. 1962. *Christianity in Africa as Seen by the Africans.* Denver: Allan Swalow.

Dickson, Kwesi A. 1996. *Methodist Times* (September): 4.

———1995. Presidential Speech. *Methodist Times* 9 (September-October.): 1, 5.

———1995. The Church and the Quest for Democracy in Ghana. In *The Christian Churches and the Democratisation of Africa.* Leiden, Netherlands: Brill. Pp. 261-275.

———1991. *Uncompleted Mission: Christianity and Exclusivism.* Maryknoll, N.Y.: Orbis Books.

———1984. *Theology in Africa.* Maryknoll: N.Y.: Orbis Books.

———1982. Mission in African Countries. In *Christian Mission-Jewish Mission,* eds. Martin Cohen and Helga Crone, 187–206. New York: Paulist Press.

——— 1978a. The African Theological Task. In *The Emergent Gospel*, eds. Sergio Torres and Virginia Fabella, 76–89. Maryknoll, N.Y.: Orbis Books.

———1978b. Christian and African Ceremonies. In *Readings in Missionary Anthropology,* ed. William Smalley, 435–41. Pasadena, Calif.: William Carey Library.

——— 1977a. *Aspects of Religion and Life in Africa.* Accra, Ghana: Ghana Academy of Arts and Sciences.

———1977b. The Minister—Then and Now. In *Religion in a Pluralistic Society,* ed. John Pobee, 166–89. Leiden, Netherlands: E. J. Brill.

———1975. African Theology—Whence, Methodology and Content. *Journal of Religious Thought* 33 (Fall-Winter): 34–44.

——— 1970. *Religions of the World.* Accra, Ghana: Ghana Publishing.

Dolphyne, Florence Abena, ed. 2000. *Ten Women Achievers from the Ashanti Region of Ghana.* Kumasi, Ghana: Centre for the Development of People.

———1994. Ethnicity and Ethnic Identity. In *The Church, Ethnicity and Democracy*, eds. David A. Dartey and Vesta Nyarko-Mensah, 41. Mid-year Seminar Report, Christian Council of Ghana.

———1989. *The Emancipation of Women: An African Perspective.* Accra, Ghana: Ghana Universities Press.

Dong, Peter M., Mary S. Bambur, and the Reverends John P. Bambur and Ayuba N. Bambur. 2000. *The History of the United Methodist Church in Nigeria.* Nashville, Abingdon.

Donovan, Vincent J. 1978. *Christianity Rediscovered.* Maryknoll, N.Y.: Orbis Books.

Dovlo, Elom. 1998. The Church in African and Religious Pluralism: The Challenge of New Religious Movements and Charismatic Churches. *Exchange* 27 (1): 52–69.

Dovlo, Elom, and Solomon S. Sule-Saa. 1999. The Northern Outreach Program of the Presbyterian Church of Ghana. *International Bulletin of Missionary Research* 23 (July): 112–16.

Dijk, Rijk A. Van. 1999. From Camp to Encampment: Discourse of Trans-subjectivity in the Ghanaian Pentecostal Diaspora. *Journal of Religion in Africa 27* (2): 135–57.

Edusa-Eyison, Joseph M. Y. 1999. Native Initiative in the Planting of Christianity in Ghana 1835–1961—The Methodist Contribution. *Trinity Journal of Church and Theology* 9 (July): 40–54.

———1997. Women in Church Leadership: Focus on the Methodist and Presbyterian Churches in Ghana. *Trinity Journal of Church and Theology* 6 (July): 57–65.

Ekechi, Felix K. 1993. Studies on Missions in Africa. In *African Historiography: Essays in Honour of Jacob Ade Ajayi*, ed. Toyin Falola, 145–65. Ikeja, Nigeria: Longman.

Ellis, Stephen. 2002. Writing Histories of Contemporary Africa. *Journal of African History* 43: 1–26.

Ephirim-Donkor, Anthony. 2000. *The Making of an African King: Patrilineal and Matrilineal Struggle among the Effutu of Ghana*. Trenton, N.J.: Africa World Press.

———1977. *African Spirituality: On Becoming Ancestors*. Trenton, N.J.: Africa World Press.

Ela, Jean-Marc. 1988. *My Faith as an African*, trans. J. P. Brown and Susan Perry. Maryknoll, N.Y.: Orbis Books.

———1986. *African Cry*, trans. Robert R. Barr. Maryknoll, N.Y.: Orbis Books.

Ellingworth, Paul. 1997. Mr. Freeman's Case. *Journal of Religion in Africa* 26 (1): 50–58.

Elsbernd, Alphonse. 2000. *The Story of the Catholic Church in the Diocese of Accra*. Accra, Ghana: Catholic Book Centre.

Essamuah, Colin B. 1996a. Boahen's Magnum Opus. *Statesman* 5 (July 14): 4, 9.

———1996b. Book Review. *Daily Graphic* (July 10): 5.

———1996c. Book Review. *Weekly Spectator* (July 6): 13.

Essamuah, Samuel B., comp. 1965. *Ebibindwom*. Accra, Ghana: Bureau of Ghana Languages.

Fabella, Virginia, and Mercy Oduyoye. 1988. *With Passion and Compassion: Third World Women Doing Theology*. Maryknoll, N.Y.: Orbis Books.

Fabian, J. 1971. *A Charismatic Movement in Katanga.* Evanston, Ill.: Northwestern Univ. Press.

Fage, John. 1966. *Ghana: A Historical Interpretation.* Madison: University of Wisconsin Press.

Familusi, M. M. 1992. *Methodism in Nigeria (1842-1992).* Ibadan, Nigeria: NPS Educational.

Fashole-Luke, Edward, Richard Gray, Adrian Hastings and Tasie Goodwin, eds. 1976. *Christianity in Independent Africa*. Bloomington: Indiana University Press.

Fiedler, Klaus. 1994. *The Story of Faith Missions*. Oxford: Regnum Books.

Fisher, Eugene J. 1982. Historical Developments in the Theology of Christian Missions. In *Christian Mission-Jewish Mission,* eds. Pp. 187-207. Martin Cohen and Helga Croner. New York: Paulist Press.

Fisher, Robert B. 1998. *West African Religious Traditions: Focus on the Akan of Ghana.* Maryknoll, N.Y.: Orbis Books.

Foli, Richard. 2001a. *Church Membership Trends in Ghana*. Accra, Ghana: Methodist Book Depot.

———2001b. *Church Growth in Ghana*. Accra, Ghana: Methodist Book Depot.

———2001c. The *Church in Ghana Today*. Accra, Ghana: Methodist Book Depot.

———2001d. *The Future of the Church in Ghana*. Accra, Ghana: Methodist Book Depot.

———2001e. *The Ghanaian Church in Retrospect*. Accra, Ghana: Methodist Book Depot.

———1994. Contemporary Wesleyan Methodism in Ghana: A Study of Problems of Church Growth. Accra, Ghana: Methodist Book Depot.

Folson, B. D. G. 1977a. The Marxist Period in the Development of Socialist Ideology in Ghana, 1962–1966. *Universitas* 6 (May): 3–23.

———1977b. The Development of Socialist Ideology in Ghana, 1949-1958. *Ghana Journal of Social Science.*

Ford, Leighton. 1991. *Transforming Leadership: Jesus' Way of Creating Vision, Shaping Values and Empowering Change*. Downers Grove, Ill.: Intervarsity Press.

Forde, C. D., ed. 1965. *African Worlds: Studies in the Cosmological Ideas and Social Values of the African Peoples.* London: Oxford University Press.

Forson, Matthias. 1995. *5 in '95.* Department of Evangelism, Mission and Renewal of the Methodist Church, Ghana.

Freeman, Thomas Birch. 1968. *Journal of Various Visits to the Kingdoms of Ashanti, Aku, and Dahomi in Western Africa*. London: Wesley Missions House. (Reprint, 1844).

Fyfe, Christopher. 1985. Reform in West Africa: The Abolition of the Slave Trade. In *History of West Africa*, vol. 2, eds. J. F. A. Ajayi and Michael Crowder. New York: Columbia University Press.

Fynn, John K. 1987. The Political System of the Fante in Ghana during the Time of the Pre-colonial Period. *Universitas* (University of Ghana,) 9, (November): 108–20.

Gates, H.L. 1999. Wonders of the African World. New York, NY: Alfred A. Knopf.

Geertz, Clifford. 1974. "From the Native's Point of View": On the Nature of Anthropological Understanding. *Bulletin of the American Academy of Arts and Sciences*, Vol. 28, No. 1 (Oct., 1974), Pp. 26-45.

Gehman, Richard J. 1989. *African Traditional Religion in Biblical Perspective*. Kijabe, Kenya: Kesho.

Gerlof, Roswith. 1997. The Significance of the African Christian Diaspora in Europe (with special reference to Britain). Paper presented at the African Initiatives in Christian Mission, UNISA, Pretoria, South Africa (January 13–17).

Ghana Evangelism Committee. 1987. National Church Survey. Accra, Ghana.

Ghunney, Joseph Kow. 1998. Ekow Ghunney Refutes Daily Graphic Story. *Methodist Times* (March).

———1993. Ghana. In *Pastoral Counseling in a Global Church: Voices from the Field,* eds. Robert Wicks and Barry Estadt, 82–104. Maryknoll N.Y.: Orbis Books.

Gilliland, Dean S. 2000. "Contextualization" in *Evangelical Dictionary of World Missions,* Eds. A Scott Moreau et al., Grand Rapids, Baker, 2000. p. 225-227

———1989. New Testament Contextualization: Continuity and Particularity in Paul's Theology. *In The Word among Us*. Dean S. Gilliland, ed., Pp 52-73. Dallas, TX: Word Books.

———1986. *African Religion Meets Islam: Religious Change in Northern Nigeria.* Lanham, MD: University Press of America.

Gifford, Paul. 1998. *African Christianity: Its Public Role*. Bloomington: Indiana University Press.

———1995. *The Christian Churches and the Democratization of Africa*. Leiden, Netherlands: E. J. Brill.

———1994. Ghana's Charismatic Churches. *Journal of Religion in Africa* 24 (3): 241–65.

———1992. *New Dimensions in African Christianity*. Nairobi, Kenya: All Africa Conference of Churches.

Gocking, Roger S. 1999. *Facing Two Ways: Ghana's Coastal Communities under Colonial Rule*. Lanham, Maryland: University Press of America.

Gollock, G. A. 1938. *Sons of Africa*. London: Student Christian Movement Press.

Gray, Richard. 1990. *Black Christians and White Missionaries*. New Haven, Conn.: Yale University Press.

Gyekye, Kwame. 1987. *African Philosophical Thought: The Akan Conceptual Scheme*. Philadelphia: Temple University Press.

Hackett, Rosalind I. J. 1998. Charismatic/Pentecostal Appropriation of Media Technologies in Nigeria and Ghana. *Journal of Religion in Africa* 28 (3): 258–77.

Halliburton, Gordon M. 1971. *The Prophet Harris: A Study of an African Prophet and His Mass Movement in the Ivory Coast and the Gold Coast, 1913–1915.* London: Longmans.

Hanciles, Jehu. 2008. *Beyond Christendom: Globalization, African Migration, and the Transformation of the West.* Maryknoll, N.Y.: Orbis Books.

Hansen, Holger, and Michael Twaddle, eds. 2002. *Christian Missionaries and the S tate in the Third World*. Oxford: James Currey.

Harmon, N.B. 1974. *The Encyclopedia of World Methodism*. Nashville, TN: United Methodist Publishing House.

Hastings, Adrian. 1994. *The Church in Africa 1450–1950.* Oxford: Clarendon Press.

______1990. Christianity in Africa. In *Turning Points in Religious Studies. Essays in Honour of Geoffrey Parrinder*, ed. Ursula King, 201–210. Edinburgh, Scotland: T & T Clark.

_______1979. *A History of African Christianity*. Cambridge: Cambridge University Press.

———1976. *African Christianity: An Interpretation*. London: Chapman

Haynes, Jeff. 1996. *Religion and Politics in Africa*. London: Zed Books.

Hayford, J.E.C. 1903. *Gold Coast Native Institutions: With Thoughts upon a Healthy Imperial Policy for the Gold Coast and Ashanti*. London: Sweet and Maxwell.

Healey, Joseph, and Donald Sybertz. 1996. *Towards an African Narrative Theology*. Nairobi: Paulines.

Hempton, David N. 1999. Methodism on the March: Messages from Distant Past. *Focus—Boston University School of Theology* (Fall): 7–20.

——— 1996. *The Religion of the People; Methodism and Popular Religion c. 1750–1900*. London and New York: Routledge.

Hiebert, Paul G. 1987. Critical Contextualization. *International Bulletin of Missionary Research* 11 no. 3 (July): 104–12.

Hillman, Eugene. 1977. *Polygamy Reconsidered: African Plural Marriage and the Christian Churches*. Maryknoll, N.Y.: Orbis Books.

Hinderink, J and J. Sterkenburg. 1975. *Anatomy of an African Town: A Socio-Economic Study of Cape Coast*. State University of Utrecht, Geographical Institute: Netherlands.

Hollenweger, Walter J. 1996. From Azusa Street to the Toronto Phenomenon: Historical Roots of the Pentecostal Movement. In *Pentecostal Movements as an Ecumenical Challenge. Concilium* 30: 4.

———1972. *The Pentecostals*. Peabody, Mass: Hendrickson.

Horton, R. 1975. On the Rationality of Conversion. *Africa* 45:219–35, 373–99.

———1971. African Conversion. *Africa* 41: 85–108.

———1964. African Traditional Thought in Western Science. *Africa* 34: 85–104.

Hunter, George G. 1994. Donald A. McGavran 1897–1990: Standing at the Sunrise of Missions. In *Mission Legacies: Biographical Studies of Leaders of the Modern Missionary Movement*, eds. Gerald H. Anderson, Robert T. Coote, Norman A. Horner, and James M. Phillips. Pp. 516-522. Maryknoll, N.Y.: Orbis Books.

Idowu, E. Bolaji. 1973. *African Traditional Religion*. London: SCM Press.

———1965. *Towards an Indigenous Church*. London: Oxford University Press.

Imasogie, Osadolor. 1983. *Guidelines for Christian Theology in Africa*. Achimota, Ghana: African Christian Press.

Isichei, Elizabeth. 1995. *A History of Christianity in Africa: From Antiquity to the Present*. London: SPCK.

Jahoda, G. 1961. *White Man: A Study of the Attitudes of Africans to Europeans in Ghana before Independence*. London: Oxford University Press.

Jenkins, Paul. 1986. The Roots of African Church History: Some Polemic Thoughts. *International Bulletin of Missionary Research* 10 (April): 67–70.

———1974. The Anglican Church in Ghana, 1905–24. *Transactions of the Historical Society of Ghana* 15 (June).

Joseph, Richard. 1993. The Christian Churches and Democracy in Africa. In *Christianity and Democracy in Global Context*, ed. John Witte, 231–47. Boulder: Westview Press.

Kaba, Lansine. 2001. The Slave Trade Was *Not* a Black-on-Black Holocaust. *African Studies Review* 44 (1): 1–20.

Kalu, Ogbu. U. 2002. Shape, Flow and Identity in Contemporary African Christian Historiography. *Trinity Journal of Church and Theology* 7 (July-December): 1–22.

———. 2000. Passive Revolution and Its Saboteurs: African Christian Initiative in the Era of Decolisation. Position Paper # 134, *Currents in World Christianity Project*, 7. Faculty of Divinity, University of Cambridge

———1996. *The Embattled Gods: Christianization of Igboland, 1841–1991.* Lagos, Nigeria: Minaj.

———1993. African Church Historiography. In *African Historiography: Essays in Honour of Jacob Ade Ajayi*, ed. Toyin Falola, 166–79. Ikeja, Nigeria: Longman.

———1989. African Church Historiography: An Ecumenical Perspective. *Encounter* 50 (Winter): 69–78.

——— ed. 1988. African Church Historiography: An Ecumenical Perspective. Papers presented at a workshop on African Church History held in Nairobi, August 3–6, 1986. Bern, Switzerland: Evangelische Arbeitsstelle Okumene Schweiz.

———ed. 1980. *The History of Christianity in West Africa*. London: Longman.

———1978. *Divided People of God: Church Movement in Nigeria, 1867–1966.* New York and London: Nok.

Kaplan, Steven. 1995. The Africanization of Missionary Christianity: History and Typology. In *Indigenous Response to Western Christianity*, ed. Steven Kaplan, 9–28. New York: New York University Press.

Kato, Byang H. 1985. *Biblical Christianity in Africa.* Achimota, Ghana: African Christian Press.

———1975a. *Theological Pitfalls in Africa*. Kisumu, Kenya: Evangel.

——— 1975b. *African Cultural Revolution and the Christian Faith.* Jos, Nigeria: Challenge Publications.

Keeley, Robin, ed. 1985. *Christianity in Today's World: An Eerdmans Handbook.* Grand Rapids: Eerdmans.

Kimble, David. 1963. *A Political History of Ghana: The Rise of Gold Coast Nationalism, 1850–1928*. Oxford: Clarendon Press.

King, Noel Q. 1970. *Religions of Africa: A Pilgrimage into Traditional Religions*. New York: Harper & Row.

Kinoti, George H. 1994. *Hope for Africa and What the Christian Can Do*. Nairobi: Aisred.

Kisembo, Benezeri, and L. Magesa, A. Shorter, eds. 1977. *African Christian Marriage*. Nairobi, Kenya: Paulines.

Klutse, A. K. P. 1977. The Proclamation of a Death of a Chief among the Ewe. *Universitas* 6 (May, new series): 128–45.

Kpobi, David Nii Anum. 2001. *Saga of a Slave: Jacobus Capitein of Holland and Elmina.* Legon, Ghana: Sub-Saharan.

———1999. Renewal and Reformation: Ghanaian Churches in Mission in the 21st Century. *Trinity Journal of Church and Theology* 9, no. 2.

Kraft, Charles H. 1996. *Anthropology for Christian Mission.* Maryknoll, N.Y.: Orbis Books.

———1979. *Christianity in Culture: A Study in Dynamic Biblical Theologizing in Cross-Cultural Perspective.* Maryknoll, N.Y.: Orbis Books.

Kraft, Charles H., and Tom N. Wisley, eds. 1979. *Readings in Dynamic Indigeneity*. Pasadena, Calif.: William Carey Library.

Kudadjie, Joshua N. 1996. Integrating Indigenous African Worship and Customary Practices with Christian Worship and Practice: An Illustration with the Outdooring and Naming Ceremony of a Baby among the Ada of Ghana. Paper presented at the Symposium on African Independent/Indigenous Churches and New Religious Movements, University of Witwatersrand, South Africa (June 26–27).

———1995. *Moral Renewal in Ghana: Ideals, Realities and Possibilities*. Accra, Ghana: Asempa.

———1971. Does Religion Determine Morality in African Societies? *Ghana Bulletin of Theology* 4 (5): 30–49.

Kurewa, John Wesley Z. 1997. *The Church in Mission: A Short History of the United Methodist Church in Zimbabwe, 1897–97*. Nashville: Abingdon.

Lang' at, Robert K. 2001. The Doctrine of Holiness and Missions: A Pietistic Foundation of Evangelical Christianity. *Evangelical Review of Theology* 25 (4): 350–61.

Larbi, E. Kingsley. 2001. *Pentecostalism: The Eddies of Ghanaian Christianity*. Accra, Ghana: Center for Pentecostal and Charismatic Studies.

———2000. History of Central University College. *Pathfinder* 2.

Larom, Margaret S. 1994. *Claiming the Promise: African Churches Speak*. New York: Friendship Press.

Lartey, Emmanuel Y., D. Nwachuku, and K.W. Kasonga, and K. W. Kasonga, eds. 1994. *The Church and Healing: Echoes from Africa*. Frankfurt am Main, Germany: Peter Lang.

Latourette, Kenneth Scott. 1997. *A History of Christianity*, vol. 2. Peabody, Mass.: Prince Press.

Lingenfelter, Sherwood G. 1992. *Transforming Culture. A Challenge for Christian Mission.* Grand Rapids: Baker Book House.

Lossky, Nicholas, José Bonino, John S. Pobee, Tom F. Stranky, Geoffrey Wainwright and Pauline Webb. Eds. 1991. *Dictionary of the Ecumenical Movement*. Geneva: World Council of Churches.

Luzbetak, Louis J. 1988. *The Church and Cultures: New Perspectives in Missiological Anthropology*. Maryknoll, N.Y.: Orbis Books.

Maddox, Randy L. 1999. Respected Founder/Neglected Guide: The Role of Wesley in American Methodist Theology. *Methodist History* 37 (January): 71–88.

Magoti, Evaristi W. F. 1997. An African Theology of Death: The Plenitude of Human Life. In *Constructive Christian Theology in the Worldwide Church*, ed. William Barr, 272–83. Grand Rapids: Eerdmans.

Martey, Emmanuel. 1996. *African Theology: Inculturation and Liberation*. Maryknoll, N.Y.: Orbis Books.

Martin, David. 2002. *Pentecostalism: The World Their Parish*. Oxford: Blackwell.

Masamba ma Mpolo, Jean, and Daisy Nwachuku, eds. 1991. *Pastoral Care and Counseling in Africa Today*. Frankfurt am Main, Germany: Peter Lang.

Mbiti, John S. 1986. *Bible and Theology in African Christianity*. London: Oxford University Press.

———. 1973. *Love and Marriage in Africa.* London: Longman.

———1970a. *African Religions and Philosophy*. New York: Doubleday.

———1970b. *Concepts of God in Africa*. New York: Praeger.

———1968. *New Testament Eschatology in Relation to Evangelization of Africa*. Nairobi: University College Press.

McCaskie, Thomas C. 1990. Nananom Mpow of Mankessim: An Essay in Fante History. In *West African Economic and Social History,* eds. David Henige and T. C. McCaskie, 113–50. Madison: University of Wisconsin.

McCutchan, Robert G. 1947. A Singing Church. *Methodism*, ed. William K. Anderson, 148–64. Nashville: Methodist.

MacPherson, R. 1970. *The Presbyterian Church in Kenya*. Nairobi, Kenya: Presbyterian Church of East Africa Publications.

McGavran, Donald. 1986. My Pilgrimage in Mission. *International Bulletin of Missionary Research* 10 (April): 53–58.

———1983. The Priority of Ethnicity. *Evangelical Missions Quarterly* 19 (January): 16–17.

McKown, R. 1973. *Nkrumah: A Biography*. New York: Doubleday.

Mensah, Atta Annan. 1960. The Akan Church Lyric. *International Review of Mission* 29 (April): 183–88.

Meyer, Birgit. 1999. *Translating the Devil: Religion and Modernity among the Ewe in Ghana.* Edinburgh, Scotland: Edinburgh University Press.

———1998a. Make a Complete Break with the Past: Memory and Postcolonial Modernity in Ghanaian Pentecostal Discourse. *Journal of Religion in Africa* 27 (3): 316–149.

———1998b. The Power of Money: Politics, Occult Forces and Pentecostalism in Ghana. *African Studies Review* 41 (December): 15–37.

———1992. "If You Are a Devil, You Are a Witch, and If You Are a Witch, You Are a Devil." The Integration of Pagan Ideas into the Conceptual Universe of Ewe Christians in Southeastern Ghana. *Journal of Religion in Africa* 22 (2): 98–131.

Meyerowitz, Eva L. 1958. *Akan of Ghana: Their Ancient Beliefs*. London: Faber and Faber.

Milum, John. 1875. *Thomas Birch Freeman: Missionary Pioneer to Ashanti, Dahomy and Egba*. London: S. W. Partridge.

Mobley, H. W. 1970. *The Ghanaian's Image of the Missionary: An Analysis of Published Critiques of Christian Missionaries by Ghanaians 1897–1965*. Leiden, Netherlands: E. J. Brill.

Moss, Arthur Bruce. 1974. Ghana. In *The Encyclopedia of World Methodism*, ed. Nolan B. Harmon, 1:1001. Nashville: United Nashville Methodist.

Muller, Karl. 1997. *Dictionary of Mission: Theology, History, Perspectives*. Maryknoll, N.Y.: Orbis Books.

Muzorewa, Gwinyai Henry. 1990. *An African Theology of Mission.* Lewiston, N.Y.: Edwin Mellen Press.

———*The Origins and the Developments of African Theology.* Maryknoll, N.Y.: Orbis Books.

Namwera, L., Aylward Shorter, Anne Nasimiyu-Wasiye, John M. Waliggo, Laurenti Magesa, Anthony Bellagamba, Andre McGrath, Raphael Wanjohi, Paul Tiyambe Zeleza, Dorothy McCormick, Joseph Kariuki, eds. 1990. *Towards African Christian Liberation*. Nairobi, Kenya: St. Paul's.

Neill, Stephen. 1966. *Colonialism and Christian Missions*. New York: McGraw-Hill.

———1964. *A History of Christian Missions*. London: Penguin Books.

Nelson, Martin L., ed. 1976. *Readings in Third World Missions: A Collection of Essential Documents.* South Pasadena, Calif.: William Carey Library.

Newbigin, Leslie. 1997. The Dialogue of Gospel and Culture: Reflections on the Conference on World Mission and Evangelism, Salvador, Bahia, Brazil. *International Bulletin of Missionary Research* 21 (April 2): 50–52.

———1996. *Truth and Authority in Modernity*. Valley Forge, Pa.: Trinity Press International.

———1994. *A Word in Season: Perspectives on Christian World Missions*. Grand Rapids: Eerdmans.

———1989. *The Gospel in a Pluralist Society*. Grand Rapids: Eerdmans.

Ngewa, Samuel, Mark Shaw, and Tite Tienou, eds. 1998. *Issues in African Christian Theology*. Nairobi: East African Educational Publishers.

Nicholls, Bruce J. 1979. *Contextualization: A Theology of Gospel and Culture*. Downers Grove, Ill.: Intervarsity Press.

Nida, Eugene A. 1993. *Customs and Cultures: Anthropology for Christian Missions*. Pasadena, Calif.: William Carey Library.

———1990. *Message and Mission: The Communication of the Christian Faith.* Pasadena, Calif.: William Carey Library.

Niebuhr, H. Richard. 1975. *Christ and Culture*. New York: Harper & Row.

Ninsin, Kwame A. 1996. *Ghana's Political Transition, 1990-1993: Selected Documents*. Freedom Publications (GA).

Nketia, J. H. 1958. The Contribution of African Culture to Christian Worship. *International Review of Missions* 47 (October): 265–78.

Nkrumah, Kwame. 1958. Speech given at the Conference on Independent African States. Accra, Ghana (April 15).

Noll, Mark. 1998. The Potential of Missiology for the Crises of History. In *History and the Christian Historian*, ed. Ronald A. Wells. Pp. 106-123. Grand Rapids: Eerdmans.

Northcott, William C. 1963. *Christianity in Africa*. Philadelphia: Westminster Press.

Nthamburi, Zablon. 1982. A *History of the Methodist Church in Kenya*. Nairobi: Uzima Press.

Nugent, Paul. 1995. *Big Men, Small Boys and Politics in Ghana: Power, Ideology and the Burden of History 1982-1994*. Accra, Ghana: Asempa.

Nussbaum, Stanley, 2003. The three-self formula in light of the emergence of African Independent Churches. In *Frontiers of African Christianity. Essays in Honour of Inus Daneel*. Eds. Greg Cuthbertson, Hernie Pretorius, and Dana Robert. Pp. 86-102. Pretoria, South Africa: University of South Africa.

Obeng, Pashington. 1996. *Asante Catholicism: Religious and Cultural Appropriation among the Akan of Ghana*. Leiden, Netherlands: E. J. Brill.

Obiri-Addo, Ebenezer. 1997. *Kwame Nkrumah: A Case Study of Religion and Politics in Ghana.* Lanham: University of America Press.

Ocquaye, Mike. 1980. *Politics in Ghana, 1972-79*. Accra, Ghana: Tornado

Odonkor, Stephen. 2000. Interview with the Leaders of the Methodist University College, Ghana. *Methodist Times* 14 (November): 6–7.

Odoi, Miriam Hornsby. 1999. Health Services of the Methodist Church of Ghana. *Methodist Times* (November-December): 8–9.

Oduyoye, Mercy Amba. 2001. *Introducing African Women's Theology*. Cleveland: Pilgrim Press.

———1999. A Coming Home to Myself: The Childless Woman in the West African Space. In *Liberating Eschatology: Essays in Honor of Letty M. Russell,* eds. Margaret A. Farley and Serene Jones, 104–20. Louisville, Ky.: Westminster John Knox Press.

———1988. Be a Woman and Africa Will Be Strong. In *Inheriting Our Mothers Gardens*, ed. Letty M. Russell. Philadelphia: Westminster Press.

———1986. *Hearing and Knowing: Theological Reflections on Christianity in Africa.* Maryknoll, N.Y.: Orbis Books.

Oduyoye, Mercy Amba, and Musimbi Kanyoro, eds. 1992. *The Will to Arise: Women, Tradition and the Church in Africa*. Maryknoll, N.Y.: Orbis Books.

Oduyoye, Modupe. 1969. *The Planting of Christianity in Yorubaland, 1842-1888*. Ibadan, Nigeria: Daystar Press.

Ojo, Matthews A. 1998. Gospel Music and Social Reconstruction in Nigeria. *Missionalia* 26 (August): 210–31.

Okine, Naomi. 2000. The Minister in the Eyes of the Laity in the Context of Episcopacy. Address given at the All Ministers' retreat (January 5), Kumasi.

Oliver, Roland. 1991. *The African Experience*. San Francisco: Icon Editions.

Oliver, Roland, and J. D. Fage, eds. 1995. *A Short History of Africa*. London: Penguin.

Olson, Duane A. 1990. Contextualization — Everybody's Doing It. *Word and World* 10 (Fall): 349–55.

Olupona, Jacob with Regina Gemignani. 2007. *African Immigrant Religions in America.* New York: New York University Press.

Omenyo, Cephas N. 2002. Charismatic Churches in Ghana and Contextualization. *Exchange* 33 (July 3): 252–77.

Oosthuizen, Gerhardus C. 1968. *Post-Christianity in Africa: A Theological and Anthropological Study.* London: C. Hurst.

Opoku, K. Asare. 1978. *West African Traditional Religion*. Accra, Ghana: FEP International.

Oppong, Christine. 1974. *Marriage among Matrilineal Elite: A Family Study of Ghanaian Civil Servants*. New York: Cambridge University Press.

Orobator, Emmanuel A. 1977. The Idea of the Kingdom of God in African Theology. In *God's Kingdom and Mission.* Pp. 327-357. Editrice Pontifica Universita Gregoriana Roma: Publication of the Faculty of Missiology.

Outler, Albert. 1971. *Evangelism in the Wesleyan Spirit*. Nashville: Tidings.

Owoahene-Acheampong, Stephen. 1998. *Inculturation and African Religion: Indigenous and Western Approaches to Medical Practice*. New York: Peter Lang.

Owusu-Ansah, David and D.M. McFarland. eds. 1995. *Historical Dictionary of Ghana*. Lanham, MD: Scarecrow.

Padilla, Rene. 1979. Contextualization of the Gospel. In *Readings in Dynamic Indigeneity*, eds. Charles Kraft and Tom N. Wisley, 286–312. Pasadena, Calif.: William Carey Library.

Paris, Peter J. 1995. *The Spirituality of African Peoples: The Search for a Common Moral Discourse*. Minneapolis, Fortress.

Parratt, John. 1995. *Reinventing Christianity: African Christianity Today*. Grand Rapids: Eerdmans.

———1987. *A Reader in African Christian Theology.* London: Latimer Trend & Co.

Parrinder, Edward G. 1976. *Africa's Three Religions*. London: Sheldon Press.

———1974. *African Traditional Religion*. London: Sheldon Press.

Parsons, Robert. T. 1963. *The Churches and Ghana Society 1918–1955: A Survey of the Work of Three Protestant Mission Societies and the African Churches, Which They Established in Their Assistance to Social Development.* Leiden, Netherlands: E. J. Brill.

Pellow, Deborah, and Naomi Chazan. 1986. *Ghana: Coping with Uncertainty.* Boulder, Colo: Westview Press.

Petersen, John. 1968. The Sierra Leone Creole: A Reappraisal. In *Freetown: A Symposium*, eds. Christopher Fyfe and Eldred Jones. Freetown: Sierra Leone University Press.

Phillips, James M., and Robert T. Coote, eds. 1993. *Toward the 21st Century in Christian Mission.* Grand Rapids, Mich: Eerdmans.

Platvoet, J. G. 1979. The Akan Believer and His Religions. In *Official and Popular Religions: Analysis of a Theme for Religious Studies*, eds. Peter Hendrik Vrihof and Jacques Waardenburg. Pp. 544-606. The Hague: Mouton.

Pobee, J. S. 2000. The Anglican Church in Ghana and the SPG. In *Three Centuries of Mission: The United Society for the Propagation of the Gospel 1701–2000,* ed. Daniel O'Connor, Pp. 409–21. London: Continuum.

———1996. A Passover of Language: An African Perspective. In *Mission in Bold Humility: David Bosch's Work Considered.* Eds. W Saayman, K Kritzinger. Maryknoll, NY: Orbis Books.

______1991*a. Religion and Politics in Ghana*. Accra, Ghana: Asempa.

______1991b. *AD 2000 and After: The Future of God's Mission in Africa*. Accra, Ghana: Asempa.

———1991c. Africa. *Dictionary of the Ecumenical Movement*, Vol. 5, eds. Nicholas Lossky, José Bonino, John S. Pobee, Tom F. Stranky, Geoffrey Wainwright and Pauline Webb. Geneva: World Council of Churches.

———1979. *Toward an African Theology.* Nashville: Abingdon.

———1976. *Religion in a Pluralistic Society: Essays Presented to Prof. C. G. Baeta.* Leiden, Netherlands: E. J. Brill.

———1974. Church and State. *Legon Journal of the Humanities* 1:104–15.

———1972. The Church's Attitude to Indigenous Beliefs. *History of Ghana,* ed. M. Dodd, 83–92. Accra, Ghana: State.

Pobee, John. S., and Barbel von Wartenberg-Potter, eds. 1986. *New Eyes for Reading: Biblical and Theological Reflections by Women from the Third World*. Geneva: World Council of Churches.

Pobee, J. S., and Gabriel Ositelu II. 1998. *African Initiatives in Christianity: The Growth, Gifts and Diversities of Indigenous African Churches—A Challenge to the Ecumenical Movement.* Geneva, Switzerland: World Council of Churches.

Pobee, J. S., and J. N. Kudadjie, eds. 1990. *Theological Education in Africa: Quo Vadimus?* Geneva: WCC Publications and Accra, Ghana: Asempa.

Pope-Levison, Priscilla, and John R. Levison. 1992. *Jesus in Global Contexts*. Louisville: Westminster/John Knox.

Prickett, Barbara. N.d. *Island Base: A History of the Methodist Church in the Gambia. 1821-1969.* Gambia: The Methodist Church, Gambia.

Quaison-Sackey, Alex. 1963. *Africa Unbound: Reflections of an African Statesman*. Foreword by Kwame Nkrumah. New York, NY: Praeger.

Quartey-Papafio, Comfort R. 2000. Relations among Ministers and Their Flock. Address given at the All Ministers' retreat (January 3–7), Kumasi.

Ramey, Lauri. 2002. The Theology of the Lyric Tradition in African American Spirituals. *Journal of the American Academy of Religion* 70 (June): 347–63.

Ramo, Joshua Cooper. 2002. Five Virtues of Annan. *Time*. September 4.

Ranger, Terence. New Approaches to the History of Mission Christianity. In *African Historiography: Essays in Honour of Jacob Ade Ajayi*, ed. Toyin Falola. Ikeja, 180–94. Nigeria: Longman.

Reid, John, Lesslie Newbigin and David Pullinger, eds. 1996. Modern, Postmodern and Christian. Occasional Paper, 27, Lausanne Committee for World Evangelization. Carberry, Scotland: The Handsel.

Robert, Dana L. 2000a. Holiness and the Missionary Vision of the Woman's Foreign Missionary Society of the Methodist Episcopal Church, 1869–1894. *Methodist History* 39 (October): 15–27.

———2000b. Shifting Southward: Global Christianity since 1945. *International Bulletin of Missionary Research* 24 (April): 50–58.

———1998a. Christianity in the Wider World. In *Christianity: A Social and Cultural History*, eds. Howard Clark Kee and J.W. Frost. Trenton City, N.J.: Prentice Hall.

———1998b. "History's Lessons for Tomorrow's Mission": Reflections on American Methodism in Mission. *Focus—Boston University School of Theology* (Fall).

———1997. *American Women in Mission: A Social History of Their Mission Thought and Practice*. Macon, Ga.: Mercer University Press.

———1996. The Methodist Struggle over Higher Education in Fouzhou, China, 1877–1883. *Methodist History* 34 (April): 173–189.

———1995. The Methodist Episcopal Church, South, in Siberia/Manchuria 1920–1927. In *Methodism in Russia and the Baltic States: History and Renewal*, ed. S. T. Kimbrough Jr., 7–83. Nashville: Abingdon.

_____ed. 2003. *African Initiatives in Christian Mission: The Mission Churches*. Vol. 2. Pretoria: South African Missiological Society.

Saayman, Willem, and Klippies Kritzinger, eds. 1996. *Mission in Bold Humility: David Bosch's Work Considered*. Maryknoll, N.Y.: Orbis Books.

Sackey, Brigid. 1999. The Evangelization of Ghana: Historical and Contemporary Roles of Women. *Research Review* (University of Ghana) 15 (1): 39–59.

Safo-Kantanka, Osei. 1989. *Can a Christian Become a Chief?* Accra, Ghana: Pentecost Press.

Sam, Cramer. 2000. The Methodist University College: A Vision Realized. *Christian Sentinel* 9, no. 3.

Sampson, Philip J. 2001. *6 Modern Myths about Christianity and Western Civilization*. Downers Grove, Ill.: Intervarsity Press.

Samuel, Vinay, and Chris Sugden, eds. 1983. *Sharing Jesus in the Two-Thirds World: Evangelical Christologies from the Contexts of Poverty, Powerlessness and Religious Pluralism.* Grand Rapids, Mich: Eerdmans.

Sanneh, Lamin. 2000. The CMS and the African Transformation; Samuel Ajayi Crowther and the Opening of Nigeria. In *The Church Mission Society and World Christianity, 1799–1999,* eds. Kevin Ward and Brian Stanley, 173–97. Grand Rapids: Eerdmans.

———1999. *Abolitionists Abroad: American Blacks and the Making of Modern West Africa*. Cambridge: Harvard University Press.

———1996a. *Piety and Power: Muslims and Christians in West Africa*. Maryknoll, N.Y.: Orbis Books.

———1996b. Theology of Mission. *The Modern Theologians,* 2nd ed., ed. David Ford, 555–74. Oxford: Basil Blackwell.

———1993. *Encountering the West: Christianity and the Global Cultural Process: The African Dimension.* Maryknoll, N.Y.: Orbis Books.

———1989. *Translating the Message: The Missionary Impact on Culture.* Maryknoll, N.Y.: Orbis Books.

———1983. *West African Christianity: The Religious Impact*. Maryknoll, N.Y.: Orbis Books.

Sarpong, Peter 1971. *The Sacred Stools of the Akan*. Accra: Ghana Publishing Corp.

______1974. *Ghana in Retrospect: Some Aspects of Ghanaian Culture*. Accra: Ghana Publishing Corp.

_______1997. Asante Culture and the Kingdom of God. *God's Kingdom and Mission.* Editrice Pontificia Universita Gregoriana Roma: Publication of the Faculty of Missiology.

Sawyerr, Harry. 1970. *God: Ancestor or Creator? Aspects of Traditional Belief in Ghana, Nigeria and Sierra Leone*. London: Longman.

Scherer, James A. 1987. *Gospel, Church and Kingdom: Comparative Studies in World Mission Theology*. Minneapolis: Augsburg.

Schineller, Peter. 1992. Inculturation and Syncretism: What Is the Real Issue? *International Bulletin of Missionary Research* 16 (April): 50–53.

Schreiter, Robert. 1994. Inculturation of Faith or Identification with Culture? In *Christianity and Cultures: A Mutual Enrichment*, eds. Norbert Greinacher and Norbert Mettem, 15–24. London: SCM Press.

———1991. *Faces of Jesus in Africa*. Maryknoll, N.Y.: Orbis Books.

Schweizer, Peter A. 2000. *Survivors on the Gold Coast: The Basel Missionaries in Colonial Ghana*. Accra: Smartline.

Serequeberhan, Tsenay, ed. 1991. *African Philosophy: The Essential Readings*. New York: Paragon.

Shank, David A. and Jocelyn Murray. 1994. *Prophet Harris, the "Black Elijah" of West Africa*, Leiden, Netherlands: E. J. Brill.

Sharp, Eric. 1989. Reflections on Missionary Historiography. *International Bulletin of Missionary Research* 13 (April): 77–81.

Shenk, David W. 1994. *God's Call to Mission*. Scottsdale, Pa.: Herald Press.

Shenk, Wilbert R. 1997. Mission, Renewal, and the Future of the Church. *International Bulletin of Missionary Research* 21, no. 4 (October): 154–59.

———1996. The Role of Theory in Mission Studies. *Missiology: An International Review* 24 (January): 31–45.

Shorter, Aylward. 1996. *Christianity and the African Imagination: After the African Synod—Resources for Inculturation*. Nairobi: Paulines.

———1988. *Toward a Theology of Inculturation*. Maryknoll, N.Y.: Orbis Books.

———1973. *African Culture and the Christian Church: An Introduction to Social and Pastoral Anthropology.* London: Geoffrey Chapman.

Simensen, Jarle. 2002. Christian Church, "Native State" and African Culture: The Presbyterian Mission in Akim Abuakwa, Ghana. In *Christian Missionaries and the State in the Third World*, eds. Holger B. Hansen and Michael Twaddle, 39–51. Oxford: James Currey.

Sithole, Ndabaningi. 1977. *Roots of a Revolution: Scenes from Zimbabwe's Struggle.* London: Oxford.

———1959. *African Nationalism.* London: Oxford University Press.

Southon, Arthur E. 1934. *Gold Coast Methodism: The First Hundred Years 1835-1935*. London: Cargate Press.

Stephens, Jacob S. A. 1997. Profile of the President-Designate: Rev. Dr. Samuel Kwame Asante Antwi. *Christian Sentinel* 6 (October): 4–6.

Stott, John R. W. 1978. *Christian Counter-Culture*. Downers Grove, Ill.: Intervarsity Press.

———1975. *Christian Mission in the Modern World: What the Church Should Be Doing.* Downers Grove, Ill.: Intervarsity Press.

Straughn, James H. 1947. The Episcopacy. In *Methodism*, ed. William K. Anderson, 251–260. Nashville: Methodist.

Strawson, William. 1983. Methodist Theology 1850-1950. In *A History of the Methodist Church in Great Britain*, eds. Rupert Davies, A. Raymond George, and Gordon Rupp, Pp. 182–231. London: Epworth Press.

Sundkler, Bengt G.M. 1960. *The Christian Ministry in Africa*. Uppsala: Swedish Institute of Missionary Research.

Sundkler, Bengt G. M., and Christopher Steed. 2000. *A History of the Church in Africa*. Cambridge: Cambridge University Press.

Taber, Charles R. 1979. The Limits of Indigenization in Theology. In *Readings in Dynamic Indigeneity*, eds. Charles Kraft and Tom N. Wisley, 372–399. Pasadena, Calif.: William Carey Library.

Taylor, J. V. 1965. *The Primal Vision: Christian Presence amid African Religion*. London: Student Christian Movement Press.

Telford, Tom. 2001. *Today's All Star Missions Churches: Strategies to Help Your Church Get into the Game*. Grand Rapids, Mich.: Baker.

Ter Haar, Gerrie. 1994. Standing Up for Jesus: A Survey of New Developments in Christianity in Ghana. *Exchange* 23, no. 3. Pp. 221-40.

———1995. *Strangers in the Promised Land: African Christians in Europe*. Exchange 24, no. 1. Pp 1-33.

——— 1998a. *Halfway to Paradise: African Christians in Europe.* Cardiff, U.K.: Cardiff Academic Press.

———, ed. 1998b. *Strangers and Sojourners: Religious Communities in the Diaspora.* Leuven, Belgium: Peeters.

Thomas, J. Christopher. 1974. Society and Liturgical Reform. *Ghana Bulletin of Theology* 4 (June).

Tienou, Tite. 1992. Which Way for African Christianity? *African Journal of Evangelical Theology* 10 (2): 3–11.

———1991. The Invention of the Primitive and Stereotypes in Mission. *Missiology* 19 (3): 295–303.

———1990. *The Theological Task of the Church.* Accra, Ghana: Achimota Christian Press.

Tucker, Karen B., ed. 1996. *The Sunday Service of the Methodists: Twentieth-Century Worship in Worldwide Methodism: Studies in Honor of James F. White.* Nashville: Kingswood Books.

Tufuoh, Isaac. 1968. Relations between Christian Missions, European Administrators, and Traders in the Gold Coast, 1828–1874. In *Christianity in Tropical Africa*, ed. C. G. Baeta. London: Oxford University Press.

Tutu, Desmond. 1975. Black Theology/African Theology: Soul Mates or Antagonists? *Journal of Religious Thought* 33.

Turkson, Adolphus R. 1995. Contrafactum and Parodied Song Texts in Religious Music Traditions of Africa: A Search for the Ultimate Reality and Meaning of Worship. *Ultimate Reality and Meaning* 10 (3): 160–75.

Turner, Harold W. 1967. *History of an African Independent Church*, 2 vols. Oxford: Clarendon Press.

———1967. A Typology for African Religious Movements. *Journal of Religion in Africa* 1 (1): 1–34.

Twesigye, E. K. 1987. *Common Ground: Christianity, African Religion and Philosophy*. New York: Peter Lang.

Ukpong, Justin S. 1999. Towards a Holistic Approach to Inculturation Theology. *Mission Studies* 25: 100–124.

Verstraelen, F. J., ed. 1995. *Missiology: An Ecumenical Theology: Texts and Contexts of Global Christianity*. Grand Rapids: Eerdmans.

Verkuyl, Johannes. 1978. *Contemporary Missiology: An Introduction*, trans. and ed. Dale Cooper. Grand Rapids: Eerdmans.

Vickers, John A. 1996. One-Man Band: Thomas Coke and the Origins of Methodist Missions. *Methodist History* 34 (April): 135–47.

———1969. *Thomas Coke, Apostle of Methodism*. London: Epworth.

Wainwright, Geoffrey. 1995. *Methodists in Dialogue*. Nashville: Kingswood Books.

Walker, F. Deaville. 1929. *Thomas Birch Freeman—The Son of an African.* Cape Coast:

Wesleyan Methodist Book Depot.

Walker, Sheila S. 1983. *The Religious Revolution in the Ivory Coast: The Prophet Harris and the Harrist Church*. Chapel Hill: University of North Carolina Press.

Wallace, Janet. 1989. *Contributions to Church and Society. Roots and Branches: Historical Essays on Methodism in Southern New England*, ed. Jerry O. Cook, 164–212. Boston: New England Methodist Historical Society.

Walls, Andrew F. 2002. *The Cross-Cultural Process in Christian History. Studies in the Transmission and Appropriation of Faith*. Maryknoll, N.Y.: Orbis Books.

———1996. *The Missionary Movement in Christian History: Studies in the Transmission of Faith*. Maryknoll, N.Y.: Orbis Books.

———1976. Towards Understanding Africa's Place in Christian History. In *Religion in a Pluralistic Society; Essays Presented to Prof. C. G. Baeta*, ed. J. S. Pobee, 180–189. Leiden, Netherlands: E. J. Brill.

Ward, Kevin. 1999. Africa. In *A World History of Christianity*, ed. Adrian Hastings. Grand Rapids: Eerdmans. Pp. 192-233.

Ward, Kevin, and Brian Stanley, ed. 2000. *The Church Mission Society and World Christianity, 1799–1999*. Grand Rapids: Eerdmans.

Ward, W. 1967. *A History of Ghana*. London: George Allen & Unwin.

Warner, Laceye. 2002. Towards a Wesleyan Evangelism. *Methodist History* 40 (July): 230–45.

Warren, M. 1967. *Social History and Christian Mission*. London: SCM Press.

Weber, Charles. 1997. Christianity and West African Decolonisation, 1945–1960. Position Paper # 80, *Currents in World Christianity Project*, 7. Faculty of Divinity, University of Cambridge.

Whiteman, Darrell. 1997. Contextualization: The Theory, the Gap, the Challenge. *International Bulletin of Missionary Research* 21 (January): 2–7.

Whiteside, J. 1906. *History of the Wesleyan Methodist Church of South Africa*. London: Methodist Book Room.

Wilks, Ivor. 1996. *One Nation, Many Histories: Ghana Past and Present*. Accra, Ghana: University of Ghana, Legon.

Williams, Peter. 2002. "Not Transplanting": Henry Venn's Strategic Vision. In *The Church Mission Society and World Christianity, 1799–1999*. Eds. Kevin Ward and Brian Stanley, 147–72. Grand Rapids: Eerdmans.

Williamson, Sidney. G. 1965. *Akan Religion and the Christian Faith*. ed. Kwesi A. Dickson. Accra, Ghana: Ghana University Press.

———1958. The Lyric in Fante Methodist Church. *Africa* 28 (April).

———1955. *Christianity and African Culture. Proceedings of a Conference held at Accra, Gold Coast, May 2–6*. Accra, Ghana: Christian Council of the Gold Coast.

Willimon, William H. 1990. *Why I Am a United Methodist*. Nashville: Abingdon.

Wiltgen, R. 1956. *Gold Coast Mission History, 1471–1880*. Techny, Ill.: Divine Word Publications.

Winter, Ralph. *The Twenty-Five Unbelievable Years: 1945–1969*. Pasadena, Calif.: William Carey Library.

Witte, John, ed. 1993. *Christianity and Democracy in Global Context*. Boulder: Westview Press.

Wyllie, Robert W. 1980. *Spiritism in Ghana. The Spirit-Seekers: New Religious Movements in Southern Ghana*. Missoula, Mo.: Scholars Press.

Yalley, Ebenezer A. 1992. *The Episcopacy in the Ministry of the Church*. Tema, Ghana: Hacquason Press.

Yirenkyi, Kwesi. 1992. The Church and the Quest for African Modernization. In *Twentieth Century World Religious Movements in Non-Weberian Perspective*, ed. William H. Swatos Jr., 143–58. Lewiston, New York: Edwin Mellen Press.

Young, Josiah U. III, 1983. *African Theology: A Critical Analysis and Annotated Bibliography*. Westport, Conn.: Greenwood Press.

———1986. *Black and African Theologies: Siblings or Distant Cousins?* Maryknoll, N.Y.: Orbis Books.

Yrigoyen, Charles. 2002. *The Global Impact of the Wesleyan Traditions and Their Related Movements*. Lanham, MD.: Scarecrow Press.

THESES

Adubofuor, Samuel B. 1994. Evangelical Parachurch Movements in Ghanaian Christianity: 1950–Early 1990s. Ph.D. diss., University of Edinburgh.

Aryee, Seth A. 1989. The Bible and the Crown: Thomas Birch Freeman's Synthesis of Christianity and Social Reform in Ghana, 1838–1890. Ph.D. diss., Drew University.

Asamoah-Gyadu, J. Kwabena. 2000. Renewal within African Christianity: A Study of Some Current Historical and Theological Developments within Independent Indigenous Pentecostalism in Ghana. Ph.D. diss., University of Birmingham.

Asimpi, Kofi. 1996. European Christian Missions and Race Relations in Ghana, 1828–1970. Ph.D. diss., Boston University.

Boafo, Paul Kwabena. 1999. An Examination of the Theology of John Wesley with Particular Reference to His Sociopolitical Teaching and Its Relevance to the Ghanaian situation. Ph.D. diss., Queen's University of Belfast.

Edusa-Eyison, Joseph M.Y. 1994. The History of an Autonomous Methodist Church, Ghana, 1961–1991. M.Phil. thesis, University of Ghana, Legon.

Essamuah, Casely B. 1995. Cultural Interpretations of Christianity among the Akan of Ghana. M.Div. thesis, Harvard Divinity School.

Essamuah, Colin B. 1982. The Intellectual as Politician: The Impact of Dr. Kofi Abrefa Busia on Ghanaian Politics. B.A. thesis, history, University of Ghana.

Forson, Matthias K. 1993. Split-Level Christianity in Africa: A Study of the Persistence of Traditional Religious Beliefs and Practices among the Akan Methodists of Ghana. D.Miss. diss., Asbury Theological Seminary.

Larbi, Kingsley. 1995. The Development of Ghanaian Pentecostalism: A Study in the Appropriation of the Christian Gospel in the 20th Century Ghana Setting with Special Reference to the Christ Apostolic Church, The Church of Pentecost, etc. Ph.D. diss., University of Edinburgh.

Nkrumah, Patrick K. 1992. The Interaction between Christianity and Ashanti Religion. Ph.D. diss., Drew University.

Quayson, Margaret. 1997. Renewal in the Methodist Church of Ghana —A Case of the Accra New Town Circuit. B.A. thesis, religions, University of Ghana.

Wright, Juanita Bass. 1984. Mission in the 1980s and Beyond. D. Min. project, Drew University.

LIST OF INTERVIEWS

Abaidoo, Daniel Yaw, Attorney, Presbyterian Lay Leader and Director of Administration, Scripture Union, Ghana (a student evangelism and discipleship organization). 2000. Interview by author, January 14. Tape recording. His office. Accra.

Aboagye-Mensah, Robert (Very Rev. Dr.), General Secretary, Christian Council of Ghana and Seminary Professor. 2000. Interview by author, January 19. Tape recording. Accra.

Achamfuo-Yeboah, Samuel Osei (Very Rev.), Managing Director, Methodist Book Depot, General Director, Board of Administration, Methodist Church, Ghana. 2000. Interview by author, January 15. Tape recording. Labone.

Agbeti, John K. (Rt. Rev. Dr.), former Chairman of the Cape Coast District, Methodist Church, Ghana and University Lecturer in church history. 2000. Interview by author, January 19. Wesley House. Accra.

Ahiable-Addo, Cosmos H. Head of Department, Department. of General and African Studies, Kwame Nkrumah University of Science and Technology, Kumasi. 2001. Interview by author, July 26. Tape recording. His office. Kumasi.

Aryee, Seth (Rt. Rev. Dr.), Bishop, Tema Diocese, Methodist Church, Ghana. 2000. Interview by author, January 8. Tape recording. Tema.

Asamoah-Gyadu, J. Kwabena (Very Rev. Dr.), Lecturer in New Religious Movements and World Religions, Trinity Theological Seminary, Legon. 2001. Interview by author, July 4. Tape recording. Pretoria.

Asante, Emmanuel Kweku (Very Rev. Dr.), President, Trinity Theological Seminary, Legon. 2000. Interview by author, January 13. His office. Legon.

Asante-Antwi, Samuel (Most Rev. Dr.), Presiding Bishop, Methodist Church, Ghana, former Principal, Trinity College, Legon, and former Chairman, Kumasi District Methodist Church, Ghana. 2000. Interview by author, January 11. Tape recording. Wesley House. Accra.

Asare-Kusi, Emmanuel (Very Rev.), Superintendent-Minister, Wa Missions Circuit, Methodist Church, Ghana. 2000. Interview by author, January 7. Tape recording. Kumasi.

Asiedu, Morgan, Bank attorney and Church Lay Leader. 2000. Interview by author, January 8. Tape recording. Dzorwulu, Accra.

Baiden, Ebenezer K. (Rt. Rev.), retired former Chairman Tarkwa District, Methodist Church, Ghana, 2000. Interview by author, January 15. Tape recording. Tema.

Bannerman, Joseph Yedu (Rt. Rev.), former Chairman of Koforidua and Winneba districts, Methodist Church, Ghana, and Renowned Expert on Akan traditions, especially proverbs. 2000. Interview by author, January 8. Tape recording. Ashiaman.

Bartels, Victor (Mr.), Lay Leader and Evangelist, Calvary Methodist Church, Abura. 2000. Interview by author, January 20. Tape-recording. Abura.

Bediako, Kwame (Rev. Dr.), Founder and Executive Director, Akrofi-Christaller Memorial Center for Mission Research and Applied Theology, Akropong-Akwapim. 2000. Interview by author, January 17. Tape recording. His office. Akropong-Akwapim.

Blankson, William (Very Rev.), Superintendent-Minister, Dansoman Mount Olivet Circuit, Methodist Church, Ghana. 2000. Interview by author, January 19, Dansoman.

Boafo, Paul Kwabena (Rev. Dr.), Superintendent-Minister of the New Achimota Circuit, Methodist Church, Ghana, and Part-Time Lecturer in Christian Beliefs and Methodist Studies, Trinity Theological Seminary, Legon. 2000. Interview by author, January 13. Tape recording. Legon.

Boamah, Francis Yaw, Methodist Lay Leader and General Secretary, Ghana Fellowship of Evangelical Students , 2000. Interview by author, January 14. Tape recording. SU Centenary House. Accra.

Bortey, Emmanuel A.B. (Rev.), Methodist minister and General Manager, Asempa Publishers. 2000. Interview by author, January 24. Tape recording. Bubuashie.

Brew-Riverson, Ebenezer H. (Rt. Rev. Dr.), former Chairman, Sekondi District and former Conference Secretary, Methodist Church, Ghana. 2000. Interview by author, January 7. Tape recording. Attafua, Kumasi. (Before joining the ordained ministry, he served as Principal, Wesley College for 22 years.)

Dickson, Kwesi Abotsia (Most Rev. Prof. Emeritus), President, All Africa Conference of Churches, past President, Methodist Church, Ghana, and Leading Theologian in Christianity in Africa. 2000. Interview by author, January 17. Tape recording. Accra.

Dovlo, Elom (Rev. Dr.), Head of Department for the Study of Religions, University of Ghana, Legon. 2000. Interview by author, January 13. Tape recording. His office. Legon.

Edusa-Eyison, Joseph M.Y. (Rev.), Methodist Historian and Lecturer in Church History and Liturgics, Trinity Theological Seminary. 2000. Interview by author, January 21. Tape recording. His residence. Accra.

Ekem, John. Rev. (Dr.), Translation-Consultant, Bible Society of Ghana and University Lecturer in Old Testament. 2000. Interview by author, January 19. Tape recording. James Town.

Essamuah, Ernestina , Methodist Lay Leader, former president, Women's Fellowship; Methodist Ministers Wives Association, and widow of the late Reverend Samuel B. Essamuah, fifth President, Methodist Church, Ghana. 2000. Interview by author, January 16. Tape recording. Korle Bu Teaching Hospital. Accra.

Gongwer, Cameron M.D., American Missionary, Mission Society for United Methodists, and Physician, Ankaase Methodist Faith-Healing Clinic, Ankaase. 2000. Interview by author, January 6. Tape recording. Kumasi.

Harvey, Alan and Pam, British Methodist missionaries. (Alan is the Chaplain to Schools and Colleges in Cape Coast and Pam is the headmistress, Nkanfua Methodist School.) 2000. Interview by author, January 20. Tape recording. Abum, Cape Coast.

Fosua, Sofia (Rev. Dr.) and Kwasi Kena (Rev. Dr.), American Missionary (Board of Global Ministries, United Methodist Church), Lecturers, Freeman Center for Leadership Development; and Devotional Literacy Experts. 2000. Interview by author, January 6. Tape recording. Kumasi.

Jonfia, William (Rt. Rev. Col. Rtd.), Bishop, Winneba Diocese, Methodist Church, Ghana, and former Chaplain-General of the Ghana Armed Forces. 2000. Interview by author, January 18. Tape recording. Winneba.

Koomson, Thomas Wallace (Most Rev.), Second President, Methodist Church, Ghana (the oldest living minister of the Methodist Church, Ghana). 2000. Interview by author, January 15. Tape recording. North Kaneshie.

Larbi, E. Kingsley (Rev. Prof.), Vice Chancellor, Central University College, Accra, Ghana. 2001. Interview by author, August 7. Tape recording. Mataheko.

Martey, Emmanuel (Rev. Dr.), Lecturer in Systematic Theology, Trinity Theological Seminary, Legon; and Chair of the Bible Society of Ghana. 2001. Interview by author, August 7. Tape recording. Legon.

Oduyoye, Mercy Amba (Prof.), Founder and Executive Director, Institute of African Women in Religion and Culture, Trinity Theological Seminary, Legon. 2000. Interview by author, January 24. Tape recording. Legon.

Ofoe-Wright, Albert (Rt. Rev.), Administrative Bishop, Methodist Church, Ghana. 2000. Interview by author, January 11. Tape recording. Wesley House. Accra.

Omenyo, Cephas (Rev.), Lecturer in Church History, New Religious Movements, and Christianity and African Culture, Department for the Study of Religions, University of Ghana, Legon. 2000. Interview by author, January 13. Legon.

Orleans-Pobee, Robert, former Headmaster, Adisadel College, Cape Coast. 2000. Interview by author, January 8. Tape recording. Osu Ako Adjei.

Orleans-Pobee, Comfort (Mrs.), Anglican Lay Leader and retired Educationist. 2000. Interview by author, January 8. Tape recording. Osu Ako Adjei.

Quartey-Papafio, Comfort (Very Rev.), Assistant to Administrative Bishop, Methodist Church, Ghana. (The highest-ranking woman Minister in Ghanaian Methodism at the time, formerly Divisional Head, Christian Council of Ghana, and chaplain, Wesley Girls' High School. 2000. Interview by author, January 11. Tape recording. Methodist Head office. Accra.

Stephens, Rev. Jacob S. A., MCG Sixth President 1985-90. 1999 videotaped interview by the Ghana Methodist Historical Society, Accra.

Tekyi-Ansah, Joseph Kow (Rt. Rev.), Bishop, Northern Ghana Diocese, Methodist Church, Ghana. 2000. Interview by author, January 7. Tape recording. Kumasi.

Tinsari, Edison K. (Very Rev.), former Chairman, Northern Ghana District, Methodist Church, Ghana. 2000. Interview by author, January 6. Tape recording. Kumasi.

Wie-Addo, Kow Agyapanyin (Rev.), Education Officer; (Bivocational Minister, Methodist Church, Ghana), and formerly Chaplain, Apam Secondary School. 2000. Interview by author, January 7. Tape recording. Kumasi.

INDEX